THE RIGHTS OF SUBORDINATED PEOPLES

THE RIGHTS OF
SUBORDINATED PEOPLES

edited by
OLIVER MENDELSOHN
and
UPENDRA BAXI

DELHI
OXFORD UNIVERSITY PRESS
BOMBAY CALCUTTA MADRAS

Oxford University Press, Walton Street, Oxford OX2 6DP

Oxford New York
Athens Auckland Bangkok Bombay
Calcutta Cape Town Dar es Salaam Delhi
Florence Hong Kong Istanbul Karachi
Kuala Lumpur Madras Madrid Melbourne
Mexico City Nairobi Paris Singapore
Taipei Tokyo Toronto
and associates in
Berlin Ibadan

ISBN 0 19 563928 6

Published in association with
The Book Review Literary Trust

Typeset by Rastrixi, New Delhi 110070
Printed in India at Rajkamal Electric Press, Delhi 110033
and published by Manzar Khan, Oxford University Press
YMCA Library Building, Jai Singh Road, New Delhi 110001

Contents

Notes on Contributors

HALEH AFSHAR was educated in Iran and the UK, and currently teaches in the Politics Department, University of York. She has published widely on political problems in Iran and elsewhere, including the particular situation of women. She has edited *Iran: a Revolution in Turmoil* (1985); *Women, Development and Survival in the Third World* (1991); (with B. Agarwal) *Women, Poverty and Ideology in Asia* (1989); and (with C. Dennis) *Women and Structural Adjustment in the Third World* (1992).

DIANE BELL is currently Henry Luce Professor of Religion, Economic Development and Social Justice at the College of the Holy Cross, Worcester, MA., USA. Her books include *Law: the Old and the New* (1980); *Daughters of the Dreaming* (1983); *Generations: Grandmothers, Mothers and Daughters* (1987); and *Just Dreams: Aborigines in Australian Society* (forthcoming). She has edited *Gendered Fields: Women, Men and Ethnography* (1993).

MARTIN CHANOCK was educated in Witwatersrand and Cambridge, and has taught in Malawi, Nigeria, the UK, and the US. He is now Professor of Legal Studies, La Trobe University. His publications include *Unconsummated Union: Britain, Rhodesia and South Africa, 1900–45* (1977); and *Law, Custom and Social Order* (1985). He is currently writing a book on the origins of the South African state.

JAMES CRAWFORD is Whewell Professor of International Law at Cambridge and former Dean of the University of Sydney Law School. His books include *Australian Courts of Law* (1982); and *The Rights of Peoples* (1988). He was Commissioner in charge of the Australian Law Reform Commission's reference on the Recognition of Aboriginal Customary Laws.

VEENA DAS is Professor and Head of the Department of Sociology at the University of Delhi, and has taught in the US and Germany. Her books include *Structure and Cognition: Aspects of Hindu Caste and Ritual* (1977); and the edited volumes, *The Word and the World:*

Fantasy, Symbol and Record (1986); and *Mirrors of Violence: Communities, Riots and Survivors in South Asia* (1990).

RAMACHANDRA GUHA is currently a Professorial Fellow at the Nehru Memorial Museum and Library, New Delhi, and has taught at Yale University. Much of his work has been on the ecological history of India. His books include *The Unquiet Woods* (1990) and (with M. Gadgil) *This Fissured Land* (1993).

MARIE-AIMEE HELIE-LUCAS was educated in Algeria and France. She manages *Women Living Under Muslim Laws*, an international solidarity network, and has written widely on the matter of women's rights.

DAVID MAYBURY-LEWIS is Professor of Anthropology at Harvard and the founder of *Cultural Survival*, which works for the rights of indigenous peoples. His books include *The Savage and the Innocent* (1965); *Ake-Shavante Society* (1967); and *Millennium* (1992), the book of his multi-part television series on indigenous peoples of the world.

OLIVER MENDELSOHN has taught politics in the USA and Australia, and is now in the School of Law and Legal Studies at La Trobe University. Many of his publications are in the field of Indian politics and the sociology of law.

JOHN MILLER graduated from Cambridge and studied at Heidelberg, Sofia, Glasgow and Moscow. He has taught at the Institute of Soviet and East European Studies, Glasgow, and now teaches Politics at La Trobe University. His books include (with R.F. Miller and T.H. Rigby) *Gorbachev at the Helm* (1987); and *Mikhail Gorbachev and the End of Soviet Power* (1993).

COLIN TATZ is Professor of Politics at Macquarie University, Sydney. His special fields of teaching and research are race politics, comparative genocide studies and the history and politics of sport. He has conducted research in South Africa, Canada, the USA, Britain, Israel and New Zealand.

MARIKA VICZIANY studied in Australia, Germany and the UK, and now teaches economic history at Monash University, Melbourne. She has published on Indian historical demography, untouchable women and international trade. She is completing a book with Oliver Mendelsohn on the Untouchables today.

Introduction

OLIVER MENDELSOHN AND UPENDRA BAXI

The origins of this volume lie in discussions in Delhi in early 1988.[1] We began from a cluster of related thoughts about oppression and resistance and the situation of particular people, including the Aborigines of Australia and the Untouchables of India. By anyone's reckoning Australian Aborigines had been a terrible casualty of European settlement in Australia. Early genocidal attacks may have ceased but Aborigines had been reduced to the status of the poorest Australians and were subject to illnesses unknown in the rest of Australia. Even worse, Aboriginal culture had been attacked and, at least until recently, dismissed as of no value by the dominant European culture. Similarly but in very different circumstances, the Untouchables represented a people who had historically been subjected to almost unimaginable discrimination. Although apparently in the same cultural community as other Hindus, the Untouchables had been assigned to a material world of drudgery and a social world of exclusion and subordination. Both these peoples, then, were culturally and ideologically rejected and despised. They were largely powerless.

At the same time we knew that there was a greater self-consciousness in these people than before, and we had a sense that the state would incur steeply rising damage to its own interests if it continued to deny such people their rights as ordinary human beings. So, although these people represented a cause for some despair, their situation was far from static or terminal.

From this starting point we began to construct the colloquium which has led to the present volume. Our object was to group a number of peoples whose experience could be meaningfully and usefully

[1] A colloquium on the subject of this book was held at La Trobe University, Melbourne, on 16–18 November, 1988, under the joint auspices of the Department of Legal Studies, La Trobe, and the Indian Law Institute, New Delhi. The meeting was sponsored by the Ford Foundation, and we thank R. Sudarshan for his unfailing encouragement. Kate Mustafa efficiently and with dedication organized the event in Melbourne and typed manuscripts. Ronald Mendelsohn prepared the index.

compared. The Brazilian Indians and New Zealand Maoris seemed an obvious point of comparison with the Aborigines as further examples of the meeting of European colonialism and the indigenous people of the New World.[2] Similarly the Indian Adivasis or tribals were the other major Indian people who lay outside the mainstream of Indian culture and who were clearly subordinated by both British colonial power and its successor regime.

It was a short step from these cases to the Blacks in South Africa. Like our paradigm cases of Aboriginal Australia and Untouchable India, South African Blacks had been subjected to a regime which denied not only their equality with white South Africans but even their common human experience. Here was a system of great ideological subordination enforced through the mechanism of a particularly powerful state. The case of Soviet peoples of the north-east emerged from a concern to look at comparable (not to say the same) problems in a socialist society. The question was whether there was space for ideological and cultural subordination within a conceptual system premised on egalitarianism. Are there social masks which allow such subordination under different rubrics?

The last two areas of consideration point in somewhat different directions. The first of these is the position of women under fundamentalist Islam, and we adopted this issue partly because it was one case in the more general matter of women's rights. There was already to be a paper by Diane Bell on the position of women within Aboriginal Australia. There was, perhaps it needs to be said, absolutely no intention to posit Islam as a subordinating religion relative to others. The point of interest in the present context is the strong ideological justification, by fundamentalists, of differential gender worth. There are two papers on this subject here and the differences between them reflect the distinctive nature of the issue itself. Marie-Aimee Helie-Lucas' paper takes an approach that sees contemporary fundamentalist Islam as a very powerful ideology working systematically to subordinate women. This paper, like that of Diane Bell, proceeds from the view that feminism provides a firm basis for a critique of the subordination of women in highly disparate social and cultural settings. Haleh Afshar's paper is less sweeping in its ethical stance and seeks to interrogate and understand the justifications of those articulate

---

[2] Two papers on the experience of the Maoris of New Zealand were presented at the colloquium but it has not proved possible to include them in this volume.

women who themselves embrace fundamentalism. Her position is that feminism is a peculiarly Western ideology which has been judged deficient by such women, and that we have to be serious about asking why.

The paper by Veena Das is more free-ranging and conceptual in approach than the others. It proceeds from three examples drawn from the Indian context to make some general observations about state, society and subordination. The examples do not necessarily suggest themselves as cases of subordination, and perhaps that is their utility here. Das is able to show that cultural oppression and questions of self-determination are widely present in multi-ethnic, multi-cultural nation states. We will return to her more particular themes shortly.

It will now be apparent that we are not using 'subordination' or 'subordinated peoples' as terms of any great precision, such that we can rigorously and objectively assign some people to this category and exclude others. The terms belong to the same family as 'oppression', 'repression', 'exploitation' and 'subjugation', but are used here in order to facilitate discussion of some particular examples and themes. We certainly wish to resist discussions as to who constitute so oppressed a people that they merit the label 'subordinated'. The point of this volume is not to counterpose the experience of the people about whom we are writing with the experience of more privileged others, some of whom claim to be historical victims.

A strong theme of the colloquium was the need to create a sense of common struggle rather than reinforce divisions between people. There was concern that we avoid creating hierarchies of suffering, such that one people's bitter experience can be ranked relative to another's. It is of no use, indeed it is positively alienating, to tell an Armenian that his/her people's calamitous losses of 1916 are quantitatively less significant than the number of Jews lost in Nazi Europe. Conversely, it scarcely helps the Australian Aborigines if we try to rank their plight relative to these experiences or to the situation of other indigenous peoples. What would be the point of such ranking, even if it were to place the Aborigines at the very bottom of the heap? The very impulse to rank order, or to downgrade the suffering of others, arises partly, in the view of Das, because we do not possess languages of suffering which are morally orienting. Instead of empathy we find a scrambling competition to be heard. Bell notes that moral sympathy is in chronically short supply and that there is no ready-made formula for its expansion: we will return to this theme shortly.

Despite our wariness about separate categories of social suffering, this volume does have a particular focus, namely communities and people who are culturally and ideologically subordinated. We take this to be a very powerful form of subjugation. Since culture is a source of power as well as a system of shared values and customs, one of the defining characteristics of these subordinated people is their powerlessness. But even here we need to be careful to avoid a category that is too static and supine. James Scott has brought to our attention a whole world of resistance in his work *Weapons of the Weak*.[3] Scott is able to show that poor and seemingly powerless Malaysian villagers habitually resist their own subjugation in ways that are subtle rather than confrontational. The weak choose their own ground of resistance. While we cannot assume as a matter of definition that the resistance Scott writes about is present in all situations of subordination, at the very least we need to avoid the assumption that the weak are always acquiescent in their own subordination.[4]

Although held in an academic setting, the colloquium that led to this book was deliberately composed of both academics and activists. The concern was to keep close to the problems as they presented themselves to activists, including people from the subordinated communities themselves. And, of course, we entered into this enterprise with the hope that we could provide encouragement to a number of struggles for human rights. This collection is built on the premise that ideas matter, that they can be distilled out of experience and become part of further experience.

But if ideas matter, it was also clear that the major funds of ideas were almost bankrupt in providing support for subordinated peoples. Revolutionary Marxism, the dominant ideology of egalitarianism, has

---

[3] New Haven, Yale University Press, 1985.

[4] Scott is sceptical about the long-run benefits of revolution for those at the bottom of the social order. For a somewhat different approach to people he calls subalterns, see the influential work of Ranajit Guha, particularly *Elementary Aspects of Peasant Insurgency in Colonial India* (Delhi: Oxford University Press, 1983). Guha has also edited seven volumes of Subaltern Studies published by Oxford University Press during the 1980s and early 1990s. Guha's own starting point was Marxist theory, though there is no consistent theoretical approach in all the contributions to the Subaltern Studies series. A major difference of emphasis between Scott's work and that of Ranajit Guha (and most of the essays in his edited volumes) is Scott's concentration on what he calls forms of everyday resistance rather than organized political movements. But the two have in common a preoccupation with social groups at the very bottom of society.

in its orthodox formulations been too narrow and insensitive a language to take account of cultural specificity or of groups framed by race and gender rather than class. The developmentalist centre of Marxism has also found difficulty assimilating ideas about the primacy of environmental protection. On the other side, liberalism too in its many variants has tended to sweep up issues of race, gender equality, and the rights of indigenous people into an assimilationist individualism. (Prosperity may sometimes trickle down, but only sometimes.) Nor has liberalism been much more concerned about issues of physical sustainability. And if we turn to the partially distinct ideology of nationalism—never absent since the nineteenth century but currently rampant—this can be seen to be disastrously insensitive to matters of cultural and social differentiation and to equality. In short, these available ideologies (all mature a century ago) are now more clearly than ever limiting rather than liberating.

We would argue that the value of approaching particular issues through the idea of 'subordination' is that it cuts across the conceptual divisions of race, class and gender, without denying the importance of these perspectives. Our effort has been to move towards a more inclusive conception of oppression or subordination than is possible under any one of these rubrics. Thus it is possible to see subordination arising from a number of sources: colonialism/imperialism, including a considerable diversity of examples such as European colonization of the New World and the 'internal' colonialism of India (relative to the 'tribals') and of the USSR; patriarchy; religion; developmentalism, with its devastating ecological and human consequences; and something as broad as statism. All these forces have in common an ideological and cultural drive to subordinate social formations that stand in their way.

In the several years since this project was first conceived, there have been extraordinary changes in the world. The communist world of Europe and the USSR has collapsed and this has coincided with an efflorescence of ethnic and national assertiveness throughout Eastern Europe and Soviet Asia. Challenges to the authority of the state are now stronger than at any previous time in the twentieth century.

This does not and cannot mean that ethnic groups or nationalities will reconstitute themselves as somehow independent of the state altogether. What is in negotiation is the nature of the state appropriate to a social world whose cultural traditions have been formed outside and prior to the modern state. These developments lend our own small enterprise even greater relevance than at the stage of conception. The papers in this collection are about the experience and struggles of social groups which have had to contend with a state apparatus which, in turn, has very often been a major proponent of the very process of subordination. One of the central themes of the colloquium was the extent to which a nominally benevolent state has acted in practice as oppressor rather than liberator.

But if it is possible to imagine more human political arrangements emerging relatively quickly from the present flux in Eastern Europe and Central Asia, resolutions for most of the peoples who are the subject of this volume will not be so available. John Miller's discussion of the indigenous peoples of the (former) Soviet north-east is an apt illustration. These hunter-gatherer peoples have had their language and culture suppressed for generations by the Soviet authorities. While the neutral language of socialism failed to single them out for special oppression, the engine of development had been working to crush their livelihood and culture. Regrettably, nothing has changed for the better with the collapse of the USSR. There is no indication at all that the newly powerful groups of the regions will constitute a less oppressive regime for hunter-gatherers. Indeed it is quite possible that these indigenous peoples' condition will be further impaired at the hands of the newly empowered non-Russian people who are no more sensitive and physically far closer to them than their old masters in Moscow.

Events in the USSR over recent years have largely destroyed that nation's claim to have solved the task of satisfactorily enclosing diverse ethnicities, nationalities and religious communities within a single political framework. This general problem is taken up in the Indian context by Das, whose programmatic object is to promote cultural rights by developing 'legal structures within which the collective dimension of human existence may be given clearer shape and form'. In her view we need to move beyond a jurisprudence of rights which is premised primarily on the individual and his/her relation to the state. In so doing we will be challenging the hegemony of the state, 'especially the notion that the state is the sole giver of values'. In India it is now the state itself which is seen as the principal threat to the life of particular communities.

Das takes three examples from contemporary India, itself a field nonpareil for supplying quantitatively huge examples of ethnic, cultural (including religious) diversity. The actual examples are not ones that the colloquium organizers were themselves concerned to commission for this volume, in the sense that they do not suggest themselves as peoples to be conceived as subordinated. But Das is able to show that these examples exemplify more general tendencies at work in contemporary social life, and in this sense they are directly relevant to social groupings which are very obviously oppressed. The three examples are the Shah Bano case involving questions of a divorced Muslim woman's right to maintenance; the cult of sati or widow immolation represented in the Deorala case; and the case of Sikh militants.

The protagonists in the Shah Bano case included the Supreme Court of India, which was bent on asserting a common law for all Indians; orthodox Muslim opinion, concerned to protect the sovereignty of the Sharia; and women's groups, outraged by oppression in the name of religion. For Das the real issue of the case is

not that of secularism versus communalism or national integration versus national disruption. It is rather a question as to whether powers of the state should be extended to encroach on the sphere of the family . . . [If] the state is to intervene in order to correct the injustice against women in such institutional structures as the family, then the focus of its legislative and adjudicatory labours has to be women themselves. The rights of subordinate groups such as women to break the power of traditions which subordinate them to men, on the one hand, and the radical recognition of the right of minorities to exist as cultural entities, on the other, are not capable of being resolved through any easy solutions. But minimally, it is necessary that these issues are addressed on their own terms, and they do not become a contest between the passions of the state (national integration, patriotism) and the passions of the community (its cultural survival in the form given to it by the dominant male culture).

This is a useful statement in locating the themes of this volume. What links all the papers is a judgment that the process of overcoming the subordination of whole communities entails recognition of their collective right to order their own affairs. In this sense it is appropriate to talk of group rights or community rights, including the fundamental right to self-determination. The most powerful enemy of self-determination is the modern state, which has its own culture and its own interests. But if self-determination is elevated to the status of an unqualified right to dominate the community, other interests will undoubtedly be compromised—the interests of women, most obviously. There is also the question of the individual. Surely no-one should want to deny the right of an individual to shape his/her own life out of personal choice. Whatever the limitations of liberal jurisprudence, there is a core of individualist ethics which remains of crucial significance.

The centrality of the state in enforcing social subordination is a theme taken up by most of the papers in this volume, whether the state is constituted by the USSR, India, South Africa, Brazil or Australia. For the Brazilian Indians, for example, the state has organized and legitimated drastic incursions into the Amazonian forests, thereby destroying their way of life and providing absolutely no alternative livelihood. In the case of the so-called tribal people in India—hunter-gatherers and practitioners of slash-and-burn agriculture—Ramachandra Guha shows that first the colonial British state and then independent India have laid bare vast tracts of forest and turned them into agricultural land, impoverishing and subordinating the tribals and simultaneously creating ecological disaster. In Australia it was the state which took Aboriginal children away from their parents to be brought up by 'civilized' (white) people, and the state which imposed a legal system to punish but never help. In a new twist, in New Zealand the 'dry' economics of the 1980s has become an engine of further oppression for the Maoris.

One of the most disturbing pieces of evidence reported in several cases in this volume is the contemporary identification of indigenous people as actual enemies of the state. In Brazil, for example, David Maybury-Lewis reports that the resistance of Indians and their supporters to the Amazon forests being cut down was called by one newspaper in 1986 a 'Conspiracy against Brazil'. The Indians represent a threat to development and also, in their demand to maintain a distinctive identity, a denial of the national myth of the racial and cultural melting pot. In Australia, where Aborigines oppose mining developments on territories that they have traditionally occupied, they and their supporters have been condemned for sabotaging the export drive and contributing to the nation's balance of payments problem. This was the case in relation to the recent political battle over Coronation Hill, a potential gold mine which was opposed by local Aborigines for spiritual reasons. In India, as Ram Guha shows, shifting cultivators have been denounced and practically hounded out of existence—in the mid-nineteenth century there may have been a million of them, now there are less than 50,000. Ideologically, these cultivators have been unacceptable to both the colonial and the independent Indian authorities. Economists, the new authorities of the post-colonial world, pronounce that shifting cultivators 'destroy the ecological balance'. Since this claim has gone hand-in-hand with the same authorities' appalling deforestation, the status of the judgment has to be other than empirical.

While the state can often be conceptualized as a major part of the structure of social subordination, this is not to say that oppression necessarily arises primarily from the state rather than civil society, or that the state has a single and always oppressive character. The example of the Indian Untouchables is instructive. Whatever the precise origins of the system of untouchability, it was clearly constituted and also sustained over centuries by economic and social forces rather than any state structure—not discounting the possibility that raja (ruler) as well as brahman (priest) had an interest in the system. In our own time, for more than half a century now, the Untouchables have become the beneficiaries of the world's largest scheme of positive discrimination in public employment and educational assistance. These measures have been an important source of livelihood and mobility for a large number of Untouchables. This said, it has to be conceded that even the Untouchables remain only a partial exception to propositions about the centrality of the state to the structure of subordination. Thus the scheme of 'compensatory discrimination' has been comparatively free of controversy precisely because it is calculated to make at best a marginal rather than a frontal attack on the position of Untouchables within Hindu society. And certainly there are innumerable instances of oppression of Untouchables at the hands of the state. Encounters with the police in relation to the now increasing conflicts with higher caste/class forces are routinely unfavourable to Untouchables. And the behaviour of officials, some of them charged with administering benefits, again tends to reflect local structures of dominance. By the end of his life Karpoori Thakur, the socialist politician and one-time chief minister of the state of Bihar, could say that what shocked him most about the contemporary Indian condition was the violence that was being done by the state, which his political education had schooled him to treat as the potential liberator of the oppressed.[5]

But it is crucial not to become too cynical about the state. Thus,

[5] Oliver Mendelsohn, Last Interview with Karpoori Thakur, *Times of India*, 18 February 1988.

Diane Bell observes that the state is not to be seen merely as an instrument of action (and therefore liable to control by the powerful) but also as an arena of conflict without invariably predetermined outcomes. At least in liberal democratic regimes, representation in institutions and rights of political action are not to be dismissed as of no value even to the relatively powerless. Aside from bureaucratic action, such structures can be used to further a discourse favourable to the interests of the subordinated. Democratic institutions can in this sense work as a crucial bridge to reach and influence public opinion.

Even if we concentrate on the state as a simple instrument, we cannot ignore its potential for constructive work. The contributions on the Aborigines of Australia, notably those of Colin Tatz and James Crawford, implicitly assume the possibility of some straightforward and beneficial action on the part of the state. (Indeed, as Law Reform Commissioner in charge of the recognition of Aboriginal 'customary law', James Crawford was himself a part of the state apparatus.) These two contributors are not naive about the contributions of officials and police to the historical and contemporary problems of the Aborigines, but they clearly believe that the state has the capacity to contribute to the solutions too.

If we turn to the theme that self-determination ought not proceed to the extent of impinging on other basic rights, this volume is rich in discussion. Martin Chanock's paper discusses the most radical (he calls it pathological) case of pluralism, namely South Africa. 'In the history of South Africa equality and differentiation have been in constant opposition. Oppression has been based on differentiation: liberation holds out promise of equality.' He rightly points out that, by contrast, 'in many of the post-colonial states it is the assertion of cultural uniqueness and validity, and the consequent legitimacy of the claims for differentiated political and legal institutions, as opposed to the (usually unconfessed) messianism of liberal assimilationism which is a core problem'. The white South African state defined non-whites as so inferior that a ruthless separation was the appropriate stance. In the sphere of law, the drive for separation was expressed through the construction of a 'customary law' applicable to Blacks alone. This divided legal system suited not only the interests of the white South African state but sections of the black population too. In the name of 'custom' a highly authoritarian and sexist legal regime has been put in place for Black South Africans. This regime, in turn, has had an impact on Black identity itself: traditionalism learned from a manufactured customary law has been channelled back into the construction of Black identity. Varying forms of traditionalism represent one of the two major streams of Black political organization in contemporary South Africa, the other stream being based on concepts of class rather than race.

Chanock is one of a number of contributors making the point that we must avoid representation of subordinated communities as inherently virtuous in contradistinction to an evil oppressor. We have been aware of the fallacy of turning colonialist anthropology on its head. That anthropology, Chanock reminds us by quoting Clifford, 'dichotomizes and essentializes its portrayal of others and . . . functions in a complex but systematic way as an element of colonial domination'. Colonial anthropology produced 'replying representations of the dominated: as with Primitive Man, so with Negritude'. None of the present papers propounds anything like a contemporary version of Negritude.

Indeed, perhaps the most controversial aspect of the collection is its willingness to point to severe fractures within the subordinated communities. Thus the paper by Bell is mainly directed to what is seen as the disastrously declining situation of women within Aboriginal Australian society. In her words, 'rape is occurring at a rate that qualifies as an abuse of human rights and on a scale that constitutes a crisis'. For Bell rape is not an inevitable price that women must pay; she explicitly rejects the sociobiology school's view of 'man the aggressor'. Rape takes places in a social context and it is that context which must be interrogated. But to raise the question of its occurrence within Aboriginal society is to incur disapproval from some quarters, particularly when it is a white person who is doing the questioning. But

not to engage with the questions intra-racial rape cases raise is to leave rape shrouded in myth, the subject of spirited legal defences based on spurious anthropological evidence by lawyers or the stuff of repressive law-and-order campaigns. Although it could be said this is 'not my business', it is very much my business. I hold to the position that no matter how unpleasant, feminist social scientists do have a responsibility to identify and analyse those factors which render women vulnerable to violence.

For her,

the most productive framing of the issue of intra-racial violence is to see the experience of Aboriginal women as refracted through the twin prisms of

gender and race. As women they are disproportionately vulnerable to violence
. . . As Aborigines they are marginal to the political process . . . (The) self-
determination movements of indigenous peoples necessarily privilege race
over gender. Their survival as a people is paramount and gender inequalities
within embattled minority groups (traditional or recent in origin) are not up
for scrutiny.

In words similar to those used by Veena Das in an essay with a very
different starting point, Bell talks about the 'impaired enjoyment of
human rights'.

This warning that self-determination may fly in the face of gender
justice is substantially the same theme pursued by Marie-Aimee Helie-
Lucas in her analysis of the condition of women within fundamentalist
Islam. She points to a very close convergence of approach to women's
rights across highly divergent Muslim societies and regime types. Far
from a movement towards greater freedom, she identifies a developing
subordination of women in the name of Islam. This can be seen in
matters of dress, sexual freedom, marriage, divorce, maintenance,
child custody, economic independence and so on. For Helie-Lucas,
who herself manages an international network concerned with these
issues, the way ahead is through 'internationalism'. The problems for
Muslim women are generated from within these societies, though
habitually the leaders of fundamentalism are able to justify their
actions by reference to external oppression. In Helie-Lucas' view it
is therefore naive to expect a satisfactory resolution to arise solely
from women's efforts within these societies. She understands those
Muslim women who buy some legitimacy through rejecting concerns
of western women as irrelevant and dangerous, a stance she calls
'entryism'. But her own view is that without international solidarity
among women, the march of fundamentalist subordination of women
will not be arrested.

A rather more cautious approach to the problem of Islamic fundamentalism is taken by Haleh Afshar. Much of her paper is concerned
with understanding the approach of those Muslim women who adopt
the veil, and in particular the women who have emerged as articulate
defenders of fundamentalism. These are the people Helie-Lucas calls
the 'entryists'. Afshar is sympathetic to this position in the sense that
she discerns value in the attempt to make an acceptable place for
women within contemporary Islam. Such a position is not difficult to
achieve in a doctrinal sense: 'If we accept the well known fact that
all religions endorse a patriarchal structure and discriminate against

women, we may be able to argue that in terms of degrees of oppression Islam may be one of the better faiths.' She warns against the assumed relevance of Western feminism to Muslim women. At the same time, she notes the convergence of a good deal of Western feminist and fundamentalist discourse. In particular, they share the view that 'both capitalism and socialism have come to exploit women as sex objects . . . '

The fundamentalism of female thinkers in Iran and elsewhere has taken a milder form: 'There is a major difference between male and female Muslim commentators of the new devout generation on the question of nature or nurture, with women seeing reproduction as natural and subordination as nurtured and most of the men viewing the women as naturally inferior and physically and mentally unequal.' But in the end these 'entryists' have failed. The fundamentalist men have had the power and they have put in place a more authoritarian and sexist form of Islam which licenses polygamy and other structures clearly unfavourable to women.

If fundamentalists have been busy 'reforming' Islamic practice by seeking to 'tighten up' the interpretation of frozen legal texts, James Crawford is a law reformer of an altogether different stripe. As a Commissioner of the Australian Law Reform Commission, Crawford brought to conclusion the reference on Recognition of Aboriginal Customary Laws. The basic question was whether, and if so to what extent, the Australian legal system should recognize Aboriginal customary law. Conceptually and politically this is an enormously difficult subject in the Australian context, and this is a large part of the reason why the reference took almost a decade to complete. The Commission rejected as a 'counsel of despair' submissions which argued that it was too late and inappropriate to recognize Aboriginal law. It was true, the Commission agreed, that many Aboriginal communities did not practise old ways and that many had been integrated into the flow of Australian life. And it was also true that the Australian state should not endorse discriminatory practices (against women, for example) or punishments which are regarded as harsh and unconscionable by Australian law and international instrument. But the Commission concluded that this was only an argument against particular kinds of recognition, notably an apartheid style of recognition of parallel legal systems for Aborigines and for other Australians of whatever colour, religion or ethnicity.

In the end, the Commission's recommendations for recognition of Aboriginal law are quite modest. They amount to an ordinary submission of Aborigines to the Australian legal system but a tempering of the impact of that system by appropriate reference to Aboriginal systems in matter such as marriage, the criminal law and hunting rights. The Commission argued against the creation of a general defence to a murder charge to the effect that the killing was sanctioned by Aboriginal law. But it recommended the creation of a partial defence, in effect reducing a payback killing recognized in Aboriginal custom to the status of manslaughter, as well as routine reference to questions of Aboriginality at the stage of sentencing a convicted Aborigine.

Acceptance of the Commission's findings would have represented a symbolic as well as practical move towards a deep reconciliation between white and Aboriginal Australia. But the meticulously researched and argued findings of the Law Reform Commission have met with a deadly silence from the Australian government over the succeeding years since publication in 1986. One can only speculate about the reasons for this silence, but clearly the government is avoiding an issue in which there are no votes and virulent opposition from conservative forces. Despite the modesty—some would say excessive modesty—of the Commission's recommendations, it would be easy to run a campaign that acceptance will amount to two systems of law for Australia, one for the general population and a more permissive system for Aborigines. Cultural pluralism at the level of recognition of customary law will strike dissonant chords in too many quarters for the comfort of government.

Crawford's service as an Australian Law Reform Commissioner has a philosphical connection with his writings on the rights of peoples, as opposed to individuals, in international law.[6] In this instance the Australian government rather than an international body was being asked by the Law Reform Commission to recognize the distinctiveness of Aboriginality in Australia, in order to temper some of the malign consequences of the Australian legal system for Aboriginal life. The failure of a relatively progressive government to act in this matter probably says something about governments in general. Our conclusion ought not to be that legislative and court systems are unpromising instruments for subordinated groups: the overall rhetoric of human rights can be a powerful support towards effective recognition of

[6] See James Crawford (ed.), *Rights of Peoples* (Oxford: Clarendon, 1988).

hitherto unrecognized rights. But in the end, the legal system is part of the larger political world and subject to the constraints of that world. Action by and through lawyers is only one of many avenues that need to be trodden.

Beyond the failures and political pressures that lie upon governments, Colin Tatz demonstrates that government does not have anything like the whole means to resolve the complex of problems inherent in Aboriginal society. Tatz presents an awful picture of the state of Aboriginal society today: 'gang rape, self-mutilation, attempted suicide, homicide, incest and child-molestation'. Alcohol consumption has reached disastrous proportions. True, it is possible to find all these within mainstream Australian society, but they are disfiguring Aboriginal society in a quite unique way. Violence has become almost the distinguishing characteristic of Aboriginal communities.

Tatz is sure that the solution will not lie in simply throwing more of the considerable amounts of money that are currently being dumped into Aboriginal affairs. It is not just a matter of money or even facilities. He talks about what looks like a collective surrender of the Aborigines themselves at the very historical moment when the worst excesses of white racism are abating. Aborigines have had important parcels of land restored to them and facilities such as health are now better than they have ever been, even if lagging terribly behind the Australian norm. There is anti-discriminatory legislation, greater participation in politics than before and considerable teaching of Aboriginal culture in the schools. But 'when I see a gambling mother pour petrol on a blanket and then suffuse her crying infant's face to quieten it while she deals the cards, I know that calamity is taking place'.

Tatz has no prescriptions to offer for an awful despair which erupts in such heedless inhumanity. By now it scarcely helps to know that the despair is born of the disastrous (for Aborigines) meeting between European man (not woman) and Aboriginal Australia. In the end, 'somehow, internally, Aborigines have to initiate and practise the controls that are essential not just to their survival but to the enjoyment of those characteristics which Turnbull says are the luxury of ordered societies'. If we can abstract ourselves for a moment from the immediate press of human tragedy such as this, we can also recall Ranajit Guha's moving statement of the need to devise means of ending the solitary quality of human suffering. We may feel helpless before one human being's experience but in the end the experience is of a human tragedy knowable by us all. What runs through all the papers and contributions to this collection is a sense that not only must subordination be primarily overcome by the subordinated peoples themselves, but also that others have a crucial role to play in facilitating and not obstructing such transformations.

Oliver Mendelsohn and Marika Vicziany's paper on the Untouchables makes this point strongly. In their telling, the Untouchables have already to some extent experienced the self-confidence which is a prerequisite to overcoming their subordinate status. But what is left is a vast edifice of discrimination and poverty that will be monumentally difficult to transcend. The tens of millions of Untouchables are by far the largest collection of people discussed in this volume, and they are spread throughout Indian society rather than concentrated in isolated communities such as the Indians of Brazil or traditional Aborigines. As Maybury-Lewis reminded us, there need to be quite different strategies for dispersed as opposed to concentrated communities. In a word, the problem of organization is far more difficult for dispersed people. And, we can add, there need to be different strategies where the numbers involved are so huge. In common with the other contributors, Mendelsohn and Vicziany have been unable to offer any simple prescription to overcome the continuing subordinations they identify. But like all the other contributions to this volume their analysis rests on a belief that progress is attainable only through a combination of self-help and a supportive environment. Self-consciousness, self-respect and self-confidence are prerequisites to successful social action for subordinated people. But in no case are these enough. Diane Bell put the matter succinctly in saying that there needs to be a discourse of responsibilities as well as a discourse of rights.

We need to resist the idea that the contributions to this volume are marginal to the more central debates which will shape the world over the next period. As we write this introduction, India is suffused with violent division over the question of showing preference to the 'backward classes': this issue is now at the centre of Indian national life. (Somewhat unsatisfyingly this issue has presented itself as a push for bureaucratic benefits from the state, thereby exemplifying the domination of matters of state over community control.) In what is left of the USSR and in countless other political formations, questions of ethnic and cultural pluralism and its relation to the nation state are now the leading issues of public life. What we have taken up here is some of the most disastrous examples of cumulative subordination, but the connections with these other issues is direct.

Similarly, there are basic connections with broader ecological issues. Ramachandra Guha's discussion of Indian tribals; David Maybury-Lewis' account of Brazilian Indian problems; and John Miller's discussion of Soviet people of the north-east have in common a preoccupation with the dialectical relationship between environmental spoliation and social injustice. Ramachandra Guha is able to show that wrong-headed forestry policies have stripped forests of their trees and people of their livelihood. Environmental and social carelessness have run together. The same formulation applies almost exactly to the case of the Brazilian Indians. And destruction of their livelihood through deforestation and the crude destructions wrought by a burgeoning oil industry are part of the story told by John Miller writing on Soviet peoples of the north-east. In Australia too, the parlous Aboriginal condition has been partly brought about by a senseless dealing with a fragile environment nurtured by the Aborigines for some 50,000 years.

There is little enough cause for optimism in the examples we discuss in this volume. Ranajit Guha summed up the problem by saying that the experience of subordination is 'deeply desolate like a cry, and solitary like silent weeping'. For Guha it is not only the institutions of the law but also the formulations of social science which have worked to prevent such cries from being heard. But the editors and almost all the contributors are optimists to the extent that we believe it possible to intervene in processes whose unfolding is currently so disastrous. The naivete of the immediate post-colonial era has given way to a realization of the extent of social injustice and the weight that keeps it in place. But there are hopeful signs too, above all the hope that resides in a heightened resistance among subordinated people in the most diverse situations. There has always been much more resistance on the part of the weak than official accounts allowed, as James Scott has so forcefully shown. But through mechanisms that include international solidarity, the weak are now developing new weapons that quite often force authority to take them more seriously. Swami Agnivesh, activist and politician rather than academician, spoke eloquently of the possibilities inherent in internationalization of issues of subordination.

The labour historian Charles Bergquist pointed to the instruction that could be had from labour organization at an earlier time in the

West. Historically, consciousness among labour begins with a small and isolated minority. In order to be a successful industrial force it must not only develop consciousness throughout larger groups of labour, but also show that 'its struggle as a class has meaning for the democratic values and interests of the majority in the nation. It has been in those periods that labour has been much more successful'. The Dalits (radical Untouchables) of Karnataka state have already learnt the same lesson from the failures of the Dalit movment in neighbouring Maharashtra state. They see a need to establish contact with other movements from different communities in order to muster a more concerted political force. These Karnataka Dalits have also been busy creating a literature, some of it particular to their own communities but much of it reaching out through popular culture to a more general society. In Australia, Aboriginal artists (now celebrated in the salons of New York) and rock bands have seized forms (canvas, acrylic paint, electric guitars) that belong to the dominant culture and have used them in ways that revive their own culture and represent it outside.

The environment movement holds out some of the strongest possibilities for the politics of overcoming subordination. Thus the plight of the Brazilian Indians has begun to register on international consciousness arising from environmental concerns about destruction of the Amazon rain forests. But more important than such instrumental assistance, environmentalism represents evidence that at the end of the twentieth century it is possible for new and putatively non-divisive ideologies to establish themselves. Environmentalism has emerged from its early phase of widespread condemnation as a middle-class, Western ideology concocted by people who cared nothing for the enduring concerns of social justice. Events like Chernobyl have demonstrated that environmental issues are everyone's concern. Similarly, it ought to be possible to build movements arising from a sense that no decent and enduring society can be built on the basis of social subordination.

POSTSCRIPT

Since this (and the chapters on Aboriginal Australia) were written, a highly significant change has taken place in the legal landscape of Australia's Aborigines. In the case of *Mabo and Others v Queensland*

(1992) 107 ALR 1 the High Court of Australia for the first time recognized an interest in land which did not derive from the Australian state but from circumstances and traditions which ante-dated the European settlement of Australia beginning in 1788. The Court called this interest *native title*, following the practice in other colonized countries of the common law world. This decision entailed the overthrow of the doctrine that in legal terms Australia was *terra nullius* or the land of no one prior to European settlement. Both in symbolic and practical terms *Mabo* has had a powerful if initially divisive impact on Australian public life, and has instilled new heart into the Aborigines. The prospects for true reconciliation between Aboriginal and European Australia may now be better than at any previous time.

Fighting for the Forest: State Forestry and Social Change in Tribal India

I

Over the past decade there has been an intense debate over the orientation of forest policy in India. Established in 1864, the forest department is the country's biggest landlord, having effective territorial control of one-fifth of India's land area. By virtue of this control, it has the power to affect, for good or ill, the life of virtually every Indian. Although it has for the most past worked away from the public gaze, with growing shortages of forest produce (in both urban and rural areas) the department has come under close scrutiny.

This essay studies the competing claims over the forest exercised by the Indian state and tribal communities, respectively. The core of the paper, sections II and III, successively examines, for the colonial and post-colonial periods, state forest policies and their impact on the tribal population of peninsular India. I lay special emphasis on the formation, during the colonial period, of stereotypical attitudes towards tribal uses of the forest (in particular, shifting agriculture)—attitudes that undermined tribal rights even as they prepared the way for commercial forestry. My focus throughout is on the ecological basis of discrimination, namely how traditional patterns of forest use have been delegitimized and replaced with patterns favoured by more powerful political and economic forces.

A word of caution here: in the Indian context 'tribal' is a contentious and by no means unambiguous term. While the Constitution of India has designated hundreds of endogenous groups, amounting to approximately 8 per cent of the country's population, as 'scheduled tribes', a longstanding debate among anthropologists concerns the extent to which these tribal communities are (or have been) culturally distinct from Hindu caste society.

The question of cultural distinctiveness is not taken up by this paper, which focuses on the impact of forest policies on 'modes of resource use' that are characteristically, though not exclusively, tribal. These modes of resource use—hunting and gathering and shifting or *jhum* agriculture[1]—are, from an ecological perspective, quite different from the dominant culture of plough cultivation that is the bedrock of Hindu caste society. Moreover, these modes of resource use are not merely particular strategies of making use of nature—they were embedded in cultural traditions which also differ from those found in caste society and are, in the broadest sense, distinct ways of life.

Of course, some important aboriginal communities, notably the Gonds and Santhals, have been skilled plough cultivators, while at least some Hindu castes, for example along the west coast, depended on jhum until well into the nineteenth century. Despite the lack of firm quantitative evidence, however, it is clear that the overwhelming majority of hunter-gatherers and swidden agriculturists were (and are) 'tribals'. For the last century, the practitioners of these modes of resource use have been fighting a rearguard battle against another mode of resource use, commercial forestry, which rests on a radically different set of priorities. This paper outlines the salient characteristics of this conflict, which originated in the colonial period but has in many respects intensified since India gained independence in 1947. My geographical focus is restricted to peninsular India: the tribes of northeastern India, many of whom had virtually no contact with Hindu civilization before an accident of history deposited them in the Indian nation, are outside this purview. Even so, the paper covers a large area and a long time span, and the presentation will necessarily be both selective and schematic.

II ECOLOGY AND COLONIALISM

In his study of white colonization of the New World, Alfred Crosby argues that the plants, animals and diseases which accompanied the migrating Europeans were as important in ensuring their success as superior weaponry. The extermination of native ecosystems and human populations by the complex of weeds, animals and microbes which the European vanguard brought with it paved the way for the creation of 'Neo Europes'—the extensive and enormously productive

---

[1] Shifting cultivation is known variously as *jhum, dhya, bewar, podu*, etc. in different regions of India. I shall use *jhum* and *jhumiyas* (to denote the communities practising it) throughout.

agricultural systems that dominate the New World today. In his fascinating yet chilling account of the biological expansion of Europe, Crosby pauses briefly to investigate the areas he believes were 'within reach' but beyond grasp—the complex Old World civilizations in the Middle East, China and India. He argues that population densities, resistance to disease, agricultural technology and sophisticated sociopolitical organization all made these areas more resistant to the ecological imperialism of Europe. Thus 'the rule (not the law) is that although Europeans may conquer the tropics, they do not Europeanize the tropics, not even countrysides with European temperatures'.[2]

The advancing Europeans did have to adopt a more sophisticated strategy in older, more ecologically resistant, civilizations like India and China. This does not mean, however, that European colonialism had an insignificant impact on these ecosystems, as Crosby's treatment seems to suggest. In India, the Europeans could not create neo-Europes by decimating the indigenous populations and their natural resource base; yet they did radically undermine the ecological viability of existing food production systems. If in the New World ecological imperialism paved the way for political consolidation, in India the causation ran the other way, their political victory preparing the British for an unprecedented intervention in the ecological and cultural fabric of Indian society. Moreover, by exposing their subjects to the seductions of the industrial economy and consumer society, the British ensured that the processes of ecological change they initiated would continue, and indeed intensify, after they left Indian shores.

By far the most important aspect of the ecological encounter between Britain and India was the new systems of forest management introduced by the colonizers. Whereas the first century of British rule was characterized by a total indifference to forest conservancy, by 1860 Britain had emerged as the world leader in deforestation, devastating its own forests and the forests of Ireland, South Africa, northeastern United States, and parts of coastal India to draw timber for shipbuilding, iron smelting and farming. In India, a generally hostile attitude to forest preservation was reinforced by the belief, widespread among colonial administrators, that forests were an impediment to the expansion of agriculture and consequently to the generation of land revenue. Their early treatment of Indian forests reinforces the belief

---

[2] Alfred Crosby, *Ecological Imperialism: The Biological Expansion of Europe* (New York, 1986).

that the 'destructive energy of the British race all over the world' was rapidly converting forests into desert.[3] The process of forest destruction in nineteenth-century India greatly accelerated in the early years of the building of the railway network (c. 1853 onwards). Contemporary accounts present vivid descriptions of the transformation in the landscape wrought by the railway, as timber contractors laid bare vast tracts of forest to meet the railway companies' seemingly insatiable demands for fuel wood and timber.[4] Yet the pace of railway expansion (from 1349 kms of track in 1860 to 51,658 kms in 1910) forced the governor-general to call for the establishment of a department that could meet the enormous requirements of the different railway companies for sleepers, which had 'made the subject of forest conservancy an important administrative question'.[5] As Britain itself had no tradition of forest management, German experts were called in to start the Imperial Forest Department in 1864. The awesome task of checking the deforestation of the past decades and then providing a sustained supply of timber for the railways and other commercial users required, first and foremost, the forging of legal mechanisms to assert and safeguard state control over forests. This was provided by the Indian Forest Act of 1878, a comprehensive piece of legislation that served as a model for other British colonies and continues to be in operation today. The sine qua non of the 1878 act was an absolute state monopoly, with peasants and tribals allowed only a limited access to forests and forest produce. The Act paved the way for the constitution of massive areas of reserved forests—covering nearly one-fifth of the subcontinent's land area by the turn of the century—and their subsequent working on commercial lines.[6]

We can now turn to the impact of state forest management on

[3] Thomas Weber, *The Forests of Upper India and their Inhabitants* (London, 1902).

[4] See, for example, Thomas Cleghorn, *Forests and Gardens of South India* (London, 1860), and G.F. Pearson, Sub Himalayan Forests of Kumaun and Garhwal, in *Selections from the Records of the Northwestern Provinces* (Allahabad, 1870).

[5] Lord Dalhousie, quoted in C.G. Trevor and E.A. Smythies (ed.), *Practical Forest Management* (Allahabad, 1923).

[6] For a fuller account of the origins and character of colonial forestry, see my article, Forestry in British and Post British India: A Historical Analysis, in two parts, *Economic and Political Weekly*, 29 October and 5–12 November 1983, Sections I and III (hereafter Forestry).

tribal communities of hunter-gatherers and shifting cultivators. While colonial game laws made their traditional activities illegal, the state monopoly over trade in forest produce also seriously affected hunter-gatherer communities for whom the collection and sale of produce such as honey was critical to subsistence.[7] Lacking both numbers and organization, hunter-gatherers were unable to effectively challenge these new incursions into their domain. One of the few options available to them was to become part-time employees of the forest department. Another option, equally precarious in an economic sense but which afforded them at least some measure of autonomy, was to take to banditry. Both the Chenchus of Andhra Pradesh and the Lodhas of Bengal turned to robbery after being evicted from their forest home, thereby fulfilling a grim prophecy: for when the 1878 Act was being framed, villagers had warned that the likely consequences of cutting off traditional sources of livelihood to forest tribes would ultimately be faced by them. After the bill became law, they pointed out, 'it will be extremely difficult for [the forest tribes] to earn their maintenance without a resort to unlawful means such as plundering the helpless inhabitants of the villages'.[8]

The communities practising swidden or jhum cultivation were a rather more difficult proposition for the state. Jhum cultivators were far better organized than hunter-gatherers, and were known to possess a proclivity for militant confrontation. At the same time, the state wanted—for reasons which will become clear presently—to restrict jhum as far as possible. These reasons were both practical and ideological, and since they also seem to underlie the policies of the present government, I shall spell them out at some length.

The deep-seated prejudices of colonial officials stemmed above all from their unfamiliarity with a form of agriculture that had sustained its practitioners for thousands of years. Influenced by the agricultural revolution in Europe, the British deplored the seeming waste of land and resources involved in cultivating plots for a few years

---

[7] The classic ethnographic studies of hunter-gatherers in the colonial period are S.C. Roy, *The Birhors* (Ranchi, 1925), C. von Furer Haimendorf, *The Chenchus* (London, 1943) and U.H.R. Ehrenfels, *The Kadars of Cochin* (Madras, 1952).

[8] Memorial to Baron Lytton, Viceroy of India, from the inhabitants of Kolaba collectorate (signed by about 5000 people), dated 21 December 1877, in B. Progs no.54, March 1878, Department of Revenue and Agriculture (Forests) (hereafter DRAF), National Archives of India, New Delhi (hereafter NAI).

before leaving them fallow. They believed this to be neither efficient agriculture—which they equated with fixity of cultivation; nor good forestry—for the methods of burning adopted by jhumiyas rarely allowed trees to attain a 'marketable' girth. The British further held that the rotational system of cultivation—and the frequent moving of homesteads it entailed—bred a wayward and lazy cast of mind. 'These erratic and wasteful clearings', exclaimed the first inspector-general of forests, Dietrich Brandis, 'give unsettled habits to the people, and make all improvement of their moral and material well-being difficult if not impossible'.[9]

A more practical reason for such hostility was that jhum often prevented alternative economic uses of hilly or forest land. The growth of state forestry coincided with the expansion of plantations in tea, coffee and rubber, and in areas such as Coorg and the Nilgiris the latter interests predominated. Where jhum inhibited the growth of plantations, its abolition could conceivably solve what was at that time one of the plantation economy's most pressing problems—a guaranteed labour force. One coffee planter combined self-interest with a shrewd appeal to the commercial instinct of the colonial state:

With regard to Kumari [shifting] cultivation, the Government, in my opinion, is the great loser, there being very seldom more than one crop of ragi taken from any one patch, which, if cultivated with coffee, would have yielded something every year for half a century, in the way of rent or tax . . . The more I think of Kumari, the more surprised I feel that it has been tolerated for such a length of time. It is carried on by a set of savages in every sense of the word, who would be much more profitably employed on public works or on coffee plantations.[10]

The territorial competition between commercial forestry and jhum cultivation was, however, clearly the most important reason for the state's opposition. Throughout the 1870s forest and revenue officials were worried that the effective control over vast forest areas enjoyed by jhumiyas was a precedent the state could ill afford, envisaging as it did an act which would once and for all vest all forest areas in the

---

[9] Note by Brandis, dated 22 July 1874, in Progs No.1, August 1874, DRAF, NAI. The collector of the southern district of Canara wrote in August 1845: 'it [jhum] has no doubt some attraction for those who are impatient of control, and are fond of a wild roving life, but it leads to unsettled habits, and takes many away from the regular cultivation of a fixed spot.' Quoted in Cleghorn, p. 128.

[10] Quoted in Cleghorn, p. 129.

state. Brandis and his boss, the agricultural secretary, Allan Octavian Hume (better known as one of the initiators of the Indian National Congress), were outraged when both the Bombay and Madras presidencies allowed the continuance of jhum in certain areas. Hume warned the Bombay government that its policy of extending jhum was 'likely to be productive hereafter of the most serious evils'.[11] He was even more upset by the reported decision of a senior Madras official, W. Robinson, to grant rights of ownership over 740 square miles of forest to one family of shifting cultivators in South Kanara. Hume estimated that in fifty years' time that area would be worth 5 pounds an acre, or over two million pounds all told. 'It was the duty of the Government of India', he sarcastically observed, to 'watch carefully and satisfy itself that [Robinson's] kindly and warm-hearted sympathy for the welfare of the semi-savage denizens of the Kanara forests does not lead him into a too lavish dissipation of the capital of the state.'[12]

A further problem was that the forests controlled by jhumiyas often contained commercially valued timber species such as sal and teak. While deeming it unwise to completely ban shifting cultivation by the Baiga tribe, the government of the Central Provinces tried, with some success, to remove Baigas from the more valuable sal forests. The Baigas were permitted to continue cultivation in inaccessible areas and where the timber was 'less valuable'.[13] Likewise, the Madras government was unwilling to completely ban jhum, but at the insistence of their conservator of forests, Henry Cleghorn, they agreed it should not be allowed in localities where teak and blackwood flourished.[14]

The Madras government's transparent reluctance to go along with Cleghorn's proposals arose out of a fear of losing control. As an anthropologist working for the same government nearly a century later pointed out, although 'the forest department would welcome the complete stoppage of [jhum] it is not done for fear of fituris [tribal uprisings]'.[15] While detailed regional studies on the interaction between the colonial state and shifting cultivators are awaited, it does appear

---

[11] See B Progs no. 30, March 1878, DRAF, NAI.

[12] Note by A.O. Hume, dated 24 June 1876, in B. Progs no.10, September 1876, DRAF, NAI.

[13] See B Progs nos. 4–5, March 1874, DRAF, NAI.

[14] See Order of Madras government, no.737, dated 1 June 1859, in Cleghorn, pp. 134–6.

[15] A. Aiyappan, *Report on the Socio-Economic Conditions of the Aboriginal Tribes of the Province of Madras* (Madras, 1948), pp. 16–17.

that the state adopted a flexible policy, balancing the largely conflicting imperatives of the maximization of a timber output and revenue and the minimization of popular discontent. Depending on the relative pressures of commercial forestry and the maintenance of social control, three different strategies seem to have been adopted in different regions.

Firstly, wherever possible jhum was totally banned. Thus Cleghorn finally succeeded in removing shifting cultivators from the evergreen forests of the Western Ghats. A total ban was also implemented in portions of Coorg and Kerala, presumably to facilitate the growth of the plantation industry.

Where such radical measures were unfeasible, cultivators were removed from valuable forests and allowed to practise jhum in other areas. This was the case, as noted earlier, with the Baigas of the Central Provinces. In 1890 the state set aside 23,920 acres of forest on the Ramgarh tahsil of Mandla district. But as Verrier Elwin pointed out, even this chak or reserve was not 'a sort of national park where the Baiga would be allowed to carry on their ancient tribal life, but a Reformatory where the Baiga, under strict supervision and increasing official pressure, would be slowly "weaned" from their primitive habits' and induced to take up plough cultivation'.[16]

Perhaps the most innovative strategy was adopted in regions where even a partial ban was felt to be inadvisable. This was the taungya system of agri-silviculture, in which jhum cultivators were allowed to grow food crops in the forest, provided they planted 'useful' trees alongside. After a few years, when the cultivator had moved on to the next patch of forest, a commercially valuable forest crop had been established on the vacated ground. Originally used for teak cultivation in Burma, the method soon spread to other parts of India. Apart from enabling social control, it had the added advantage of solving at a 'comparatively low cost' the problem of labour supply in interior forest regions.[17]

The prohibition of jhum, whether partial or total, and the loss of forests generally, created an acute sense of deprivation among tribal communities. The new rulers had made them outlaws in their own land. Not only did forest regulations curb traditional forms of cultivation, they also restricted access to hunting and gathering for all classes.

[16] Verrier Elwin, *The Baiga* (London, 1939), p. 118.
[17] See H.R. Blanford, *Regeneration with the Assistance of Taungya in Burma*, Indian Forest Records, vol. xi, part III (Calcutta, 1925).

The affirmation of state control violated the aboriginals' notion of property, wherein forests and forest produce belonged to the community, 'every member of which had a prescriptive right' to harvest ` what they needed for subsistence.[18] Baulked at every turn, the aboriginals quickly found themselves on the wrong side of the law. Commenting on the extraordinarily high number of forest 'offences' in tribal districts of the Central Provinces, Elwin observes:

At every turn the Forest Laws cut across his life, limiting, frustrating, destroying his self confidence . . . It is obvious that so great a number of offences would not occur unless the forest regulations ran counter to the fundamental needs of the tribesmen . . . A Forest Officer once said to me: 'Our laws are of such a kind that every villager breaks one forest law every day of his life.'[19]

The resistance to colonial forest management spanned the continuum from 'avoidance' to 'confrontation'.[20] The first type of protest included such activities as covert defiance of the law, the continuance of hunting and cultivation in forest areas too remote for inspecting officials, and voting with their feet, i.e. migrating to forest areas where forest laws were less stringent. With variations in the intensity of forest operations and thereby of restrictions on jhum, the geographical interspersing of British ruled areas with princely states was effectively used by jhumiyas—cases were reported of migration both to and from princely states, depending on where jhum was permitted. At the same time, the new forest regime was directly responsible for a number of major tribal rebellions. These included a series of uprisings between 1879 and 1924 in the Gudem Rampa hills of present-day Andhra Pradesh, a rebellion in 1911 in Bastar which engulfed half the state (an area of about 6000 square miles), and a revolt by Gonds and Kolams in 1940 in Adilabad district of the State of Hyderabad. Both 'avoidance' and 'confrontational' modes of protest had deeper cultural roots, as aboriginals tried desperately to hold on to ways of life that had sustained them for thousands of years.[21]

[18] Cf. H.C.F. Ward, *Report on the Land Revenue Settlement of the Mundlah District of the Central Provinces (1868–69)* (Bombay, 1870), p. 90.
[19] *The Tribal World of Verrier Elwin: An Autobiography* (Bombay, 1964), p. 115.
[20] Cf. Michael Adas, 'From Avoidance to Confrontation; Peasant Protest in Precolonial and Colonial Southeast Asia', *Comparative Studies in Society and History*, vol. XXIII, no. II, 1981.
[21] For a detailed analysis of popular resistance to colonial forest management

III The March of Commercial Forestry

The edifice of colonial forestry was inherited by the government of independent India, and immediately put to work in the service of the state's primary goal of rapid industrialization. The national forest policy of 1952 underlies the continuity of colonial and post-colonial policies: upholding the 'fundamental concepts' of its predecessor, the forest policy of 1894, it reinforced the claim of the state to exclusive control over forest protection and production. Significantly, this policy identified shifting cultivation, which it held responsible for 'large scale destruction', as one of the main threats to state forestry.[22]

Since 1947 the industrial orientation of forest policy has passed through three distinct stages. In the first stage the forest department relied on the existing 'selection' system to harvest marketable species. Simultaneously, large industry was supplied raw material at highly subsidized rates. When these methods failed to meet the growing industrial demand, a second stage commenced in which large tracts of natural forests were clearfelled and planted over with monocultures of exotic species such as eucalyptus and Caribbean pine. The failure of plantation forestry (in one state, Karnataka, yields were between 14 to 43 per cent of those projected) forced industry to partially abandon the forest department and look elsewhere. In this third stage both government and industry have offered handsome subsidies to private farmers to plant eucalyptus as industrial raw material.[23]

How have tribal communities responded to the march of commercial forestry? The forest law has continued to be a formidable deterrent; at the same time, commercial felling has radically altered the species mix of the forests (usually in favour of species with little use to the local economy) or made many formerly tree-clad areas totally bare. In the circumstances, most hunting and gathering communities have only one survival strategy open to them: to put their enormous knowledge of flora and fauna at the service of the new owners of their habitat, the forest department. Thus the Jenu Kurubas of Mysore, with

---

and relevant references, see Ramachandra Guha and Madhav Gadgil, 'State Forestry and Social Conflict in British India: A Study in the Ecological Bases of Agrarian Protest', *Past and Present*, no. 123, May 1989.

[22] Anonymous, *The National Forest Policy of India* (Delhi, 1952), p. 7.

[23] See Madhav Gadgil, S.N. Prasad, and Rauf Ali, 'Forest Management and Forest Policy in India: A Critical Review', *Social Action*, New Delhi, vol. XXVII, no. II.

a tradition of helping the state in the capture of elephants, now collect honey and other forest produce on behalf of the forest department and merchants. In one taluk, Heggen Deve Kote, the department was earning revenue of Rs 25 million per year from minor forest produce in the 1970s, collected mostly by Jenu Kurubas working for a small daily wage. These tribals have very little freedom of choice with respect to work—they either work for the department or face the threat of eviction. This near-total dependence led one anthropologist to characterize the forest department and Jenu Kuruba relationship as 'feudalistic'. The Hill Pandaram in Kerala, who also depend heavily on the collection of minor forest produce, are equally afraid of the forest department. Living in what are now legally 'reserved forests', they live in terror of government officials who often extract favours from them. Even where hunter-gatherers are comparatively autonomous of the forest department, ecological changes have forced new adaptive strategies—for example the sale of small animals, honey and plants to nearby markets.[24]

On the whole a stronger and better organized group, jhum cultivators have continued to resist forest policies. In Madhya Pradesh jhum was banned in all areas covered by the Indian Forest Act, including large tracts earlier under the princely states. Undeterred, tribals continued to follow the traditional rotations, although these areas had now been constituted as state reserves. When prosecutions and monetary fines failed to stop jhum cultivation, the forest department turned to the police, who made several arrests. The release of the jhumiyas was made conditional on a promise that they would take to plough cultivation.

The transparent unwillingness to give up their traditional occupation was illustrated by the case of the Baigas. While the forest authorities were 'hopeful of persuading [the] younger generation of Baigas to give up bewar [jhum] altogether', the older generation was unyielding. It believed 'the Baigas were born to be the kings of the jungle and the soil' and did not at all want to give up jhum, which provided 'the link with the past and with their ancestors'.[25]

[24] See P.K. Mishra, 'The Jenu Kurubas', in Surajit Sinha and B.D. Sharma (eds.), *Primitive Tribes: The First Step* (Delhi, 1977); Brian Morris, *Forest Traders: A Socio-Economic Study of the Hill Pandaram* (London, 1982).

[25] R.N. Datta, in *Indian Forester*, vol. 80, 1954: National Council of Applied Economic Research, *Socio-economic Conditions of the Aboriginals of Madhya Pradesh* (Delhi, 1963), pp. 77–8.

Over many areas the specific issue of jhum has been submerged in the larger question of tribal rights in the forest. Anthropologists were hopeful that the new nation would redress the injustices which the tribals had suffered in colonial times. While their concerns found their way into important policy documents (including the Indian Constitution), there continued to be a wide gulf between policy and implementation. A special commission set up in 1960 to enquire into tribal problems was everywhere 'flooded with complaints from the tribals and their representatives against the forest administration'. Despite nearly a century of government control, the tribals were unshakeable in their belief that 'the forest belonged to them'.[26]

Viewing the forest department as a comparatively recent interloper, and undeterred by the provisions of the forest act, many tribal groups mounted a sustained challenge to the continuing denial of their rights. In 1957 a movement broke out among the Kharwar tribals of Madhya Pradesh which called upon the people 'to stop payment of rent to revenue-collecting agents, utilise timber and forest produce without making any payment, defy magistrates and forest guards, and flout the forest laws which violated tribals' customary rights'. The movement's slogan, *Jangal Zamin Azad Hai* (forests and land are a free gift of nature) succinctly expressed the opposition to external control and commercial use. For a time the movement brought forest operations to a standstill, dissipating only after the arrest of its leaders. Forest grievances also played a major part in a tribal revolt, led by Maoist revolutionaries, that broke out in the late sixties in the district of Srikakulam in Andhra Pradesh. Restrictions on jhum, oppression by forest officials and the state's reluctance to allow forest labourer co-operatives were all cited as reasons for tribals joining the communist-led movement, which was crushed only with the use of substantial police force.[27]

More recently, attempts by the state to convert the mixed forests of Central India into monocultural plantations have met with stiff resistance. The Bihar Forest Corporation's policy of replacing sal and mahua forests with teak has been bitterly opposed by Ho, Munda and Santhal tribals in the Chotanagpur area. In August 1979 the tribals, armed with bows and arrows, began cutting down the newly planted

---

[26] Government of India, *Report of the Scheduled Areas and Scheduled Tribes Commission* (Delhi, 1961).

[27] K.S. Singh (ed.), *Tribal Movements in India, Volume II* (Delhi, 1983); Leslie Calman, *Protest in Democratic India* (Boulder, 1985).

teak saplings, asking simultaneously for their replacement with trees of species more useful to the local economy. The opposition to teak drew sustenance from the wider movement for a separate state of Jharkhand. A slogan of the movement, 'Sal means Jharkhand, Sagwan [teak] means Bihar', captures these links between economic and ecological exploitation. Outside Bihar, a World Bank aided project for raising Caribbean pine as raw material for a new paper mill was stopped as a consequence of local opposition. And in the Midnapur district of Bengal, tribals have opposed both the auction of forests and attempts to clearfell sal to raise eucalyptus.

Changes in the proprietary status of the forests, as well as changes in its ecology, have clearly undermined the capacity of forest-dependent modes of subsistence to reproduce themselves. At the same time, the continuing resistance of tribals to state control has been no more than a holding operation. And as commercial forestry continues its apparently unstoppable march, many forest-dependent communities— both hunter-gatherers and shifting cultivators—have been forced to accept the new systems of forest working. The only option available to them—wage employment in commercial forestry—ironically, concedes the inevitability of the new forest regime. One can see a classic process of proletarianization at work: divorced from the means of production (forests and land) previously under their control, forest dwellers are forced to accept a subordinate place in the new (state) 'capitalist' system of production. This process has generated a new set of conflicts characteristic of capitalism, in which labourers seek to improve their wages, while capitalists seek to maintain high profit margins.[28]

The basis of such conflicts lies in the very mode of forest working in India, the so called 'contractor' system. Although the state owns the forests, until very recently it has played little part in the actual extraction of timber and other forest produce. The procedure most widely followed is to mark, according to silvicultural prescriptions, the trees to be felled in any given year. The trees are then collectively sold and auctioned to the highest bidder, who is then issued a contract by the state. This 'contractor' is responsible for organizing labour, conducting felling operations and transporting the converted logs directly to the actual user. A similar procedure is followed with respect to minor forest produce, wherein yearly contracts are offered to the

[28] Nirmal Sengupta (ed.), *Jharkhand: Fourth World Dynamics* (Delhi, 1982); Peoples Union for Democratic Rights, *Undeclared Civil War* (Delhi, 1982).

highest bidder for the collection of any particular item—e.g. sal seeds —from a designated patch of forest.

Corruption and waste are inherent in the contractor system. It is well known that at departmental auctions the contractor often bids a price far higher than the actual value of the marked trees, and then goes on to disregard silvicultural prescriptions by felling both marked and unmarked trees. By depressing wages, contractors realize staggering profit margins of up to several hundred per cent. Similar profit margins are realized by the processing industry, especially in the case of low bulk, high value items (e.g. perfumes) processed from minor forest produce.[29]

Policy documents have acknowledged that contractors exploit both forests and their labour—the need to replace contractors by forest labour co-operatives has been stressed by all the five-year plan documents. A committee set up in 1967 to look into the tribal-contractor-forest nexus cynically observed that in this case they did not 'envisage the need for any changes in the wording of the existing [forest] policy'. The cynicism was warranted—for even in the one state, Maharashtra, where forest labour co-operatives had been encouraged by the state following tribal movements in the 1940s, their share in forest operations has been slowly dwindling.[30]

The state's unwillingness to replace the contractor system has given rise to militant movements of forest labourers. Protesting low wages, tribals have repeatedly struck work, refusing to deposit bundles at collection centres. In heavily forested areas such as Srikakulam in Andhra Pradesh and Gadchiroli in Maharashtra, tribals are being organized by Marxist revolutionaries—the so-called 'Naxalites'. Despite some successful struggles for wage increases, tribals continue to get only a tiny share of the gains from commercial forestry. Nor have they benefited from the abolition of the auction system in some states and the takeover of forest working by government co-operatives. Nor is the state a model employer. As the commissioner of scheduled tribes found, the forest department frequently violated the minimum wages act in dealing with tribal forest labourers.[31]

[29] For examples, see Guha, 'Forestry'.

[30] Government of India, *Report of the Committee on Tribal Economy in Forest Areas* (Delhi, 1967), p. 13; S.W. Muranjan, 'Impact of Some Policies of the Forest Development Co-operation on the Working of the Forest Labourers Co-operatives', *Artha Vijnana*, vol. 22, 1980.

[31] See *Report of the Commission for Scheduled Castes and Scheduled Tribes for 1986–87* (Delhi, 1988); Ranjit Gupta et al., *Tribal Unrest and Forestry*

I should briefly mention two additional threats to aboriginal populations. A powerful impetus for forest destruction in recent decades has come from the siting of large dams, for both irrigation and power generation, which often submerge large areas of forest apart from displacing thousands of people. The craze for dam-building has reached its apogee with the Narmada Valley Project, a gigantic enterprise which envisages the construction of thirty major dams and several thousand medium and minor dams. When completed, this project will displace up to 200,000 people, a substantial proportion of whom are tribals, and submerge 40,000 hectares of some of the finest forests in the subcontinent. The opposition to large dams is gathering ground in different parts of the country, and the politics of water-use is likely to overtake forestry as the most hotly debated subject on the Indian environmental agenda.[32]

The second threat stems ironically not from intensive resource use but from its obverse—the sharp curbs in certain areas on commercial and subsistence uses of the forest. I refer to the massive network of wildlife sanctuaries, covering over 3 per cent of the country's land area, almost all established after 1947. Internationally acclaimed as showpieces of conservation, these sanctuaries have often had an adverse effect on the lives of nearby human populations. While the populations of large mammals, around which the most important sanctuaries are centred, have prospered, villagers both aboriginal and non aboriginal living on the periphery of the reserves are inadequately protected from crop damage, man slaughter and other hazards. There are also serious curbs to the gathering of forest produce within the boundaries of sanctuaries, including the ban in several areas on the ritual hunt central to the religious life of many tribal communities.[33]

IV

This paper has documented the decline and fall of two systems of

---

Management in Bihar (Ahmedabad, 1981).

[32] Kalpavriksh, *The Narmada Valley Project: A Critique* (Delhi, 1988); Anil Agarwal and Sunita Narain (ed.), *India: the State of the Environment 1984–85; A Citizens Report* (Delhi, 1985).

[33] Centre for Science and Environment, *India: The State of the Environment 1982: A Citizens Report* (Delhi, 1982), chapter IX; Ministry of Home Affairs, *Report of the Committee on Multipurpose Tribal Blocks* (Delhi, 1960), chapter VIII.

resource use once widely prevalent in peninsular India. For all practical purposes, hunter-gatherers are extinct on the Indian mainland, although small communities exist in the Andaman and Nicobar islands. Yet in numerical terms the decline of shifting cultivators has been even more dramatic. It is likely that as late as the mid-nineteenth century, over a million people depended on jhum in peninsular India; today the number is less than 50,000.

While hunter-gatherers have been powerless to resist the forces of the state and the modern economy, shifting cultivators, as we have seen, have been capable of militant resistance. In the circumstances, ideology has continued to play a key role in the state's bid to wipe out jhum cultivation. In independent India the mantle of the forest official, in this respect, has been taken up by the high priests of development planning, the economists. They claim that jhum has 'adverse physical consequences' which are 'well accepted'. It 'destroys the ecological balance, results in substantial soil erosion which subsequently leads to flooding of rivers [and] dries hill springs'.[34]

Analogous to the stereotypes created by colonial officials, the picture development economists paint of jhum is deeply tainted with prejudice—it is certainly not based on any first hand acquaintance with its system of production. The work of anthropologists provides abundant documentation that under conditions of stable population growth shifting agriculture is in fact a highly efficient and sustainable use of resources.[35] A major study of the Hill Marias of Abujmarh, one of the few surviving tribal communities in peninsular India who still depend exclusively on jhum, demonstrates that under the long fallow system practised by the Marias both soil fertility and forest vegetation have sufficient time to recuperate.[36] And as Furer-Haimendorf and his

---

[34] T. Gupta and S. Sambrani, 'Control of Shifting Cultivation: The Need for an Integrative Approach and Systematic Appraisal', *Indian Journal of Agricultural Economics*, vol. XXXI, no.1, 1978.

[35] The best-known studies are probably Clifford Geertz, *Agricultural Involution* (Berkeley, 1963), and Harold Conklin, *An Ethno-ecological Approach to Shifting Agriculture* (1954), reprinted in Andrew Vayda (ed.), *Environment and Cultural Behaviour* (New York, 1969). Conklin is generally credited as the first anthropologist to provide a defence of swidden, based on his own fieldwork in the Philippines; Verrier Elwin's ecological defence of jhum, though certainly not as sophisticated in its approach or as detailed in its documentation, was made two decades earlier in his study, *The Baiga* (London, 1936).

[36] Savyasachi, *Fields and Farms: Shifting Agriculture in Bastar*, mimeo, World Institute of Development Economics Research, Helsinki, May 1987 (part of a

colleagues observe, 'some of the largest natural forests exist in areas inhabited by slash-and-burn cultivators for centuries, whereas plough-cultivation has destroyed forests wherever it is practised'.[37]

As Verrier Elwin and other anthropologists have pertinently observed, jhum is not merely an economic system with certain ecological impacts; to its practitioners it is a way of life, the core of their mental and material culture. While its critics are quick to show population growth as the most important reason why jhum can no longer be allowed, they usually ignore the takeover of vast areas by the state which first undermined the ecological viability of jhum through most of peninsular India. In any case, most areas earlier controlled by jhumiyas and taken over by the state have been subject to greater, not lesser, forest exploitation, chiefly for the market.

This retrospective defence of the ecological and cultural integrity of jhum cultivation is perhaps largely for the record. Of the 640,000 jhum cultivators in the country today, 95 per cent are in north-eastern India. Faced with ecological decline, continuing political opposition and rising populations, including the invasion of their territory by outsiders, it is only a matter of time before the last jhum cultivators in peninsular India are forced to accept a subordinate position within the dominant system of agricultural production. Reconciled to this collapse, radical political organizations working among the tribals in central India are now concentrating on forging alliances with other groups left behind by the 'development' process. One section of the Jharkhand movement, for example, is keen on overcoming the identification of the movement with tribals, trying instead to build a broad-based coalition in which dispossessed tribals rub shoulders with industrial, agricultural and mining labour. The focus of the Jharkhand movement as a whole is on the creation of a separate province within the Indian Union. Apparently, tribal organizations have accepted as a *fait accompli* the destruction of their way of life, demanding instead territorial control over land traditionally inhabited by them. In any case, ecological degradation, population growth, and the expansion of mining and industrial operations in tribal areas have long since made the revival of jhum a forlorn hope.

Ph.D. dissertation completed at the Department of Sociology, Delhi University).

[37] Urmila Pingle, N.V. Rajareddy, and C. von Furer-Haimendorf, 'Should Shifting Cultivation be Banned?', *Science Today*, Bombay, March 1982. Furer-Haimendorfs own major ethnographic study of shifting cultivators is titled *Hill Reddis* (London, 1943).

It is the task of historians and anthropologists, among others, to document the pain and suffering that flowed from the collapse of a once vibrant cultural and ecological system. However, detailed regional studies of the decline of jhum cultivators and hunter-gatherers may be of more than academic interest. For in many respects the history of state-forest relations in peninsular India has anticipated a similar process in the forest regions of the north-east. Here too the state has repeatedly expressed its desire to completely do away with the 'primitive' system of shifting cultivation and introduce the tribals of the north-east to more 'modern techniques' of agriculture.[38] At the same time, the last great forest frontier in the country, the north-east, is being invaded by the same plywood and paper companies which have decimated the bamboo and hardwood forests in central and southern India. In this unequal encounter the state is following its penchant for condemning jhum while allowing 'scientific' forestry to take its place. It is possible, though perhaps not probable, that at least in some areas the rights of tribals to land, water and forests will be protected. A great deal will depend on the tribal leaders who are now in control of the provincial legislatures and ministries, and the effectiveness with which they can resist the blandishments of the state and its desire to integrate what it views as more 'backward' regions into the national 'mainstream'. The battle has not yet been lost or won.

[38] See for example, 'Change Sought in Tripura Farming', *Times of India*, 3 March 1988; Usha Rai, 'Jhum as an Ecological Disaster', *Times of India*, 15 November 1987; 'Plan to Control Jhum Cultivation', *The Statesman*, 20 September 1987.

From Savages to Security Risks: The Indian Question in Brazil

DAVID MAYBURY-LEWIS

HISTORICAL BACKGROUND

The Portuguese arrived in Brazil in 1500 and were received in a friendly fashion by the Indian tribes along the coast. These amicable relations soon soured as the Indians discovered that they were expected to work for the invaders and would be forced to do so if necessary. While the Portuguese footholds on the Atlantic coast of South America were still weak and being contested by France, Holland and England, the Indians managed to maintain their independence. They were sought as allies in European disputes. But as the Portuguese established themselves more firmly, they subdued and enslaved the coastal Indians.

The total population of Portugal in the early sixteenth century was approximately one million and the nation already had overseas commitments in Africa and the East Indies. Unlike England, Portugal had no surplus population of its own to send out to the Americas and, unlike Spain, it did not find large settled Indian populations in its American territories. There was therefore a shortage of colonists and labour in Brazil from the very beginning.

At first the crown toyed with the idea of educating the Indians to become its loyal citizens and to hold its Brazilian territories for it; but such ideas were soon abandoned in the face of settler opposition. The settlers wanted slaves and became expert at sending out slaving expeditions to capture and bring in Indians. These expeditions were known as *bandeiras* (flags) and the *bandeirantes*, or people who showed the flag, later became the explorer-heroes of Brazilian history books. Their role as enslavers is glossed over in modern Brazilian schoolbooks by stating that the work of the Indians was essential to the progress and prosperity of the colony.[1]

[1] See David Maybury-Lewis, 'Images of the Indian in Brazil and the Southern Cone', to appear in M. Gutierrez-Estevez, Leon-Portilla, Gossen and Klor de Alva

The Jesuits, led by the remarkable Father Antonio Vieira, opposed this policy on both moral and practical grounds. They argued that Indians should not be enslaved without just cause and that if one wished to Christianize and civilize them, one should gather them in properly run settlements under Jesuit tutelage. They did persuade the king to abolish Indian slavery for brief periods in the seventeenth century and to permit them to run Indian settlements, which did indeed flourish. But the settlers objected, to the point of rebellion, and the Jesuits were forced to compromise. Indians in Jesuit settlements were exempt from slavery but they had to be rented out to work for the colonists at illusory wages for six months of the year. Meanwhile, other Indians could legally be held as slaves.

In the mid-eighteenth century the powerful Marquis of Pombal instituted a series of reforms that were intended to modernize Portugal. He too thought of abolishing Indian slavery but eventually preferred to abolish the Jesuits instead. They were expelled from the Portuguese empire in 1759. Pombal had already freed all Indians from Jesuit control (in 1755), and shortly after he decreed that they be settled in directorate villages.

These were so called because the crown appointed directors of the settlements, who were expected to put the Indians to work. They could be rented out to colonists, put to labour on public works, or sent as paddlers and porters to man the flotillas of canoes that made official journeys along the great waterways in the interior of Brazil. Indians particularly feared and hated being conscripted for this task because it took them away from their own subsistence farming for months at a time and caused great hardship to their families. It was also back-breaking work from which some of them never returned at all. In this system of state-sponsored forced labour the profits were allocated to a whole series of people, from the king down to the director himself. The Indians, if they were paid at all, often received their wages in negligible amounts of cloth, a commodity they did not particularly want but which their masters thought they ought to use.[2]

Brazil was not densely populated with Indians to begin with, and

---

(eds.), *In Word and Deed: Inter-ethnic Images and Responses in the New World* (Madrid, Mexico City, Siglo 21).

[2] For accounts of policies toward the Indians in colonial Brazil, see John Hemming, *Red Gold: The Conquest of the Brazilian Indians* (London: Macmillan, 1972); and John Hemming, *Amazon Frontier: The Defeat of the Brazilian Indians* (Cambridge: Harvard University Press, 1987).

the effects of the conquest reduced that population drastically, there as elsewhere. It is estimated that there may have been 2–4 million Indians in Brazil in 1500 and that this number had been reduced by warfare—but mainly through disease and the brutalities and starvation of slavery and forced labour—to approximately 100,000 by the beginning of the nineteenth century.[3] Indian labour thus became less and less significant in the economy of the colony. Blacks had been imported in large numbers to toil on the sugar plantations of the northeast, and by the beginning of the nineteenth century it was the black slaves who were working in the plantations in Brazil. The relative numbers are important. When a dissident branch of the Portuguese royal family declared Brazil an empire independent of Portugal in 1822, almost a third of its population was white: about two-thirds of it consisted of Blacks and Mulattoes (the majority of them slaves), and only about 5 per cent of it was Indian, with many of these living beyond the frontier of settlement.[4]

In imperial Brazil during the nineteenth century the official policy of the crown was still to bring Indians into settlements and put them to work under court appointed overseers. But these settlements were seen as a means of solving remote local problems by civilizing savage Indians who would otherwise threaten the frontier. Meanwhile the Indian question had become a minor issue, economically and politically.

At the end of the nineteenth century the major social issues in the country were Black slavery (abolished in 1888), the monarchy (overthrown in 1889), republicanism (the republic was proclaimed in 1889), regionalism and the rights of the rural oligarchs who intended to control the new republic. The Indian question was not on the national agenda.

The Portuguese did not sign treaties with Brazilian Indians nor were Indian rights to land ever recognized, either in colonial or imperial times. It is true that there were those who felt that these rights

---

[3] It is extremely difficult to calculate the number of Indians who lived in what is now Brazil in 1500. For a discussion of various estimates and how they were calculated, see Hemming, *Red Gold*, pp. 487–92. My figure for the number of Indians in Brazil at the time of Independence is drawn from Dauril Alden, 'Late-Colonial Brazil, 1750–1807: Demographic, Economic and Political Aspects', in Leslie Bethell (ed.), *The Cambridge History of Latin America* (Cambridge: Cambridge University Press, 1984).

[4] Hemming, *Amazon Frontier*, p. 176.

ought to receive some sort of recognition. The Jesuits referred to the Indians in the seventeenth century as the 'natural lords of the land'. Jose Bonifacio de Andrada e Silva, sometimes known as the patriarch of Brazilian independence, argued that the settlers were usurpers, who owed it to the Indians to respect their rights.[5] But these views received little political support. The crown wavered but always came round to the settlers' view that Indians were savages who should be civilized by being put to work for the Portuguese. In the nineteenth century, when Indian labour had been largely replaced by Black labour, the prevailing view changed. Indians were still considered savages, but they were now looked on as savages who should be eliminated to make way for the advance of civilization.

FROM SPI TO FUNAI: INDIAN POLICIES IN THE TWENTIETH CENTURY

The Indians became a national issue at the beginning of the twentieth century when German immigrants, clearing new land in the south, clashed with Indians in the state of Santa Catarina. The Germans hired professional Indian hunters to rid themselves of the Indians who were harassing them. The atrocities committed by these men were denounced at an International Congress in Vienna in 1908. Professor von Ihering, the German-born director of the Museum of the State of São Paulo, one of Brazil's prestigious research institutions, defended the colonists, saying they had a right to protect themselves. The Indians, he argued, were bound to disappear anyway. Indeed they had to make way for civilization.

His view was opposed by liberals, supported by scientists from the National Museum in Rio de Janeiro. They rallied round a young army officer, Candido Mariano da Silva Rondon, himself part Indian, who had become a Brazilian hero by leading an expedition to the north-western extremity of the country to lay the first telegraph line in those parts. Rondon was a deeply religious positivist. He believed sincerely in progress and was convinced that the Indians, whom he considered to be at an earlier stage of this process than their white neighbours, could and should be helped to move up the ladder. During his expedition he told his men that their motto as regards the Indians

---

[5] Jose Bonifacio de Andrada e Silva, *Apontamentos para a Civilização dos Indios Bárbaros do Reino do Brasil* (Lisbon: Agencia-Geral do Ultramar, 1963/ 1823).

was to be 'die if need be, but never kill'. In this way he made friends with the Indians along the route and the success of his expedition was in no small measure due to this policy. Rondon therefore returned to Rio, preaching a gospel of kindness toward the Indians.

The pro-Indian faction managed to get public opinion on its side by playing on Brazilian nationalism. Rondon's policy was held to be in the best tradition of Brazil's own Christian values, and it was depicted as contrasting sharply with the imperialist and racist views of the Germans.[6] This nationalist view won the day and in 1911 the government set up the Service for the Protection of the Indians and the Settlement of National Workers (hereafter SPI). The enabling legislation for the Service was extraordinarily liberal, guaranteeing to Indians the continued use of their lands and the right to maintain their own cultures. The SPI was expected to protect Indian peoples and to enforce these guarantees. Rondon became its first President.

The SPI was founded in an era when the federal government in Brazil was weak and took a minimalist view of its role. The Service was, however, consistently overextended and underfunded. It offered Indians some protection by the very fact of its existence and its ability to threaten federal intervention in matters which local settlers would rather deal with themselves. But the greatest protection enjoyed by the Indians in the first half of the twentieth century was that the majority of them lived in areas remote from the national life.

Meanwhile some SPI officials perfected the techniques of making friends with remote Indian tribes. The Service adopted Rondon's motto, 'die if need be, but never kill', as its own and its experienced agents ventured into the wilds to search for uncontacted Indians. When they found traces of them they left presents along the trails and continued doing so until the Indians made contact with them of their own free will. The technique, if carried out with a great deal of patience, usually worked. When the opening up of the interior began in earnest, however, the SPI agents began to worry that they were 'bringing in' Indians whose societies would then be destroyed by the colonists flooding into the backlands.

[6] The national debate that led to the creation of the SPI is discussed in David H. Stauffer, 'The Origin and Establishment of Brazil Indian Service, 1889–1910', Ph.D. Dissertation, University of Texas at Austin, 1955; and also in D. Maybury-Lewis, 'Becoming Indian in Lowland South America', in *Nation-states and Indians in Latin America* (University of Texas Press, 1991); and Darcy Ribeiro, *Os Indios e a Civilização* (Rio de Janeiro, Civilização Brasileira, 1970).

The first attempt to open up the west came under the administration of President Getulio Vargas who assumed power in 1930. But Vargas was preoccupied with other matters, including the industrialization of Brazil, and his march to the west petered out. It was not until the administration of President Juscelino Kubitschek (1956–61) that the opening up of the interior began in earnest. Kubitschek inaugurated the nation's new capital at Brasilia in 1960, which in turn was connected by an all-weather road to Belem, at the mouth of the Amazon. This provided regular north-south overland communication for the first time in Brazil's history and opened up central Brazil to settlement.

By the early sixties the country was torn between its developmental euphoria and the festering social problems near the coast. The north-east of Brazil was a poverty-stricken area containing nearly thirty million people. Land hunger was growing elsewhere. The rural poor were swelling the slums of the big cities to dangerous proportions. When a populist leader acceded to the presidency by accident in 1962 and appeared to be trying to rally the masses against the oligarchs, the military overthrew him and took power in 1964.[7]

The military government suppressed all opposition, crushed the outspoken union organizations and moved to solve the problems of the coast by opening up the interior. Development was their aim and those who opposed or stood in the way of their development plans were considered subversives and dealt with accordingly. The Indians fell into this category and were ruthlessly treated, so that Brazil found itself being accused of genocide in the world's press. Agents of the SPI were accused of selling out the Indians to the colonists and even of collaborating with the colonists in killing the Indians they were supposed to protect. The government reacted by disbanding the SPI and replacing it in 1967 with FUNAI (The National Indian Foundation). It also sponsored an inconclusive inquiry into the atrocities against the Indians but punished no one.

In retrospect it is remarkable that the SPI was founded at all, and even more remarkable that it should have been brought into existence by the terms of legislation that would be considered liberal even today and was well ahead of its time in 1910. We should remember however

---

[7] At that time Brazilians voted for the president and vice-president on separate slates. When Janio Quadros won the presidency, the opposition candidate João Goulart was elected to serve as his vice-president. Goulart acceded to the presidency after Quadros' surprise resignation in 1962.

that even those who sympathized with the Indians at the turn of the century thought that their days were numbered. The Indianist writers of the late nineteenth century, who wrote feelingly about the injustices done to the Indians and about their noble and tragic struggles to preserve their freedom, wrote of them in the past tense. Their literature was an extended elegy for a dying race.[8]

When the famous debate between von Ihering and the Indianists took place later, both sides felt that they were speaking of small numbers of people at the frontier who would have to make way for civilization. The argument was really about the process and not about the end result. Von Ihering thought that the Indians would vanish— probably die out or be killed as a result of their own intransigence. Rondon respected them and their intelligence. He therefore felt that they could eventually become as civilized as other Brazilians. In the meantime their lands and their customs would need to be protected. Either way the Indian way of life would eventually disappear.

As for the legislature in 1910, it was dominated by the rural oligarchy that held power in Brazil. They welcomed a federal agency to deal at federal expense with Indians at the frontiers, who might otherwise become a nuisance for the states. Guaranteeing their lands was of little significance for these lands were remote and undesirable and beyond the frontiers of settlement. Guaranteeing their customs was likewise an insignificant gesture, for the Indians would eventually abandon them anyway, as they became civilized.

Brazilian policy towards the Indians has thus always rested on the presumed need to civilize them, and the assumption that this would lead to their eventual absorption into Brazilian society. Brazilians had always been uneasily aware of the fact that theirs was a society that had tolerated a great deal of miscegenation. After the influential works of Gilberto Freyre, which started appearing in the 1930s, this was seen as something to be proud rather than ashamed of.[9] Brazil, according to Freyre's thesis, had avoided the nastier extremes of racism to be found elsewhere in the world, because of the Portuguese tolerance for other races and other cultures. Brazil had thus become a racial and

---

[8] The most important of the Indianist writers were the poets Antonio Goncalves Dias and Gonçalves de Magãlhaes, and the novelist José de Alencar.

[9] See Gilberto Freyre [*Casa-Grande e Senzala*, 1937], *The Masters and the Slaves: A Study of the Development of Brazilian Civilization*, translated from the Portuguese from the fourth and definitive Brazilian edition (New York: Knopf, 1946).

cultural melting pot. Yet Freyre too wrote of the Indians as if their culture had already vanished, leaving behind only Indian traits such as beliefs, recipes and rhymes that had now been absorbed into the dominant Brazilian culture. This thesis still exerts a powerful hold on the Brazilian imagination, as we shall see, and continues to affect Brazilian policy towards the Indians.

FUNAI AND THE TREATMENT OF INDIANS BY THE MILITARY REGIME 1964–1985

FUNAI has been caught in a dilemma since its inception. It was supposed to protect the Indians, but it was also the agency of a government committed to development and not squeamish about the rights of those whom it felt 'stood in the way' of development. Like the SPI before it, FUNAI has not been able to protect the Indians from the consequences of the government's own policies. On the contrary, the government expects FUNAI to oversee the smooth execution of those policies.

The first presidents of FUNAI, all military officers, stressed that the motto of their agency was '(national) Security and Development'. In the early 1970s the government was encouraging cattle ranching on a massive scale in the interior and the ranches were encroaching on Indian lands. FUNAI did little to protect Indian lands. Instead it concentrated on making sure that the Indians too contributed to national development through the notorious system known as the 'Renda Indigena' (Indian Fund). Under this system, reminiscent of the Directorate, Indians would be gathered into villages under the tutelage of FUNAI and put to 'productive' work. The proceeds from their work would go to FUNAI, which would then use them 'on behalf of the Indians', i.e. to defray the operating costs of FUNAI itself.

These policies aroused fierce opposition. An Indian movement began to take shape.[10] The Catholic church, through its newly created indigenist arm known as CIMI (The Indianist Missionary Council), helped Indian leaders get together to discuss their common problems. A number of national organizations were formed to support the Indian

[10] See Roberto Cardoso de Oliveira, 'Indian Movements and Indianism in Brazil', *Cultural Survival Newsletter*, 5(1), 1981; and David Maybury-Lewis, 'Indian and Pro-Indian Organisations', *Cultural Survival Quarterly*, vol. 8, no. 4, 1984.

cause. These included pro-Indian commissions, set up largely by anthropologists, which worked closely with nascent Indian organizations; CEDI, a São Paulo based organization that collects and analyses information on the Indian question and thus acts as an intellectual centre for the Indian movement; CETI, a São Paulo-based organization that hoped to sponsor projects that would be genuinely helpful to Indian communities; and ANAI, the National Association for Support of the Indian, that set up chapters in various cities. Meanwhile international organizations continued to take a close interest in Brazil's treatment of its Indians.

For a while the government temporized. It appointed a moderate director of FUNAI, General Ismarth de Oliveira, who sought to collaborate with Indians and anthropologists in development programmes that would benefit the Indians. But the balancing act could not be sustained for long. The government soon proposed that all Indians who could be considered acculturated should be 'emancipated. General Ismarth de Oliveira resigned and was succeeded by others who were willing to implement this policy.

Emancipation in one form or another has since become the central theme of Brazil's Indian policy. It was originally presented as a progressive measure, similar to the emancipation of the Blacks in 1888. It was Rangel Reis, the minister of the interior, who drew this parallel but, as Indians and others were quick to point out, 'it was a false analogy.'[11] The Indians were not slaves, who needed to have their servile status altered in law. On the contrary, they were people whose rights to their own lands and own cultures were already guaranteed under Brazilian law. FUNAI was the government agency responsible for enforcing those guarantees. The Indians wanted FUNAI to do its job of protecting their rights. The government's proposal of 'emancipation' would not accomplish this. It would only free the Indians from FUNAI's tutelage and leave them to take their chances without official assistance against the forces arrayed against them.

FUNAI's tutelage of the Indians has always been an ambiguous and haphazard affair. Under Brazilian law all Indians were technology minors and FUNAI was their legal guardian. The Indians demanded FUNAI's help in protecting their rights, but rejected FUNAI's attempts to control their lives. The government wanted it the other way

[11] Beltrao, Luiz, *O Indio, um Mito Brasileiro* (Petropolis: Editora Vozes, 1977), p. 47.

round, seeing FUNAI primarily as an instrument of control that would keep the Indians quiet and in their villages, except where those villages had to be moved to make way for 'progress'. In fact FUNAI found it impossible to exercise the control that the government desired, except in places so remote that the Indians depended on FUNAI for transport to get out.

Meanwhile FUNAI tried, also unsuccessfully, to prevent the formation of Indian organizations. It had the police break up meetings of Indian leaders, alleging that such meetings were illegal unless they had been authorized by FUNAI. The agency gained further notoriety by trying to prevent Mario Juruna, a prominent Xavante, from obtaining a passport to travel to Amsterdam, where he was invited to serve on the Russell Tribunal to hear evidence of atrocities against tribal peoples around the world. Lawyers came to Juruna's aid and he got his passport.

Juruna came to prominence in the late 1970s, during the period of the *abertura* (opening), when the country went through a lengthy transition from military to civilian rule. He set himself up as a sceptical mediator between his people and the whites. He bought himself a tape recorder out of his earnings as a ranch-hand and used it to tape the promises made to the Xavante by visiting dignitaries. He would step forward and inform them that they could not renege, since he had their promises taped. The press was delighted by this outspoken Indian who was willing to tell generals to their faces that he did not believe what they said, and he became a celebrity. In 1982 he became the first Indian in Brazil to hold federal office, when he was elected a federal deputy representing the state of Rio de Janeiro in the first elections held since the military took power.

FUNAI was unsuccessful in controlling Mario Juruna, but it still struggled to control the Indians. It maintained its policy of distinguishing between 'real' Indians—isolated and unready for civilization, who would be protected on FUNAI's reserves—and acculturated Indians, who should give up being Indian and accept emancipation as soon as possible.

FUNAI's most famous reserve was the Xingu National Park, established as a refuge in the heart of Brazil by the Villas-Boas brothers. They had worked initially for President Vargas' Central Brazil Foundation. Later their reserve became the official responsibility of the government Indian agencies, though the Villas-Boas brothers continued to administer it with their well-known personalist flair. FUNAI liked to point to the reserve as an example of how well Brazil's protective policy was working and how misguided therefore were its critics. But the reserve was in fact the exception to the rule of what was happening to Brazil's Indians. Moreover it was not a wholly admirable exception, for the Indians who lived in it were maintained in a kind of picture-postcard isolation. In fact they became an attraction for affluent tourists and postcards of them were sold all over Brazil. Meanwhile, little attempt was made to prepare them for a future alongside the whites.[12]

In this the Xingu peoples presented a dramatic contrast with most of the other Indian groups in the country, for FUNAI was determined to emancipate the others as soon as possible. It put pressure on individual Indians to declare themselves emancipated, and thus no longer Indian. It insisted that Indians who earned diplomas and qualifications that would permit them to work in Brazilian society should not receive them unless they were willing to sign that they were emancipated. In this way FUNAI hoped to persuade ambitious Indians to give up their Indianness and at the same time to make sure that educated Indians did not lead the Indian movement, for they could only use their education by renouncing their Indianness. FUNAI even tried, unsuccessfully, to persuade Brazilian anthropologists to help it to establish the criteria of Indianness that would enable the agency to distinguish scientifically between real Indians and acculturated Indians who no longer deserved FUNAI's assistance.

Meanwhile the pressure on Indian lands continued unabated. There was a gold rush in the northern state of Pará. Large reserves of tin, cassiterite and bauxite were discovered, so that mining companies as well as ranchers now coveted Indian lands. FUNAI had never had most of these lands formally demarcated and allotted to the Indians; nor had it succeeded in protecting them against invasion by outsiders. There was thus an outcry when FUNAI announced that it was studying ways to allow mining companies to operate on Indian lands under FUNAI supervision.

As the political opening progressed FUNAI became increasingly demoralized. The Indians had by now learned to come to Brasilia to present their grievances in person. Delegations of Indians came to the

---

[12] See Eduardo Viveiros de Castro, 'When the Mask is Removed: What is the Truth about the Xingu Park?', in *Brazil*, Cultural Survival Special Report No. 1 (Cambridge: Cultural Survival, 1979).

nation's capital, where they met opposition deputies and pro-Indian sympathizers. The pressure on Indian peoples and Indian lands was now regularly discussed in Brazilian newspapers. In fact this became a way of alluding to the burdens placed by the Brazilian model of development, not just on the Indians but on the rural poor as well. The plight of Brazil's Indians now received international attention once again. At the urging of Cultural Survival and other organizations that had been supporting the struggle of the Brazilian Indians, the World Bank adopted guidelines for the protection of the environment and of the rights of tribal peoples in areas affected by its loans.[13] Brazil accepted funds from the Bank to improve its road system to the north-west, along the famous route of Rondon's telegraph line. FUNAI agreed to do its part to protect the many small Indian tribes that would be affected along the way. In fact the project turned into an ecological disaster and FUNAI so significantly failed to fulfil its obligations towards the Indians that the World Bank actually halted disbursements on the loan for a time.

The government responded to this national and international concern in characteristic fashion. FUNAI took placatory measures. It appointed more Indians to visible positions in FUNAI itself, including Megaron, a Kaiapo, appointed as director of the Xingu National Park, from which the Villas-Boas brothers had retired. FUNAI also funded development projects to assist some particularly outspoken Indian tribes.[14]

But the substance of the government's policy remained unchanged. It continued to insist that development was its overriding priority and that Indians should not be allowed to stand in the way of it, but should be integrated into Brazilian society as soon as possible. Meanwhile it took the process of demarcating Indian lands out of the hands of FUNAI and made it infinitely more complex than before. FUNAI had to initiate the process, but was required to submit its documentation to an interministerial council which often demanded fresh studies. Eventually, if the council approved, the demarcation

---

[13] World Bank, *Economic Development and Tribal Peoples: Human and Ecological Considerations* (Washington, D.C.: World Bank, 1981).

[14] The best known and most ambitious of them was the now defunct Xavante project. For a critique of that project, see David Maybury-Lewis, 'Brazilian Indianist Policy: Some Lessons from the Shavante Project', in Theodore Macdonald, Jr. (ed.), *Native Peoples and Economic Development*, Occasional Paper 16 (Cambridge: Cultural Survival, 1985).

decree was sent to the president of the republic for his signature. As a result, the demarcations, which were already badly in arrears when FUNAI was responsible for them, were virtually paralysed.

The period of military rule in Brazil (1964–85) combined developmentalism with repression of dissent. When the military encouraged aggressive development of the interior in the sixties, the Indians, along with others, suffered severely. The international reaction to this caused the government to take steps to repair the damages—not to the Indians but to the image of Brazil. Since those early days the government has proceeded more cautiously. Rather than admit that it is uninterested in demarcating and guaranteeing Indian lands, it has made the procedure impossibly complicated and does it rarely and only when obliged to. Meanwhile it insists that it has the best interests of the Indians at heart by campaigning steadfastly for their integration into Brazilian society. Their policy is one of encouraging all the forces that threaten Indian rights, while only pretending to protect those rights. This policy is however complicated by the fact that the Indians have mobilized to defend themselves and have elicited considerable support both nationally and internationally. It is this fact that has precipitated the crisis in Indian affairs which I will discuss in the next section.

THE INDIAN QUESTION AND NATIONAL SECURITY

In recent years, under successive civilian administrations, Indian affairs in Brazil have been treated as a matter of national security. This is extraordinary enough to call for some explanation. Indians, after all, constitute a fraction one per cent of the country's population and they live scattered in its remotest areas. Furthermore, as we have seen, the Indian question has not figured prominently on the national agenda since early colonial times. The Portuguese never clung to the legal fiction that Brazil was an unoccupied land.[15] Indian labour was too important in the colonial economy for this to be plausible. But the Portuguese crown never formally recognized the rights of the Indians. Nor were these rights mentioned at the time of independence. Brazil did not gain its independence by fighting a war against the mother country in the name of freedom. It was achieved without ringing

---

[15] As did the British, for example, in Australia: see Kenneth Maddock, *Your Land is our Land* (Melbourne: Penguin Books, 1983).

declarations concerning the rights of man, when a branch of the Portuguese royal family separated to rule over the Brazilian empire. In the nineteenth century the Indians became less and less important as a national issue. In this respect Brazil contrasts with other American countries, such as Chile, Argentina and the United States, which likewise had sparse Indian populations that were not large or central enough to provide a significant pool of labour for the state. All of these countries, with the exception of Brazil, ruthlessly suppressed the Indian populations at their frontiers in the nineteenth century. These campaigns cannot be explained as reactions to threats that the Indians were thought to pose. Only in Argentina did a relatively small number of Indians harass the frontiers of the state and bar the way to the pampas. It is rather to the national agenda of each state in the mid-nineteenth century that we must look to understand their treatment of their Indian populations.[16]

Towards the end of the nineteenth century Chile had secured its northern borders by defeating Peru in the War of the Pacific. New technology and new world markets now offered lucrative profits to landowners who exploited the fertile southern regions of the country. The new technology also, and at last, gave the Chilean army the power to defeat the Mapuche Indians, who had halted Spanish expansion in the sixteenth century and had defended their autonomy ever since. The Mapuche could have been left alone, but Chile was in a period of national consolidation and unwilling to allow the country to be bisected by a semi-autonomous Indian territory. It therefore moved against the Mapuche and seized the greater part of their lands in the name of progress.

Similarly, Argentina at the end of the nineteenth century had come through the war with Paraguay and its own civil wars to embark on a phase of national consolidation. New technology and new markets offered enormous profits to landowners if they could establish themselves on the pampas. As in Chile, the technology also gave the army the weapons to defeat the Mapuche's Araucanian cousins who controlled the fertile grasslands. General Roca's famous 'conquest of the desert' was planned as an expedition to 'cleanse the country of savages'. The land controlled by those same 'savages' was divided up in advance between landowners, speculators and the officers and men of Roca's army.

[16] For a comparative discussion of the treatment of Indians in Chile, Argentina and Brazil, see Maybury-Lewis, 'Becoming Indian in Lowland South America'.

By contrast, Brazil had no grand project to open up new lands in the late nineteenth century. It was a society that hugged its own huge coastline. Up until the mid-twentieth century 80 per cent of its population lived within 200 kilometres of the coast. In this effective national territory an oligarchic and agrarian way of life was firmly established. The interior of the hinterland continued to be explored but it was not exploited. Most of the Indians lived there and were left more or less alone, deemed irrelevant to the life of the nation. Brazil did not consider it a necessity at that time to defeat and dispossess the Indians at its frontiers.

Brazil's liberal Indian legislation of 1910 can be seen therefore as a statute passed by conservative oligarchs jealous of their class privileges and regional interests, the effect of which was to transfer responsibility for Indian affairs to the federal government. The laws were a high-minded gesture, thought at the time to have little practical significance. When Brazil embarked on its own push to the west half a century later, measures similar to the ones that the oligarchs had approved of so calmly in 1910 were hotly opposed by conservatives, who claimed that they would undermine the very fabric of the nation.

The opening up of the interior has been a perennial dream among Brazilian politicians and planners and, as we have seen, it was set in motion by two of Brazil's most energetically modernizing presidents, Getulio Vargas and Juscelino Kubitschek. But it was when the military took over in the mid-sixties that the westward expansion began in earnest. The military brought a sense of manifest destiny to the development of Brazil's Amazonian regions which was incorporated into the teaching at the *Escola Superior de Guerra* (the Advanced War College) and given theoretical expression in the writings of General Golbery de Couto e Silva.

The military did not, however, move outright to 'cleanse the country of savages'. Such rhetoric was used without embarrassment in official circles in Argentina and the United States in the nineteenth century. But Brazil recognized Marshall Rondon as a hero and repeatedly recommended him for the Nobel Peace Prize.[17] Even the military could not easily turn its back on the legacy of Rondon, nor casually repudiate Brazil's claim to be a country free of racial dis-

[17] It is said that the nomination was regularly rejected on the technicality that Rondon's work, in mediating between Brazil and its Indians, was not 'international' in the sense required by the prize committee.

crimination. Besides, times had changed. In the late twentieth century tribal peoples are still regularly dispossessed and killed in the name of 'progress', but this is no longer viewed internationally as a normal part of the process of 'civilizing' remote areas. Most governments therefore (Brazil's included) prefer to claim that, if such things happen, they are not deliberate, but are regrettable incidents which they are anxious to prevent.

Furthermore, the Indians were mobilizing to defend themselves and garnering national and international support as they did so. The mobilization did not come easily. Indians, after all, do not see themselves as 'Indians'. The blanket term is applied to them by the people who invade their territories, a lingering result of Christopher Columbus' famous confusion. Indian peoples do not automatically feel kinship with each other and the European invaders of the Americas systematically exploited the enmities between them for their own ends. In modern times, Indians who think of themselves as Xavante or Kaiapo or Yanomami have to learn to act together 'as Indians' in order to defend themselves within the political arena of the nation.

This was especially difficult in Brazil, where distances are huge, the Indians scattered and the authorities anxious to prevent contact between them. In the early seventies it was CIMI, the Indianist arm of the Catholic church, that initially helped Indian leaders get together to discuss their problems and work out common strategies of action. Other organizations soon offered their assistance as well. This help is still important, but the Indians have increasingly moved to take charge of the defence of their own rights.

Yet they have to proceed with caution, as the examples of what happened in Chile and Argentina clearly demonstrate. In those countries the Indians were defeated and massacred at the frontier. The survivors reorganized painfully over the years to protect themselves. They discovered their common Indianness within the nation, a quality that set them apart from the rural poor, whose lot they shared. They hesitated as to whether they should support the parties claiming to represent the rural poor within the political process. Eventually they did so and suffered savage repression as a consequence.[18]

The Indian peoples of Brazil are thus caught in a familiar quandary. If they forge political alliances to defend their interests, they are considered subversive by the authorities. If they do not, then they

[18] See Maybury-Lewis, op. cit.

are too weak to defend themselves. This became abundantly clear during the writing of Brazil's new constitution. President Sarney, who presided over the first civilian administration after the military had formally relinquished power, convened a large group of legislators to draft a new constitution for the country. The convention had, of course, to deal with the question of Indian rights. Pro-Indian advocates opposed FUNAI's policy of emancipation and that agency's attempts to redefine Indianness in such a way that the category of Indian would eventually be abolished in Brazil altogether. They wanted the new constitution to confirm the legislation of 1910, guaranteeing that Indian lands and Indian ways of life would be protected. They even wanted the constitution to go a step further and declare Brazil officially to be a multi-ethnic nation. Their opponents echoed the official view of the government that Brazil was a melting pot society in which there should be no permanent recognition of special status for the Indians. They urged that the constitution should provide for the rapid 'integration' (i.e. disappearance) of the Indians into the Brazilian population at large.

In support of the latter position Brazilian newspapers, using data supplied by FUNAI itself, argued that Indians, who comprise a tiny fraction of the population of Brazil, had far too much land. A study of these allegations carried out by Brazilian anthropologists in São Paulo and Rio de Janeiro demonstrated, however, that they were based on misleading manipulation of gross statistics.[19] Only 7.9 per cent of the lands counted by FUNAI as 'Indian lands' have actually been registered as such. FUNAI has not even initiated the process of demarcation for over half of the lands it lists as Indian lands. Much of the supposed Indian land has already been invaded and is neither used nor controlled by Indians. Moreover, FUNAI and the newspapers compared the amount of land per person supposedly controlled by the Indians with the national average, when it should have been compared with the rural average, since all Indians live in rural areas. When compared with the rural average, even the inflated figures for the Indians show them as controlling less land per head than is the rural norm. In any case, such figures are quite misleading since land in Brazil is unequally distributed. There is severe land hunger in most

[19] CEDI, *Terras Indígenas no Brasil*, Report prepared by the Centro Ecumenico de Documentação Indígena (São Paulo), and the Museu Nacional, Rio de Janeiro (São Paulo, CEDI, 1987).

rural areas, which is not reflected in gross figures of hectares divided by total population. Yet these statistical slanders are mild compared with other accusations in the campaign against Indian rights. In 1987, just before the constitutional convention was due to vote on the articles dealing with Indians, the Estado de São Paulo, the major newspaper in Brazil's major state, ran a series of front-page articles for a full week denouncing the supporters of the Indian cause for being engaged in what was headlined as a *Conspiracy against Brazil*.[20]

The Estado accused CIMI (and thus the Brazilian Catholic church) of taking instructions from a so-called 'Christian Church World Council' that was said to be co-ordinating an international conspiracy to restrict Brazilian sovereignty, especially in the Amazon. This would benefit foreign mineral companies at the expense of Brazilian ones. CIMI and other pro-Indian organizations were accused of manipulating the Indian issue to advance an internationalist cause that was profoundly harmful to Brazilian interests. The articles were picked up by newspapers all over the country, so that the accusations were broadcast nationwide.

The church responded immediately by initiating legal action against the newspaper, insisting on a Parliamentary Commission of Inquiry to investigate the accusations and publishing its own response.[21] The reply argued that the newspaper had misinterpreted the constitutional provision for Brazil to be a multi-ethnic society as one of 'dividing Brazil'. It also showed that much of the 'evidence' on which the Estado's sensational articles were based came from articles and reports that were partially and misleadingly quoted or were themselves suspect. For example, their documentation of the implausible link between CIMI and a non-existent Christian Church World Council (presumably a clumsy attempt to implicate the World Council of Churches) was a forgery. The campaign appeared to have

---

[20] See the *Estado de São Paulo*, whose series entitled 'The Indians under the New Constitution' ran from 9 August 1987 to 15 August 1987. The *Estado's* story on 9 August ran under the headline, 'The Indians under the New Constitution: A Conspiracy against Brazil'. On 11 August their headline was 'CIMI does not Live by Indians Alone'; on 12 August, 'CIMI and its Tin-mining Brothers'; on 13 August, 'Indians—The Way to Mining'; on 15 August, 'The Gospel According to CIMI: Indians, Gold . . . '

[21] CNBB-CIMI, *A verdadeira conspiração contra os povos indigenas e a igreja no Brasil*, Report prepared by the Conferencia Nacional dos Bispos do Brasil and the Conselho Indigenista Missionario, Brasilia (CNBB-CIMI, 1987).

been inspired by Brazil's largest tin-mining company, the Grupo Paranapanema, whose mining rights on Indian lands, granted by the outgoing military president João Figueredo, were being challenged by CIMI in courts.

In spite of the church's prompt response and of widespread scepticism about the Estado's charges, the campaign had its effect. It put the Indianists on the defensive and frightened away middle-of-the-road members of the constitutional convention who might have voted in favour of the Indian articles without giving them too much thought. The pro-Indian activists had to mount an all-out campaign to save what they could at the convention. In this they were aided by a contingent of Indians, mostly Kaiapo, who sat, painted and feathered, day in and day out, inside the parliament buildings, impressing the framers of the new constitution with their fortitude and persistence. In the end the article proclaiming Brazil a multi-ethnic society was voted down. Indian lands were not constitutionally protected against mining interests, though it was stipulated that they could only be mined under special circumstances with specific government authorization. But at least the rights of the Indians to their lands and their ways of life were written into the constitution and FUNAI's more objectionable policies of emancipation were excluded.

This partial victory for the Indians in law has to be set against the violence that continues to be perpetrated in present-day Brazil. Mining interests and agri-businesses encroach on their lands and Indians are killed in the process. This is done, moreover, with government encouragement, for, while the government officially deplores Indian deaths, it continues to encourage the process that causes them without giving Indians adequate protection.

The most notorious recent example of this process is what is happening to the Yanomami, who live astride the border between Brazil and Venezuela. These Indians had had comparatively little contact with the outside world before their lands were invaded by miners who first came to extract tin and then to dig gold. Supporters of the Yanomami in Brazilian society urged the government to designate and protect their territory as an Indian reserve. This was never done. FUNAI, occasionally supported by the federal police, did in fact make occasional and ineffective attempts to control the massive influx of miners. Meanwhile the Indians were decimated by disease, starvation caused by loss of their plantations and outright attack. Eventually the government virtually sided with the miners. President Sarney appointed Romeo Juca Filho, who as head of FUNAI had implemented the most hardline anti-Indian policies, to be governor of the territory (soon to be the state) of Roraima, where the Yanomami live. The result was predictable. The miners, tough and armed to the teeth, refused all suggestions that they leave and were supported in this by the governor of the state. Indian and pro-Indian organizations obtained an injunction in a federal court in Brasilia ordering the miners to leave Yanomami territory. The federal government argued that it was powerless to enforce the measure. President Sarney's successor, President Collor de Melo, responded to growing international concern about the rain forests and the Yanomami by stating that he would if necessary blow up the landing strips that were the lifeline of the miners. But the miners are still there in force. Meanwhile the government has expelled all missionaries and pro-Indian advocates from Yanomami territory, leaving the miners and their supporters in control of the situation.

It is clear that the civilian administrations that succeeded the military have not found it in their political interest to act firmly on behalf of the Indians. This shows up a cruel feature of the Indians' situation in countries like Brazil, where they are a small and scattered minority. Civilian governments are much more susceptible to pressure from anti-Indian forces than from the Indians and their allies. Military regimes, which are not so susceptible to pressure, are not usually sympathetic to the Indians.

In Brazil at present the Indians have the worst of both worlds, since Indian affairs have been militarized under a civilian regime. This militarization is especially evident in Amazonia, where the armed forces have been permitted by the civilian administration to plan and put into effect the *Calha Norte* or Northern Drainage project in virtual secrecy from 1986 until the present. A working group of the National Security Council elaborated the plan, calling for a series of interrelated activities sponsored by various government agencies and spearheaded by the military. Its purpose is to establish an effective military presence in Brazil's Amazonian region, to develop it, to guarantee its frontiers and to adopt a new policy towards the Indians who inhabit it.[22]

The proposals for the Indians are particularly revealing. The working group stresses that the development of the Amazonian region will depend on mining, but notes that much of its mineral

[22] See João Pacheco de Oliveira, 'Projecto Calha Norte: Militares, Indios e Fronteiras', *Série Antropologia e Indigenismo*, #1 (Rio de Janeiro.; Editora UFRJ, 1990).

wealth lies in territory occupied by Indians. It proposes therefore that the laws controlling mining on Indian territory (and indeed the very definition of what constitutes Indian territory) be altered so that development may proceed without Indians being permitted to stand in its way. Meanwhile the plan calls for FUNAI to construct new agencies and airstrips in northern Amazonas as part of the new presence that the state and the military are seeking to establish there. There is little attention given, or money allocated, to measures that would benefit the Indians themselves (as opposed to FUNAI). The Indians are supposed to be acculturated and thus to disappear as soon as possible.

Consistent with this aim is FUNAI's stated resolve that it will in future only protect the lands of unacculturated Indians. Since FUNAI sets itself up as the judge of which Indians are acculturated (i.e. no longer Indian) and which are not, this enables FUNAI to 'emancipate' Indians administratively from its protection, even though such measures are not sanctioned in the constitution. Indians who FUNAI decides are acculturated—and such a determination may be made if they can so much as speak Portuguese—will not have their rights to land defended by the government. The most they can hope for is to be removed to 'colonias indigenas' (Indian settlements) where FUNAI will run their lives and turn them into mainstream Brazilians as rapidly as possible.

The determination of successive governments, the military and FUNAI to do away with the Indians altogether is part of a long tradition of ethnic suppression in the Americas. Since the nineteenth century the elites of Spanish and Portuguese America have been trying to abolish the category of *indio*. Reformers sometimes hoped that if this category, with all its pejorative connotations, could be eliminated from the law and even from the language, then those who had previously suffered from its stigma could blend with the rest of the population and become ordinary citizens, usually *campesinos*. This has not happened, for two reasons. First, the host populations have not been very welcoming to Indians, even if they were no longer called Indians. Second, a substantial number of Indians throughout the hemisphere cherish their heritage and struggle to preserve it. They do not want to be assimilated. In countries with large Indian populations, many Indians have maintained their Indian identities, despite all efforts to have them obliterated. Even in El Salvador, where Indians went underground and concealed their Indianness for many

years after the massacres of 1932, the indigenous population of the country has not been assimilated.[23]
In countries with sparse Indian populations another strategy was possible. The majority of the Indians could be annihilated and the rest absorbed. This was the solution pursued by Argentina. Brazil does not seek to annihilate its Indians physically, although it encourages development policies that may result in Indians getting killed. It does however strive hard to eliminate Indians culturally and socially, out of conviction that Brazil is a melting pot in which minorities must disappear.

The ideology of development is as important as that of the melting pot in Brazil's image of itself. The military and the technocrats who ran the country from 1964 to 1985 justified their authoritarian regime in terms of national development. Even to-day it is a serious matter to be accused of standing in the way of development, which is normally the charge that is levelled against the Indians. People who oppose development or those policies which the authorities say are intended to promote development are accused of being unpatriotic or downright subversive. Indeed, as current events in Brazil show, Indian peoples are often defined as being impediments to development simply by being who they are and where they are.

Such arguments are regularly used against indigenous peoples worldwide and are all too often accepted uncritically. In Brazil they cannot withstand informed scrutiny. The Brazilian model of development produced what was once called 'the Brazilian miracle' in the early 1970s, namely growth rates of up to 10 per cent per annum in the gross national product. It depended on export-driven growth, coupled with government assistance to agri-business, mining and certain kinds of industry. It neglected to build up the internal Brazilian market or to bring about the structural changes that would modernize Brazilian society and make it less inequitable. The model also relied on the military's ability and willingness to stifle all opposition to it, since it imposed considerable sacrifices on the bulk of the population. The strategy failed over the long term. Only specialists remember 'the

23 See Thomas P. Anderson, *La Matanza: El Salvador's Communist Revolt of 1932* (Lincoln: University of Nebraska Press, 1971); Theodore Macdonald, 'El Salvador's Indians' in *Cultural Survival Quarterly*, vol. 6, no. 1, 1982 (Cambridge, Cultural Survival), pp. 14–16; and Mac Chapin, 'The Five Hundred Thousand Invisible Indians of El Salvador', *Cultural Survival Quarterly*, vol. 13 (3), 1989 (Cambridge: Cultural Survival), pp. 11–16.

Brazilian miracle' now. Instead Brazil is notorious for its gargantuan foreign debt and its ongoing economic crisis.

None of this is the fault of the Indians. Nor is the rape of Indian lands likely to produce an upturn in the Brazilian economy now. It cannot therefore be defended on those grounds. These lands are being invaded simply because that is part of the dynamics of a development process sponsored by the government and encouraged and enforced by the military.

Nor can this flawed development strategy be defended on the grounds of equity. It certainly has not worked for the greatest good of the greatest number. On the contrary, Brazil's distribution of income is worse than that of India. Its maldistribution of land is reminiscent of Mexico before the revolution. Its social inequities have spawned despair, crime and death squads to deal with it. Amnesty International has recently issued a special report about the human rights violations taking place in Brazilian cities. It is clear that this is a society where 'development' has benefited a few and the costs of that process have been passed on to the many. It is equally clear that resources seized from the Indians will not be redistributed for the benefit of Brazilian society as a whole and it is also clear that the Indians are not expected to share in the wealth that may be produced off their lands.[24]

The developmental argument against indigenous peoples is normally as hollow in other parts of the world as it is in Brazil. It is rarely used alone, however. It is usually buttressed by the contention that minorities, if they are permitted even limited autonomy, pose a threat to the nation state. I have examined these arguments elsewhere and shown that they are usually self-serving.[25] The Indians pose no threat

[24] The argument from equity is criticized in David Maybury-Lewis, 'A Special Sort of Pleading: Anthropology at the Service of Ethnic Groups', in Robert Paine (ed.), *Advocacy and Anthropology: First Encounters* (St. John's Memorial, University of Newfoundland Press, 1985). From the extensive literature on the Brazilian model of development the following works are particularly relevant to the points made here: Albert Fishlow, 'Some Reflections on Post 1964 Brazilian Economic Policy', in Alfred Stepan (ed.), *Authoritarian Brazil* (New Haven: Yale University Press, 1973); and Joe Foweraker, *The Struggle for Land: A Political Economy of the Pioneer Frontier in Brazil from 1930 to the Present Day* (Cambridge: Cambridge Latin American Studies No. 39, 1980).

[25] David Maybury-Lewis, 'Living in Leviathan: Ethnic Groups and the State', in Maybury-Lewis (ed.), *The Prospects for Plural Societies*, Proceedings of the American Ethnological Society (1982) (Washington: American Ethnological Society, 1984).

to Brazil, economic or otherwise, but they do present an uncomfortable ideological challenge. Their demand to have their lands protected challenges the oligarchical assumptions of Brazilian society, both traditional and modern. Their demand to be allowed to retain their cultures, while nevertheless being accepted as Brazilians, challenges the self-image of the nation, for it insists that Brazil should not be a melting pot but rather a multi-ethnic nation based on pluralism and tolerance.

The elites and the military who run the country show little sign of being interested in either pluralism or tolerance in this sense. On the contrary, they appear to feel that Brazil is currently threatened and that firm measures are necessary to deal with the threats. The Amazon is a particular focus of their concern. They view with disquiet the international concern being expressed over the deforestation of the Amazon and react with understandable anger to calls for the internationalization of the region, arguing that Brazil is only doing what other countries (notably the United States) have done in order to develop. This had led to a determination to develop the Amazon quickly and to link it effectively and rapidly with the rest of the nation.

The Amazon, moreover, is a region in which Brazil borders on no less than seven other countries. The military is concerned about the effective defence of those frontiers against subversion of various kinds. The documents outlining the *Calha Norte* plan mentioned a possible threat from leftist regimes in Guiana and Surinam, which could very well join up with the east bloc countries to establish a communist foothold in South America.[26] The military is also worried about subversion from leftist guerilla movements in Colombia and Peru and even more so about the spread of drug trafficking into the Brazilian Amazon.

The combination of drugs, guerrillas and leftist regimes on its borders adds upto a powerful image of 'subversion'. The military worries that this contagion will link up with Brazil's internal 'subversives' and that this will destabilize the country by undermining the established order. The armed forces continue to insist on their special mission to protect the order and stability of the nation. Hence they throw their weight against all those who oppose the establishment, accusing them as often as not of 'subversion'.

This is particularly evident in current disputes over land. The

---

[26] Pacheco de Oliveira, p. 19.

concentration of land in the hands of relatively few owners and the desperate land hunger of the rural poor had reached crisis proportions by the time the military gave up formal control of the government in 1985. The first civilian administration to take office put land reform at the top of its agenda, but soon backed away from it in the face of conservative opposition. Government policy continues to favour development through agri-business and mining in rural areas, so the military cracks down on advocates of land reform. It does nothing, however, to curb the continuing violence of large landowners against smallholders and the rural poor. Instead it declares those parts of the country where the rural poor—usually supported by the liberal wing of the Catholic church—are really aroused over the land issue to be 'areas of national security' and places them under special restrictions.

All of these sensitivities implicate the Indians, who have become scapegoats at a time of national crisis in Brazil. Most Indians live in the Amazonian regions (broadly defined). Many of them are near the frontiers or occupy lands coveted by miners and businessmen or are in areas where the drug trade might take root. They are said to impede access to the nation's mineral and other resources and therefore to 'stand in the way of development'. Worst of all, their plight has been compared to that of the rural poor and used as an object lesson to show the severe costs of the Brazilian model of development.

Until now the Indians have had difficulty organizing a broad-based indigenous movement to protect themselves, and there has been comparatively little effort by indigenous groups to make alliances with labour associations or rural trade unions. Such alliances are now being made. Indians and rubber tappers are working together in the state of Acre, notorious as the place where Chico Mendes, the tappers' leader was gunned down by a local landowner. The Indians who organized a week-long protest meeting at Altamira to protest a dam that would inundate their lands used the occasion to raise the consciousness not only of the world but also of the local people of the region who were likewise imperilled.

The major support for the Indian cause inside Brazil is still coming however from religious and other non-governmental organizations and from a number of federal deputies and senators in the opposition. The anti-Indian campaign which was most blatantly expressed in the stories run by the *Estado de São Paulo* portrayed the Indians and their allies as conspiring against Brazil. This is precisely the definition of subversion used by the military. The official view implies that the nation has to choose between the nation and its destiny on the one hand and Indians and their rights on the other. This choice is, however, based on a false antithesis. In Brazil, as elsewhere, there is no necessary incompatibility between development and indigenous rights, between progress and pluralism. There is only incompatibility between indigenous rights and indeed the human rights of large segments of the population and the social arrangements and development policies that are currently being enforced. These could be changed. Indeed many people in Brazil are crying out for change, as the strong showing by 'Lula' Ignacio da Silva, the trade-union leader who was defeated in the final run-off in the last presidential election, indicated. Yet it is precisely these changes in the nation's thinking and the nation's social structure that are resisted by the conservatives and the military and their advocates classified as subversive.

The Indian cause attracted national attention during the 'opening' when the military were getting ready to relinquish formal power. At that time the plight of the Indians came to symbolize the hardships of the poor and the dispossessed under Brazil's model of development. When the violence being done to Indians attracted international attention as well, the authorities in Brazil took steps to protect the image of Brazil abroad and to deal with the subversives at home whom they accused of tarnishing that image, if not actually conspiring against the nation. The Indian question thus came to be treated as a matter of national security.

This does not mean however that the Indians in Brazil have lost the battle to protect their rights. Indian peoples are forming their own organizations and beginning to work out relationships with regional and national indigenous associations. These organizations are in turn supported by national and international associations as they engage in the political struggle on which the survival of indigenous cultures depends. Their success in this struggle will depend in turn on the extent to which the nation as a whole is able to adopt new ways of thinking and acting. But that is what the current turmoil in Brazil is all about and it is not only the Indians who are hoping against hope for a better future.

The Untouchables

OLIVER MENDELSOHN AND MARIKA VICZIANY

During the present century the Untouchables have been both invented and all but discarded as a political issue, while the circumstances of their living have undergone no comparable transformation.[1] Fifty years ago the practice of untouchability was the great moral issue for India but today this concern is no more than residual. This paper sets out to explore the construction of the Untouchables as a social and political category and the later conversion of this potentially radical grouping into a bureaucratic and welfare category in post-independence India. The paper will argue that in the process the Untouchables have failed to lose their status as a subordinated people.

Somewhat arbitrarily we can cite three grounds for the judgment that the Untouchables remain deeply subordinated, despite the undoubted progress they have made over the last half century. The first ground is their overwhelming poverty—as a category they form a large and disproportionate share of the poorest of the Indian population. They are at the bottom of Hindu society—in wealth, social status, education, health and cultural amenities. Secondly, Untouchables continue to suffer discrimination ranging from the routine denial of access to goods and services in social life and at the hands of the state, to occasional acts of inhuman violence. This discrimination is not merely the kind of treatment suffered by the poor in general but also proceeds from the uniquely low social standing of Untouchables. And thirdly, there is a widespread sense among Untouchables themselves that their low status marks them off from the rest of Hindu society. Significant, if isolated and fitful, mobilization of Untouchables as a separate political entity is a continuing phenomenon.

WHO ARE THE UNTOUCHABLES?

The Untouchables do not exist as a legal category, since the Constitu-

---

[1] The research on which this paper is based was made possible by a grant from

tion of India (1950) purported to abolish the condition of untouchability and made its practice an offence. But this was a formal and instrumental declaration, not a sociological statement. The same Constitution recognized the persistence of the problem of the Untouchables by laying the legal basis for a scheme of compensatory action for the so-called scheduled castes.[2]

By and large the scheduled castes were the 'depressed classes', itself a synonym for Untouchable castes, of the 1931 Census of India.[3] They now constitute almost 16 per cent of the Indian population—over 130 million persons.[4]

To what extent is this huge population a unit of political or social action rather than a mere bureaucratic category? In arguing that the Untouchables are a subordinated people, we have committed ourselves to the view that they have an identity distinct from other Indians. But this view is a contested one. There is no controversy that the Untouchables are descended from people who in the recent past have suffered significant discrimination. But what is not universally agreed is that there is today a body of people who are so ill-treated and so distinct from other Hindus that they should be separated out and labelled Untouchable. To run together a range of attitudes expressed over a number of years, the following propositions typify this approach. The so-called Untouchables are a regular part of Hindu society, which is an untidy aggregation of multiple compartments or statuses varying over both region or culture group and time. These people are distin-

---

the Australian Research Grants Scheme, and support and leave from La Trobe and Monash Universities.

[2] This term became potentially available in 1936, with the passage of the Government of India Act: certain castes were námed in a schedule to that Act. The followers of B.R. Ambedkar were the first to adopt the term, and it came into common usage after Ambedkar formed a party for Scheduled Castes in 1942: Eleanor Zelliot, 'Dr Ambedkar and the Mahar Movement', unpublished Ph.D. thesis, University of Pennsylvania, 1969, pp. 191–2.

[3] See Mohinder Singh, *The Depressed Classes—Their Economic and Social Condition* (Bombay: Hind Kitabs, 1947), chapter I and Appendix 1; Marc Galanter, *Competing Equalities: Law and the Backward Classes in India* (Delhi: Oxford University Press, 1984), chapters 5 and 6. The chief change from the 1931 list to the post-independence schedule is the addition of Sikh Untouchables: Galanter, p. 135.

[4] Government of India, *Selected Statistics on Scheduled Castes* (New Delhi: Ministry of Home Affairs, June 1984), Table 7, p. 9. In 1981 there were about 105 million scheduled caste persons in India, and by the 1991 census some 25 million would have been added assuming a decadal growth rate of 24 per cent.

guished by being generally poor and of very low status, but not so low that they should be identified as a collective grouping opposed to the remainder of higher-status Hindu society. Beneath all the differences among Hindus there is a profound unity, which binds the lowest to the highest. This unity is one of belief, culture and social interdependence. The practice of untouchability has been a serious moral problem for Hindu society but reform is now well under way. There remains some discrimination in various parts of India but this is only the anachronistic residue of a system which is now defunct. Progress is measurable by the fact that there is no widespread politics of untouchability; rather, the ex-Untouchables are by and large integrated into the general electoral politics of India. As the economic condition of the Untouchables improves, so will the residue of discrimination tend to disappear.

This characterization of the Untouchables' situation is not shared by the present writers, but the point of view is not implausible. Any contention that the Untouchables are a separate grouping at the bottom of Indian society is problematic. Thus, the Untouchables are not by themselves a class. The great majority of them are field labourers or workers in a range of other so-called unskilled occupations. Increasingly, they look like a particularly downtrodden proletariat and, in the cities, lumpen proletariat. But they share this social situation with many millions of Indians from different religious or caste backgrounds. So even if the concept of class is useful in analysing Indian society—and we believe it is increasingly useful—it will not do service in distinguishing Untouchables from other people.

If the Untouchables are not a class, then they are clearly not a people of any single ethnic identity; they possess no common physical form or cultural outlook. They speak the language of their region rather than any common language. Their forms of worship are usually recognizably Hindu, albeit skewed towards local folk traditions and usually stripped of discriminatory concepts like karma. And crucially, they are divided into castes which are organized on a regional basis. To talk about *the* Untouchables is not to identify a particular caste but to locate a large category within which there are many hundreds of castes. This variety of social life among the many millions of Untouchables makes the idea of a single grouping less than straightforward.

What the Untouchables do have in common is a unique form of discrimination at the hands of high-caste society, and this is the primary basis for regarding them as a distinct grouping within India.

In other words it is the oppressor rather than the victim who has primarily determined the Untouchables' identity *qua* Untouchable. It is true that millions of other low-caste Indians also suffer various ritual debasements, but these do not compare in severity with those suffered by the Untouchables; this is what makes the Untouchables different. The experience of untouchability does not constitute the whole of any person's social identity, but it is appropriate to see it as the most defining social characteristic.

Of course, common experience does not necessarily lead to common consciousness or common action—this is what led Marx to deny that the European peasants were properly speaking a class. In the case of the Untouchables, the formal political record is limited in scope and concentrated in particular historical periods. There has been only one high point of the political struggle, an almost opportunistic success on the part of B.R. Ambedkar some sixty years ago. For the rest, the political energies of the Untouchables have either been poorly organized or frittered away in endless internal divisions. This was the fate of the one significant Untouchable political party, which in any case was based only on Ambedkar's Mahar community of western India. Mostly, the Untouchables have been incorporated into electoral coalitions engineered by the Congress Party or, increasingly, other broad-based parties—for example, the Communist parties in the States of Kerala and West Bengal.

While the Untouchables have enjoyed little success in formal politics, they have conversely failed to disappear as a political force. It is possible to detect a strong Untouchable consciousness bubbling away below the surface of Indian political life. Sometimes this consciousness erupts in political demonstrations, violent actions or attempted party formation. Even in backward Bihar, for example, the lowly Musahars (the rat catchers) have for a number of years staged armed resistance to what they see as their agrarian oppressors. Everywhere, Ambedkar's potency as a symbol of Untouchable resistance has grown over the years; as one simple measure, his stone statue now stands in innumerable Indian streets. The most impressive expression of Untouchable resistance does not take strict organized form but consists in what James Scott has called the everyday resistance of the weak.[5] The image of the Untouchable as acquiescent in his/her

---

[5] James Scott, *Weapons of the Weak—Everyday Forms of Peasant Resistance* (New Haven: Yale University Press, 1985), pp. 28–48.

own subordination is no longer an accurate one. Where, for example, Untouchable women were often at the sexual beck and call of high-caste men, nowadays this occurrence is much resisted and hence much reduced. This resistance sometimes shades into more organized political activity: in Bihar, for example, the demand for social respect has been at the core of the so-called Naxalite activities for years.

If discrimination and resistance are the twin bases of an Untouchable identity, then their cultural and linguistic heterogeneity and relative lack of formal political organization no longer appear so critical. Clearly, these qualities represent a barrier to effective political mobilization but they scarcely serve as a denial of existence. The contrary position sometimes rests on the proposition that 'the Untouchables' are an observer category rather than an action grouping. Presumably the leading example of an action grouping is caste. Undoubtedly the Jats of Uttar Pradesh, for example, are an important action group in local and even national politics, in the sense that they collectively set out to maximize parliamentary representation from their own community and to promote policies which putatively benefit the group as a whole. The Untouchables, by contrast, clearly have no such common purpose or organization, though there are comparable examples of individual Untouchable caste organizations (for example, the Pulaya Mahasabha of Kerala). But none of this serves to render the Untouchables an 'observer' category—a term used to denote a category of analysis rather than action.[6] When the considerable political action is read in the context of the common consciousness of subordination we have identified, the distinction between observer and action categories is falsely drawn.

Part of the problem of fixing the social and political identity of the Untouchables arises from their ambiguous place within Hindu society. Thus we have already noted that the Untouchables are divided into many castes, but this is not something that arises directly from the great books of Hinduism. From the standpoint of orthodox (or Brahmanical or Vedic) Hinduism, Untouchables have no caste at all. Ostensibly every Hindu belongs to one of the four varnas, each of which has a distinct social occupation and identity. The varnas are Brahmin (priest and teacher), Kshatriya (prince and warrior), Vaishya (trader) and Sudra (servant). But not the whole of the population of

---

[6] Lloyd Rudolph suggested that this might be the appropriate way of looking at the grouping during a seminar on the present theme delivered by the authors to the South Asia Studies Center, University of Chicago, 18 October 1989.

the time was seen to be part of this order. The people without varna included those who incurred pollution from the work they perform— for example, the flaying of cowskins and fabrication of leather articles. To come into close contact (touch, smell, even proximity) with these permanently polluted persons was to be infected by the pollution (though this persists only for so long as purity has not been reinstated through ritual exercise). Ostensibly, then, the Untouchables—all 130 millions of them today—are descended from these polluted persons. Another way of putting it is to say that the Untouchables are 'without caste' or outcastes, for varna is the idea of caste which emerges from the great Hindu books.

But varna is not what one can see at work in village India today, though the categories can still have importance as ideology.[7] What is commonly understood by the word caste (itself a European term rather than a translation from Indian languages) most closely corresponds to the jati form. There are hundreds if not thousands of jatis in India, the largest containing millions of persons and the smallest perhaps only hundreds. The salience of jati rather than varna in everyday life can be reconciled with the view in the books by seeing jati as an elaboration of varna.

So where do the Untouchables fit in? If jati were simply an elaboration of varna, then there would be no Untouchable jatis. But the Untouchables are in fact divided into jatis in the same way that so-called caste Hindus are. Bhangi, Chamar, Dom, Dhobi, Paswan, Mahar, Madagi, Pulaya are some of the many hundreds of Untouchable castes or jatis named under the Constitutional Schedule as entitled to preferential treatment. In the local context everyone knows and operates on the basis that the Untouchables are part of their particular caste community. Despite the Hindu logic, then, the Untouchables possess caste as much as any other Hindu does.

The ambiguity of the Untouchables' situation is not confined to contrasts between the Hindu books and social practice. At an attitudinal and behavioural level high-caste Hinduism has been deeply unsure of just who the Untouchables are and what they represent. Sometimes, perhaps usually, they have been seen as part of the Hindu fold—despite the practice of the grossest discrimination. This has been particularly true at times of tension between Hindus and Muslims. But at other times the Untouchables have been regarded as a polluted and

[7] See Louis Dumont, *Homo Hierarchicus* (Chicago: Chicago University Press, 1970), chapters 2 and 3.

subordinate people which has pretensions but no claim to the status of being Hindu. Take the following example as one small illustration of this outlook. The British Census of 1881 reported a problem with some of its high-caste enumerators: they were refusing to sully the name of Hinduism by listing Untouchables as Hindus. The census commissioner of the Central Provinces said this:

Many of the more bigoted high caste Hindoos employed as census enumerators or supervisors objected to record such low persons as of the Hindoo religion. This was illustrated by numerous instances brought to my notice of such persons having been recorded as of the Dher, Mang, or Chandal religion by mere repetition of their caste in the column for religion. Possibly some in their humility and ignorance may not have claimed to be of the Hindoo religion. More probably they were not asked.[8]

It was far from coincidental that problems such as this surfaced in the course of an intrusive British presence in India. What we have called the ambiguity of the Untouchables' situation was not new, but the transformation of ambiguity into an intellectual and ultimately a political problem was very much an artefact of British rule.

THE EMERGENCE OF THE UNTOUCHABLES AS A POLITICAL GROUPING

Although there were earlier surges of interest in the position of the Untouchables,[9] the modern problem was framed in the context of the British intrusion into India. The British impact was accomplished without their having directly taken up the Untouchables as a moral cause; they had set out to preserve the social status quo, though their Christian missionaries had seen a magnificent opportunity in the oppressed Untouchables. Even without systematic intention, their interventions had the effect of allowing the Untouchable issue to emerge

---

[8] *1881 Census of India*, Census of the Central Provinces, General Report, p. 17.

[9] Untouchability as it is known today, had become entrenched in Indian society by about AD 200. Almost immediately a tradition of dissent was born in the Bhakti movement which, for many centuries thereafter, produced a large number and wide variety of bards who attacked the daily injustices of the caste system and offered those oppressed by it the solace of equality before God if not before Man. Some of the bards were themselves Untouchables—a good example is Chokhamela (*c.* thirteenth and fourteenth centuries). See, for example, Charlotte Vaudeville, 'Cokhamela, An Untouchable Saint of Maharashtra', *South Asian Digest of Regional Writing*, vol. 6, 1977, pp. 60–79.

as it never had. One of these interventions was the seemingly neutral and innocent institution of the census.

From the moment the British rulers began to count Indians, they began inventing criteria to classify and delineate the multiple religions, castes and tribes. The appropriate location of what were later called the Untouchables was a problem from the first full census of 1871/72 to the last of 1941. With the partial exception of the 1881 census, all the censuses ended up counting them as Hindus. But they were never seen by the British census officials as ordinary Hindus of particular caste. Nor were they viewed as a single entity with any internal coherence. The terms used to fix their status were primarily plural and adjectival: they were the depressed classes, inferior castes, menial castes, excommunicated castes, and so on.

The most controversial census was the 1911 one conducted by Gait. As preparation for the census, Gait issued a circular asking officials in the various provinces to comment on a list of questions to resolve the issue of which castes and tribes could properly be called Hindu. The questions included: 'are the members of the caste allowed to enter Hindu temples or make offerings at the shrine?' Another asked, 'will good Brahmans act as their priests?' And again, 'do they cause pollution (a) by touch; (b) by proximity?' Gait noted that once the appropriate tests had been ascertained, the next step would be to prepare a list of the castes and tribes 'which do not satisfy them and cannot therefore properly be regarded as Hindus'.[10]

Gait's approach provoked loud protest from Hindu leaders in the context of the emergence of a separate Muslim nationalism concerned to maximize the proportion of Muslims to Hindus. He had to abandon any effort to read any of the 'depressed castes' out of Hinduism and in his summary report he left the questions hanging as a kind of lame academic query beyond the powers of the census to pursue.

The motives of the British for their probings into the religious and caste structure of India are of no direct interest here. Suffice it to say that conclusive evidence of a primary concern to 'divide and rule' is hard to find. G.S. Ghurye's view is that 'the intellectual curiosity of some of the early officials is mostly responsible for the treatment of caste given to it in the Census, which has become progressively more elaborate in each successive Census since 1872'.[11] This is not

---

[10] *The Tribune*, 12 November 1919.

[11] G.S. Ghurye, *Caste and Class in India* (Bombay: Popular Book Depot, 1957), p. 193.

a view favourable to the British, since Ghurye regards the curiosity as gratuitous and resulting in 'a livening up of the caste-spirit'.[12] Whatever the British motives, the impact of the decennial census was diffuse but profound. One of the early effects of emphasizing the degraded condition of the huge population of 'depressed classes' was to bolster high-caste fears about Hindu vulnerability to Muslim and Christian conversion activities. The most determined response came from the Arya Samaj, a new Hindu reformist organization which carried out a campaign of ritual purification of Untouchables in the late years of the nineteenth century and the early years of the twentieth. There was no doubt some genuine concern about the condition of these people in the context of modernist ideas about equality. But the major inspiration was fear of a Christian and Muslim takeover. Some of this Hindu fear arose directly from missionary activities but it was the census which regularly focused, indeed stampeded, Hindu opinion.[13]

Beyond the subversive effects of the census, the impact of British rule on the Untouchables was often either indirect or confined to small numbers of people. In comparative terms, the Untouchables were less beneficially affected than many high-caste communities. True, some Untouchables got access to education, but this was no more than a trickle relative to the more respectable and prosperous communities. Recruitment into the army was significant for those who enjoyed it, but again the numbers were not large.[14] Comparatively few Untouchables were able to put down roots in the growing towns and cities of the nineteenth century;[15] this was a significant drawback in view of the relative prosperity possible in the urban situation for people (including many Brahmins and Kayasthas) from a landless background.

If the second half of the nineteenth century was the great period of social ferment for the Hindus in general, it was not until the second

---

[12] Ibid.

[13] As one example, see Shraddhananda Swami, *Hindu Sangathan, Saviour of the Dying Race*, March 1924, pp. 16–20.

[14] About 17 per cent of the Bombay Army recruits were Mahars in the late part of the nineteenth century, but Untouchables in the Madras and Bengal regiments constituted only about 5 per cent: Stephen F. Cohen, 'The Untouchable Soldier: Caste, Politics and the Indian Army', *Journal of Asian Studies*, May 1969, vol. 28 (3), p. 455. But even the higher Mahar total represented only a tiny proportion of the caste's population.

[15] As late as 1961 only 11 per cent of India's untouchables lived in urban areas and that percentage had risen to a mere 16 by 1981.

decade of the twentieth century that Untouchable communities were sufficiently conscious to begin serious social action. The first targets were Hindu temples of general worship, which in most parts of India excluded Untouchables from attendance. Demands for temple entry began in 1917 in Kerala, a region with some of the most inhuman traditions of Untouchable oppression. But the idea of Untouchables walking into Hindu temples was far too radical even for a protest movement, and so the Vaikom Satyagraha of 1924–25 diverted the question of temple entry into a struggle to allow Untouchables free access to the roads which converged on the Vaikom Temple.[16] Throughout the 1920s and into the early 1930s the issue of temple entry was bitterly fought for and led to considerable violence, even bloodshed in the case of western India.[17] At this stage Ambedkar's movement was in the forefront of the temple entry campaign, but Congress remained aloof. Although the nationalist movement was philosophically committed to temple entry, even the personally sympathetic Gandhi was not prepared to press for admission of Untouchables in the face of opposition of the temple membership, even if that opposition represented only a minority opinion.[18] This was a measure of the severity of opposition and also an index of Gandhi's own strategy of adopting causes which would consolidate rather than divide Indian opinion. In these circumstances progress was slow, if symbolically important: the first gains were the opening up of roads adjacent to temples in Travancore. But the temple entry movement itself came to nought. In western India Ambedkar and his followers were exhausted and disillusioned after a number of ineffective campaigns. By the early 1930s the Ambedkarites were ready to switch from social

[16] Mahadev Desai, *The Epic of Travancore* (Ahmedabad: Navajivan Karyalaya, 1937), pp. 10–23.

[17] The protesters at Vaikom had lime thrown into their faces (*Young India*, 3 July 1924), quoted in M.K. Gandhi, *The Removal of Untouchability*, compiled by Bharatan Kumarappa (Ahmedabad: Navajivan Publishing House, 1954), pp. 126–127; violent reaction to the Ambedkarite struggle for temple entry is documented by Atul Chandra Pradhan, *The Emergence of the Depressed Classes* (Bhubaneswar: Bookland International, 1986), pp. 123–24 and Dhananjay Keer, *Dr Ambedkar, Life and Mission* (Bombay: Popular Prakashan, 1987 edition), p. 138.

[18] This was clear in the campaign to enter the Guruvayur temple in 1931–32, when Gandhi devised a number of complex strategies to reconcile orthodox opposition to the notion of untouchables using the temple: M.K. Gandhi, pp. 90–2, and B.R. Ambedkar, *What Congress and Gandhi Have Done to the Untouchables* (Bombay: Thacker & Co., 1964), p. 116.

campaigns to political manoeuvering closer to the centre of institutional power.

The great political successes of the Untouchables are almost all concentrated in the short period from 1919 to 1932. By the end of this period the Untouchables had been firmly recognized as a grouping distinguishable from ordinary Hindus, such that they deserved special electoral arrangements. This recognition spilled over into the provision of special welfare benefits as early as the thirties, and in the post-independence period fed the creation of the world's largest scheme of compensatory discrimination or affirmative action. The scale of resources committed to compensatory discrimination in the post-independence period rightly makes the scheme seem the creation of independent India, but the crucial gains were made earlier.

The political successes of this period can mainly be attributed to three factors—first, the underlying support of half a century of British intellectual preoccupation with the bottom strata of Indian society; secondly, the emergence of a strong Muslim nationalism which presented the Untouchables with companion opportunities; and thirdly, effective new Untouchable leadership in the form of B.R. Ambedkar. Importantly, the victories were not achieved through any mass mobilization of Untouchables across different regions but essentially through elite action.

The first small victory came in 1919, as part of the Montagu-Chelmsford reforms to concede some limited Indian representation in government. Provision was made in the 1919 Government of India Act for the nomination of seven members of the depressed classes to the Legislative Council, the first recognition that the Untouchables had an interest separate from that of other Hindus. This result came about largely because of representations from Untouchables themselves, acting through their own organizations scattered throughout India.[19] For the British, the depressed classes were now a recognized and significant Indian minority.[20] The early institutional successes were built on during the period 1929 to 1932, encompassing the Simon Commission, the two Round Table Conferences and the Poona Pact. These have come to represent the great set-piece of Untouchable politics, pitting Gandhi against the Untouchable Ambedkar. Although

---

[19] See Atul Chandra Pradhan, pp. 99–103, and Dhananjay Keer, p. 33.

[20] India Office, Report on Indian Constitutional Reforms (presented to both Houses of Parliament), Cd. 9109 (London, 1918). pp. 188–9.

Ambedkar had been politically active among his own Mahar community and more widely among Untouchables, he was substantially unknown to nationalist leaders when he gave evidence before the Simon Commission in 1929/30.[21] The Commission handed him his first victory when it adopted his 'golden mean' of multi-member joint electorates with seats reserved for Untouchables. The principle of electorates for Untouchables was now won. The Simon Commission went so far as to declare that the election of Untouchable candidates was needed to 'train them in politics'.[22]

The rest of the story is well known. The recommendations of the Simon Commission were rejected by the Congress and the depressed classes but, on the strength of his showing before that Commission, Ambedkar was invited to the Round Table Conferences as one of two representatives of the Untouchables. He emerged from these with a concession by the British that the Untouchables were to have electorates constituted of Untouchables alone. But, more important, he succeeded in making a credible claim to lead a united Untouchable constituency.[23] Gandhi's reaction can be gauged from the following words in a speech he made to the Second Round Table Conference:

I can understand the claims advanced by other minorities, but the claims advanced on behalf of the Untouchables, that to me is 'the unkindest cut of all' . . . I claim myself in my own person to represent the vast mass of the Untouchables . . . (T)here is a body of Hindu reformers who are pledged to remove this blot of untouchability . . . *Those who speak of the political rights of Untouchables do not know their India . . .* [24]

Gandhi was outraged that Ambedkar was politicizing untouchability and thereby denying the sincerity of Hindu reformers led by himself

[21] Ambedkar's biographer goes so far as to maintain that Gandhi thought that Ambedkar was a Brahmin rather than an Untouchable until the time of the second Round Table Conference in 1931: Dhananjay Keer, p. 168.

[22] HMSO, Report of the Indian Statutory Commission, Recommendations, Cmnd. 3569 (London, 1930), vol. I p. 65.

[23] Ambedkar fought for political recognition of the Untouchables through the Minorities Committee at the Round Table Conferences and at the end of the Second Round Table Conference when that Committee had reached a stalemate he signed the controversial Minorities Pact between the depressed classes, Muslims, Indian Christians, Anglo-Indians and British Indians. These minorities all pledged to support each other.

[24] Indian Round Table Conference, 2nd session, 1931, Proceedings of Federal Structure Committee and Minorities Committee, London, H.M.S.O., p. 544; italics added.

and threatening the very integrity of Hinduism at its moment of trial by the Muslim leadership. His outrage was the greater by virtue of his ignorance of political organization among the Untouchables: Ambedkar's stand wrongly seemed to him to be built on no foundation of public support. It was almost as if Ambedkar was some kind of Trojan horse, so unhinged by 'the great wrong under which he has laboured' that he denied the unity of Hinduism itself.[25]

The conflict reached maturity in India the following year, when the British proceeded as part of their Communal Award to declare in favour of separate electorates for Untouchables. Gandhi's response was to enter into one of his 'fasts unto death' on 20 September 1932. Faced with the martyrdom of the great Mahatma, Ambedkar had no option but to back down.[26] He agreed to scrapping of the separate electorates for Untouchables in return for a substantial increase in the number of general seats to be reserved for candidates from the Untouchable castes.

Both sides were unhappy with this result, though by most reckonings Gandhi won.[27] But in the larger struggle of some three years' duration, Ambedkar had used the opportunities thrown up by British invitations and Muslim communalism to mount a credible challenge to Gandhi's claim to represent the Untouchables. He had seemingly transformed the untouchability question from a moral problem dominated by reformist Hindus led by Gandhi into a matter of political rights for a subordinated segment of Indian society.

Ambedkar's achievements were extraordinary, even astonishing, but they proved to be more of an end than a beginning. Ambedkar was unable to consolidate the gains in two vital political areas. First, the victories won at an elite level could not be translated into any mass mobilization of Untouchables on an all-India basis. For the next quarter century until his death in 1956 Ambedkar was in almost absolute command of his own Mahar caste, and he led them into permanent opposition to the mainstream nationalist movement represented by the Indian National Congress. Although he enjoyed great prestige at least among educated Untouchables throughout India, he was unable to prevent the alignment of most other Untouchable castes

---

[25] Ibid.

[26] This account is based on Eleanor M. Zelliot, *Dr Ambedkar and the Mahar Movement*, pp. 174–91.

[27] See Ravinder Kumar, 'Gandhi, Ambedkar and the Poona Pact', *Occasional Papers on History and Society*, no. XX (New Delhi: Teen Murti House, 1985).

with Congress or with the Communists in Kerala and West Bengal. Secondly, and connected with this first failure, Ambedkar did not manage to make the issue of the Untouchables a central concern for any extended period. With the partial exception of Gandhi himself, the key Indian politicians continued to see untouchability as a marginal issue which could not be allowed to divert the nationalist movement from its anti-colonial struggle. Indeed when Gandhi showed a willingness to align himself more closely with the Untouchables' struggle during 1933–34, he was forced out of the nationalist leadership for a time.[28]

Despite the overall weakness of the movement against untouchability, major changes in institutional behaviour began to be put into effect during the thirties. The movement against ritual untouchability gained new momentum, particularly the fight for the right of temple entry. In 1936 the Maharajah of Travancore issued a proclamation that all temples in his State were open to Hindus of all castes, and this example was widely followed in other parts of India in subsequent years. But the really fresh achievement of the 1930s consisted in the first steps towards what had become the scheme of compensatory discrimination for Untouchables, now styled scheduled castes under the Government of India Act 1935.[29] Madras Province, for example, initiated a scheme of special arrangements and benefits designed to promote the education of Untouchables. And the national elections of 1937 delivered for the first time a large number of Untouchable legislators occupying seats reserved for Untouchable candidates.[30] The seal on this mode of recognition was seemingly fixed by Nehru's concession to Ambedkar of the position of chief draftsman of the constitution for independent India. This document duly provided a legal basis for compensatory action in relation to the scheduled castes

[28] Judith Brown, *Gandhi and Civil Disobedience, the Mahatma in Indian Politics 1928–1934* (Cambridge: Cambridge University Press, 1977), pp. 330–79. Opposition came from many quarters, including local party bosses who were often landlords (and therefore interested parties in issues affecting agricultural labour) or orthodox Hindus deeply opposed to social reform.

[29] The Poona Pact also said that all states should set aside a part of their education budgets for the Untouchables, and in 1944 this idea was activated at the central level.

[30] The 1935 Act gave Untouchables 9.5 per cent of the total seats in the provincial legislatures (i.e. 151 out of 1585). See B.A.V. Sharma, 'Development of Reservation Policy' in B.A.V. Sharma and K. Madhusudhan Reddy (eds.), *Reservation Policy in India* (New Delhi: Light and Life Publishers, 1982), p. 16.

and tribes and also 'the other backward classes'. We will look at the impact of this and other post-independence policies following a review of the condition of the Untouchables today.

THE UNTOUCHABLES TODAY—POVERTY AND DISCRIMINATION

Earlier we characterized the Untouchables as a subordinate people with reference to three criteria: poverty, discrimination and consciousness. The first two represent an external measure, and they are discussed in this section. An initial word of caution is needed. Since the Untouchables number some 130 million people and are spread throughout diverse situations in India, any characterization of them as a whole is bound to be superficial. This said, it is possible to describe certain characteristics that are common to a high proportion of this vast body of people.

To assert that the Untouchables are generally marked by poverty is to risk entering the often fruitless debates about defining this condition. The criteria for identifying poverty are necessarily mobile across society and time; there are degrees of poverty but not all can usefully be fitted onto a single scale. Poverty does not always announce itself in simple material terms. At the margins, its physical presence is no doubt self-evident: a chronically hungry family dressed in rags and living in a mean structure without possessions, will qualify as 'poor' by any definition. A great many Indians—and therefore a great many Untouchables—live in conditions of this kind, and so understandably the most common approach to poverty measurement in India has been the 'rock bottom' one of calorie intake.[31] But even in India, calorie measurement is a very blunt approach to the problem of identifying poverty. Indian poverty, like American or French poverty, can also sometimes be represented as absence of choice. With these qualifications and for the present purposes, Indian poverty can be

---

[31] The Indian poverty line is an absolute one: it is based on estimating how much income is needed in order to buy sufficient food to meet the calorie needs of different individuals. The Nutrition Advisory Committee estimates the calorie norms and these are then translated into money values via the evidence in the National Sample Survey on Private Consumption Expenditure. For a clear exposition of how these calculations are made, see S.P. Gupta, 'Poverty', in J.N. Mongia (ed.), *India's Economic Development Strategies, 1951–2000* AD (New Delhi: Allied Publishers, 1986), pp. 499–505.

defined as the sum of low standards of nutrition, housing, clothing, health care and formal education. These, in turn, lead to a lack of social and political effectiveness.

THE BASIS OF UNTOUCHABLE POVERTY

The poverty of Untouchables arises predominantly from their position in the productive process. Untouchables fall mainly into two occupational groups, though in practice the groups overlap. The first group is artisans engaged in tasks reserved for their jati, such as skinning animal carcasses, tanning leather and shoemaking; butchery of animals; playing in musical bands; scavenging and cleaning; coconut plucking; and toddy tapping. These are ritually polluting occupations and the list of them is somewhat longer than this, but still remarkably short for a population so large as the Untouchables. Yet these occupations are ostensibly the basis of the ritual untouchability of all the people from the affected jatis.

Today the predominant occupation of the Untouchables is agricultural work rather than the so-called 'traditional' tasks. The majority of Untouchables now never perform the polluting work of their jati, and this may always have been the case. Moreover, those who do perform the caste work also tend to do agricultural work on a seasonal basis—again, this is not new. While the question of the origins of untouchability as a phenomenon lies beyond this paper, the non-polluting nature of most of the work performed by Untouchables suggests that the prime ideological function of the concept of untouchability may always have been to sanctify and therefore justify labour exploitation. In Kerala, for example, the agrestic slavery of the Pulayas was partly enforced by pollution rules which conveniently prohibited their free movement along public roads.[32] A person who lacks freedom of movement is at the mercy of his/her employer/owner.

In agriculture Untouchables are almost always paid labourers or sharecroppers, rather than self-employed landowners. The distinction between sharecropping and straight-out labouring is not a sharp one: sharecroppers tend also to work part of the time as paid labourers for other farmers. Moreover, the customary terms of sharecropping in

[32] See K. Saradamoni, *Emergence of a Slave Caste* (New Delhi: People's Publishing House, 1980), pp. 61–2, 147–8.

regions like Bengal and Bihar are highly unfavourable: usually the sharecropper provides all the labour and most of the inputs, in return for which he may be entitled to keep half his production. Of course, there have always been individual Untouchables recognized as proprietors of land. They may have acquired land through the royal patronage of a local lineage. In Maharashtra, Untouchable Mahars served as general village servants and were entitled to a collective portion of land called *watan*.[33] Today, some Untouchables have been ceded small parcels of land freed by the limited land reform that has taken place in independent India. But these are essentially details. The figure of the landless labourer remains the motif of Untouchables today. Since villagers without land tend to be poorer than landed ones—the most obvious exceptions are traders—the material poverty of the Untouchables can be seen to arise primarily from their state of landlessness.

Of course, there are many rural workers from non-Untouchable backgrounds who are also landless and poor. This is the situation for a great many of the 'backward backwards', to use a Bihari term for ritually low and economically backward castes such as the fishermen of that state. The travelling blacksmiths of Rajasthan are another low caste, landless and in this case rootless people locked into desperate poverty. Certainly it would not be appropriate to try to argue that Untouchables are always worse off than these people. But what we can say is that there is no category of persons of comparable numerical weight with the same clear identity as labourers tilling fields for the benefit of others. Throughout India if the man tilling a field and the woman cutting the crop are not of the legal proprietor's family, then there is a strong likelihood that they are Untouchables. And conversely, we know that a large proportion of families dependent on agricultural labour belong to the poorest strata of Indian society. Their daily income is low and the availability of work is seldom more than six months in a year.

Although far more agrarian in character than the population as a whole, the Untouchables too are increasingly being sucked out or pushed out—the distinction is a fine one—from their villages into small and large towns, and also regions where the 'green revolution' has produced labour shortages. So the figure of the landless labourer

---

[33] See Jayashree Gokhale-Turner, 'From Concessions to Confrontation—The Politics of the Mahar Community in Maharashtra', Ph.D. thesis, McGill University, 1980, pp. 183–9 for a discussion of the institution of the watan.

in his/her own village is increasingly being joined by the Untouchable labourer in mines and stone quarries, brick kilns, construction sites, road building and other enterprises which use up large quantities of menial labour.[34] The rickshaw puller of Patna, Calcutta, Delhi or a myriad of small towns in India is more likely to be an Untouchable than a person from all the other communities of India put together. And these figures are increasing at a fast pace, as the swelling towns and cities demand houses, roads, offices, hotels and transport. The extra employment is not only welcome but often crucial to an Untouchable population which is growing at the same time as rural opportunities are contracting because of factors like mechanization; the transfer of land from high-caste to lower-caste self-cultivating families; and the growth in size of the latter families, such that their need for hired labour is reduced.

The new employment for Untouchables is generally not the kind that will produce lasting benefits for their families. Work and conditions tend to be harsh, and so health and safety suffer. Financial conditions may be better than at home, though when all the expenses are deducted even this is not always true. The phenomenon of bonded labour is notorious in the quarries and brick kilns, for example. In these circumstances it often becomes impossible to provide better opportunities for one's children. Life continues to be a question of survival.

Statutory reservation of public jobs had made only a marginal difference to overall employment among the Untouchables. By definition, a share in public employment proportional to their share in the overall population cannot benefit more than a fraction of Untouchables. There are simply not enough government jobs to go round. This is not to say that such employment is useless or merely token. In addition to the benefits flowing to individuals and their families, appointments to the higher levels of public employment are working towards creating a relatively prosperous and influential group which may have an important role to play in the future politics of the Untouchables. But such an impact is distinct from alleviating poverty directly through public employment.

The geographical spread of Indian, and therefore Untouchable, poverty is not even across the country. Its highest concentration is in

[34] See Oliver Mendelsohn, 'Life and Struggles in the Stone Quarries of India: A Case Study', *Journal of Commonwealth and Comparative Politics*, vol. XXIX, no. 1, March 1991, pp. 44–71.

the northern-eastern parts of the subcontinent: almost half of India's 130 million Untouchables live in the four states of Uttar Pradesh, W. Bengal, Bihar and Orissa and on average about 70 per cent of these people live below 'the poverty line'.[35] Punjab and Haryana, the leading states of the green revolution, stand out as the two exceptions in the picture of extreme poverty among the Untouchables. Less than 30 per cent of the Untouchables in these states fall below the poverty line. The explanation is that shortage of labour in the context of cash cropping has led to far higher rates of pay than elsewhere.

The incidence of poverty is higher in rural than urban areas for all sections of the population, including Untouchables: again Punjab and Haryana are the main exceptions. So concentration of Untouchables in agriculture is itself a pointer to their predominant poverty.[36]

One of the best quantitative measures of poverty is literacy. The proportion of literate Untouchables is now rising but is still very low. By 1981 the figure had reached only 21 per cent, while a decade earlier it was 15 per cent. The figure for females was an appalling 6 per cent in 1971 and 11 per cent in 1981.[37] These high levels of illiteracy are a particularly potent indicator of both present and future levels of poverty. Since the majority of Untouchable families are without land or other productive assets, the only logical avenues of private advancement are enhanced remuneration for traditional manual labour or the acquisition of jobs requiring new skills. The first is a possibility mainly for rural workers in highly productive agricultural zones utilizing modern techniques: the rates of pay for agricultural labour are far higher in Punjab than, say, in Bihar. For the rest, it would be naive to believe that agricultural workers will manage markedly to increase their share of agricultural income in the short run. Greater prosperity will arise predominantly through distribution of public benefits and

[35] See Oliver Mendelsohn and Marika Vicziany, 'The Untouchables Today', in J. Masselos (ed.), *India, Creating a Modern Nation* (Delhi: Sterling, 1990), Table I, p. 257.

[36] Ibid., Table 2, p. 258. Also see ibid., Table 3, p. 259 showing that most Untouchables in the populous states are agricultural labourers or cultivators. Source: Primary Census abstract, Scheduled Castes, Part 11B (ii), Census of India, series 1, 1983.

[37] Selected Statistics on Scheduled Castes, op. cit., Tables 15–20, pp. 27–32. The literacy rate for the rest of the population (i.e., excluding scheduled castes and tribes) was in both censuses roughly double that of the Untouchables. In the case of female literacy, the rate was three times higher than for Untouchable females.

the acquisition of new skills. In the present Indian circumstances (and unlike the situation for English or Japanese workers in the last century), such skills will generally be acquired only by literates.[38]

The only other social indicator for which it is possible to develop reliable figures is the most basic indicator of all, namely mortality. Here the position appears rather less bleak for the Untouchables. Census figures over about a century can be used to show that the life expectancy of what are now called the scheduled castes has risen proportionally more than that of the population as a whole.[39] With poorer than average nutrition, housing, clothing, health care and general amenities, Untouchables can be presumed to have been particularly vulnerable to infectious disease and, of course, starvation in times of famine. Considerable success in combating epidemics of cholera and other infectious diseases and better famine relief may well be the principal reasons for the disproportionate increase in Untouchable life expectancy. This expectancy, however, is still considerably below the Indian average.[40] Infant mortality, for example, rises with the degree of poverty and illiteracy. And although increased life-expectancy clearly rests on material progress, it fails to represent more than a fragment of prosperity. After all, we are still talking about a life expectancy which is very low by world standards.[41]

[38] This is true even in the states where agricultural labour is comparatively well paid, since labour absorption in agriculture will decline. So it is scarcely promising to note that untouchable literacy in 1981 was 23 per cent in Punjab and 20 per cent in Haryana, against a general literacy rate of 59 per cent and 36 per cent respectively: *Census of India, 1981*, series 17 Punjab and series 6 Haryana, Part IX (i), Special Tables for Scheduled Castes.

[39] See Marika Vicziany, 'The Demography of Untouchability, Bihar 1872–1971', paper presented to the Asian Studies Association of Australia, 5th National Conference, Adelaide, May 1984.

[40] In 1978 the general infant mortality rate was 136 in rural areas, 70 in urban areas and 125 combined rural-urban. For untouchables the rates were 159 in rural areas and 90 in urban areas. The discrepancy persists beyond the first year of life. The number of untouchable child deaths (age 1–5 years) per 100,000 population in 1978 was 286 (rural) and 199 (urban), compared with the general rates for Hindus of 228 (rural) and 94 (urban): Office of Registrar General, Ministry of Home Affairs, Survey on Infant and Child Mortality, A Preliminary Report, New Delhi, pp. 32–39.

[41] During the 1980s infant mortality was 5.5 per 1,000 in Japan, 9.9 in Australia, 30 in S. Korea, 50 in the Philippines, 55 in Vietnam and 61 in China. At the same time it was 101 in India, and of course far higher for the untouchable population of India.

THE QUESTION OF DECLINING POVERTY

The next obvious question is whether the poverty of Untouchables is declining and, if so, at what rate. This question is partly bound up with the more general matter of poverty amelioration in India, and the evidence is far from clear. Reliable data are sparse for our own period and still more limited for earlier times. Clearly, the subject is too large for a full assessment here, but some summary comments are possible. Thus the mortality and literacy data; the existence of emergency relief measures, including food-for-work programmes;·the gradual extension of public health and welfare facilities; pockets of relative prosperity in areas like Punjab; a trickle of public employment and urban opportunities—these are pointers to a somewhat more prosperous category at the bottom of Indian society. Against this, the decline of exploitative but still sometimes secure relationships characteristic of the old (some would say feudal) regime has tended to lead to an equally—and sometimes even more—ruthless capitalism.[42] There is also a different but parallel argument that the origins of mass poverty coincide with the experience of European imperialism. On this view, the independent Indian state has to contend with a poverty created by colonialism; if poverty is either growing or not abating very quickly, then the blame must be laid at the feet of the British conquerors of India.[43]

Our own view is that mass poverty, which has its roots at least as far back as the early sixteenth century, has become less desperate but more widespread during the last 150 years. But whatever general rise in living standards there has been for Untouchables, it has still fallen tragically short of meeting their basic human needs. One need only examine the situation in Kerala—the state which has done most to meet basic health, housing and education needs for its poorest people—to realize how far most of the rest of India falls short. And even in Kerala, the gap between the life chances of those at the bottom and those at the top has not necessarily closed. The Untouchables of Kerala are well

[42] See Jan Breman, *Patronage and Exploitation, Changing Agrarian Relations in South Gujarat, India* (Berkeley: University of California Press, 1974), pp. 124–48, 187–218, 218–31; and Oliver Mendelsohn, 'Life and Struggles in the Stone Quarries of India', pp. 59–62.

[43] See Tapan Raychaudhuri, 'Historical Roots of Mass Poverty in South Asia, A Hypothesis', *Economic and Political Weekly*, vol. XX, no. 18, 4 May 1985, pp. 801–6.

off by all-India standards but as a category they seem to be now fixed in a proletarian mould of menial labour.[44] Their performance in higher education is weak and they generally appear to have poor prospects of raising their children to a life of greater amenity and higher status.[45] The Untouchables have been singularly absent from the millions of Kerala people who have found prosperity from employment in the Persian Gulf region: they seem to lack a network of useful connections which can serve as a lever of social advancement.

In the quite different situation of Haryana state, the Untouchables have clearly benefited from mounting agrarian prosperity. They receive much higher wages than obtain in less prosperous agricultural regions—Haryana does seem to bear out some of the predictions of the 'trickle down' economists. At the same time, there is insufficient evidence that these higher incomes will work to restructure radically the overall social condition of the Untouchables of Haryana. Haryana scores relatively well on the social indicators of literacy, health and infant mortality, though not so well as Kerala with its lower per capita incomes but higher commitment to public health. But in common with Kerala, the Untouchables of Haryana seem unable to emerge from their very limited position as agricultural labourers. In sum, even in those states where there has been a relatively dramatic increase in material consumption and/or provision of needed facilities, the comparative position of Untouchables does not seem to have undergone any radical improvement. This judgment needs to be set beside the more basic observation that most states of India have made appallingly poor progress in meeting the basic needs of their poorest people, among whom the Untouchables are a large proportion.

DISCRIMINATION

If the poverty of Untouchables can fairly easily be established from both observation and quantitative data, the question of discrimination is more difficult. As we noted earlier, there is no disagreement about the severity of mistreatment suffered by Untouchable castes in earlier periods—say a century ago. It is now a matter of notoriety, for example, that in parts of the South Untouchables were forced to ring

---

[44] For the purpose of this discussion the Ezhavas are not treated as Untouchables.

[45] See Oliver Mendelsohn and Marika Vicziany in Masselos op. cit., pp. 272–3.

bells to announce their presence, which could pollute from specifically prescribed distances, and wear spittoons around their necks to prevent the ground from becoming defiled. Throughout the whole of India Untouchable houses were usually segregated on the outskirts of village settlements, such that a caste Hindu need not so much as pass through the quarter. In most places Untouchables were denied the right to share common wells or to enter temples frequented by the higher castes. The ubiquitous Hindu rules proscribing dining with inferior castes were most rigorously applied to the untouchable castes. This rigour of exclusion delineated the Untouchables from all other Hindus—not merely from the high castes—even in comparatively benign regions like Bengal.

The ritual denial of common humanity was paralleled by economic subordination, which took a variety of forms. In parts of the South it was possible to find people who have reasonably been called 'slaves': the Pulayas of Kerala are a commonly cited example, and certainly these people were heritable and transferable. Vast numbers of Untouchables lived in a 'bonded' condition which varied only marginally from the status of slavery. Such persons were unfree in the sense that they lacked the right as well as the practical power to leave the family for whom they worked and to whom they were perpetually indebted. The coercion was not merely economic but arose from a variety of overlapping inferior statuses, and ritual untouchability was a crucial source of the subordination. Sexual exploitation of Untouchable women by their high-caste masters appears to have been so common as to have been habitual.

No broad brush can faithfully depict the condition of all Untouchables. There were gradations of status between different Untouchable castes and regional variation was significant. In northern India association with Rajput potentates afforded some Untouchables a superior economic condition—the Dusadhs of Bihar sometimes fell into this category. It was also possible to find individual Untouchables who had escaped the degree of subordination common to their fellows through particular circumstances or achievements. A pointer to this phenomenon can be picked up from the stories of many of the most prominent Untouchable leaders today. Almost to a man, these people emerge from families at least one generation, sometimes many generations, removed from the usual grinding poverty of Untouchables.[46]

---

[46] Oliver Mendelsohn, 'A "Harijan Elite"? The Lives of Some Untouchable

Often the family has been able to acquire a parcel of land sufficient to break the bonds of landless subordination. In a surprisingly large number of cases such figures arise from families with a tradition of particular professional service to other Untouchables, notably the practice of medicine or priestly function. In the British period, army service began to multiply the number of fortunate Untouchable families: B.R. Ambedkar and Jagjivan Ram, the most prominent Untouchables of the century, both came from army families.[47]

With all the variation that can be found in so vast a category of human beings residing in multiple localized social systems, the historical image of Untouchable subordination remains sharp. But just how much of this system of discriminatory treatment remains in place? The broad answer to this question is less equivocal than questions about the direction of Untouchable poverty. Without doubt, subordination arising from the practice of ritual untouchability has greatly declined over the twentieth century. The idea of Untouchables in Kerala now being forced to travel on out-of-the way tracks rather than highways to avoid polluting the good Hindu citizen, is simply unthinkable. Public ideology in contemporary Kerala is Marxist-derived egalitarianism, an outlook which does not exist in the same intellectual universe as casteist Hinduism. Throughout India Untouchables now go to the same schools as do caste Hindu children, they attend the same hospitals and travel in the same buses. In the cities they drink at the same teashops, eat in the one cafe. All of this·represents a sea change and not merely a minor amelioration of the Untouchable condition.

Once we look closer at particular social situations, the precise pattern of change begins to emerge more clearly. The areas of social life which have been most securely opened up to Untouchables are those directly under the auspices of the state. Undoubtedly the most important of these is the school system. Untouchable children are provided access to all government schools in India and apparently with only rare exceptions are treated without formal segregation in the schoolroom. Obviously this transformation did not occur overnight, and resistance was considerable. Older Untouchables are today

---

Politicians', *Economic and Political Weekly*, vol. XXI, no. 12, 22 March 1986, pp. 501–9.

[47] Ambedkar's background is well known. Details about Jagjivan Ram come from an interview with the author, New Delhi, 5 January 1983. Jagjivan Ram's grandfather owned seven acres of land and his son bought more during service in the British army.

able to relate ludicrous incidents from their childhood, like the case of a Brahmin teacher flinging the disciplinary rod at an offending Untouchable boy. The Brahmin was here giving vent to his anger without risking the pollution believed to be had from beating the Untouchable with stick in hand.[48] But these incidents now belong firmly to the past. Gross displays of discriminatory treatment are no longer a general feature of Indian schoolrooms, discouraged as they are by criminal sanctions and the heightened assertiveness of Untouchables themselves. At the same time, the persistence of ritual untouchability makes it likely that isolated examples of the vilest discrimination will still occur. And, of course, we are not suggesting that the experience of the Untouchables within the educational system is 'equal'. Similarly, the programmes for recruitment of Untouchables into government service have ensured that Untouchables are no longer shut out from such employment. Untouchables may still be under-represented at the highest levels of government service but again this is a distinct, albeit connected, matter.

If we turn to social life, the picture is more varied. Untouchables are subject to less discrimination in the cities than in the villages, and this is essentially an aspect of a more general homogenization of standards in the cities. It is not possible to maintain traditional standards of purity/pollution in a teashop in Bombay: if you pay your money you get a cup of tea, whoever you may be.[49] The traditional Brahmin must either avoid the teashop—avoidance strategy is the mark of a great deal of Indian social life today—or conveniently suspend old notions of ritual purity, at least while he is in Bombay. Similarly, one cannot afford to be choosy about whom one is packed together with in a Bombay train. But Bombay teashops and even Bombay trains account for very little of the total social life of India.

[48] Interview with A.C. Das, MP from Madhya Pradesh, New Delhi, 24 December 1982. The same experience happened to Pan Durang Dharmaji Jadhav, a nominated member to the Rajya Sabha from Maharashtra: interview, 24 December 1982.

[49] But as late as the mid 1970s Bangalore factory workers from the powerful Vokkaliga caste themselves poured coffee (when they felt like it) for Untouchable Madiga labourers. They did this rather than allow the Madigas to pollute the common pot supplied by management by helping themselves. When the Madigas rebelled and began to help themselves, there was labour unrest on the part of the Vokkaligas. Ultimately management could see no way out but to back the Untouchables: interview with Chandraprasad Tyagi, State Convener, Karnataka Dalit Sangharsh Samiti, Bangalore, 7 January 1988.

Perhaps the best survey of the modern incidence of ritual un-touchability was conducted by I.P. Desai in rural Gujarat, some twenty years ago. Gujarat is an economically and socially progressive region by comparative Indian standards, but Desai found that the practice of untouchability was still widespread and serious in the villages he surveyed. It was least practised in what he calls the 'public situations' of bus travel, seating arrangements in school and post office service. Desai treats these as 'public' matters because he suggests that they are directly governed by legislation. His finding was that in only one village out of fifty-nine was there discrimination in the arrangement of seating in a school classroom: since his inquiry was undertaken twenty years ago, it is probably safe to assume that even this single instance would not be found today. Postal discrimination was higher: only 4 per cent of post offices discriminated against Untouchables in the sale of stamps and like matters, but 17 per cent of postmen were discriminatory during their delivery of mail. The one 'public' area of high discrimination was in seating arrangements at statutory panchayat meetings.[50]

In the so-called 'private' sphere, the incidence of discrimination soared. In 90 per cent of the villages Untouchables were not allowed into the houses of caste Hindus. An even higher percentage of barbers did not serve Untouchables in their concern not to lose high-caste patronage. Sixty per cent of village shopkeepers took care to avoid touching anything to do with them, even their money, in conducting transactions. Seventy per cent of the potters did not allow the Un-touchables to touch pots while going about their purchases, and in 89 per cent of the villages Untouchables were prohibited from entering temples frequented by caste Hindus.

For Desai the heart of the untouchability question is whether water sources are treated as polluted by Untouchable use. The water question is clearly more relevant than any question about food pollution, since the latter occurs in multiple Hindu social situations that do not involve Untouchables. Denial of access to common water sources seems to be a discrimination particular to Untouchables, though it is possible to find the denial affecting some tribals too. In view of the 'conser-vatism' evident in matters like temple entry, Desai finds it 'surprising' that 26 per cent of villages allowed Untouchables access to common

50 I.P. Desai, *Untouchability in Rural Gujarat* (Bombay: Popular Prakashan, 1976), p. 258.

water sources.[51] In 10 per cent of villages the water source was considered polluted if used by Untouchables, and Untouchables were dependent on the grace and favour of caste Hindu users to acquire water. Untouchables had to wait near the well until someone agreed to pour water in their containers, taking care that the two containers did not touch. (If a caste Hindu's clay vessel was touched, it became irredeemably polluted and had to be thrown away or given to an Untouchable). But in the largest number of villages, 64 per cent, this problem was averted through the provision of separate water facilities for Untouchables. If these had not existed, the Untouchables would apparently also have been at the mercy of caste Hindus. The difference is not one of attitude towards pollution but of preparedness to ease the lot of Untouchables by having separate wells constructed. Desai concludes that the behaviour of caste Hindus has changed but their beliefs have not. On the other hand, Untouchables have certainly benefited because 'they do not have to suffer humiliation every day at the hands of the savarna (clean castes)'.[52]

Desai's findings in a relatively progressive region help fill out the context of our earlier observation that there has been a 'sea change' in the practice of ritual untouchability. That one can talk of such a change and simultaneously identify an intact edifice of inhuman discrimination is testament to the awesome dimensions of the untouchability system. What Desai uncovered was an increasingly subtle behavioural system able to accommodate radically opposed ideological systems by confining them to different social sites. In this way it is possible for a Brahmin child to sit next to an Untouchable in the classroom, while the Untouchable continues to be denied access to the well from which the Brahmin draws water. There is no doubt that compartmentalization is greatly to be preferred to the previously cumulative and comprehensive untouchability. It prepares the ground for a measure of social and even material comfort for Untouchables and breaks the cycle of relentless subordination. But while it persists, such compartmentalization acts as a severe limit to the prospects of Untouchables.

Observers of the United States have sometimes made comparable remarks about the progress of race relations in that country. Certain kinds of overt discrimination against African-Americans have become

---

[51] Ibid., pp. 62–3.
[52] Ibid., p. 114.

unacceptable behaviour following the gains of the civil rights movement and the militancy of African-Americans. At the same time, more subtle discrimination in employment and other areas of social life persists and shows few signs of abating. There are parallels, albeit far from complete, between this development and what has happened to the Untouchables. The concept of 'racism' is suggestive of the common outlook, despite the fact that the Untouchables are not distinct from other Hindus in any anthropometric sense. The idea of Untouchables as polluted tends to constitute them as a separate and subordinated race.

On the side of the Untouchables, there is decreasing willingness to put up with an order which outwardly concedes them equality but which masks the persistence of structural barriers to their advancement. The last decade and a half has been a period of increasing violence as Untouchable resistance to the old order has asserted itself with a vigour not seen before. This refusal to continue with the old subordination has in turn produced savage reaction from their social superiors. It is far too early to predict where this new resistance will take the Untouchables. They remain the prisoners of a grossly imperfect political mobilization, discussed at length below, and this severely limits the possibility of political and social gain. But the ferment at the bottom of Indian society now seems endemic and not easily containable by the present regime.

The following case study illustrates the persistence of gross discrimination and resistance by the Untouchables. This is an example of what has come to be called a Harijan atrocity, or outrage perpetrated by caste Hindus against Untouchables. In this instance the outrage consisted of a group of Untouchables (and a caste Hindu who was caught up in the affair) being forced to consume human faeces. The event took place in a village in Belgaum district of Karnataka state during August 1987 and we examined it in January 1988 on the basis of reports and interviews with some of the participants in the village.[53] The location of the problem in Karnataka is notable, for this is a state with a reputation for being peaceable and moderate in its social complexion.

There were a number of factors in the chain that led to the outrage. The first factor was an election in 1987 for the statutory panchayats

[53] Interviews with Holeyas and the Lingayat Pradhan in Bendegeri Village, Belgaum District, 14 January 1988.

or local government bodies, which were being clothed with much greater power to disburse development funds. The electoral system had also been changed to provide for reservation of seats for scheduled castes/tribes and for women. In the village in question the three seats on the panchayat were all won by the Janata party against fierce opposition from a locally-based peasant party. The position of pradhan or head of the panchayat was taken by a Lingayat, the most powerful caste in Karnataka, and the scheduled caste seat went to a Holeya (a large Untouchable caste in Karnataka). The unsuccessful candidate for pradhan was also from the dominant Lingayat caste and was said to be the main organizer of the atrocity. One of the victims was the son of the successful Untouchable candidate. Apparently the defeated Lingayat blamed the Holeyas for his defeat and many bitter words had been exchanged since the election.

A second destabilizing factor was the Integrated Rural Development Plan (IRDP), an anti-poverty programme built around the idea of transferring assets rather than mere sustenance funds to poor people (see below). In the present case the successful Untouchable in the election had received IRDP assistance to buy a milch buffalo. But the advent of the buffalo increased as well as reduced the Untouchable's dependence on high-caste farmers. The new owners did not have sufficient agricultural land to feed the buffalo, so they were dependent on caste Hindus and the Lingayats in particular to allow them to cut green fodder from their fields. Presumably there were reciprocal arrangements whereby the fodder was paid for in labour.

On the day in question Subhash, son of the newly elected Untouchable, had gone to the fields with three other Untouchables and a Maratha (caste Hindu) friend to cut some fodder for the buffalo. Night was falling and it had started to rain. Out of prior agreement, mischief making, or simple laziness—the version varies with the witness—they began to cut fodder from a field belonging to someone in the unsuccessful Lingayat candidate's family. The latter were furious and managed to capture the five young men and herd them to the chief accused's house. Along the way the Lingayats forced Subhash to pick up some human faeces that lay by the roadside and carry it in a piece of paper. When they got to the accused's house, Subhash and his friends were forced to eat the faeces. They had to comply for fear of death at the point of a scythe.

The victims told us that they wanted to commit suicide out of a sense of shame for what they had been forced to do. Feelings were greatly inflamed in the village—particularly among the Marathas, since one of their number had by chance been part of the affair—but no general violence—broke out. The incident became a major issue throughout Karnataka and the Dalit Sangharsh Samiti (the principal Dalit or radical Untouchable organization in Karnataka) organized a number of rallies demanding government action against the culprits.[54] In late January the latter were officially expelled from the village pending charges being heard in a court.

This incident is instructive on a number of counts. Of course, the grotesque action was quite out of proportion to any provocation caused by the cutting of fodder. Even when the aggravated feelings following the election are taken into account, there is a gap in reconstructing causation. That gap cannot be filled, we believe, by more empirical material on the incident itself—there would always remain an empirical gap. The degrading incident can only be understood by reference to the outraged feelings of people such as these particular Lingayats at the rise of Untouchables in the village. How dare they own buffaloes, contest and win elections and act against the interests of their moral superiors! Who do these uppity people think they are?

The incident is also interesting for what it says about the dangers of programmes like IRDP. A programme which seeks to engineer independence through asset formation as opposed to relieving poverty temporarily through wage labour is fundamentally flawed if it succeeds in producing a new kind of dependence. This incident in Belgaum district is not an isolated example of this kind of problem.

Atrocities like this are not a daily occurrence, nor are they so exceptional as to shed no light on the general problem. Acts of gross violence against Untouchables can be seen as the culmination of severe tensions that arise in the context of routine discrimination and subordination of Untouchables. Clearly, such violence is not new, and some of the recent reportage reflects heightened sensitivity on the part of both Untouchables and other activists. But there also appears to have been an increase in the actual occurrence of violence, arising from a heightened assertiveness among Untouchables. The mid-to-late 1970s —coinciding with initial Janata (non-Congress) rule at the centre and a number of the states—seem to have marked a turning point. After this period there has been a steady flow of information about violent

[54] 'Press Handout' by the State Convener of the Karnataka Dalit Sangharsh Samiti, Bangalore, n.d. (c. 18 January 1988).

incidents involving Untouchables, punctuated by a number of unusually shocking stories of mass murder and rape. If there is a common thread in these incidents, it seems to be the phenomenon of resistance to subordination. Sometimes the resistance is to violence itself—rape or assault, for example. At other times it is the Untouchables offering 'provocation', in the form of demand for land, the payment of statutory minimum wages, or some other objective which would seem reasonable in a less hierarchical context.

PUBLIC POLICY AFTER INDEPENDENCE

It will now be clear that the post-independence policies directed at ending the condition and basis of untouchability have failed to achieve their putative object. This failure, it is equally clear, is one of design and not merely administrative performance. Even without 'slippage' during administration, the programmes would not have worked. The fundamental reason for this failure is political: the elite which had the task of devising and carrying through the anti-untouchability programme would have been directly disadvantaged by its comprehensive success. Not only were the class interests of the elite antagonistic to those of the Untouchable population, but so were their more diffuse *caste* interests. In the absence of a powerful Untouchable political movement, the Untouchables were simply bound to end up with programmes that did not meet anything like their full needs.

We should make clear that our argument is not that there has been a conspiracy to prevent any transformation of the Untouchable condition, only that there have been reasons of self-interest which have inhibited the formation and implementation of policy directed to that end.

COMPENSATORY DISCRIMINATION

The centrepiece of post-independence policy in relation to the Untouchables has been the scheme of compensatory discrimination, or 'reservation' as it is popularly known. This scheme has three main components: scholarships for schooling (predominantly at secondary and tertiary levels) and guaranteed places in scarce educational institutions, particularly medical and engineering schools; guaranteed public employment; and seats reserved in parliamentary and elected local institutions. These measures grew out of the fledgling British schemes of the thirties and forties but have been immensely magnified since independence. Curiously, the scheme has been built with neither an initial blueprint nor a later assessment of its success or failure. The compromises struck sixty years ago at the time of the epic struggle between Gandhi and Ambedkar have been progressively and almost thoughtlessly translated into a giant scheme whose principal characteristic is relentless and often senseless bureaucracy. True, significant and not merely token benefits have been delivered to many millions of Untouchables under the various programmes. But if the yardstick is substantial success in overcoming the disabilities of the scheduled castes, then the scheme has been highly deficient.

A measure of the unthreatening nature of the reservation scheme is that in a nation where the smallest of public benefits are the object of the most intense competition, until quite recently no substantial political objection had been raised on the ground of the scheme's discriminatory nature. In 1990 the Government of India's decision to implement the Mandal Commission's recommendations to extend similar compensatory benefits to the backward (but not Untouchable) castes caused widespread rioting and even self-immolation among people who could not qualify, and was a prime factor in the fall of the V.P. Singh government.[55] The strength of this reaction has no analogue in historical reactions to preference for the Untouchables, though by now the Untouchables too have to some extent been caught up in the backlash against compensatory action.

Part of the explanation for this variable reaction is the knowledge that Untouchables, as opposed to backwards, will not be able to use their preference to bring about any substantial redistribution relative to their social and economic superiors. Beyond straightforward material calculations, there is also a large symbolic dimension to the recent politics of compensatory discrimination. Groups representing the backward castes have come to constitute a political bloc that has the potential to capture power at state and even national levels. Rivalries between high-caste, traditionally dominant communities and once subordinate castes (like the Yadavs of Bihar and Uttar Pradesh) are

[55] See *India Today*, 15 September 1990. On the debate surrounding the Mandal Commission, see Asghar Ali Engineer (ed.), *Mandal Commission Controversy* (Delhi: Ajanta Publications, 1991).

bitter and often violent.[56] In these circumstances any shift in policy which delivers scarce public benefits to the backwards is bound to engender serious opposition from the 'forwards'. But in the case of the Untouchables no such symbolic politics come into play. In a word, the Untouchables do not need to be taken seriously by the high-castes.

At some risk of cynicism, it is possible to mount a case that the principal achievement of reservation has been its capacity to satisfy the Untouchables sufficient to discourage radical politics. Certainly, the Untouchables have been a crucial support base for the Congress Party at the national level. Only in 1977 (and possibly 1989) did the Untouchable vote in northern India go overwhelmingly to anti-Congress forces, and on those two occasions Congress lost national office.

Reservation of parliamentary seats has been particularly disappointing. Under the scheme arrived at in the Poona Pact and refined in the early 1950s, the Untouchables are guaranteed legislators in proportion to their share of the population. Constituencies are set aside for Untouchable candidates but not for Untouchable voters: the whole of the population chooses between the Untouchable candidates. This scheme is criticized for not allowing an independent Untouchable voice to emerge. The argument is that the candidates are forced to be mainstream party figures without any particular identification with the minority Untouchable population from which they come. While there may be something in this essentially mechanical argument, the separation of Untouchable electorates from general seats would not of itself have created a separate Untouchable political voice. In the absence of other forces working in that direction, the tendency would still have been for an assimilation of Untouchables into mainstream party politics.

Whatever the reason, there can be no doubt that electoral politics have not thrown up strong Untouchable leaders.[57] The one Untouch-

---

[56] On the new political formations, see Oliver Mendelsohn, 'Is There a New Politics Waiting to be Born?', in *India, Prospects for the Future*, Briefing Paper No. 1, Indian Ocean Centre for Peace Studies, Perth, June 1991, pp. 15–9.

[57] The process of candidate selection by parties is often a kind of anointing of plausible, if publicly unknown, candidates for seats which must have an Untouchable candidate. This is to be distinguished from the perhaps more common Indian model of a powerful caste imposing its nominee on the party. Thus Bhargavi Thankappan, Deputy Speaker of the Trivandrum Assembly and from the Untouchable Sidhanar caste, notes that she was 'picked up by the CPI, which was looking for an educated lady to run for a reserved parliamentary seat': interview, Trivandrum, 23 December 1987. (In this instance the candidate did prove to have

able politician to have played at the highest level is Jagjivan Ram who came to occupy the position of defence minister and finally deputy prime minister in the Janata government of 1977–80. Jagjivan Ram was an important symbol for Untouchables and particularly for his own Chamar community, the largest of the Untouchable castes. The huge Untouchable population behind him must have been an important source of his power within Congress, but overall Jagjivan Ram operated as an orthodox Congress politician rather than someone specially devoted to the cause of the Untouchables.[58] As an Untouchable he was a particularly useful symbol for successive Congress governments (and the Janata government of 1977–80) to deploy,[59] but he was either not allowed to or did not himself seek a role as the voice of the Untouchables.

In present-day politics the only Untouchable politician to have achieved high prominence is Ram Vilas Paswan. He was a senior minister in the short-lived V.P. Singh government of 1989–90 and was one of the architects of that government's decision to implement reservation for the backwards.[60] Paswan represents a new generation of Untouchable politicians who are beginning to effect a more radical and assertive style,[61] though none has yet managed to stay close to the centre of power for any length of time.

Despite the weak impact of mainstream Untouchable politicians, we need not conclude that reservation of parliamentary seats is either useless or even counter-productive to the Untouchable cause. Without reservation there would have been precious few Untouchable legislators—what pressures would have induced the political parties to select Untouchables? The proposition that a discriminatory absence of Untouchable legislators might have disturbed the minds and therefore concentrated the political energies of the Untouchable population, is implausible. Moreover, it would be too cynical to suggest that

---

some considerable political capacity.) Clearly a party is unlikely to anoint a candidate who looks as if she will rock the boat.

[58] For some of his own views, see Jagjivan Ram, *Caste Challenge in India* (Delhi: Vision Books, 1980), pp. 43–9.

[59] For a short biography of J. Ram, see V.S. Kulkarni, et al. (eds.), *India's Parliament 1971, Who's Who of Indian M.P.s*, pp. 131–2.

[60] In the early 1980s Ram Vilas Paswan was leader of the Lok Dal (K) in the Lok Sabha, and became Minister for Welfare and Labour in V.P. Singh's government in 1990.

[61] A number of interviews with Ram Vilas Paswan in the period 1985–1991.

Untouchable legislators have accomplished nothing of value to their communities. Particularly in recent years, there has been a trend for these legislators to be increasingly assertive, as for example, on the issue of continuing violence against Untouchables, the Harijan atrocity issue.

Reservation of public employment for the scheduled castes has had greater impact than electoral reservation. Tens of thousands of Untouchables have benefited from the quota of public jobs made available to them. When the wider impact of this employment on families and whole communities is computed, the beneficial impact has been considerable. At the same time, the overall experience of job reservation has been disappointing. The great concentration of Untouchables is in the lowest grade of public positions, many of them in the 'sweeper' category. This grade entails cleaning work of a ritually polluting nature, which is traditionally performed by particular Untouchable castes. Persons from these castes are only too delighted to perform their habitual work at much higher rates of pay and with security of tenure in a government position. Conversely, no one else wants their job. While these sweeper positions have increased the welfare of many individual families, there is no evidence of any structural change in their situation. The sweeper castes lie at the very bottom of the status hierarchy among Untouchable castes, and the enlarged source of family income has generally not provided the base from which to promote the education and therefore upward mobility of the succeeding generations.[62]

At the other end of the scale, many of the senior civil service positions reserved for scheduled caste persons have in the past not been filled. The justification was a claimed insufficiency of qualified candidates. But nowadays Untouchables are enthusiastically taking up these high status jobs in many regions of India.[63] Gradually a useful

[62] Mary Searle-Chatterjee, *Reversible Sex Roles: The Special Case of Benares Sweepers* (Oxford: Pergamon Press, 1981). The lack of social and political aspirations amongst the sweepers is attributed by the author to their preoccupation with improving their immediate economic and working conditions. Their occupational mobility is said to be very restricted because the high visibility of their polluting work makes them turn in upon themselves.

[63] And where the acquisition of such jobs is blocked by the higher castes, the Untouchables are learning to complain—even in backward states like Bihar. In early 1983, the All India Backward Harijan Adivasi and Religious Minority Federation demanded that positions be reserved for these groups in the judicial system: *The Searchlight*, 2 February 1983.

pool of senior Untouchable administrators is being created. Indeed, the claim is now increasingly heard that there is a 'Harijan elite' which has cornered the benefits of reservation and now passes them on from one generation to the next. The claim is that these people are devoted to furthering their personal interests and have no concern for the larger Untouchable population. This is not the place to debate this question; suffice it to say that the whole 'Harijan elite' thesis rests on an essentially hypocritical demand that the beneficiaries of reservation be both especially talented and extraordinarily noble.[64]

Measured against the scale of the problem, job reservation can only be a marginal attack on unemployment among the Untouchables. There are simply far too many Untouchables, far too few government jobs.[65] Nor has the government moved to require private firms to practise reservation, a development which would begin to break the upper-caste domination of all but the most menial private sector positions. But even this change would not affect the condition of the vast majority of Untouchables living and working in village fields.

By far the most important prong of the policy of compensatory discrimination has been the provision of educational benefits to the scheduled castes (and the scheduled tribes too). Part of this assistance has taken the form of reservation of scarce places in elite faculties— particularly medicine and engineering.[66] But by far the more significant part has been financial assistance to school and college students in the form of special stipends and, more occasionally, hostel accommodation away from home. This scheme was originally administered at the upper secondary and tertiary levels but now extends even to primary education. Unfortunately, the scheme suffers pitfalls of administration common to all welfare programmes in India, as for

[64] For an extended discussion of these arguments, see Oliver Mendelsohn, 'A "Harijan Elite"?'

[65] The organized sector of the Indian economy represents some 10 per cent of the total job market, and of this some 7 per cent is public sector employment: Gail Omvedt, 'Twice Born Riot Against Democracy', in Asghar Ali Engineer, p. 12.

[66] This has been the most likely form of reservation to provoke violent resistance. One example was on the campus of the Darbhanga Medical College in January 1983. Untouchable and tribal students were 'ragged' and beaten in retaliation against an order by the Supreme Court in 1982 that they be admitted to the college: *The Searchlight*, 17, 18, 20, 21 January 1983. Acts of violence also marred life in the Bangalore Medical College Hostel and the Agricultural University in the mid 1970s: V.T. Rajshekar Shetty, *Dalit Movement in Karnataka* (Madras: The Christian Literature Society, 1978), pp. 111–13.

example, chronic delays in delivering stipends and the pocketing of a portion of funds by intermediaries.[67] These deficiencies have quite severely limited the scheme's capacity to aid any but the most motivated Untouchable students. Still, the assistance must have been one factor in turning around educational culture among Untouchables throughout India. A related factor has been the widespread ambition of Untouchable children to achieve a 'service' position in the category of government jobs reserved for scheduled castes. All but the bottom rung positions are open only to those with a comparatively high level of education.

Even without special assistance, the Untouchables' interest in education would clearly have risen in step with the approach of the larger Indian population. What has changed for the Untouchables as a special group is the decline in active deterrence of their participation in education. Blatant discrimination in the classroom persisted well into the post-independence period but has now declined, though undoubtedly arrogant and insensitive treatment of children does persist in many parts of India. The engine of change would seem to have been legislative prohibition of discrimination and political and bureaucratic pressure. This removal of barriers has been far more important an incentive for Untouchable families than any positive financial assistance. But of course it is not enough of an incentive: there remains the disabling influence of severe poverty and a weak tradition of formal learning.[68] It is precisely these problems that special financial assistance schemes could have confronted, if not entirely solved.

Land Reform—The Greatest Failure

Compensatory discrimination has effectively characterized the Untouchables as a welfare problem. They have been afforded a scheme of benefits which is at once monumental in terms of the human number

[67] See High Power Panel on Minorities, Scheduled Castes, etc., Report on Scheduled Castes, vol. I, Ministry of Home Affairs, New Delhi, December 1983, pp. 11–12.

[68] Even the incidental costs of schooling represent a considerable burden on Untouchable families. For example, as institutions which represent middle class values, schools compel students to dress and groom themselves in a way which is quite costly to the very poor. Then there is the additional cost of contributions towards festivals and celebrations in school: interviews with Untouchable women in Patna, January 1983.

affected and utterly benign towards the holders of power and privilege in India. Meanwhile, the one measure calculated to transform the condition of the Untouchables has been utterly neglected. There has been no programme to deliver 'land to the tiller'. True, the Untouchables are not merely poor or landless: their condition is perpetuated by elaborate structures and attitudes which are not reducible to any single material cause. But equally, their social position is inescapably bound up with their condition as a predominantly landless people condemned to work on the land of others. Any scheme of reform which fails to address the issue of land control is bound to produce piecemeal change rather than systematic transformation.

Abolition of intermediaries and associated measures of land reform during the fifties did have important consequences for the rural hierarchy. In very broad terms, the principal beneficiaries were the medium-to-large peasant proprietors of the British period. Their tenure was either made newly secure or at least reaffirmed, and their prosperity augmented by the effective cessation of taxation payments to the state. In the context of the 'green revolution', this class has been one of the two most successful in independent India (the other being the urban middle class). This peasant class has progressively expanded its holdings through buying up land from non-cultivating high-caste families; the process has amounted to a redistribution through the marketplace. A large proportion of this rising stratum of the peasantry were from the middle-ranking castes, others from high-caste and Muslim backgrounds. Their political strength has grown with their economic power, and they have dominated non-Congress governments in several states (including Uttar Pradesh and Bihar, the two largest) and even the Indian government formed after the 1989 elections.[69]

Since Indian-style land reform entailed very little redistribution of land to the landless, it was of little or no benefit to the predominantly landless Untouchables. Indeed, the kind of de facto redistribution from

[69] The above account is based on fieldwork in Rajasthan and Bihar extending over the period 1971–1990 and is confirmed by numerous published accounts. See Oliver Mendelsohn, 'The Indian Courts and Radical Redistribution: The Problem of Land Reform', unpublished paper, Conference, 'Room to Manoeuvre', Institute of Development Studies, Sussex University, 1980. There are numerous published accounts for example, Francine R. Frankel, *India's Political Economy 1947–1977: The Gradual Revolution* (Delhi: Oxford University Press, 1978), pp. 190–92.

high-caste landlords to their ritual and class inferiors has often harmed Untouchable interests. The change has effectively removed any prospect of a more radical redistribution at the hands of the state; Indira Gandhi's state of emergency in the mid-1970s was the last time that redistribution became a serious issue, and very little redistribution actually took place during this period. Meanwhile the sharpening conflicts between the rising peasantry and those at the very bottom of the rural hierarchy—the Untouchables, among others—make life increasingly uncomfortable in the countryside.

It is difficult to exaggerate the importance of land ownership in India. To give a simple example, the best prevailing division of production between sharecropper and owner in Bihar or West Bengal has been 50:50. In other words, for supplying nothing but his land, an owner has been entitled to half the production.[70] Since sharecropping is almost invariably more lucrative to the cultivator than straight-out labouring, the exploited nature of the labourer's situation follows without question. To possess land is not merely to gather the full product of one's labour but also to have a base from which to acquire other skills. Interviews with Untouchable 'success stories' very often reveal possession of a plot of land as the crucial asset which laid a base for a child to be sent to school and then on to college and a job in the reservation category.

Land reform would not only have had an immediate impact through increasing the income and life chances of labourers and their children, it would also have created a less dependent and therefore less exploitable Untouchable population. Land control is the basis of the agrarian hierarchy and therefore the means by which the dominants have subordinated Untouchables in the villages. Small resources like a home site of one's own and even a very small plot of productive land can effect a powerful liberation of the subordinate Untouchables from total and arbitrary dependence on their oppressor.[71] This, in turn, would have important ramifications in the character of the Indian state:

[70] Since Operation Barga implemented during the late 1970s and 1980s in West Bengal, many sharecroppers have received security of tenure and therefore capacity to enforce a far higher statutory entitlement than the prevailing rate. See Mendelsohn, ibid., and Atul Kohli, *The State and Poverty in India—The Politics of Reform* (Cambridge: Cambridge University Press, Bombay, 1987).

[71] See, for example, Ronald J. Herring, *Land to the Tiller, The Political Economy of Agrarian Reform in South Asia* (New Haven and London: Yale University Press, 1983), p. 213 and n. 48.

it would disrupt the influence habitually exercised by dominant land-holders. Thus the police force can often be relied on to support landed power in struggles with workers—this has been an everyday occurrence in Bihar during struggles over demands for the payment of statutory rates for day labour. Even with goodwill, diligence and probity (not always to be assumed), isolated administrators posted at district and sub-district sites cannot be successful in pushing through programmes which challenge local power. There are isolated examples where a state administration has carried through genuine, if limited, redistributive measures in the villages. The most recent case is Operation Barga in West Bengal, and this was done only with the crucial assistance of Communist Party organization at the grassroots level. And moreover, this operation was successful because it confronted comparatively easy targets.

If there had been a transfer of land to Untouchable cultivators, it would therefore have entailed a political redistribution too: Untouchables as even minor landholders would be more secure and effective both in the village and in relation to the state. It might be thought that this was precisely the reason why no significant land redistribution was ever possible in post-independence India. No doubt there is much truth in this, while at the same time there is reason to believe that more resolute intervention on the side of the landless was a possibility in the early years of independence. Thus West Bengal contrived to acquire a significant parcel of land for redistribution in the 1950s, and so did the apparently most 'feudal' state of Rajasthan. If a strong reformist administration had taken charge in the other states during the first years of independence, the dismal story of land reform might well be different. But by now it is difficult to be anything but intensely pessimistic about land redistribution. Most of the largest estates have gone and landholding now tends to be concentrated in communities which either work the land themselves or at least take an intense supervisory interest in agriculture. To part these groups from their land will require something approaching revolution, not reformism.

THE ANTI-POVERTY PROGRAMMES

As commitment to land reform has waned, the emphasis has shifted to a number of 'anti-poverty programmes'. These have not been officially described as an alternative to land reform measures but this has been their function for the ruling parties. By the time of the Sixth Five Year Plan (1980–5) three particular programmes formed the core of the anti-poverty strategy: the Integrated Rural Development Plan (IRDP), the National Rural Employment Plan (NREP) and the Special Component Plan (SCP).

The earliest and within its own terms most successful programme is NREP.[72] This is the latest variant of the conceptually simple food-for-work programmes first instituted in the 1960s. All that is done under these programmes is to provide relief in the form of daily wages for labour on public works: road and dam building are two of the favourite projects. The object is to site employment in areas and periods where alternative employment is not available.

Despite articulate supporters,[73] public works programmes have never lost the status of being mere emergency measures. What did emerge for a time as a programme promising permanent escape from poverty is the Integrated Rural Development Plan. Over a period of time, IRDP was transformed from a general programme of rural development inspired by Gandhian principles into a highly specific scheme to provide poor persons with income-producing assets. The theory was that these assets would so supplement income from labour that the beneficiaries would be permanently raised out of poverty. The ambition was nothing short of abolishing mass poverty in India by the beginning of the twenty-first century.

There is no comprehensive analysis of IRDP but there is a very large number of studies conducted in different parts of India, and none of them claims any major reduction in the scope of Indian poverty through the programme. The studies are not unanimous in their judgments but most of the independent studies (themselves usually directly funded by government research money) reveal fundamental flaws in design which guarantee only a marginal impact on poverty.[74]

[72] For a discussion of the literature on NREP relative to the other anti-poverty programmes, see Marika Vicziany, 'India's Anti-Poverty Drive and the Poorest of the Poor: An Assessment of Recent Trends', in John Browett, et al. (eds.), *Rethinking Development Issues: Opportunities and Constraints in the 1990s*, Conference Papers Series No. 5, Centre for Development Studies, Flinders University, March 1988, pp. 125–55.

[73] Two notable examples are Professors Dandekar and Rath of the Gokhale Institute, Poona. See Nikantha Rath, 'Garibi Hatao: Can IRDP Do It?', *Economic and Political Weekly*, 9 February 1985, p. 241.

[74] For an influential and sharply critical view of IRDP, see Rath. A broadly similar approach is taken in K. Sundaram and Suresh D. Tendulkar, 'Integrated

In many ways IRDP represented an attractive new approach to poverty eradication in India. Whatever the practical utility of public works programmes as a source of employment for the poor, there is something more appealing in the idea of transforming Untouchables and other poor people into small businessmen. One official has reasonably noted that it gives the poor a taste of freedom. But conceived as an isolated dropping of 'assets' from on-high, the scheme is obviously ludicrously ill-equipped to conquer rural poverty. It is difficult to escape the conclusion that the national government has abandoned any serious attempt to come to grips with the poverty of the poorest Indians, among whom the Untouchables loom large.[75]

But the numbers are so large that some obeisance must always be made to the issue of mass poverty.[76] The latest effort is the Special Component Plan, whereby all government programmes and departments must be administered so as to spend at least as much on the scheduled castes and tribes as their proportion in the population. We have seen no reliable evaluation of this programme (if that is the correct term), but there is no reason to believe that it will yield significant results. A common argument which is used to justify the

---

Rural Development in India', *Social Action*, vol. 35, no. 1, Jan.-March 1985. For a more positive (but still modest) view of the merits of IRDP, see the evaluation of one of the principal officials concerned with the policy in New Delhi: D. Bandyopadhyaya, 'An Evaluation of Policies and Programmes for the Alleviation of Rural Poverty in India', in Rizwanul Islam (ed.), *Strategies for Alleviating Poverty in Rural Asia* (Bangkok: ILO (ARTEP), 1985), pp. 99–151.

[75] Even if we accept the more optimistic picture of a rapid decline in Indian poverty during the 1980s, the position of the Untouchables has lagged behind. According to Hanumantha Rao, between 1977/78 and 1983/84 rural poverty fell by 12.5 per cent but for Untouchables by only 7.6 per cent and in the case of urban poverty Untouchable poverty increased by 1 per cent against an all-India fall of 7.8 per cent: Hanumantha Rao, 'Changes in Rural Poverty in India: Implications for Agricultural Growth', Dr Rajendra Prasad Memorial Lecture, 39th Annual Conference of the Indian Society of Agricultural Statistics, Punjabrao Krishni Vidyapeeth, Akola, Maharashtra, p. 4.

[76] This is not to say that the acknowledgment will be translated into resources reasonably calculated to address the problem. According to Dandekar the anti-poverty programmes cannot make a 'visible impact' on poverty because expenditure on them represents, at best, a mere 2.5 per cent of Net National Product generated by agriculture and the unorganized manufacturing sectors, the sectors in which the poor are located: V.M. Dandekar, 'Agriculture, Employment and Poverty', in Robert E.B. Lucas and Gustav F. Papanek (eds.), *The Indian Economy: Recent Development and Future Prospects* (Boulder and London: Westview Press, 1988), pp. 102–3.

neglect of the Special Component Plan is that development projects are not divisible into bits of value to Untouchables as distinct from the rest of the population. In the absence of concerted government attention backed by an effective political movement, anti-poverty programmes will continue to exist at the margins of Indian public policy.

THE ANTI-DISCRIMINATION LEGISLATION

As in the case of compensatory discrimination, the basic spadework for anti-discriminatory legislation outlawing untouchability had been done prior to independence.[77] This legislation was subsumed in and expanded by the Untouchability Offences Act 1955 which was designed to give teeth to the Constitutional prohibition of the practice of untouchability. In 1976 the act was amended and renamed the less specific Protection of Civil Liberties Act, perhaps in celebration of what had been accomplished. The only other significant anti-discriminatory legislation has been the Prevention of Atrocities Act of 1989, designed to single out 'Harijan atrocities' for particular legislative attention.[78]

The potential effectiveness of the Untouchability Offences Act was limited by a number of judicial interpretations which made prosecutions difficult to sustain.[79] But, more importantly, there are serious doubts as to how effective any anti-discrimination legislation can be in the Indian (and perhaps any) context. Certainly, utilization of the Act was slight in comparison to the magnitude of the problem: Galanter estimates that there were on an average 520 cases a year from 1955–64, and markedly fewer after this.[80] This is true despite the offences being 'cognizable' and therefore requiring mandatory prosecution by the state. There is no doubt a complex of reasons for this weak performance, including lack of knowledge and resources on the part of Untouchable victims; hostility from dominant groups in

[77] See Marc Galanter, 'The Abolition of Disabilities—Untouchability and the Law', in M. Mahar (ed.), *The Untouchables in Contemporary India* (Tucson: University of Arizona Press, 1972), pp. 239–40.

[78] For an assessment of its significance: Upendra Baxi, 'Historic New Law: Protecting SC/STs Human Rights', *Times of India*, 15 September 1989.

[79] Marc Galanter, 'The Abolition of Disabilities', pp. 249–61.

[80] Ibid., p. 266.

the locality; and the reluctance of police and other government authorities to take up unpopular causes which can do themselves little good. The 1976 Protection of Civil Liberties Act has not been more effective.[81]

It seems likely that the major impact of the anti-discrimination legislation has been to contribute to a general de-legitimation of untouchability. But this has been partial and, as we have seen, mostly concentrated in the areas of education, transport and road use—all of these are areas of strictly secular activity and are also controlled directly by the state. On the other side, the picture of rural society drawn by Desai has probably not changed substantially over the succeeding years. The most basic issue of access to water has been predominantly sidestepped by providing Untouchable settlements with their own separate water facilities. And there is no reason to believe that Untouchables are now welcome (or sometimes even tolerated) to make regular use of temples in those regions from which they were shut out in the past. On the side of the Untouchables, by and large there seems no point in making an issue of these matters—Ambedkar took this view in as early as the 1930s. It is not that matters of social respect are considered unimportant by organized Untouchable groups but that other individual issues—including the treatment of women and the very manner in which Untouchables are addressed in speech—have taken precedence over access to religious sites where one will be made to feel uncomfortable. And provided one has convenient access to water, it seems not so vital to insist on using a well where again one will feel unwelcome.

THE FAILURE OF UNTOUCHABLE POLITICAL MOBILIZATION

The greatest failure of the Untouchables has been the inability to organize themselves as a strong and durable political movement. Instead, their progress has had to depend on larger political forces which have only been partially and intermittently committed to the transformation of their condition. Mahatma Gandhi was the best of

---

[81] When a high level committee investigated the working of this Act in the early 1980s, they got no cooperation and no information from a number of the States in which the practice of untouchability remains a major problem, including Bihar, Uttar Pradesh, Madhya Pradesh, and Gujarat: High Power Panel on Minorities, etc., pp. 94–5.

these external aids, animated as he was by a deep abhorrence of untouchability. But for much of his political life Gandhi could not afford to embrace the Untouchable cause to an extent that would disrupt his larger practice of a politics of consensus. Moreover, Gandhi was scarcely a radical critic of Hinduism: his rejection of untouchability, for example, did not lead to a more general rejection of caste.[82] Even Jagjivan Ram—himself far from a radical—came to view Gandhi as being concerned in maintaining the structure of caste Hindu society at the cost of justice for the Untouchables.[83]

Gandhi brought such criticisms on himself with his insistence that he alone could sufficiently represent the Untouchable cause. But Jagjivan Ram's view also lacks self-criticism. He himself was a leading player in Indian politics over almost half a century and yet his overall contribution to progress for his people was slight. The potential strength of his position was revealed only once, when he left Congress and Indira Gandhi on the eve of the 1977 election. That act of desertion probably delivered the election to the Janata coalition, since it appears that the great majority of Untouchables voted against Congress for the first time.[84] Probably only a portion of that swing would have occurred without Jagjivan Ram's switch. So what did he do all those years when he was a leading figure in the Nehru and Indira Gandhi governments? The answer is that he was a good administrator in important posts like that of defence. Besides that, he is said to have managed to give a disproportionate number of jobs to his own Chamars during his tenure as railways minister. And no doubt he had importance as a symbol both for Chamars and, to some extent, for Untouchables in general. This is obviously pretty limited stuff relative to the overall problem.

Since Jagjivan Ram was by far the leading Untouchable to have played within the post-independence political system, his limited achievements are an important comment on the record of this 'insider' style of politics. Unfortunately, the achievements of political groupings that have operated independent of the major parties have been

---

[82] Gandhi did eventually reject caste towards the end of his life, during the 1940s. Jagjivan Ram admired Gandhi for his change of heart (op. cit., p. 52) but the new view could not displace three decades of his earlier instruction.

[83] Interview, op. cit.

[84] Paul Brass, *The Politics of India since Independence*, New Cambridge History of India, vol. IV (Cambridge: Cambridge University Press, 1990), pp. 208–9.

even less. The leading example is the Mahar movement of Maharashtra state. In a final act of disgust and despair at Untouchable prospects, Ambedkar led some millions of his Mahar followers out of Hinduism and into Buddhism shortly before his death in December 1956.[85] This same movement inspired the creation of the Republican Party in 1958,[86] and, in the seventies, the Dalit Panthers modelled on the Black Panthers of the United states.[87] All of these acts are impressive testament to the depth of consciousness among the Mahars, but again none of them met with great political or social success. The quitting Hinduism by a unilateral act—some would assert this to be an impossibility—has been judged by one writer to have led to heightened self-esteem but to have been all but useless as a means of improving the community status or prospects.[88] Indeed, because Untouchable Buddhists became preoccupied with proving their status as scheduled castes and therefore their rights to reservation,[89] conversion diverted attention from the more important question of mass political organization.[90] The Republican Party collapsed amid internal dissension by the early 1970s,[91] and the Dalit Panthers suffered a similar end.[92] But

[85] On the conversion movement, see Dhananjay Keer, pp. 481–513 and Jayashree B. Gokhale-Turner, 'From Concessions to Confrontation', chapter V.

[86] On the relationship between the conversion movement and the Republican Party, see Owen Lynch, *The Politics of Untouchability* (New York/London: Columbia University Press, 1969), pp. 94–109.

[87] Jayashree B. Gokhale-Turner, 'The Dalit Panthers and the Radicalisation of the Untouchables', *Journal of Commonwealth and Comparative Politics*, vol. 17 (1), 1979, p. 77. Also see 'Dalit Panthers Manifesto, Bombay, 1973', in Barbara Joshi (ed.), *Untouchable! Voices of the Dalit Liberation Movement* (New Delhi: Selectbook Service Syndicate, 1986), pp. 140–7.

[88] Jayashree Gokhale-Turner, 'From Concessions to Confrontation', chapter V.

[89] This right was partially conceded in 1969 when untouchable converts to Buddhism became eligible for educational benefits: Barbara R. Joshi, *Democracy in Search of Equality: Untouchable Politics and Indian Social Change* (Delhi: Hindustan Pub. Corporation, 1982), p. 106.

[90] Gokhale-Turner, 'From Concessions to Confrontation', pp. 317–18. Conversion also divided the Mahars and those Untouchables (especially Mangs and Chambhars) who staunchly insisted on their Hindu identity.

[91] An index of the insignificance of the Republican Party is that it does not even get a mention in Paul Brass's relatively comprehensive survey of parties in *The Politics of India Since Independence*.

[92] Ideological differences have been the cause of internal dissension according to Gokhale-Turner, 'The Dalit Panthers and the Radicalisation of the Untouchables', pp. 89–91. According to the Dalits in Karnataka, the Maharashtrian movement was weakened by internal disputes and a too narrow support base which

as a movement the Mahars' remains very much alive. In 1987 tens of thousands of them marched in protest against the Maharashtra government's decision to stop distribution of one of the unpublished works of Ambedkar which the government itself had published in August 1987 as part of its project to bring out all the unpublished manuscripts of Ambedkar. The work, *Riddles in Hinduism*, was claimed by the high-castes to be defamatory of Hinduism.[93]

The radical spirit of the Dalit movement of Maharashtra has now spread to other states, notably neighbouring Karnataka. Again it is Ambedkar whose teaching and example is studied by these Dalits (most of them young men), but the immediate inspiration for the movement was a speech by an Untouchable minister in the Congress government of Devaraj Urs, Basavalingappa, at a Dalit conference in 1973.[94] His fame arises from a single image that he projected—an image of Kannada (the language of the region) literature as *boosa* or cattle fodder, by virtue of its ignorance and falsification of the lives of Untouchables. His speech was like a match to tinder and, extraordinarily, a whole literature and movement of resistance was born virtually overnight.[95] Many years later this Dalit literature of Karnataka continues to flourish and grow in complexity and quality.[96] It has given an entirely new voice to subordinated Untouchables.

More recently, the Bahujan Samaj has been established to fight elections in north India and has enjoyed some surprising early success: in the national election of 1989 it actually won three seats. The party's leader, Kashi Ram, is based in Delhi and is a self-styled radical whose rhetoric is closely focused on Brahmanism as the great subordinator of Untouchables. Reputedly he begins his political meetings with cries to any Brahmin attenders to identify themselves, so that they can be

---

did not reach out to enlightened people among caste Hindus: interview with Indudan Honnapur, dalit writer and editor, Bangalore, 10 January 1988.

[93] This was the title of the 4th volume of *Dr Babasaheb Ambedkar, Writings and Speeches* (Education Department, Government of Maharashtra). In 1987 some eleven volumes had already been published or were in press.

[94] From 1972 to 1980 Urs cultivated support of the OBCs and Untouchables and appointed at least three Untouchable ministers: Interview with E. Raghavan, journalist, *Times of India*, Bangalore, 5 January 1988.

[95] Immediately after the conference the Dalit Sangharsh Samiti was formed: interviews with Indudan Honnapur, op. cit., and Chandraprasad Tyagi, op. cit.; and Basavalingappa himself, Bangalore, 7 January 1988.

[96] For example, Indudan Honnapur is the editor of *Sugathi*, a Kannada weekly (circulation 65,000) which is a family magazine with a Dalit twist.

tossed out of the meeting. This focus on Brahmanism is reminiscent of Ambedkar. The support base of the Bahujan Samaj appears to be the now considerable number of Untouchables occupying positions reserved for the scheduled castes.

More impressive in human terms is the political activity of Untouchable agricultural labourers in Bihar.[97] For a number of years now there has been a melange of radical political organization and action at a grassroots level. This Left politics has tended to be lumped together as 'Naxalite', and indeed some of it has ideological and even some organizational roots in the insurrectionary Naxalite movement of West Bengal which operated in the late 1960s. But most of the time this identification sheds no light into what is happening in a number of districts of central Bihar. What is singular about the developments in Bihar is the resoluteness and durability of the agitation and resistance which low-caste and Untouchable labourers have been conducting in the seventies and particularly the eighties. The issues have been simple and immediate, including a demand for social respect (particularly in relation to women, who have been routinely sexually abused by their social superiors); the payment of statutory minimum wages; and ownership of disputed lands. But simple and essentially moderate as these demands are, they are explosive in the context of Bihar.

The history of grassroots political action on the part of Untouchables and some backwards runs parallel with increased reportage of 'Harijan atrocities': Bihar has become synonymous with this term. From the mid-seventies the Indian newspapers have been full of stories detailing such violent incidents: the names Parasbigha, Belchi, Pipra and many others live on with images of the most ghastly acts of violence perpetrated on Untouchables by caste Hindus.[98] It is all too easy to be glib in providing explanations of these phenomena, each of which has its own distinctive incidents. But a study of many of the cases must convince any serious observer that the traditional status of the Untouchables is a prime ground of the peculiarly savage nature of these attacks. We can give a simple hypothetical example (in fact modelled on an actual incident). If a Bhumihar girl is molested by a group of Rajput boys, this will provoke great Bhumihar fury which

[97] The following account is based on fieldwork in a number of districts of Bihar on several occasions during the period 1980–85.

[98] For examples of these atrocities, see N.D. Kamble, *Atrocities on Scheduled Castes in Post Independence India, 19 August 1947 to 15 August 1979* (New Delhi: Ashish Pub. House, 1981).

could lead to serious violence. But if the molesters are Untouchable Chamars or Musahars, the Bhumihar fury will take on a demented character. The lowly have not only dared to raise their heads but they have defiled their social superiors.

So Untouchables have become part of the new violence of Bihar because they are not prepared to suffer subordination to the extent they once did. In a situation of competitive party politics and breakdown of the old caste order, Untouchable discontent and assertiveness have taken a more active character. The Untouchables are met with massive retaliation for any aggression. Clearly, this is fertile ground for political organizers with a revolutionary programme. Thus the problem of untouchability in Bihar has become a pressing political problem to a greater extent than anywhere else in India. It would be good to predict that out of this situation will arise progress for the Untouchables, but it is not yet possible to say this with any confidence. The new consciousness and solidarity among the Untouchables may be a positive sign but the larger reality of Bihari life today is ever deepening antagonisms in the context of an utterly stagnant economy. Mere political consciousness is not enough. There need to be skills and opportunities as well, if the Untouchables are to improve their material life.[99]

This short discussion of some Untouchable activity in different parts of India clearly demonstrates that the Untouchables have not disappeared in any political sense. But neither do they represent a united or a leading political force. As to their divisions, these have existed from the moment they emerged as a distinctive political presence some sixty years ago. The divisions are various, though the most obvious one is between different Untouchable castes. Thus despite the fact that Dr Ambedkar is something of an inspirational icon for Untouchable activists throughout India, his movement only developed lasting strength among his own Mahar community. The reasons for this are several, rather than lying simply in any crude primordial spirit of the Mahars or the other Untouchable castes. Linguistic heterogeneity clearly represents a formidable if not impassable barrier in the way of Untouchable unity. But it is true that even with a common language, different Untouchable castes have found it difficult to re-

---

[99] Bihari Untouchables have the lowest level of literacy in India, even amongst Untouchables: 6.5 per cent in 1971 and 10.4 per cent in 1981. Source: Selected Statistics on Scheduled Castes, Tables 17 and 19, pp. 27–31.

main part of a single organization. In Maharashtra Ambedkar's movement failed to attract lasting support from other Untouchable castes, particularly the large Mang and Chambar castes. There were leadership difficulties—Ambedkar was not a deeply talented organizer—but also more traditional rivalries about relative ritual status. Similar splits were present in the movement in Hyderabad state during the same period.[100]

The history of Ambedkar's movement gives no confidence that it will be possible to fabricate any great overarching party of Untouchables. But conversely the experience of Untouchables working within umbrella parties like Congress or the Communist parties suggests a continuing likelihood that Untouchable interests will be muffled by stronger forces. This experience has convinced many of the most committed young activists that there is no gain to be had through participation in orthodox politics which guarantees Untouchables what they see as useless parliamentary seats. This outlook is shared by groups as diverse as illiterate Musahar labourers in the central plains of Bihar and the Dalits of Karnataka who are busy practising cultural politics through literature and journalism.

Disenchantment with the politics of reservation among some of the more critical Untouchable activists has coincided with increasing high-caste resentment with the whole system of reservation.[101] There may well come a point when the limited gains to be had from the system are outweighed by the political opposition which it sets up. But the history of Untouchable political organization can give no confidence that any post-reservation era will be marked by greater political purpose or unity. Indeed, it is probably time to throw away as irrelevant the very idea of one great Untouchable political force across India as a whole. While we have defended the idea of 'the Untouchables' as having a social and not merely an analytical significance, it has to be recognized that political organization on this basis cuts across both caste (jati) and class. It is neither possible nor desirable to organize Untouchables as some kind of third force that is

---

[100] R. Venkatswamy, *Our Struggle for Emancipation* (Secunderabad: Universal Art Printers, 1955), 2 vols. This documents the long history of conflict between untouchable Malas and Madigas.

[101] It is not only radical Untouchables who are critical of reservation. Professor Parvathamma complains of the tendency for reservation to be monopolized by a privileged elite among the Untouchables and handed down from generation to generation: interview, 16 January 1988, Mysore.

neither caste nor class based. The preferable model is one of organized Untouchables pursuing a variety of strategies both within and outside mainstream political processes. They would sometimes be operating independently and sometimes within larger political organizations dominated by non-Untouchables.

For the present writers this represents a more realistic and more pluralist model than the one that prevailed in the era of Gandhi and Ambedkar, a model which was in turn heavily influenced by earlier British perceptions. Whatever their other differences, both Gandhi and Ambedkar were at one in conceiving of the Untouchables as a single identifiable stratum within Hindu society rather than as a collection of jatis or castes. Gandhi could afford to depict the Untouchables with this broad brush because he saw their degraded status as a temporary disability from which he would liberate them; any difference among them was of little relevance, since all the Untouchables would resume their rightful position as ordinary Hindus of particular caste once liberation was complete. In the case of Ambedkar, the proposition of Untouchable unity was politically suited to his ambition to be the leader of a large and enduring political force. Gandhi and Ambedkar were of course right that ritual untouchability distinguishes 'the Untouchables' from all other Indians, and the two leaders greatly contributed to the development of self-consciousness among the Untouchables through this approach. But by now it is important that Untouchable political formations explore a variety of political strategies that can take advantage of local circumstances. This can be done without their throwing away a sense of solidarity with all Untouchables throughout India.

To give one example, influential members of the Dalit movement of Karnataka have concluded that one of the reasons for the collapse of the Dalit Panther movement of Maharashtra was its exclusivity: the Panthers failed to build bridges to radical organizations drawn from communities other than the Mahars, and in particular to non-Untouchables. These Karnataka Dalits are determined to avoid the same mistake as they forge their own movement. Of course, their difficulty will be to preserve a separate identity while simultaneously pursuing the politics of coalition. They have to avoid the opposite fates of Jagjivan Ram and the Ambedkarites: foundering through isolation or through submersion in a larger organization. But whatever the difficulties of their political situation, these Karnataka Dalits are at least thinking creatively about what is undoubtedly a difficult political task.

CONCLUSION

Inequalities of esteem and wealth are present in all societies and from one viewpoint, Untouchables are simply an example of this general phenomenon. This is not the view adopted in the present paper. Our argument here is that Untouchables have retained their identity as a subordinated people within Indian society, and by this we mean to identify a condition that is far more severe than merely being bottom of an inevitable hierarchy.

All the central policies in relation to the Untouchables have failed, and failed miserably rather than marginally. The anti-poverty measures—including land reform and compensatory discrimination—have not had the effect of 'carrying' any significant proportion of Untouchables over the poverty 'line'. On the other hand, social oppression has very significantly diminished: through an interaction of legal prohibition and political and social pressure, schooling and transport have been defined as public spaces within which overt discrimination is inappropriate behaviour. And developments such as the installation of separate water facilities for Untouchables have worked to reduce the number of other stress points within Indian society. But even in the matter of ritual untouchability, the record is far less benevolent when placed under closer scrutiny. Avoidance strategy rather than fair-minded tolerance seems to characterize much of the social contact between caste Hindus and Untouchables. This is highly preferable to former tyrannies, and we would not wish our argument to be misconstrued on this point. But multiple incidents of continuing oppression suggest a broader persistence of the old hierarchical ideology.

In their dealings with government, Untouchables do not encounter a politically benign and technically effective instrument of rational social engineering. Government can be both enemy and benefactor to them—the idea of the contradictory state takes on new meaning in the context of the Indian state's meeting with the poor. Only in Kerala can government be seen to have pursued a strategy which has consistently (though still far from comprehensively) worked to reduce social gaps between Untouchables and their ritual superiors. Thus the Kerala government has clearly benefited the Untouchables through working to provide basic needs of shelter, health, education and even some social security in old age. This is a model that deserves emulation throughout India.

In common with many of the papers in this book, we have concluded that the liberation of the Untouchables is ultimately a task for themselves and that the mechanisms are political. But it would be cynical and unjustified to believe that well meaning people from other communities cannot play an important part in this liberation. Similarly, the institutions of the state must not be written off as constitutionally incapable of delivering crucial assistance. The sphere of most urgent need for the Untouchables is education, and this is an area where they cannot meet their own needs by themselves. In India formal education cannot possibly lead to guaranteed employment. But for a subordinated people like the Untouchables, education represents liberation and empowerment. Education cannot be conceived of as an alternative to politics but rather as a necessary part of the development of political consciousness. If the Indian state were to adopt resolute measures to provide a primary education to all Untouchables, it would be taking a decisive stand against the whole complex of traditions that constitute untouchability. It is doubtful that untouchability could persist as a credible social system in the context of universal literacy among the now Untouchable castes.

Cultural Rights and the Definition of Community

VEENA DAS

One of the symbolic areas around which mobilization has taken place within the political realm in modern India is 'cultural rights'. Despite the similarity of this phrase to 'political rights', I believe that cultural rights cannot be thought of as parallel or analogous to other kinds of political rights: I shall try to show that the term 'cultural rights' includes a variety of situations with very different moral implications. Further, cultural rights cannot be understood exclusively within a framework of a theory of interests, for they refer primarily to political passions. Before I explore this relationship between cultural rights and political passions further, let us see the contexts in which the problem of cultural rights has been formulated.[1]

THE SUBJECTS OF CULTURAL RIGHTS

The question of cultural rights has been formulated in national and international forums, primarily in the context of the rights of minorities. The Indian Constitution grants minorities the right to preserve and develop their culture, and to make institutional arrangements for this—for instance, by establishing educational institutions. As formulated in the Constitution, this right is in the nature of a restriction on the powers of the state.

A similar concern with preserving the culture of minorities is

[1] I am grateful to Upendra Baxi for intensive and extensive discussions on the subject of cultural rights and for many ideas most generously shared. The paper was first presented at the conference on Rights of Subordinated Groups at La Trobe University in November and subsequently at the Sudasien Institut of the University of Heidelberg (July 1989) and at the IDPAD Seminar on 'State and Society' (March 1990). In the process of these presentations it has been considerably transformed. I thank all those who commented on it. Finally, my deepest gratitude to Ranendra Das for his support.

evident in various provisions of international law concerning the rights of minorities.[2] The Commission on Human Rights, established in 1946 by the United Nations Assembly, appointed a Subcommission on Prevention of Discrimination and Protection of Minorities. Between 1947 and 1954 the Subcommission attempted to define 'minority'. Although most members were agreed that the definition ought to include an objective as well as subjective element, it failed to agree on any precise notion of this crucial concept. This partly reflected the dual character of international law in relation to human rights, where the state and the individual form the two poles around which legal personalities are organized. In international law it is states which mutually recognize each other. In certain cases individuals have a right to petition, but there has been great hesitation in granting legal personality to groups. In part, this comes out of historical circumstances under which the international community has come to recognize that the most gross violations of individual rights can occur within lawfully constituted states: witness the attempt to exterminate the Jews in Nazi Germany. Thus the first formal recognition of the crime of genocide (*crimen lesae humanitus*) was made in Nuremberg in 1945. This concrete context, within which a concern for human rights was articulated in international forums, naturally emphasized the rights of individuals against the overwhelming power of the state. These rights, according to Sacerdoti (1983),[3] fall into the following five clusters.

1.   The right of individuals, peoples, groups, and minorities to existence and protection from physical suppression. At the level of the individual this is expressed as the right to life, of which an individual may only be deprived through due process of law. At the collective level this is recognized through the convention on genocide, which makes the physical suppression of a group punishable.[4]

---

[2] On the question of rights of minorities in international law, see F. Capotorti, 1985, 'Minorities,' in *Encyclopedia of Public International Law*, vol. 4 (North Holland, 1985) and see Giorgio Sacerdoti, 'New Developments in Group Consciousness and the International Protection of Rights of Minorities', *Israel Year Book of Human Rights*, 1983, vol. 13, pp. 116–146.

[3] See Sacerdoti, op. cit.

[4] It has been noted that the Convention on Genocide made physical killing and forcible control of biological reproduction punishable, but could not reach any agreement on cultural genocide. Further, the provisions of the Convention were not applicable to groups whose members were recruited on the criterion of choice

2. The right of individuals not to be discriminated against on grounds of their membership in a minority group.

3. The right of persons belonging to racial or ethnic groups not to be the objects of hate or hostile propaganda.

4. The prohibition against actions meant to destroy or endanger the existing character, traditions and culture of such groups.

5. The right of persons belonging to ethnic, linguistic, or religious minorities to preserve their culture and language, and the right of persons belonging to religious minorities to practise and profess their religion.

It ought to be quite clear that the subjects of all these rights are individuals. Especially important in this context is the right of individuals not to be discriminated against on the grounds of their membership of a group, or not to be made the object of hatred or hostile propaganda. Yet it is also evident that the subjects of these rights cannot be treated as isolated, atomized individuals, because in order for them to preserve and enjoy their culture the collective survival of traditions becomes an important condition. To understand the complexity of the issues involved, let us pay close attention to Article 27 of the International Convenant on Civil and Political Rights:

In those states in which ethnic, religious or linguistic minorities exist, persons belonging to such minorities shall not be denied the right, in community with other members of their groups to enjoy their own culture, to profess and practise their own religion, or to use their own language.

It should be noted that the subjects of the rights in Article 27 are persons; yet we have to ask whether the rights promised to minorities can all be derived from the fundamental human rights of individuals,

---

such as political groups or homosexuals [cf. J. Lador-Ledeaer, 'The Human Rights to Groups Organization', *Israel Year Book of Human Rights*, 1983, pp. 47–54.) On major examples of genocide in the 20th century, see M. Baccianini, 'A Century of Genocide', *Telos*, 70, 1987, pp. 155–61. Crawford has noted that 'peoples' or 'groups' protected by the rules on prevention and punishment of genocide include groups which could not be classed as beneficiaries of the right to self determination. He also notes that the Genocide Convention is directed at offenders rather than victims, emphasizing *duties* of legal persons, whether these be rulers, public officials or private individuals: see J. Crawford (ed.) in his Introduction to *Rights of Peoples* (Oxford, Clarendon, 1988). But to the extent that the Convention has as its object the preservation of groups, it is meaningful to talk of their rights. As we shall see later it is precisely on the question of preservation of a group as a cultural entity that serious conflict between the rights of groups and those of individuals may come into conflict.

or alternatively whether it becomes necessary to invoke additional criteria pertaining to collectives for the protection of minorities. The crucial phrase in Article 27 is *'in community with other members of their groups'*. It would seem from this phrase that a collective dimension of rights is being recognized only in the form of associational rights so that individuals can, in community with other individuals of similar character, enjoy these rights. Yet how can this community of individuals be preserved if its cultural traditions, or language, or religion is allowed to disappear? Can one define a group as a mere aggregate of individuals? Would a Chinese, an Indian and a Bantu, when aggregated, make up a group with a culture, and can each such individual be said to be enjoying his culture in community with other members of his group?[5]

The discussions which took place among the members of the Subcommission on Protection of Minorities reflected some of these difficulties. For instance, it was recognized that the definition of minority cannot be arrived at by enumerating objective criteria. It was stated that members of a majority group must show the subjective will to preserve the traditions of their group; equally, if a group became numerically depleted, it was unlikely to show the will to preserve and live by these traditions. So it was stressed that the issue was not only of biological survival and of ensuring against discrimination towards individuals within minorities, but also that in order for individuals to be able to enjoy their culture it must be preserved in the collective conscience.[6]

[5] On the difference between an aggregative notion of totality and a distributive one as applied to human societies, see Veena Das, 'Difference and Division as Designs for Life' in Carla Borden (ed.) *Contemporary Indian Tradition: Voices on Culture, Nature, and Challenge of Change* (Washington: Smithsonian Press, 1989), pp. 45–57

[6] In its attempts to define minorities the U.N. Subcommission on Prevention of Discrimination and Protection of Minorities discussed in 1950 the following text:

(1)   The term minority includes only those non-dominant groups in a population which wish to preserve stable ethnic religious, or linguistic traditions or characteristics markedly different from those of the rest of the population.

(2)   Such minorities should properly include a number of persons sufficient in themselves to preserve such traditions.

(3)   Such minorities should be loyal to the states of which they are nationals.

The suggested definition came up for sharp criticisms. Bruegel commented that all obligations against any positive steps have been collected in a resolution supposed to define desirable positive steps. Similarly a representative of a Jewish

The following theoretical issues, then, seem to me crucial in developing the conceptual framework within which we may think about cultural rights. First, if we divide rights according to their adjectival qualities into individual rights and collective rights, then we need to ask: What is the relation of this distinction to the distinction between individual and collective as morphological categories and as subjects of rights? Second, in granting individuals the right to enjoy their culture, what obligations does the state have towards ensuring the survival of that culture? Is the state simply required to abstain from interference or does it have positive obligations towards these groups?[7] Is the dualistic structure of human rights—organized around the state and the individual as the two poles with legal personalities— adequate in the context of cultural rights? In other words, is the state the only possible organization of human collectivities which can be bestowed with legal personality in the matter of rights, or is it possible for groups and communities to be recognized as legitimate expressions of man and woman's collective existence? Finally, if we consider it necessary that rights of collectivities (as distinct from the collective rights of individuals) be recognized, then how would relations between different collectivities on the one hand, and the collectivity and the individual on the other, be governed? A strong fear has been expressed by many scholars that since there is no legally acceptable definition of 'people', the recognition of such entities as legal beings may lead to gross violation of human rights enjoyed by individuals in the interest of an abstraction such as the nation, the community, the masses, the economy or even the state.[8]

In the context of these questions, I would like to suggest that just

---

organization commented that no minority of any kind could get any rights under these provisions. See Sacerdoti, op. cit.

[7] Capotorti, op. cit., favours the interpretation that the state has positive obligations to protect the culture of the minorities. To quote him, 'If real equality of treatment is to be assured—only tolerance pure and simple will not achieve it'. He goes on to say that Article 27 would be superfluous if it only granted rights that could be basically deduced from human rights. 'With particular reference to the cultural field, it should be recalled that the obligations imposed on states by Article 13 and 15 of the Covenant on Economic, Social, and Cultural Rights (concerning every individual's rights to education and to take part in cultural life) have the features of positive obligations to be implemented through appropriate measures'.

[8] See Paul Sieghart, *The International Law of Human Rights* (London: Oxford University Press, 1983), and James Crawford, op. cit.

as the experience of the Second World War was of crucial importance for European and American societies—which arrived at a conception of human rights based on natural law theories and which essentially tried to empower the individual against oppressive state structures—so the experience of Asian societies today in the context of their struggles over culture may be crucial to develop the legal structures within which the collective dimension of human existence is given clearer shape and form. This collective dimension is recognized in the Universal Declaration of Human Rights, which refers to the 'community in which alone the free and full development of personality (of everyone) is possible'. It seems important, therefore, that we apply our intellectual resources towards developing the concepts involved, including the concepts of culture and community.

WHAT IS CULTURE?

Definitions of the term 'culture' are contested. In its anthropological use the term refers to a system of shared meanings through which collective existence becomes possible. However, as many recent critiques point out, this view of culture has no place for the notion of judgement, and hence of the relations of power through which the dominance of ideas and tastes is established. As Said says about Matthew Arnold's view of culture

what is at stake in society is not merely the cultivation of individuals, or the development of a class of finely tuned sensibilities, or the renaissance of interests in the classics, but rather the assertively achieved and won hegemony of an identifiable set of ideas, which Arnold honorifically calls culture, over all other ideas in society.[9]

The implications of Arnold's view of culture are profound; they lead us towards a position in which culture must be seen in terms of that which it eliminates as also that which it establishes. Said argues that when culture is consecrated by the state, it becomes a system of discriminations and evaluations through which a series of exclusions can be legislated from above. By such legislative enactment, the state comes to be the primary giver of values. It defines anarchy, disorder, irrationality, inferiority, bad taste and immorality: these are all located

[9] Edward W. Said, *The World, the Text and the Critic* (London: Faber, 1983), p. 10.

outside culture and civilization by the state and its institutions. This exclusion of alternatives—other forms and ways of living—is an important device by which the hegemony of the state is established. Either certain 'others' are defined as being outside culture (as in the case of madness), or domesticated (as in the case of penal servitude: Foucault's monumental studies on the asylum and the prison demonstrate this).

It is in this context that one must understand the challenge posed by the community to the hegemony of the state, especially the notion that the state is the sole giver of values. The danger, however, is that one may in the process valorize the community as representing a more 'organic' mode of organizing culture. Many scholars argue that culture occupies a place more organically related to the traditions of groups, whereas tradition is falsely invested in the hands of the state.[10] The issues are by no means so simple, for culture and tradition are not instituted in society once and forever. They are subject to the constant change which marks every living society. Indeed, the very attempt to freeze and fix cultural traditions may jeopardize their survival. Finally, in the contest between states, communities, and collectivities of different kinds on the one hand and the individual on the other, we see the double life of culture: its potential to give radical recognition to the humanity of its subjects, as well as its potential to keep the individual within such tight bounds that the capacity to experiment with one's self—which is equally a mark of one's humanity—comes to be severely at risk.

This double definition of culture as a system of shared meanings which both define collective life as well as keep the individual within strict social bounds, places the question of cultural rights squarely within the larger question of passions rather than interests.

So it is time now to define passion. After the classical work of Hirschman on political passions, it was usual to think of passions as

[10] This, for example, appears to be the case in (R.M. Unger's) conception of 'community' as he himself acknowledges in a Postscript to *Knowledge and Politics* (New York: Free Press, 1985, pp. 339–40, emphasis supplied). 'But the vision of empowerment in the classical doctrines of emancipation is clouded by unjustifiably restrictive assumptions about the possible forms of social life and in particular about the possible institutional definitions of market and democracies. *In place of the theory of organic groups, I would put a program that extends the ideal of empowerment*, and relates it to ideals that it seems to exclude, by freeing it from unnecessarily confining premises.' (Unger, 1984, pp. 339–340, emphasis supplied).

obstructions in the path of reason which had to be overcome for enlightened interest to emerge. This view of passion is extremely limited. Indeed, certain kinds of revelations, including the recognition of oneself as human become possible only through passion.[11] If the self is constituted only through the *other*—so that desire, cognition, memory and imagination become possible through the play of passion—then the revelatory role of passion must be acknowledged, not only in the life of the individual but also in the life of the collective. Passion then must play a role in politics. It is precisely through the life of passions that the question of culture and community has come to be linked in the shaping of the public sphere in modern India.

The demand for cultural rights in contemporary times has here come to be articulated in a context where cultural symbols have been appropriated by the state, which tries to establish a monopoly over ethical pronouncements. The state is thus experienced as a threat by smaller units who feel that their ways of life will be penetrated if not engulfed by this larger unit. The situation is quite the opposite of the relation between the part and the whole in hierarchical systems which were the characteristic mark of traditional politics in South Asia.[12] In a hierarchical system, *differences* between constituent units were essential for the 'whole' to be constituted. In other words, small units come to be defined by being bearers of special marks in a hierarchical entity, and although by definition they could not be equal in such a system, the very logic of hierarchy assured that they could not be simply engulfed into the higher totality. This was both a source of their oppression as well as a guarantee of acceptance (not necessarily a radical acceptance) of their place in the world. This is not an appeal for return to hierarchy as a principle of organization but an effort to

---

[11] This view of passion is developed in recent years primarily by R.M. Unger, *Passion: An Essay on Personality*, (New York: Free Press, 1984), although the history of this concept is complex.

[12] A systematic elaboration of this view may be found in Louis Dumont, *Homo Hierarchicus: The Caste System and Its Implications* (London: Weidenfeld and Nicolson, 1970). It may, however, be noted that Dumont's view has been criticized for its idealist orientation and recent studies of kingship point to various complexities both within the ideology of hierarchy as well as in the categories of the polity. David Shulman, *The King and the Clown* (Princeton: Princeton University Press, 1985); H. Kulke, *The Devaraja Cult* (Ithaca: New York University Press, 1978); Nicholas Dirks, *The Hollow Crown: Ethnohistory of an Indian Kingdom* (New York: Cambridge University Press, 1987); and Burton Stein, *All the King's Manna* (Delhi: Manohar, 1984), among many others.

locate the special nature of the threat that smaller groups feel in relation to the state in modern India.

COMMUNITY AND STATE

In order to understand contests between the community and the state in India, and thus to clarify concepts, I focus upon two different events which serve as exemplary instances. Later I will analyse some themes which pertain to cultural rights in the militant Sikh movement of Punjab.

My first event is popularly known as the Shah Bano case. This raised the whole question of the relation between secular law (as formulated and implemented by institutions of the state) and the rights of minorities and women.

My second incident is the occurrence of *sati* in 1987 in a small town of Rajasthan, when an eighteen-year-old girl was consigned to flames on the death of her husband. This led to a severe contest between women's groups and some Hindu organizations on the nature of this death, including questions about violence against women on the one hand and the rights of a community over its religious customs on the other. In both cases the state intervened and passed new legislation, although the direction of the legislative provisions was quite different in the two cases. A comparison of these cases helps us see the kinds of questions likely to arise in the political culture of India on issues relating to cultural rights, and especially the contradictions or conflict between different kinds of community on the one hand and the state and the community on the other.

THE SHAH BANO CASE

The Shah Bano case refers to the events which followed from a criminal appeal by the appellant, Mohammad Ahmad Khan, against the respondents, Shah Bano Begum and others, in the Supreme Court in 1985.[13] The appeal arose out of an application filed by a divorced

---

[13] A voluminous literature exists on the Shah Bano case, only some of which has been directly referred to in this paper. A very useful compilation of this literature is available in A.A. Engineer (ed.), *The Shah Bano Controversy* (Delhi: Orient Longman, 1987).

Muslim woman, Shah Bano, for maintenance under section 125 of the Code of Criminal Procedure. The appellant, who was an advocate, was married to the respondent in 1932 and there were three sons and two daughters born of this marriage. According to the respondent, she was driven out of the matrimonial home in 1975. In April 1978 Shah Bano filed an application against her husband under section 125 in the court of the judicial magistrate, Indore, asking for maintenance at the rate of Rs. 500 p.m. On 6 November 1978 the appellant divorced the respondent by an irrevocable *talaq* (divorce), permitted under Muslim personal law. His defence to Shah Bano's petition for maintenance was that she had ceased to be his wife after the divorce and that he had paid a maintenance allowance of two years and had deposited a sum of Rs. 3000 by way of dower during the period of *iddat*, which is normally three menstrual cycles or the passage of three lunar months for post-menopausal women. The pre-history of the case need not concern us here. What is important is to note that the husband was in the Supreme Court by special leave and the court had to give its ruling on the question of whether the provisions of section 125 of the Code of Criminal Procedure were applicable to Muslims.

The judgement given on 25 April 1985 has a heterogeneous structure which I shall analyse in a moment. The court decided that the provisions of the Code of Criminal Procedure were indeed applicable to Muslims, and therefore upheld the High Court decision as regards the provision of maintenance to Shah Bano. In the course of giving the judgment, however, the Chief Justice, Chandrachud, also commented upon several other issues, including the injustice done to women in all religions, on the desirability of evolving a common civil code as envisaged by the Constitution, and on the provisions in the Shariat regarding the obligations of a husband to provide maintenance to the divorced wife. In a way it was this very heterogeneity which allowed the judgment to become a signifier of issues that touched upon several dimensions, including the nature of secularism, the rights of minorities, and the use of law as an instrument for securing justice in favour of the oppressed.

I do not wish to suggest that the judgment by itself created these issues; the Muslim community was clearly in the midst of debating these issues itself. The very fact that Mr Yunus Saleem had appeared as counsel on behalf of the Muslim Personal Law Board and not as counsel for the defendant attests to this interpretation. The issue had become contentious at both the legislative and adjudicatory level. Baxi summarized this well when he asked

What has caused this insecurity (among the Muslims)? Surely not the affirmation by the Supreme Court of India of an order raising the maintenance of Shah Bano from about Rs.70 to Rs.130 from a husband whose earnings as a lawyer were very substantial indeed? Ahmad Khan did not resort to the Supreme Court because maintenance amounts caused great financial hardship to him. The real meaning of the Shah Bano litigation was an attempt to secure reversal of two earlier decisions of the Court allowing maintenance to divorced Muslim wives under section 125 of the Criminal Procedure Code. The litigation was devised to reinstate the Shariat. And it succeeded in the first round when Justice Fazal Ali explicitly referred to a five-bench judge the question whether the earlier decisions were in consonance with the Shariat Act, 1937, which laid down that in all matters of family, including divorce and maintenance, courts will decide the questions in the light of the Shariat.[14]

Thus it was not the judgement which created the issues, but certain complications were introduced as a result of a lack of restraint in the judicial prose.

Following this judgment there was great agitation as well as heated debates within the Muslim community—between 'progressives' and 'fundamentalists'; between women's groups and Muslim leaders; between rival speakers in parliament. The political debates, pressures and counter-pressures finally led to the passing of The Muslim Women (Protection of Rights on Divorce) Bill, 1986. This was hailed as a victory for fundamentalists by some and as a triumph of democracy by others; it was alternately seen as a betrayal of women's rights and as a document which vindicated the position of women in Islam which, it was alleged, had stood questioned in the Supreme Court judgment. Although in 1985–6 it was perhaps not possible to delineate the complexity of the issues, so that the debate on the case was seen in terms of a confrontation between 'secularists' and 'communalists', it may now be possible to break from this battle of shadows to see the varied and complex nature of the question.

The first issue is the nature of the judgment itself. On legal issues the judgment was quite clear. The judges stated quite categorically that earlier decisions of the Supreme Court had referred to whether Muslims were exempt from the application of section 125 of the

[14] Upendra Baxi, 'Text of Observations Made at a Public Meeting on The Muslim Women (Protection of Rights) Bill,' *Hindustani Andolan* (Bombay, 1986).

Criminal Procedures Act: the said section referred to the case in which a person of sufficient means refused to maintain a wife, including a divorced wife who was unable to maintain herself. Incidentally, the provisions of the Act also applied to aged parents, children and handicapped adult children. The purpose of the Act was to see that when relatives could maintain a destitute relative within the categories mentioned above, they fulfilled this duty so that the destitute person was not forced towards vagrancy.

The judges quoted from the speech of Sir James Fitzjames Stephen, who piloted the Code of Criminal Procedure, 1872, as a legal member of the Viceroy's Council, to establish the purport of the relevant sections of the code within which section 125 occurred. He had described this particular section as a 'mode of preventing vagrancy or at least of preventing its consequences'. Supporting this interpretation, the judgment said 'the liability imposed by section 125 to maintain close relatives who are indigent is founded upon the individual's obligation to society to prevent vagrancy and destitution. That is the moral edict of the law and morality cannot be clubbed with religion'.

One could take issue with this colonial piece of legislation, for its concern is not with individual rights but rather with vagrancy as a threat to public order. The creation of the legal category 'vagrants', as well as the criminalization of 'close relatives' not supporting indigent relatives, reflects some of the basic concerns of colonial rule about maintaining unproductive populations.[15] That the judges should have invested this clause with such moral fervour, without considering at any point the state's responsibility for the maintenance of indigents, is quite another story.

To return to the strictly legal issues, the judgment did not raise questions which could become symbols of the contests that were to follow. The judges said that section 125 was part of the Code of Criminal Procedures, not of civil law. They further stated they were not concerned with the broad and general question of whether a

---

[15] Responsibility for maintenance of pauper lunatics and pauper lepers was similarly placed on the family in the Lepers Act as well as the Lunatic Act. It is, however, interesting to observe that in the metropolitan countries the problem of indigent populations was sought to be resolved through institutional solutions. For a masterly account of poor laws, the category of vagrants and its relation to the growth of capitalist market systems in England and Wales, see Peter Barham, *Schizophrenia and Human Value: Chronic Schizophrenia, Science, and Society*, (Oxford: Basil Blackwell, 1984).

Muslim husband is liable to maintain his wife, including a divorced wife, under all conditions. The correct subject matter of section 125 related to a wife who was unable to maintain herself, and their ruling was limited to these cases. Clearly, given the fact that there is a uniform criminal code to which all Indian citizens are subject, the court could not take into account the religion of the persons involved. Had the judgment stopped at this point, the issue would only have been on the application of the criminal and penal codes to all citizens of India.

But the judgment went beyond this issue. It considered questions relating to the interpretation of the Quran and of Islamic law on the issue of maintenance of divorced wives. The judges also commented on the desirability of evolving a common civil code as a means of achieving national integration and gender justice.

In the opening paragraph of the judgment, it was said that the appeal did not involve questions of constitutional importance. However, the judges also said it did raise other issues that were important:

Some questions which arise under the ordinary civil and criminal law are of a far-reaching significance to large segments of society which have been traditionally subjected to unjust treatment. Women are one such segment.

They then quoted the famous line from Manu which acts like a signature for all discourses on Manu, namely *na stree swatantryam arhati*, i.e. a woman does not deserve autonomy. Having shown their critical capacity in relation to Hindus, they then criticized Islam, taking for their authority a statement of Sir William Lane made in 1843 to the effect that the fatal point in Islam is the degradation of woman.

The semiotic function of this framing paragraph in the judgment was to establish the secular and learned credentials of the judges, for, by a time-honoured tradition in our political culture, one's secular credentials are signalled by evenly handing out criticisms of the majority and minority communities.[16]

A second purpose was to show concern for gender justice:

This appeal . . . raises a straightforward issue which is of common interest not only to Muslim women, not only to women generally, but to all those who, aspiring to create an equal society of men and women, lure themselves

---

[16] I have noted the function of this rhetoric elsewhere. Veena Das and Ashis Nandy, 'Violence, victimhood and the language of silence', in Veena Das (ed.) *The Word and the World: Fantasy, Symbol and Record* (Delhi: Sage Publications, 1986).

into the belief that mankind has achieved a remarkable degree of progress in that direction.

Two moral ends are thus posited in the judgment: the creation of a society based on gender equality, and the moral duty of the individual to support destitute relatives so as to prevent society being contaminated by vagrancy. These two ends, however, do not belong to the same moral plane.

The third set of relevant observations relates to the importance of evolving a common civil code. 'It is a matter of regret', state the judges, that 'Article 44 of our Constitution has remained a dead letter.' They deplore the absence of official activity towards framing a common civil code. 'A common civil code will help the cause of national integration by removing disparate loyalties to laws which have conflicting ideologies.' Thus the case of Shah Bano becomes the occasion for an attack on the conflicting ideologies which rule family and marriage among the different communities of India. There is no attempt in the judgment to explain why different ideologies in the sphere of personal life are seen as intrinsically threatening to national integration. This is taken to be 'self evident'; to an anthropologist this appears puzzling, for the self-evidence of one culture is often the puzzle of another. One must recall here that the issue of personal law concerns not only Hindus and Muslims but also tribal communities whose family affairs have been regulated by their own customary laws, on which the intellectual discourse in India, with a few honourable exceptions, remains silent.[17]

At one level, then, the judgment is about Shah Bano and the applicability of the provisions of the Code of Criminal Procedures to all citizens, regardless of their religion. It is not about civil law or

[17] For one instance of this silence, See Gopal Krishna, 'Islam, Minority Status and Citizenship: Muslim Experience in India', *Arch. Europ. Sociol.*, vol. XXVII, 1986, pp. 353–68, in which the debate on personal law is constructed primarily as a problem concerning the Muslim community. Krishna argues that according to Islamic political theory, the relation between Muslims and the non-Muslim state is contractual, devoid of any moral obligation on the part of the former towards the latter. He singles out the Muslims as 'the one community' that felt threatened by the integrative process initiated by the Constitution. Krishna's paper is remarkable for the lack of any analysis of the ideology of integration or the processes through which the state may establish a hegemony over smaller communities. But it must be said in all fairness that Krishna is not alone among social scientists in giving unquestioned support to nation-state ideologies.

national integration. At other levels, however, it is about the unquestioned allegiance to legally created semiotic objects such as the category of 'vagrants', defined via the danger that they supposedly pose to public order. Secondly, there is complete rejection of legal pluralism in the judgment, for it is taken as self-evident that conflicting laws create conflicting ideologies which are inimical to national integration. Finally, there is the question of the rights of women which is raised but is then eclipsed by the allegiance to such abstractions as public order and national integration.[18]

From the perspective of secular and progressive opinion, opposition to the judgment of the Supreme Court was led by 'fundamentalists' and 'communalists', whose rise to power indicated 'regressive' threats to Indian society. This seems, as I hope to show, a simplistic characterization of the complex issues that were raised.

THE RESPONSE OF THE 'COMMUNITY'

The first such complex issue was the relation between community and state. I do not think that a claim was ever made on behalf of any section of the community that Muslims should be ruled in accordance with Islamic laws in matters pertaining to crime and punishment. It was, however, aggressively asserted that in civil matters pertaining to family and marriage the Muslim community recognized only the authority of the Shariat.[19]

From some of the responses given by Muslim leaders it seems clear that laws pertaining to crime and punishment were seen as

[18] The allegiance to the idea of public order is a little surprising given that there is widespread recognition among many jurists that evoking a danger to the public order in general terms rather than showing the existence of such danger in concrete and specific terms is often a pretext of the state's for the illegitimate use of its police functions.

[19] See for example, the comments of Syed Shahabuddin in Engineer, op. cit. He had criticized the competence of the judges to interpret the Shariat which he said was an exclusive right of the ullama. When questioned if he would advocate the Islamic punishment for theft (amputating the hand of the thief) he replied that such punishments could only be given by an Islamic state, and under Islamic rules of evidence, which were not applicable in the Indian case. Unfortunately most such statements were made in a highly adversarial context, whereas what is needed is one or several comprehensive position-pictures on the varieties of relationship possible between the Shariat, non-state customary law, and state law in matters pertaining to both criminal and civil law.

coming under the jurisdiction of the state; laws pertaining to family and marriage were seen as coming under the jurisdiction of the 'religion' or 'culture' of the community. One way to interpret this claim of the community over its civil matters is to see it as part of a worldwide pattern, a pattern which is connected with the decline of the idea of the nation state which pretends to full ideological and political loyalty to its own values. In challenging the state as the only giver of values, the community may be seen from one point of view as claiming authority over its private life. Nevertheless, the all-pervading presence of the state was acknowledged in the very act of the new legislation and the widespread support it received from 'fundamentalist' sections of the community. In giving support to the new bill, such sections were paradoxically reiterating the authority of the state to legislate and the courts to interpret the Shariat,[20] while simultaneously asserting their own obligation to give a direction to state law. The bill postulated that a divorced woman was to be supported by those relatives, such as sons or brothers, who were in the category of heirs, and that if such relatives were unable to support a divorced, indigent woman, then it was the responsibility of the community to support her, as a surrogate relative, through its *waqf* boards. Thus, although the category of relatives who were to support an indigent

---

[20] It should be recalled that codification of the Shariat for purposes of administration of the personal law by British Courts through the Shariat Act of 1937 was a piece of colonial legislation that took away the customary rights of Muslims and created an area of 'tradition' suitable for the British masters. The elitist assumptions behind such legislation would be obvious, as also the attempts to create a homogeneous community that could be administered with greater ease.

In the case of the Muslim Women (Protection of Rights) Bill 1986, the varying interpretations of the Shariat were manifest within the Muslim community which was homogenized through an act of the state. For example, the Islamic Shariat Board of Kerala stated in a memorandum to the Prime Minister, dated 1 February 1986, that 'views expressed by the commentators of the Quran and eminent theologians recognized by the Islamic world corroborate the verdict of the Supreme Court'. For this and other dissenting views, see Engineer, 1987, op. cit.

It is not at all surprising that there should be differences in interpretation within the Islamic community itself on the interpretation of the Shariat, for this is at the heart of the hermeneutic enterprise to which all revelation has to be subject. Even among these different voices, however, the voice of folk interpretations of theology is given no place among contemporary Islamic theologians. On the conflict between elite and folk interpretations, see Veena Das, 1985, 'Towards a folk-theology and theological anthropology of Islam', *Contributions to Indian Sociology* (n.s.), vol. 18, no. 2, 1985, pp. 293–300.

woman was altered, the right of a woman to have these provisions endorsed by courts of law of the modern state were not challenged. One could say that the forms of legal mediation instituted by the modern state were endorsed, even as the contents were being directed by the mobilization of the Muslim community in a particular direction. The community, then, can be seen not as claiming sovereignty in competition with the state, but informing the state on the direction of laws in the field of marriage and family.

The second question which arose from the judgment was whether it was legitimate and proper for personal laws to reflect the differences between different communities on the nature of conjugality. It was argued by some Muslim scholars that a Hindu woman, upon marriage, lost her rights in her natal family and became fully incorporated into the family of her husband: this was reflected in several institutional practices, including the fact that divorce was not recognized in the *Dharmasastras*.[21] Under such conditions, it was argued, even when laws were developed and provisions for divorce introduced, the liability of the husband to maintain his abandoned or divorced wife was of a piece with the concept of marriage and conjugality. In contrast, marriage under Islamic law was a contract and a woman was never fully incorporated into the husband's group. She continued, for instance, to exercise rights of property in her natal family. It was therefore considered proper that a woman should be maintained by those relatives who expected to inherit from her share, namely sons and brothers. This argument had also been put forward in the court also and been rejected as contrary to 'law' and 'life'. When codified in the new law on the Rights of Muslim Divorced it was criticized by several women's groups as the equivalent of taking away rights of maintenance from women; it was felt that a woman would never drag members of her natal family or her children to a court of law.

There were several assumptions about 'law' and 'life' implicit in the judgment, as well as in some of the responses of women activists. These are presented in the nature of 'self-evidence', which seems puzzling when seen from the eyes of another culture. Certainly, the central place given to conjugality in the life of a woman, and her primary definition as a wife rather than a daughter or a sister, is not

---

[21] Divorce was recognized in the customary regulations of many castes but it is part of the same elitist discourse referred to earlier that jurists and scholars of Islam who wrote on this issue equated Hindu law with rules of the *Dharmasastras*.

a principle one can derive from 'life' if we mean that it derives from nature. Seen in a cross-cultural context, in many societies where marriages are hypogamous a woman may be seen by her natal family as simply 'lent' to the husband's family.[22] She is never incorporated in the conjugal family and continues to exercise all her rights in her natal family. Yet there is no evidence that her status is lower than that of women in societies which practise hypergamous marriages and in which the rights of the husband override any claims by her natal kin. One must not assume that the concepts of marriage and sexuality enshrined in 'secular' laws are somehow derived from principles of life. Rather some supposedly secular laws relating to marriage, conjugality, sexuality and the family bear the stamp of ecclesiastic laws and reflect a Christian understanding of marriage and the family, rather than read as the unmediated reflections of 'law' and 'nature'.

As to the question of whether women are reluctant to take their natal family and children to a court of law, this reflects the unspoken assumption in our society, among both Hindus and Muslims, that conjugality may become a site of conflict but that conflict between a woman and her natal kin should be covered by a shroud of silence.[23] In fact, violence against a woman by her natal family, including attempts to deprive her of property rights, are by no means uncommon. In the Muslim case many studies show that though women have a theoretical right over property in their natal families, they are rarely able to exercise this right, exchanging it for the right to visit and receive gifts.[24] Thus, if woman's rights are to be strengthened against those of the family, there is no reason to exclude her rights as a daughter or sister from this arena of conflict. The very emphasis on the woman as wife reflects the almost exclusive preoccupation with her uxorial role.

[22] See Edmund Leach, 'Asymmetric Marriage Rules, Status Difference and Direct Reciprocity: Comments on Alleged Fallacy', *Southwestern Journal of Anthropology*, 1961, vol. 17, pp. 49–55. This unfortunate vocabulary has to be applied here because women are invariably seen as 'exchanged' between men at the level of ideology although they subvert this ideology in many ways in the practices of their everyday life. For a masterly account of both forms of laws of exchange and their limits, Lévi Strauss is still unequalled: Claude Lévi-Straus, *The Elementry Structure of Kinship* (London: George Allen and Unwin, 1969).

[23] This silence does not apply to conflict between brothers over property.

[24] See Z. Eglar, *A Punjabi Village in Pakistan* (New York: Columbia University Press, 1960); and Veena Das, The Structure of Marriage Preferences: An Account from Pakistani Fiction, *Man*, 1973, 8(1), pp. 30–45.

It must be evident that I believe that the real issue is not secularism vs communalism or national integration vs national disruption. It is rather a question of whether powers of the state should be extended to encroach into the sphere of the family. In the colonial period this encroachment was justified on the grounds that the state was engaged in the creation not just of a civil society but also a 'good' society.[25] This is why, though many colonial interventions concerned the rights of women, these were so enmeshed in a network of other concerns that women themselves seemed almost peripheral to the issues. Given this history, it seems pertinent to argue that if the state is to intervene in order to correct injustice against women in institutional structures such as the family, the focus of its legislative and adjudicatory labour has to be women themselves. The conflict between the rights of subordinate groups (such as women) to break the power of traditions which subordinate them to men on the one hand, and the radical recognition of the right of minorities to exist as cultural entities on the other, are not capable of being easily resolved. But minimally, it is necessary that these issues be addressed on their own terms, and that they do not become a contest between the passions of the state (national integration, patriotism) and the passions of the community (its cultural survival in the form given to it by the dominant male culture).

In the context of the debate on the Shah Bano case, several women activists pointed out that the issue was not whether women enjoyed a high status in Islam at the level of ideas; it was whether women were able to obtain reasonable security for themselves under the existing institutional structures. The high number of petitions for maintenance from women (including Muslim women) which came up every year under section 125 of the Criminal Code was a clear indicator that the family or the community were not protective institutions—as the scriptural quotations elicited from religious traditions would have us believe.

It is more than clear that the family is a site of conflict. So, when a community claims a right to practise its own culture, which includes the right to govern its members in the sphere of the family according to its own laws, then where do women or children who may be oppressed by the pathologies of the family and the community go for

[25] Gayatri Chakravorty Spivak, 'Can the Subaltern Speak? Speculations on Widow Sacrifice', *Wedge* 7/8, 1985.

redress? Clearly, the right of a community to preserve and develop its culture cannot preclude the right of individuals to move out of the community or criticize and even reject its norms. Meanwhile, the appropriation of the issue of justice to women under the master symbols of state and community almost made them disappear from view, except within the title of the new legislation.

This eclipse may be best seen if we pay close attention to Shah Bano, the woman. The facts of her personal case were as follows: married to her first cousin, she was the mother of three adult sons, the oldest being fifty-four years of age. Her husband had taken a second wife, she being another first cousin. It seems likely that Shah Bano's sons had asked their seventy-six-year-old mother to sue her husband for maintenance as part of a move in their ongoing dispute with their father and his son by his second marriage on the issue of property. After the Supreme Court decision, Shah Bano was persuaded by the 'leaders' of the community that she should reject the decision. Her letter speaks most eloquently of the way in which a woman may simply become the means by which various contests between men can be conducted: contests between father and sons; between adherents of different schools of Islamic law; and between state and community. A passage from her letter says:

Maulana Mohammad Habib Yar Khan, Haji Abdul Gaffar Saheb and other respectable gentlemen of Indore came to me and explained to me the commands concerning nikah, divorce, dower and maintenance in the light of the Quran and hadith . . . since women were getting maintenance through law courts, I also filed a suit for the same in the court of law and was successful . . . till then I had no idea about the shariat's view in this regard.

She goes on to say that after the provisions of the Shariat had been explained to her, she rejected the judgment of the Supreme Court which upheld her plea for maintenance from her divorced husband. Thus, from the lowest to the highest levels of male society, she became nothing more than a pawn through whom men played their various games of honour and shame.

As evident from the discussion above, the supreme court judgment raised several conceptual issues regarding culture and community. These can be summarized:

1. Does the constitutional right given to minorities to preserve and enjoy their culture, as well as the rights of minorities enshrined in the international instruments of the UN (e.g. the Covenant on

Human Rights), include their right to live according to their own civil laws of family and marriage? Does the existence of conflicting ideologies of marriage and family in itself pose a danger to the sovereignty of the state?

2. If legal pluralism in civil matters is considered acceptable or even desirable, so that the norms of particular communities are given not only the status of custom but of law,[26] then what are the limits to the control that such communities may exercise over individual members? In other words, how does one take into account heterogeneity *within* a community for the purpose of recognizing 'non-state law'?

3. How would one resolve conflicts which arise between the desire to preserve culture by a filiative community such as an ethnic or religious minority, and a similar but affiliative community, such as the community of women, which wishes to reinterpret that culture according to a different set of principles?

4. We have seen how the human rights movements empowered the individual against the state. If a commitment to cultural rights leads us similarly to empower the community against the state, how can one ensure that the individual is not totally engulfed by the community?

THE QUESTION OF SATI

I turn now to my second incident, which involved the ritual consignment to flames of a young eighteen-year-old girl. This took place in Deorala, a small town in Rajasthan, on 4 September 1987, when Roop Kanwar ascended or was forced to ascend the funeral pyre of her husband. The continuance of this custom of sati—a sign of India's stigmatized identity in the eyes of the British—allied with the fact that it happened when the country's women's groups were combating violence against women in the family (especially against young brides accused by their conjugal families of bringing inadequate dowry)

[26] Upendra Baxi calls this 'non-state law'. See 'Discipline, Repression and Legal Pluralism', in P. Sack and E. Minchin (eds), *Legal Pluralism: Proceedings of the Canberra Law Workshop, VII* (Canberra: ANU, 1985). This expression hardly commends itself on grounds of elegance but has the great advantage of steering the debates away from the normal sterile discussions on the difference between law and norms, or law and custom. It also disputes the claim of the state as the only legitimate maker of law.

made it a very volatile issue. It would, however, be mistaken to think that the opposing political formations which emerged around this issue can be summarized in terms of tradition vs modernity or men vs women. For one thing, Hindu leaders were themselves sharply divided on the issue of sati within Hinduism. Thus, the Shankaracharya of Puri appeared a strong supporter of the custom, whereas reform groups such as the Arya Samaj, led by Swami Agnivesh, challenged both the Shankaracharya's authority as well as his understanding of Hinduism. Similarly, in the so-called 'modern' sector there were those who saw sati as a pathology of Hinduism and others who saw it as a pathology of colonialism.[27]

It is not possible to discuss all the complex issues and their implications in the various public discourses for the present understanding of India's political culture. I only wish to point out here that there is a tradition of 200 years in which sati came to be regarded as the exemplary instance by which the whole of Indian society could be characterized, either as a land of miracles or of savagery.[28] I shall disengage from this debate in order to pose the problem of cultural rights in the contemporary context. The question of history is important but, as we shall see, it stands transformed into the issue of the organization of popular memory.

Some of the questions on the relation between cultural rights and law were similar to those in the Shah Bano case; therefore I shall concentrate on issues which raise new problems on cultural rights. The object of my analysis is the text of the Commission of Sati (Prevention) Act 1987, which the government enacted in order to prevent incidents of sati and to devise adequate instruments for the punishment of those responsible for inducing someone to commit sati. Although the Act was designed to punish those responsible for the death of a widow, paradoxically, it defined the woman herself as also punishable under the Act.[29]

---

[27] It is simply not possible to refer to the large and complex literature that grew out of this event. But see Veena Das, 'Gender Studies, Cross-cultural Comparison and the Colonial Organization of Knowledge', *Berkshire Review.* vol. 21, 1986, pp. 58–76; Nandy, 1980; Lata Mani, 'Production of an Official Discourse on Sati in Early Nineteenth Century Bengal', *Economic and Political Weekly.* vol. XXI, no. 17, 1986, and the Special issue of *Seminar* (1988).

[28] See Christina Prinz, *Sati: Ideologie und Praxis* (Heidelberg: South Asian Institute, 1988).

[29] See Vasudha Dhagamwar, 'Saint, Victim or Criminal', *Seminar*, 1988, pp. 34–39.

One important feature of this Act was that it made criminal any act of 'glorification' of sati. The act defined 'glorification' as any of the following:

(a) the observance of any ceremony or the taking out of a procession in connection with the commission of sati;

(b) the supporting, justifying or propagating the practice of *sati* in any manner;

(c) the arranging of any function to eulogize the person who has committed *sati*;

(d) the creation of a trust or the collection of funds, or the construction of a temple or other structure or the carrying out of any form of worship or the performance of any ceremony with a view to perpetuate the honour of or to preserve the memory of any person who has committed sati.

Thus the bill not only made any act or attempt towards commission of sati punishable but also made the glorification of acts of sati a punishable offence. It is this aspect of the law which raises questions different from those raised by Shah Bano. As in the latter case, where the semiotic excess of the judgment as well as certain characterizations of orthodox sections by 'progressive' opinion helped convert the issue of women's rights into one of secularism vs communalism, so in this case the language of criticism revealed much more than attitudes to women's rights.

In terms of the political unconscious, I believe that one of the confrontations was over the nature of time consciousness in the discourses of the state and the community. This may seem a very abstract issue, and one which is unlikely to raise strong passions on either side. I hope to show, however, that the ideologies of modern states do try to control the time consciousness of communities and impose upon them a singular view of time; this then gets translated into issues of control over one's own history, as well as how far a community is willing to submerge its biography into the biography of the nation state.

From the point of view of the state which enacts such legislation, time is valued as a scarce resource for a future-oriented mastering of problems left over from the past. In this time consciousness, there are no exemplary models from the past because modernity does not borrow standards from the past—it draws its normativity from itself. In many of the speeches made in parliament, as well as in the way in which this particular episode was inscribed into writing, frequent reference was made to the fear that the occurrence of sati showed us reverting to a barbaric age. Indeed, the bill itself makes the following observations on this issue:

> The recent incident of the commission of sati in the village of Deorala in Rajasthan, its subsequent glorification and the various attempts made by the protagonists of this practice to justify its continuance on religious grounds had aroused apprehension all over the country that this evil social practice, eradicated long back, will be revived. A general feeling had also grown in the country that the efforts put in by social reformers like Raja Rammohun Roy and others in the last century would be nullified by this single act in Rajasthan.

As this statement on the objectives of the bill shows, an act of sati comes to signify an anxiety about time which is typical within modernity, namely a regressive past which might recur and cancel all the 'progress' made by the modern state on behalf of society. Such a past has to be rigorously controlled and eliminated. The new legislation not only sought to control and punish future incidents of sati and abetment to commit sati but also tried to control the past.

Criminalization of the act of glorifying sati belongs to an order of events different from the actual commission of sati. This is because in all modern forms of governance the state establishes an absolute right over the death of its citizens. Within modern state structures it is only through due process of law that a person may be deprived of his or her life. In ordinary cases no death is legitimate unless certified by agencies of the state, and as for heroic deaths, the nation holds a monopoly on valorous sacrifice. The glorification of a particular social or religious practice, however, is open to a greater range of freedoms: it merges with the right to practise one's religion. Interference with this custom raises the question of whether the state has a right to control the future, or whether it may also redefine and control the past. Given these difficult questions, it was only to be expected that bringing the glorification of sati within the purview of legislative acts would not go uncontested.

The contest that we examine here is the litigation between the trustees of the Rani Sati Mandir and the government over this very question. The Rani sati temple is located in Jhunjunu, about 190 kms from Jaipur. It is owned by the Rani Sati Mandir Trust with its head office in Calcutta. According to oral tradition, the temple is dedicated to the memory of Narayani Devi, the wife of a merchant of Jhunjhunu who, during his travels with his young wife, was attacked by Muslims and died. His wife, according to legend, fought with the Muslims, defeated them, and then, having constructed a funeral pyre, consigned herself to its flames alongside the body of her husband.

As this legend shows, the sati myth has been appropriated here by merchant castes as a challenge to Rajput legends asserting that only Rajput women became true satis. This caste now found its position being challenged by the ruling introduced in the new act. The temple used to hold a *mela* on Bhadra Amavasya, in the month of September. After the passing of the Act, the district magistrate of Jhunjhunu banned the glorification of sati, in any manner whatsoever, all over the district, by any individual or group.[30] In accordance with this ruling the temple was closed in the month of August that year and preparations for the annual mela which was to fall on 10 September, were halted. The Rani Sati Mandir Trust Calcutta challenged this order in the High Court in on the grounds that the order interfered with its freedom to practise one's religion—that freedom being constitutionally guaranteed. The High Court, in an order of 17 August 1988, upheld the right of the Rani Sati Temple in Jhunjhunu to conduct daily worship (*puja*) and service (*seva*), and restored the right of individuals to worship in the temple. The court order also stated that the respondents must not cause any interruption or harassment to visitors and devotees for their daily worship of deities located in the temple. However, as far as the annual public mela was concerned, the position of the court was ambivalent, allowing individual notice to be given to members with respect to the Annual General Meeting but not permitting public announcement of the mela in newspapers. In its judgment the court clearly made a distinction between public and private religion; public aspects of religion were to be regulated by the state as 'law and order' issues, while religion in everyday life was left to individual conscience. This division by which public festivals such as melas, routes of processions, and regulation of noise in sacred places were to be treated as 'law and order' issues has been part of state repertoire for the management of crowds since the early nineteenth century.[31]

---

[30] This was reported on 22 August in all the major national dailies. For an analysis of the legal issues, see P. van den Boch, 'A burning question: the sacred centre as the object of political interest', paper presented at a symposium on *The Sacred Centre as the Object of Political Interest*, University of Groningen, 5–8 March 1989.

[31] See for example, M. Roberts, 'Noise as Cultural Struggle', in Veena

It is therefore not surprising to see that the Supreme Court, when hearing a special leave petition filed by the State of Rajasthan, stated that 'offering of puja inside the temple and holding of mela outside are certainly two different aspects and the mela may give rise to problems of law and order'.[32] In presenting their case in the Supreme Court the trustees of the Rani Sati Mandir claimed that puja within the temple did not constitute a glorification of sati, whereas in a writ petition filed by the All India Democratic Women's Association and the Janvadi Mahila Samiti this particular interpretation was questioned.[33] These organizations requested a prohibition of the chunari mahotsava in honour of Narayani Devi—the sati goddess to whom the temple is dedicated.

These questions raised by the new legislation are on two different planes. The first relates to the prevention of sati and the punishment of offenders who aid or abet such acts. Yet ambiguity is built into the heart of the legislation, for it does not quite know whether to treat the woman 'with respect to whom sati is committed' as a victim or a criminal. This difficulty is not insurmountable because, as in all hard cases, a thin line has to be maintained between legitimacy and law. From a simply legal point of view, suicide is a punishable offence in the Indian Penal Code, and symbolic recognition has to be given to this. The Act, however, clearly lays out that when determining the extent of punishment (imprisonment up to a year, a fine, or both), the special court shall 'before convicting any person take into consideration the circumstances leading to the commission of the offence, the act committed, the state of mind of the person charged with the offence at the time of the commission of the act and all other relevant factors'. Such acts must remain suspended between legitimacy and legality and it is only at the adjucatory level that we shall be able to see the working of the act. In contrast to the woman, stringent punishment, including life imprisonment, is laid out for those who aid or abet such acts, clearly moving from the definition of sati as suicide to its definition as murder.

The second question which relates to the 'glorification' of sati and the prevention of *satimata* worship raises a very different issue:

Das (ed.), *Mirrors of Violence: Communities, Riots, and Survivors in South Asia* (Delhi: Oxford University Press, 1990).

[32] Special Leave Petition (civil), no. 9922 of 1988 in the Supreme Court of India, Civil Appellate Jurisdiction.

[33] Writ Petition, Supreme Court of India, no. 913 of 1988.

whether a community has a right to construct the past in the mythic or historic mode, in accordance with its own traditions or whether the state has a complete monopoly over the past. That such a question has no straightforward answer is doubtless clear from my earlier discussion, for we have at the outset to contend with the hegemonic exercise of power by the state, which acts as the only giver of values. The truth of this became evident when even the state's most vocal critics turned to it in response to the situation. Beyond this, the construction of time in such a way that all new events are sought to be understood by mechanical analogy with the limited stock of past events often leads to hegemonic control being established over the individual by the community. This is especially true when the community draws its energy from the symbol of a divine sacrificial victim, as in the case of sati.

Finally, I want to suggest that there is a new participatory model of legislation which is introduced by the recent law. This is a model in which the state acknowledges the role of women's groups when giving direction to legislation. In the case of the Muslim Women's Bill, no acknowledgement was made of the legitimate interests of women, the community being defined solely in filiative terms, namely those born as Muslims. In the case of the Commission of Sati (Prevention) Act, women's groups and the interests they represented were given a legitimate place, making that legislation at least a triangular contest between state, community and women's groups.

There are two aspects of community identified with reference to the two cases discussed here. In the first case, the contest between community and state was over the realm of law and the possibilities of pluralism in the conduct of personal life. In the second case, it was the right to organize memory. Both cases led to challenges to the hegemony of the state as the only giver of values, but they also showed deep-rooted contests between different definitions of community itself. There was a particular polarization between the community defined on the basis of filiation, and the community defined on the basis of affiliative interests. What are the implications of this polarization?

In the debates between women's rights and the rights of the community, an implicit assumption seems to have crept in, to the effect that the culture to which the community lays claim is essentially a male creation; indeed, in one social science tradition the dominant public culture—what Simmel called the 'objective culture'—is historically a male creation. In a debate with Marianne Weber, while denying the possibility of a female culture, Simmel said women could contribute to the private and subjective spheres but could never transcend these. For Marianne Weber, in contrast, the representation of male culture as objective culture and female culture as subjective culture was a result of historical circumstances, and therefore alterable.[34]

Both the Shah Bano and the Roop Kanwar cases raise the possibility of interrogating male definitions of community. Since the organization of memory is a crucial issue for the definition of community, it is necessary to define memory both as an archive and a history. Thus, women's practices have been historically suppressed in the public culture of all communities but continue both in the private spheres of life and as an archive. If these were to be revived and given recognition in public self-portraits of the community, then questions of the heterogeneity of the community and the multiplicity of identities would become necessary. For instance, in the case of sati, women's narratives among many Rajput communities have emphasized the everyday presence of sati matas in the lives of women and have dwelt rather less on their violent deaths. Would such a cultural construction alter the community's portrait of its own culture? What appears now as a conflict between two different kinds of communities e.g. Muslims and Rajputs on the one hand and women's groups on the other, could well become a conflict *within* a community if women were to lay greater claims to the public cultures of filiative communities themselves.

The relation between a community and its culture brings two distinct sets of preoccupations in creative tension with each other. These are: first, how does the culture of a community create a shared vision of the world—a resource for questioning the ideologies of the state, including an unquestioned allegiance to it, and second, does this shared culture homogenize the community to the extent that other definitions of culture and community are effectively denied or silenced? At the heart of culture we saw an enormous conflict, not only between state and community but also between different definitions of community.

A resolution to this problem can only occur if the state ceases to demand full ideological allegiance from the various collectivities which constitute it; and communities, instead of demanding complete surrender from individual members on the pretext of the preservation

---

[34] See Marianne Weber, *Ehefrau und Mutter in der Rechtsentiwicklung: Eine Einfuchrung* (Aalen: Scientia Verlag, 1971, first published 1907)

of culture, recognize the paradoxical links of confirmation and antagonism from its members. An individual's capacity to make sense of the world presupposes the existence of collective traditions. However, selfhood demands that one is able to break from these collective traditions by being allowed to live around their limits. The simultaneous development of rights of groups and of individuals will depend upon the extent to which these paradoxes can be given voice, both in the realm of the state and in the public culture of civil society.

In our two exemplary cases we saw the relation between state and community; between alternative definitions of community; between filiative communities and affiliative communities; and finally between community and individual. These may be seen as being located within a web of creative or destructive tensions in the matter of cultural rights, and offer an opportunity to consider the problem from the perspective of two major communities, the Muslims and Hindus in modern India. Now I turn to a third situation, one which concerns the Sikhs, and see how issues of self and memory are articulated when giving shape to the notion of community among them. In the earlier cases the institutional context involved a dramatic use of agencies of the state; so also in the Sikh case the institutional context involves the law courts and a mobilization of the community through which the public sphere is sought to be transformed. But whereas in the earlier cases, in a sense, *cultural memory* (as embodying a portrait of the self) and *desire* (embodied in norms of conduct relating to sexuality and marriage) were brought from the domain of the private into a public sphere, the Sikh case is entirely different. Here, though memory and law are organizing symbols through which the hegemony of the state is sought to be challenged, there is a self-conscious rejection of any dramatic use of the agencies of the state. Instead, the production of 'subversive' literature, as well as a challenge to the state's monopoly over force through dramatic and violent acts, forms the repertoire of a militant movement. I take for analysis only the two organizing symbols of memory and self, as these are articulated in the written and oral discourse in the militant literature of the Sikhs, and treat these as a window through which to view crucial questions of culture and community in modern Indian politics.

THE COMMUNITY IN 'EXTREMIST' DISCOURSE

The emergence of a militant movement among the Sikhs is an important phenomenon of the last decade. It is not my intention to provide a comprehensive account of this complex process here. I will, instead, enumerate the salient events as summarized in the excellent introduction by Kapur.[35] India's Sikhs form a relatively prosperous community. They have participated actively in political and economic life. Yet they have a long history of struggles waged for the protection of their separate identity. What concerns me here is the period between 1981 and 1984, when Sikh leaders began a series of mass civil-disobedience campaigns against the Indian government for the fulfilment of several demands. These included greater autonomy for the state of Punjab. The demands were most clearly articulated in a document known as the Anandpur Sahib Resolution, which was adopted by the Working Committee of a major regional party of the Sikhs, the Akali Dal, in 1973.[36]

As the agitation for the fulfilment of these demands proceeded, rivalry between different Sikh leaders and the absence of a serious national forum where such demands could be negotiated led to the growth of extremism. A violent terrorist campaign developed with the avowed aim of creating the sovereign Sikh state of Khalistan. Between 1981 and 1984 a militant Sikh preacher, Jarnail Singh Bhindranwale, rose to a position of considerable influence among the Sikhs. Although considered by many to have been a protege of the Congress Party at the centre—which wished to use him in order to curtail and limit the influence of Akali leaders on Punjab politics—there is no doubt that he enjoyed considerable support among the Jat peasantry in Punjab.

[35] See A. Rajiv Kapur, *Sikh Separatism: The Politics of Faith* (Delhi: Vikas Publications, 1987).

[36] This Resolution was adopted in 1973 at Anandpur Sahib. However, its text became a subject of great controversy and confusion due to the subsequent formation of two factions. Several versions of the resolution were in circulation. The President of the Akali Dal issued an authenticated version in 1982. The term Sikh nation has been used in this resolution but then one must remember that the Punjabi term *desh kal* (country and era) has a different semantic range than the English term nation. This term has been used in different political contexts to mean a separate sovereign state as well as a Punjabi state within a federal structure of the Indian polity. See Jeswant Singh, *A Plea for a Punjabi State* (Amritsar, 1960) and Kapur, ibid.

Under his leadership a campaign of terror grew in which several prominent Hindus, moderate Sikhs, as well as servants of the state (such as policemen) were killed. While these were people especially targeted, a number of killings of ordinary Hindus in buses or crowded market places were also organized.[37]

In June 1984 the Indian government launched a massive operation against the terrorists. The Golden Temple, which had been converted by the militants into sanctuary, was stormed by the army. In this operation Bhindranwale and several other militants died, and several innocent pilgrims lost their lives. The storming of the Golden Temple led to widespread alienation among the Sikhs. Moderate Sikhs found it especially difficult to find a political voice after this event. As revenge for the attack on the Golden Temple, Prime Minister Indira Gandhi was assassinated by her Sikh security guards, which was followed by massive violence against the Sikhs during riots in Delhi and some of the other major cities of north India.[38]

Here I can only briefly analyse a selection of the written and oral discourse of Sikh militancy which was produced during this apocalyptic period. I shall try to show how the idea of cultural rights came to be articulated through the symbols of self and memory, and I hope also to examine the nature of the community as it emerged in this literature.

Some of the written discourse appeared in the monthly magazine *Shamsher Dast*, which was the organ of the All India Sikh Student Federation till it was banned in 1982; others appeared in the published reports of the Shiromani Gurudwara Prabandhak Committee in the *Khalsa Times* and the *Akal Times*. For my analysis of the oral discourse

[37] The place of violence in Indian politics, especially in the Punjab, has not received the scholarly attention it deserves. Apart from Kapur, ibid., there are journalistic writings such as Chand Joshi, *Bhindrinwale, Myth and Reality* (Delhi, 1984), and Nayar and Singh (1984) but sociological in-depth studies or even informed psycho-biographies of the leaders and actors in this political phenomenon are lacking. For an analysis of the widespread use of the rhetoric of militant nationalism during the freedom struggle of India, see Surjit Hans, 'The Metaphysics of Militant Nationalism', *Journal of Sikh Studies*, vol. XII, no. II, 1985, pp. 85–131, although the psychological explanations are somewhat superficial and hasty. See also Rabindra Ray, *Naxalites and their Ideology* (Delhi: Oxford University Press, 1989), for an analysis of the Naxalite movement and the importance of violence in the construction of the self.

[38] For an analysis of these riots, see PUDR, 1984, and the relevant essays in Veena Das, *Mirrors of Violence*.

I depend on the lectures given by Bhindranwale which, though not easily available at present, enjoyed wide circulation as recorded lectures during the extremist period.

It is the characteristic of written discourse that it strives towards a rational organization of ideas. Further, the tone of written discourse often varies according to the assumed addressee, whereas in oral discourse the 'you' of the discourse is directly present to the speaker. However, as both instances belong to political rhetoric, there are certain imperatives embedded in them both which make them closer to performative forms of speech acts. The emotional role of several tropes—such as synecdoche, irony and metonymy—in the organization of such discourse has been noted by several authors and is amply demonstrated in the militant literature.[39]

In the most direct forms of speech, the aim of the militant movement is expressed in terms of an anxiety over the preservation of a separate Sikh identity. Thus, in a written address to members of parliament, the president of the Shiromani Akali Dal, Sant Harchand Singh Longowal stated: 'All that we are seeking for the last 35 years is an arrangement to safeguard the hard core of their [sic] basic socio-religious and cultural-cum-political rights'.[40] The demand for cultural rights is articulated in the written discourse along three themes, all of which attempt a challenge to state hegemony. The first of these is an attempt to create a Sikh history as a counterpart to 'nationalist history', which is seen as the state's monopolization of narratives of the past. The second is a challenge to the state's monopoly over force and an attempt to create 'alternative legalities.' Running through these two themes is a third on space, which contrasts the place of Sikhs in the Indian nation state with the imagined utopia of a Khalistan. The semiotic web which binds these three themes is intricately woven, making separations difficult. In the interests of economy, only the theme pertaining to Sikh history and identity will be pursued in any detail here.

[39] See Paul Friedrich, 'Language, Ideology and Political Economy', *American Anthropologist*, 1989.

[40] This is a document entitled 'Exclusively for you, Members of Parliament'. There is no date on the document but it was probably circulated in 1982, after a gruesome tragedy in which one of the buses carrying thirty-four prisoners involved in demonstrations was run over by a train due to a manned railway crossing having been kept open. It was in line with the general emotions of betrayal that Sikhs experienced in this period that this accident was taken to be a direct result of a 'conspiracy' to eliminate Sikhs.

NARRATIVES OF THE PAST

Let us first consider the Sikhs' construction of their past. In this narrative, the Sikh community is defined with reference to certain key events within the past. These emphasize the building up of a community on the basis of heroic deeds. The construction of memory here is strongly tied up with the construction of a concrete identity; and as Assmann has noted, this has a positive aspect (that is how we are) as well as a negative aspect (that is our opposite).[41] In other words the self is given shape and form by contrasting it with its opposite. Two communities are posited as counterpoints of the Sikh—these are the relevant others—in the building of this narrative. The first community is the Muslims, holders of power in the medieval period, whom the Sikh gurus consistently defied but whose position in modern India as a 'minority' resembles the Sikhs. The second community is the Hindus, who are represented as weak, effeminate and cunning, people towards whom the Sikhs are shown to have had contempt but whom they consistently protected. The self of the Sikh, as it emerges from this particular organization of images, is of the martyr whose sacrifices have fed the community with its energy in the past. Indeed, even when there are differences of emphasis, an important image in all these texts is of charkhi chadhna and khopdi utarvana i.e. being slowly ground to death over a churning wheel, or offering one's head at the stake— punishments that defiant Sikhs are said to have received from the Mughal emperors.

Consider the following example in which the construction of the past and the construction of the self appear conjoint:

History has always been repeating itself. Sikh people passed through such a critical phase after the death of Banda Bahadur Baba Gurbakash Singh in 1716, that some historians called it the darkest period of Sikh history. . . . Time again took a new turn with the martyrdom of Bhai Mani Singh in 1734 a.d. . . . In this way began once again the era of struggle for the Sikhs which subsequently was converted into the golden age of the Sikhs. Which sacrifice is there in the history of the world that Sikhs had not to pay for this conversion? A terribly dark route from the teeth of 'Charhi' to the edge of the sword was traversed. Every inch of the land where we today have assembled was covered with the precious blood of the Khalsa then and then only could we

[41] See Jan Assmann, 'Kollektives Gedachtnis und Kulturelle Identitat', in Jan Assman and Tonio Holcher (eds), *Kultur und Gedachtnis* (Suhrkamp Tasenbuch Wissenschaft 724).

harness the days when Kashmir, Jamraud and Ladakh bowed before the Kesri Nisan Sahib and Nanak-Shahi coins could replace the Muslim one's [sic].[42]

Just as the heroic character of the Sikh is sought to be established through a particular reading of Sikh history, so the character of the Hindu, the negative 'other' of the Sikh, is established through a narrative of the modern period. It is the consistent complaint of the writers of these journals that the contributions of Sikhs have been undermined within the creation of modern India, and especially within the nationalist movement. By a careful choice of episodes which happened primarily in Punjab, they are able to argue that the sacrifices of Sikhs were far weightier than the sacrifices of other communities; and yet Sikh symbols such as the *nishan sahib*—the flag which flew over Lahore during the times of Maharaja Ranjit Singh—were given no recognition in modern India. The people responsible for this denial to the Sikhs of their rightful place in history are the Hindus who have bestowed modern India with their own 'effeminate' and 'cunning' character via their dominance of the state apparatus as well as the ideology of the nation.

Let me take as example a poster circulated by the All India Sikh Student Federation, entitled 'Lala Lajpat Rai di maut kiven hoi?' (How did Lal Lajpat Rai die?). Addressed to the Sikhs, the first paragraph reads as follows:

The politicians of India have always tried to keep the minorities suppressed. We have a well-known saying that a Hindu does not kill a snake. He asks the Muslim to kill the snake. The meaning of this is that if the snake dies, an enemy dies. But if the snake bites the Muslim then its meaning will also be that an enemy will die. This saying makes the character of the Hindu crystal clear—of what temperament are they the masters.

This poster then goes on to exemplify the character of the Hindus through the discussion of a historical event. It mentions the visit of the Simon Commission in 1928 and the decision taken by several prominent politicians in Punjab to boycott it. According to this poster, a procession was organized by the Akali Dal, with the help of several Muslims and Congressmen, to greet members of the Commission with black flags. Thirty thousand people came to protest against the visit of the Simon Commission, of which nineteen to twenty thousand were Sikhs.

[42] 'Message to the Delegates of the 1st Annual Dal Khalsa Conference', held at Gurdaspur on 8–9 December, 1979 by S. Gajinder Singh, Panch Dal Khalsa.

In the poster the story of Lala Lajpat Rai's so called heroism is as follows:

The procession was being led by Master Tara Singh, Lala Lajpat Rai, Dr Satpal Dang, and Abdul Kadar when a lathi charge against it was ordered. According to the poster, Gopi Chand, Satpal Dang and Abdul Kadar were wounded. Lala Lajpat Rai received one lathi blow on the head but was protected by his umbrella. This is why he could continue to lead the procession till its final destination. The procession was organized on 30th October 1928. Lala Lajpat Rai died of a heart attack on 17th November due to heart failure. Yet his death was linked with the lathi charge and it was circulated that as he lay wounded he had uttered the famous words that every lathi falling on his body would become a nail in the coffin of the British Raj.

Even as the misrepresentation of events in this and several other such posters would be easy to show, the truth that several history books link the event with Lala Lajpat Rai, and the fact that the protest organized by the Congress understated or ignored the contribution of others, can hardly be denied. Indeed, as many historians, especially those writing under the rubric of Subaltern Studies, have pointed out, there has been a tendency in nationalist historiography to assimilate local histories into the master narrative of nationalist history, with agency being vested in nationalist leadership alone.[43] What is interesting from my point of view, however, is that the author of this poster is not content with challenging the nationalist narrative and expanding the consciousness of the reader by giving voice to the silences in this narrative. There is a further move to establish that the history of Sikhs inscribed on the body of the martyr is a reflection of Sikh character, while the history of the Indian nation, when it takes the character of the Hindu as paradigmatic, becomes nothing more and nothing less than a writing of Hindu history. This point becomes clearer in the discussion of Gandhi and the ideology of non-violence.

Expressed in gentler terms in the written discourse, where the position of Mahatma Gandhi as the Father of the Nation is contested, the anxiety about non-violence and passivity implied within a movement based upon the principles of non-violence, becomes much more palpable in oral discourse. Thus, in one of his speeches, Bhindranwale propounded the idea that it was an insult for Sikhs to be included in a nation that considered Mahatma Gandhi its father, for his techniques

---

[43] See the five volumes of Subaltern Studies edited by Ranajit Guha (1982–9), published by Oxford University Press, Delhi.

of fighting were quintessentially feminine. He was symbolized by a charkha, a symbol of woman. 'Can those whose symbol is the sword ever accept a woman like the Mahatma as their *father*? Those are the techniques of the weak, not of a race that has never bowed its head before any injustice—a race whose history is written in the blood of martyrs.'

Thus the construction of the past is also a construction of the self and the other. Through the particular narrative web of Sikh history, the Sikh character is also sought to be simultaneously created. The dangers of a 'Hindu' history are not just that Sikhs are denied their rightful place in history but also, as many of the authors state, it is a conspiracy to make the martial Sikhs a weak race.

The Sikhs have been softened and conditioned during the last fifty years to bear and put up with insults to their religion and all forms of other oppression, patiently and without demur, under the sinister preaching and spell of the narcotic cult of non-violence, much against the clear directive of their Gurus, their Prophets, not to turn the other cheek before a tyrant, not to take lying down any insult to their religion, their self-respect, and their human dignity.[44]

The danger is not of a heroic confrontation with a masculine other but that the feminine other will completely dissolve the masculine self of the Sikh. 'With such an enemy', says one warning, 'even your story will be wiped out from the face of the earth'.

The effort to interpret the past in a manner consistent with the reproduction of a particular kind of character among the Sikhs is further supported by reflections on the nature of the present. It is repeatedly stated that this particular moment in history is pregnant with new possibilities, that it only requires conviction and the capacity for sacrifice to ensure that an earlier period of Sikh glory can be revived again. Precisely because the nature of time is seen as extraordinary, it is also assumed that ordinary morality does not apply. In various warnings that were issued both in written and oral forms to individuals seen as opposed to Sikhs, threats were framed by reference to the particularity of the historical moment. 'We would regret if something were to happen to you—but the time is such that every action has to be geared towards the recovery of lost Sikh glory.'

The construction of the past in this mode of defining community becomes the major cognitive tool through which complete control is

[44] See *They Massacre Sikhs*, a White Paper by Sikh Religious Parliament (Amritsar: Shiromani Gurudwara Prabandhak Committee, n.d.).

established over the individual. There is no willingness to subject the character of the community to the chances of transformation. This is directly tied up with the obsession to mechanically analogize new events with a limited stock of past events. Such a view of the past does not allow freedom from fixed preconceptions about Sikh character; nor, hence, from the *idee fixe* that every future event repeats the past and can only be understood within the framework of repetition. The assassins of Indira Gandhi are seen as reincarnations of two characters, Sukha Singh and Mehtab Singh, who once avenged the desecration of Harmandar Sahib by a small Muslim chieftain, Massarangara, in 1752, by assassinating him. Similarly, even the death of young children is eulogized as evidence of the heroic character of Sikhs, which becomes a repetition of the past sacrifices of the two young sons of Guru Gobind Singh. It is not as if outrage at such events does not exist, but simply that it becomes a muted link in the master narratives of Sikh history and Sikh character.[45]

As may be expected, such a unified master narrative, which absorbs all voices within the community to itself cannot be built without a systematic 'forgetting'. In the master narrative of Sikh history this forgetting is essentially of the close links between Hindus and Sikhs—the bonds of language, common mythology, shared worship, and the community created through exchanges in everyday life. This parallels the forgetting of their bonds with Persian, Urdu poetry, important elements of Islamic ideology, and everyday relations with Muslims during the traumatic period of communal violence of the late forties in Punjab. In fact, the participation of Sikhs in the communal riots against the Muslims, testimony of which exists not only in history textbooks but also in the personal lives of people, is not acknowledged at all. All the darker aspects of the past are purged by being projected onto the Hindus.[46]

[45] Such an incident was discussed in a letter to Giani Zail Singh who was then the President of India and a Sikh himself, by Simeranjeet Singh Mann, a high ranking police official who resigned in protest after Operation Blue Star and has been actively engaged in the militant movement and the politics of Punjab.

[46] The relation between memory and forgetting in constituting the community has been noted in many contexts in recent years. In a very interesting paper, Gross shows the importance of memory in the resistance to totalitarianism and of simultaneous forgetting for the construction of community as purged of its past evil in the case of Polish-Jewish relations during World War II. He comments powerfully on the Polish conviction that 'a half-way victory over totalitarianism's attempts to destroy social solidarity would still be won if the community's history

As one example of this kind of 'forgetting', incidents of communal tensions from the 1920s are discussed primarily in terms of Hindu-Muslim conflicts, as if Sikhs did not figure in these at all. Under the sub-heading 'It Happened Before', a White Paper prepared by the Sri Gurdwara Prabhandhak Committee entitled *They Massacre Sikhs* states:

This phenomenon in which Sikh religious sensibility is calculatedly outraged and their human dignity cruelly injured, has its historical antecedents in this part of the world. It was in the late twenties of this century that a cultural ancestor of the present anti-Sikh Hindu urban crust wrote and published a small book, purporting to be a research-paper in history under the title of *Rangila Rasul*: 'Mohammad, the pleasure loving Prophet'. . . . The entire Muslim world of India writhed in anguish at this gross insult to and attack on the Muslim community but they were laughed at and chided by the citified Hindu press of Lahore . . . But the process of events that led to bloody communal riots in various parts of India till the creation of India and Pakistan and the partition of the country itself, with tragic losses in men, money and property, is directly and rightly traceable to a section of the majority community exemplified in the matter of Rangila Rasul . . . [47]

The first act of wilful forgetting, then, is related to purging the community of an evil which is projected to 'the citified Hindu majority'. The second act of forgetting is to gather all acts of violence—both those directed *within* the Sikh community in institutional practices such as the feud and *outwards* in the form communal violence—as the violence of martyrdom. And finally, the assumption made is that the state is an *external institution*, imposed upon the Sikh community rather than created through practices prevalent in the region itself; and this assumption allows the community to absolve itself from all blame in relation to the corruption of the institutions of the state.

When reading through texts such as the *Akal Times or Shamsheer Dast* the reader can see the alienation that results from the attempt to create a national culture, including a nationalist history, in which

---

were rescued from the regime's ambition to determine not only the country's future but also its past'. Yet the same Polish people developed elaborate myths to conceal from themselves the nature of Polish-Jewish relations and the anti-semitism in Polish society which led to both covert and overt support being given to the fascist ideology of scapegoating the Jew: Jan T. Gaoss, 'Polish-Jewish Relation During the War: an Interpretation', *Archives Europeenes de Sociologie*, XXVII, 1986, pp. 199–214.

[47] See footnote 43.

groups such as the Sikhs find it difficult to recognize themselves. Clearly, a challenge to such unitary modes of constructing the past is important not only for the development of a critical consciousness of the symbols of the nation state, but also as a sign of the radical acceptance of various small groups which constitute Indian society. Such a radical acceptance requires a sign that there is a place in the world for them in which experiments in self-knowledge and self-construction are possible without courting disaster. The Indian nation state has not yet shown any maturity in this regard. Liberal opinion in India is also nervous of such cultural claims, and these tend to be assimilated too often into such categories as revivalist, fundamentalist, communalist, etc.

While accepting fully the legitimacy of such a challenge by the community to the state, however, it seems to me that the community in this case has ended up reproducing the same hegemonic character of which the state stood earlier accused. This is evident from the fact that the militant discourse denies any possibility of alternative definitions of community. It fails to give any assurance to the individual that the character which is sought to be produced for the individual does not exhaust his self. Thus, there is a denial of the self not necessarily by repression but by a valorization of the frozen character of the Sikh. Distrust of alternative definitions of community comes to the fore in the relation of the Sikh militants with communities on the peripheries of Sikhism itself. One such case is that of the Nirankaris, a sect which could be considered a sectarian development out of Sikhism. However, since the followers of this sect worship a living guru, contrary to orthodox Sikh teaching, they were declared enemies of the panth in 1973 by the priests of the Golden Temple. In April 1978 some of Bhindranwale's followers clashed violently with Nirankaris on the holy day of Vaisakhi in Amritsar. There were deaths and injuries on both sides. Some Nirankaris were arrested but later found to have acted in self defence. In April 1980 the Nirankari guru was assassinated and several Nirankaris were later murdered. In the reportage of these episodes in militant literature, the very use of Sikh symbols by Nirankaris was construed as an insult. Although it is acknowledged in such documents that the Nirankaris are a historical sect with close connections with Sikhs, their existing forms of worship are considered unacceptable and contemporary adherents are declared 'counterfeit Nirankaris'. By a mental exchange of images, it is not the Nirankaris who are seen as victims of the violence by militants, but rather the Sikh community appears as the victim. Further, Nirankaris are declared as agents of the government whose only mission is to destroy Sikhs. Yet a certain ambivalence towards the violence directed against them by militants is discernible in the phrase with which the killing of the Nirankari Baba is described: '*Akhir ona da katal ho gaya*', i.e. After all, his murder happened.' The use of the impersonal voice signals a distance from the act of violence, as if in dim recognition of the violence that this would do to the notion of the community itself.

In a remarkable book entitled *Sikh ki karan* (What shall the Sikhs Do?), Surjit Singh Hans gives us insights into various dilemmas. On the one hand, he would like to support the challenge to the state as the only giver of values; on the other hand the definition of community that is emerging, he says, is contrary to people's own experiences of the self and the other in their lived experience. I suggest that this dilemma comes from the fact that, in posing a challenge to the hegemony of the state, the community has ended up by mirroring the very structure which it had sought to oppose.

CONCLUDING COMMENTS

I started this paper by opposing the state and the community as two different kinds of repositories of culture, and by suggesting that the question of cultural rights therefore could not be dissociated from a discussion of the meaning of community itself. In looking at the literature produced by the militant Sikhs I was hoping to show the nature of the challenge that the modern state faces in its role as the sole consecrator of culture. Cultural rights, I have argued, express the concern of groups to be given a sign of their radical acceptance in the world. The definition of the self that emerges is a temporal one, although, as in the case of the militant movement, sometimes a group may feel that its own past is only secure in its own space.[48]

[48] I do not have the space to take up this argument in any detail here but elsewhere I have argued that the meaning of one's own space expands and shrinks according to political context as also between literal meaning and metaphoric meaning. For example, Khalistan—the independent Sikh state proposed in the militant movement—refers sometimes to all Gurudwaras in the world, sometimes to large parts of India and Pakistan which are resymbolized by the process of renaming, and sometimes to the present Punjab in India. The play between literal

The examination of this literature has led me to argue that, unfortunately, the critique by the community exists in the same arena of historicity as the organization it opposes. This may be expressed by superimposing the following two diagrams upon each other.

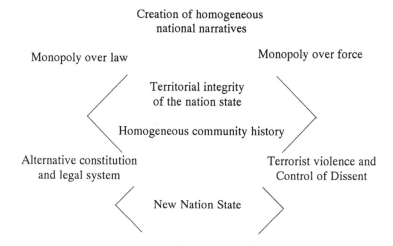

Creation of homogeneous
national narratives

Monopoly over law   Monopoly over force

Territorial integrity
of the nation state

Homogeneous community history

Alternative constitution   Terrorist violence and
and legal system   Control of Dissent

New Nation State

Clearly, a critique of the state which exists in the same arena of historicity can do little more than mirror its structures. This is why I believe that unless a very different theory of community emerges, the technology of cultural rights will not be adequate for the moralizing of those areas of life which have become denuded of all moral meaning on account of the domination by technologies of governance within modern states. All the theories of community in social-science literature are premised upon the idea that communities are spatially bound, face to face, and are thus valorized as a resource for challenging the impersonal and dehumanizing structures of the modern state. I have shown, through the three examples here, that a very different definition of community is emerging in the political culture of India, in which it is not the private sphere of intimate relations but the public sphere of law and history that is sought to be reshaped by new definitions of

---

and metaphoric meaning is well captured in the book by Hans, op. cit., when he says that Khalistan is not so much a physical space as an idea of a space in which people may be more scared of dacoits than of policemen. In this masterly description Hans captures the despair of people facing the illegality of the state in their everyday lives.

community. All of the country's major groups—Hindus, Muslims, Sikhs—seem to be experimenting with these. In such experimentation the community has created for itself a symbiotic relation with the state from which it seems unable to break.

In conclusion, I would like to take a flight of fantasy and suggest that instead of calling for complete surrender from its individual members, a community can become a vitalizing force in the shaping of public culture if it recognizes, even in the matter of cultural rights, the paradoxical links of antagonism and confirmation that it bears to its individual members. Collective existence is necessary because one's capacity to make sense of the world presupposes the existence of collective traditions. However, selfhood depends upon our capacity to break through these collective traditions, or to be able to live at their limits. The complete ownership that every community now seems in the process of establishing over its members will not allow the experimentation that is needed to create genuinely new forms.

From these experiments, however, we may learn that the most perfect communities do not necessarily exhaust all human possibilities, for these groups, together or in themselves, may be transient realizations of humanity. One of the dominant metaphors in the Sikh militant literature is that of the Sikh as the betrayed lover of the Indian state. But from this disappointment may come a further realization, that just as communities need to resist the encompassing claims of the state, so individuals need to develop an inner resistance to even the most vital communities as a condition of human freedom.

A Question of Rights and Wrongs

COLIN TATZ

'In the areas of racism, particularly to do with the Aboriginal people
. . . Australia's record seems to have worsened'—this is the view of
the United Nations Association of Australia.[1] That body castigates
Australia for having ratified only five of the thirteen major human
rights treaties, covenants and declarations, as of 1990. The conclusion
is that what was once called the 'Lucky Country' ranks fourteenth in
the world 'concerning its record on human rights'—there is no indication whether this means fourteenth best or fourteenth worst.

The United Nations Association has not got it entirely right. As
of the end of 1990, Australia had ratified at least eighteen major
conventions, including those dealing with genocide, torture, hostages,
refugees, racial and gender discrimination, 'white slave' traffic, the
rights of the child and labour matters. But the real issue is not how
many ratifications have taken place, or where Australia is placed in
the rankings. What matters is where this country's subordinated black
people are located now, in this last decade of the century, in terms of
real rather than abstract rights. If, following Rawls, the practical
meaning of 'rights' is an entitlement to fairness, then white Australia
has a long way to travel. If by 'rights' we also mean that the people
have a right to have a reason for existence, we are confronted with a
catastrophic problem. While things improve slowly on paper, the
realities remain stark.

To appreciate what is happening to Aborigines one has to look
beyond policy, which is nothing more than a set of hopes and aspirations. This paper is directed to the crisis besetting many Aboriginal
communities: its nature, the forms it takes, and some of the factors
underlying the crisis. I look at what has been attempted by way of
resolution of the crisis, and what has yet to be tried in order to win a
modicum of Aboriginal empowerment. While the present catastrophe
can and must be attributed to the legacy of past violations from a
hostile and even genocidal settler society, it is argued that much of

[1] *Sydney Morning Herald*, 11 November 1989.

the remedy now rests within the Aboriginal communities, comprising 266,000 people, or 1.42 per cent of the Australian population.

'We continue to regard them as inferior, at best to neglect their claims and at worst to despise them and impede their recovery.' This is a recent summation of white Australian attitudes by a long-time student of the Aboriginal condition, Professor Noel Butlin.[2] While I share this broad view, here we need to be more specific and much more precise.

THE CRISIS IN ABORIGINAL AUSTRALIA

We are used to identifying crises and social catastrophes in our own and previous times. What makes the situation of the Aborigines remarkable is that their crisis arises in peacetime, and in a country that is both materially rich and also a stable liberal democracy. Moreover, Australia is a society that has embraced policies of anti-discrimination, affirmative action and social justice, and has often described itself as 'the land of the fair go'. But what concerned outsiders are witnessing today is a chain of behaviour tearing Aboriginal communities apart: suicide and attempted suicide, rape (see Bell in this volume), self-mutilation, homicide, incest and child molestation.[3] Suicide has become a particularly potent symbol of the contemporary Aboriginal condition.

Colin Turnbull has argued that the human values of affection, social grouping for work or for play, systems of law and religion, respect for the old and the care of the young, are not inherent in humanity at all.[4] Rather, these values are 'a luxury of ordered societies'. Turnbull was writing with reference to the Mountain People of Kenya and Uganda, the Ik. Originally hunter-gatherers, the Ik were forbidden hunting and forced to become farmers. With poor land and drought, they struggle for bare survival. Their society was a parody of what we take to be a properly human society.

Turnbull's breakdown of values and of systems is what I saw

[2] *The Age*, 7 February 1990.

[3] See Colin Tatz, 'Aboriginal Violence: A Return to Pessimism', *Australian Journal of Social Issues*, vol. 25, no. 4, November 1990, pp. 245–60; see also Ernest Hunter, 'A Questions of Power: Contemporary Self Mutilation among Aborigines in the Kimberley', ibid., pp. 261–78.

[4] Colin Turnbull, *The Mountain People* (London: Jonathan Cape, 1973).

across Australia during extensive fieldwork during 1989 and 1990, when I visited seventy communities.[5] And if we make the appropriate substitutions—instead of forced transformation into farmers amid drought, the Aborigines suffered the calamity of incarceration on government-run settlements, Christian-run missions, and settler-owned pastoral properties—Turnbull's identification of causes is astonishingly apt for some of Australia's indigenous people.

The suicide issue came to prominence in Aboriginal minds in the early 1980s, particularly with the death in a police cell at Wee Waa, NSW, of 21-year-old Eddie Murray. Christine McIlvanie (Stafford) has examined the factors underlying what, rather than who, killed Murray.[6] She found that police information indicated fourteen attempted and six completed suicides of Aborigines in some form of custody in Australia between 1960 and the end of 1979. Yet the Committee to Defend Black Rights, founded in September 1983, could document thirty-three deaths in custody or in prison between January 1980 and their own founding less than three years later. The disparity in these calculations appears not to arise from poor police statistics before 1980 but rather a plethora of suicides post-1979. The Committee campaigned—by way of rally, picket and public forum—for a royal commission. With increased public, parliamentary and media pressure to back the Aboriginal demands, the Royal Commission into Aboriginal Deaths in Custody was established by Letters Patent in October 1987. It investigated ninety-nine specific deaths (although it had 110 cases under consideration) occurring between January 1980 and the end of 1990.

This chapter was written before the Commission's national report was published. What is known, in the broad, is stark enough: Aboriginal people die in custody at a rate more than twenty times that of non-Aborigines. At this stage, it is possible to say that some 46 per cent of the deaths were from suicide, and a further 36 per cent from natural causes. Matters examined include the character of the places to which Aborigines have been taken, the way they are treated in custody, the frequency with which they are held in custody, and the

[5] Communities visited: 14 in New South Wales, 11 in Queensland, 12 in the Northern Territory, 15 in Western Australia, and 9 each in South Australia and Victoria.

[6] Christine McIlvanie, 'The Responsibility of People: A Study of Race and Racism, Wee Waa, New South Wales', B.A. Honours thesis, University of New England, 1982.

general question of their vulnerability to the police and prison system. Inevitably, the Commission has had to consider the array of social factors that lie behind their detention by state authorities: income, employment, education, housing, ill-health, malnutrition, poverty, alcohol and violence.[7]

Amid the uproar—caused in part by misconception that the Commission was an investigation to cover-up either police or prison-officer homicide—nothing was said of Aboriginal suicide outside custody. That some deaths in custody were occasioned by neglect, and in a few instances criminal neglect, has been established; that at least half the deaths were suicide has also been documented. But we now have to consider Aboriginal suicide in general.

Ernest Hunter's recently completed study of twenty-five suicides in the Kimberley region of northern Western Australia throws light on young male deaths.[8] In the decade 1959 to 1969, there was one suicide; between 1969 and 1979, there were three; between 1979 and 1989, nineteen. The suicides are increasingly younger, and male; they are essentially urban-based and enacted in an environment of heavy drinking and violence. On the other hand, a recent Adelaide study of Aboriginal stress and destructive behaviour found fifteen para-suicides (attempted suicides) in a random sample of eighty-eight people.[9] Fourteen were female, one male.

Prior to the 1960s, the research literature reported no more than twenty instances of conscious acts of self-destruction among Aboriginal people. Yet in the seven days from 16 to 22 October 1989, the week before I visited Adelaide, the (then) Department of Aboriginal Affairs was made aware of eight Aboriginal non-custody suicide attempts in and around that city. In the seventy communities I visited, only five had been free of suicide or para-suicide in the past three years.

[7] Royal Commission into Aboriginal Deaths in Custody, 'Underlying Issues: A Preliminary Discussion of the Possible Range of Underlying Issues . . . ', November 1989 (circulated document).

[8] Ernest Hunter, 'Changing Aboriginal Mortality Patterns in the Kimberley Region of Western Australia, 1957–86: The Impact of Deaths from External Causes', *Aboriginal Health Information Bulletin*, no. 11, 1989; 'Just Happy: Myths and Realities of Aboriginal Health in Isolated Australia', M.D. thesis, University of New South Wales, 1989.

[9] Aboriginal Education Foundation and Flinders University of South Australia, *Taking Control: A Joint Study of Aboriginal Health in Adelaide with Particular Reference to Stress and Destructive Behaviours 1988–89* (Flinders University Monograph, no. 7, 1990).

Suicide, para-suicide and self-mutilation are now rampant in black Australia. This is no exaggeration. Classifying suicide is a vexed matter. Wekstein defines it as 'the human act of self-inflicted, self-intentional cessation of life'.[10] However unsatisfactory the general classifications, two 'types' interest me in this context (and in such places as Alakanuk, Alaska, where in 1988 in a population of 550, there were eight suicides, two dozen para-suicides, two murders and four drownings).[11] The first is 'chronic suicide': the masking of a death orientation by the excessive use of alcohol or drugs. Intent and method may not be in the same class, or class of drama, as the classic note-and-gun, but the common element remains self-destruction. The second type is, I believe, the key to an appreciation of what is happening. It can be called 'existential suicide', and is Camus' notion of ending the unending burden of hypocrisy, the meaninglessness of life, the ennui; it is the lack of motivation to continue to exist; it is what Victor Frankel would call purposelessness in all things, especially in future things.[12]

In sum, we have to acknowledge a grim social fact of which there is, regrettably, abundant evidence in these respects:

(1) A high degree of personal violence within Aboriginal groups, even within families.

(2) Widespread child neglect, including an insufficient supply of food and general care.

(3) Considerable damage and violence committed even in sober states.

(4) A marked increase in Aboriginal deaths from non-natural causes.

(5) Much destruction of property, both white-supplied and own-acquired.

(6) Increasing numbers of attacks, often violent, on white staff who work with the groups.

(7) The vast quantity of alcohol consumed—this is commonly offered as the sole and total explanation for the above.

What is almost as disturbing as these physical manifestations of the contemporary Aboriginal condition is the frequency with which

[10] Louis Wekstein, *Handbook of Suicidology* (New York: Brunner/Mazel, 1979).

[11] *Newsweek*, 15 February 1988.

[12] Victor Frankl, *Man's Search for Meaning* (New York: Washington Square Press, 1984).

Aborigines externalize causality and deny responsibility for any of their own actions.

THE PUZZLE

Why this violence, this response, when on the face of it things can be said to be so much better than they were thirty, certainly forty, years ago?

There is much more money from public budgets, more social service benefits and more actual employment. In the past ten years the Community Development Education Program (CDEP) has been established in many communities. Aborigines no longer receive their social service benefits as cash entitlements: they work for the number of hours required to arrive at the sums to which they are entitled. Many I talked to were thrilled to have the status of gardener or fencer rather than receive what they so aptly call 'sit-down money'. The scheme has wrought wonders of self-worth and dignity in many places. But the scheme has to be seen for what it is: essentially artificial employment for less than the normal industrial wage for that particular task.

There is more housing, through Aboriginal-run housing associations. There is language salvation in several centres; there is also indigenous language maintenance in several schools, together with literacy centres. Assimilationist Australia has yet to be convinced of the value of bilingualism and biculturalism, but enough lip-service and subsidy money have been given to enable a few programmes to survive, even thrive.

Work skills programmes as well as Aboriginal-run and owned enterprises are supported by a Development Commission. Several have come to a shuddering halt through mismanagement or misappropriation. Others have been grounded by unrealistic and inappropriate expectations or premises, like the provision of computerized financial control systems to communities where electricity itself is often a scarce commodity. Still others have triumphed over all kinds of adversity, including impossible weather conditions, great distances to markets or resources, and white mistrust or plain hostility. Mining royalties are paid to Aborigines in a handful of areas, notably for uranium in Arnhem Land and oil in Central Australia. Two or three communities now have substantial financial investments.

There are more and better educational facilities than ever before, and perhaps five or six Aboriginal-run community schools. In one case the South Australian government funds a 'government' secondary school that is designed solely for Aborigines. Study grants are available to most secondary and tertiary students.

Aboriginal Legal Aid and Aboriginal Medical Services function reasonably effectively. Both began as black reactions to and rejections of the 'normal' facilities because Aborigines were either denied service or were placed at the end of the queue. Legal Aid spends most of its time, personnel and money pleading both guilty and in mitigation of clients who are at the mercy of inherently racist police institutions, in which officers tend to see Aboriginal drunks, vagrants and resisters of arrest as 'easy pickings'.

There are now hundreds of legally incorporated Aboriginal associations across the continent. Many of the 'outstations' to which Aborigines have moved from settlements and missions have resource centres; while they are embryonic, often poorly equipped, underfunded, and often badly exploited by greedy staff, they are a form of organization that can cry out in the name of the collective.

We have seen the virtual end of the 'old guard' Native Affairs or Community Services Departments: the 'tough guys' in Aboriginal administration are going or have gone.

There is now the reality of land rights, in one form or another, in all states except Western Australia. Even there, several sheep- and cattle-station pastoral leases are held by the communities. The much disparaged system of 'Deeds of Grant in Trust' in Queensland—by which land is granted in batches of fifty years on stringent lease conditions—is working well. There are strong land councils in the Territory and in New South Wales. Even though factional clashes sap effectiveness, they have a presence and they represent strength. In New South Wales in 1990 the state government was forced to back down on its overt bid to change the land council system. Pressure politics worked well, but only because of the power base of the existing councils.

In the Northern Territory Aborigines own a television station, Imparja, and run a radio station in Central Australia. Aboriginal-based programmes, often made by Aborigines, are a regular feature of the presentations of the Australian Broadcasting Corporation. SBS, the multicultural broadcasting network, works hard at portraying the Aboriginal experience.

Black artists, theatre and writers are now recognized, not only by the media but by audiences and readers. Black dance and cultural festivals flourish, as do sports carnivals. Aboriginal sporting achievement is not only outstanding but is being recognized as such.

There is growing Aboriginal participation in political and parliamentary life, and greater local decision-making than ever before. There is anti-discrimination legislation in most states, and concerned moves towards affirmative action programmes. Northern Territory Aborigines have recently won a tortuous battle for excisions of land from leased pastoral properties on which they were born, and with which they were bought and sold as chattels when the land changed hands. Remarkably, Aborigines have won eight of their last forays before the High Court of Australia, all matters related to land rights and issues touching on 'sovereignty' (including the all-important Mabo case in 1993).[13]

Aboriginal Studies are meant to be taught in state school systems, and in New South Wales in 1991 a new Higher School Certificate subject of that name was introduced.

That all of the above represents a set of gains is not denied, not even by most Aborigines. After thirty years of observing the Aboriginal condition, I have to say that factually, rather than attitudinally, some major changes have occurred: the repressive legislation has gone, albeit leaving indelible scars that will take generations to fade; the incredible system by which Aborigines were minors in law, seemingly in perpetuity, has ended, albeit with administrative remnants and relics still evident; the old boss superintendents, replete with powers of physical punishment and imprisonment, have gone; the old prohibitions on freedom of movement, of religious and cultural practices, have ended.

Why then is the internal violence, the crisis, so marked, so widespread now? Is it possible that Aborigines perceive most of these gains as irrelevant, or meaningless, or wrongly motivated? Yes. Is it obvious that some of the 'advances' were and are to appease white guilt or international investigating teams? Yes. Is it possible, as in South Africa, that the black agenda is now at least a decade ahead of where white Australians are or are prepared to be? Yes. Is it likely that Aborigines recognize many of these programmes as flimsy, as gameplaying, as artifices? Yes. Could it be that the legacies of the past have

---

[13] See John McCorquodale, 'Aborigines in the High Court', *The Australian Quarterly*, Autumn 1983, pp. 104–13.

finally erupted in these behaviours, and that the changes have arrived too late, palliative rather than curative or restorative? Yes, I believe so. Was the violence always there, dormant or unrecognized? Certainly there were, and are, aspects of traditional life that incorporate and embrace violence, such as a man being speared for infringing a taboo or incest prohibition. But what is being discussed here is the *new* violence, the kind not seen by Aboriginal leaders or field workers even twenty years ago. Is it possible that the violence is endemic because no matter the gains, the wrongs that exist in Aboriginal life are so prevalent? Again, the answer is yes, as will be shown.

WHAT IS NOT BETTER

Aborigines remain the sickest sector of Australian society. The levels of ill-health are appalling for a 'first world' nation. High infant mortality is the order of the day, notwithstanding governmental claims of 'huge' reductions these past twenty years. Life expectation is not consonant with what prevails in the rest of this affluent, reasonably well-educated, non-peasant society. Men cannot expect to live beyond forty-five. Most don't. Trachoma abounds. Leprosy, while not as fearful or fatal as myth would have it, is rife in the north; true malnutrition is rampant. Obesity, heart disease and diabetes now figure prominently in the health profiles. The largest single cause of death is now 'non-natural' causes. At the end of 1990 the Minister for Aboriginal Affairs announced the spending of 232 million dollars over five years for Aboriginal 'health and infrastructure'. This, he said, was short of the 2.5 *billion* dollars needed for housing, water, sewerage and electricity.[14]

Aborigines are the poorest group in this society. Experts agree that while there is poverty in Australia, there is a quantifiable and tangible difference between Aboriginal and non-Aboriginal poverty. They remain the poorest, sickest, most homeless, least literate, hungriest of people. They are the most oppressed, repressed and depressed community, generally. Proportionately, they are the most arrested, the most imprisoned, the most convicted. Even in a country imbued with a sporting obsession, Aborigines have almost nothing in the way of facilities. In a country that takes pride in its 'multi-

---

[14] *Sydney Morning Herald*, 18 December 1990.

culturalism', Aborigines are most often relegated as a sub-species of ethnicity, as a subset of the migrant population. There really is no need to traverse any further the social indicators that locate Aborigines at the bottom of almost every conceivable scale.

The Israeli anthropologist Emanuel Marx asserts that 'a person resorts to appealing violence when he has reached the end of his tether, and feels unable to achieve a social aim unaided by others . . . '[15] He calls this 'a cry for help'. 'It is partly a cry for help addressed to a public, and partly an attempt to shift some of his obligations towards his dependents onto others.' In this state, in this social context, man or woman abuses self, violently, with alcohol or drugs, or through mutilation or attempted suicide; or he/she abuses others close to hand, such as partner, child, relative or even property at hand.

Alcoholic self-abuse has to be arrived at, usually through a cluster of politico-legal and/or socio-economic factors. Alcohol is not the start of the syndrome: it is the mid point, the end point of which is the abuse of self and others. What Australia so blithely ignores is the set of starting points.

In the hard-drinking, alcohol-adoring and booze-boasting ethos of Australia, Aborigines drink more and with greater consequences to self and to those close by. There is a dual white response to this. One view, all too common from those who ought to know better, is that Aborigines are born with a genetic predisposition to get drunk or with a biological, enzymal inability to handle the stuff. The other is that we should seek to explain, even applaud, the camaraderie, empowerment and social integration that accompanies, or fuels, collective drinking. The latter is certainly a preferable approach, but it does not seek explanation of why the drinking begins. In my own view alcohol is only the agent and instrument of the carnage taking place. *It is not the cause.*

Given that there is no single cause or set of causes to explain Aboriginal drinking, I suggest this aggregation of factors:

(1) The legacies of past violations which are now manifesting themselves: institutionalization; heavy-handed administration; prohibition of cultural practices and the forbidding of hunting; curfews; imprisonment for offences only Aborigines could commit; the food

---

[15] Emanuel Marx, *The Social Context of Violent Behaviour: A Social Study in an Israeli Immigrant Town* (London: Routledge and Kegan Paul, 1976), particularly on pp. 2–6.

ration system; alcohol prohibition; exiling of people to remote areas; and, in particular, the forced removal of children.

(2) Aborigines survived the trading men, the whalermen, the sealermen, the church men, the cattle men, the welfare men and, lately, the mining men, but the new challenges require something more than the sheer will to survive a cruel but often crude enemy. There is a new and sometimes disabling uncertainty about who is accountable and responsible for their lives. In the face of uncertainty, purpose may waver.

(3) Doctrines of equality have given contemporary Aborigines an enormous agenda of expectations while they lack the skills that a market society is prepared to pay for at the common rate. So their expectations are routinely dashed. This situation is scarcely unique, but is everywhere grossly destructive.

It is notable that black drinking is almost never treated as individual drinking. Like everything else to do with Aborigines, it is perceived, regarded, addressed and debated as a *collective phenomenon*. My own analysis here has proceeded on the basis that alcohol is a major problem in Aboriginal society, but of course it is also a major problem in white Australian society. But in analysis of the latter problem, the focus is usually on the individual rather than the collective. Generally, even among the academic brothers and sisters, Aborigines are always plural, never singular. This said, if my conjectures have any validity, the heavy drinking will not stop in the next quarter of a century. There is a view which holds that Aboriginal drinking is in a post-prohibition phase, exacerbated by lack of employment, and that somehow Aborigines will come out of the 'binge' fairly soon. My own view is that the unrealistic expectations and exhortations will persist, as will the ambiguity which serves bureaucratic interests. And the scars of the past will remain a source of great pain. Together, the past and the present will fuel destructive behaviour like alcohol abuse for decades to come.

WHAT IS BEING TRIED

The most obvious panacea for the problems of Aboriginal society is to spend more and more money on the now routine agenda of housing, training, employment, health and legal aid programmes. More symbolically, there has been much talk about a treaty or 'reconciliation' with Aborigines. Hope is often invested in strengthening anti-discrimination statutes and in affirmative action 'quotas'. There is still a strong lobby for a Bill of Rights to be inserted in the Constitution. More consultation mechanisms are called for, more 'community development', and generally more Aboriginal decision-making about themselves. Aborigines tend to talk of the aboriginalization of all that pertains to them. A few Aborigines even talk of a 'Black state' issuing its own passports. The majority of concerned people assert that the universal answer is more 'land rights'.

The treaty idea is based on the (white) belief that we can achieve a true reconciliation with the past, and make restitution or reparation by encapsulating high rhetoric—about rights, about a future in mutual understanding—in a publicly-posted document, a *Makarrata*, thereby producing what the post-1945 Germans called *Wiedergutmachung*, a making good again.[16] What is also intended is a recognition that two hundred years ago there ought to have been a treaty between two nations, the victorious British and the vanquished Aborigines, which conceded rights to the vanquished.

There are many problems with this. A document cannot make good that which patently cannot be made good again: life, family, the clans, marriages, parenthood, childhood, torture, maiming, enslavement. Nor can we pretend that at the end of the twentieth century Aborigines are a separate nation, rather than part of a multicultural Australian nation. For a time, the Australian government seemed committed to a treaty in the context of the then forthcoming bicentenary. But during 1989 the government shifted uncomfortably away from the word 'treaty' towards the word 'compact'. By late 1990 it had retreated even further, establishing for the next four or five years a Council for Aboriginal Reconciliation.

The belief in an Australian Bill of Rights ignores the history of the United States model.[17] Fifty-eight years elapsed between *Plessy vs Ferguson* (1896) and *Brown vs Board of Education* (1954). In short, a Bill of Rights has to be interpreted, and interpretation is cast in the political context of the era. Plainly, there is no Aboriginal salvation in a Bill of Rights. We have enough legal instruments as it is.

[16] Colin Tatz, 'Aborigines and the Age of Atonement', *The Australian Quarterly*, vol. 55, no. 3, 1983, pp. 291–306. The article analyses the whole question of treaties and suggests different models for reparation and compensation.

[17] Colin Tatz, 'Aboriginality and Human Rights', in his *Aborigines and Uranium and Other Essays* (Heinemann Educational Australia, 1982), pp. 26–56.

Australian anti-discrimination legislation leaves much to be desired.[18] Based on English legislation of the 1960s, it avoids any notion of criminality attaching to racist behaviour. It treats the phenomenon of racism as a kind of social pathology, an illness of the soul that needs negotiation, arbitration, conciliation and, above all, counselling. It eschews the adversarial process wherever and whenever possible. And when a civil proceeding is reached, as a last resort, maximum damages, at least in New South Wales, amount to 40,000 dollars. Accompanying such statutes, and in a sense integral to them, is the belief that one can educate people out of their racist attitudes and behaviours. There is not a tittle of evidence anywhere to show that education *qua* education has ever 'deracialized' a racist.

When one turns from the devices of lawyers to those of social planners, the thinking is no better. Aboriginal 'community development' has been a disaster—and it will continue to contribute to the destruction of some of their societies. Governmental agencies and church groups talk about the existence of *communities*, implying and imputing to *all* aggregations of people a social coherence and a set of functioning systems. Hence they favour and finance only 'community development', a phrase no one defines, spells out or understands (in its correct usage). Apparently derived from distorting British colonial theories in Africa, the community development school reveres the collective but ignores the plight of the individual Aborigine in a way that no white citizen's individuality would be ignored. At its lowest and meanest level, it is openly justified as a device 'to protect the taxpayer's dollar' by giving money only to legal incorporations amenable to audit. (This follows several parliamentary inquiries into alleged mismanagement of programmes and funds.)

The calls for more 'consultation' of Aborigines by policymakers are not so much an hypocrisy as a deliberate sleight of hand and of mind. Consultation has come to mean that we either tell Aborigines what we are doing to or for them (instead of just doing it, as we used to), or we insist on consulting *every single* Aborigine before we concede the representativeness of a viewpoint. We, and they, are now in the realms of absurdity: no consensus of this kind can be reached, and the 'non-consensual' Aboriginal decision arrived at by other means can be disregarded.

But equally, the Aboriginalization of all things is fraught with

18 Ibid.

both hypocrisy and improbability. The new Aboriginal and Torres Strait Islander Commission, which replaced the 'old' (1973-born) federal Department of Aboriginal Affairs, is believed to be *the* way by which the indigenous people, elected to office, will make real decisions. Their former 'bosses', the 700 or so bureaucrats, are to be their serving or servant secretariat. It is a nice idea and no doubt the framers of this, and earlier similar plans, mean well. But the reality is that Aboriginalization can only mean having Aborigines in positions within a Eurocentred system of bureaucracy, tradition and precedent. Since Aborigines contribute only between 1.4 and 2 per cent of the population, there can be no Aboriginalized parliament, bureaucracy or courts that can fully control the state in its attention to Aboriginal matters.

One major fallacy of the present period is the tendency to subsume *all* Aboriginality—past, present and future—under the phrase 'Land Rights'. Here land rights are being seen as a political and social movement highlighting the essence of Aboriginal dispossession and providing *the* avenue to repossession not only of land but of spirituality, culture, dignity, self-respect and, importantly, the respect of white Australians. But land means different things to different Aborigines.

In the Northern Territory, land rights passed into law on the major (white) premise that all Aboriginal land is inherited through mother, father, or both, and that all land is associated with spiritual feelings and ceremonial duties. But when Tasmanian Aborigines seek land rights legislation, they want the right to sell or mortgage such land. The white community and the traditional Aboriginal communities respond in horror: land is, or has been allowed to become sacred, and therefore unthinkably sellable. This is only one illustration of the dominant tendency to reduce Aboriginal experience to a plural and collective status. Aborigines are seen as a single people with a common history, an homogeneous people for whose common problems we need to find universal solutions. But while there is, of course, a common oppression, the values and states-of-being of Aboriginal groups differ enormously across the continent.

WHAT NEEDS TO BE TRIED

If there is to be a way forward from the present lamentable position, each 'side'—the several governments on one side and the Aborigines on the other—must make its own changes. In two particular instances there needs to be something of a 'joint venture' between the two sides. Here I can only sketch a few choices for change.

From the side of government, the first major change needs to be an abandonment of that misperception of Aborigines as always plural and collective. The need to individualize and so humanize the Aboriginal population is crucial. As I have noted in this chapter, the history of Aboriginal administration has been a fruitless search for the overarching universal in policy, legislation and administration. Instead we need a regional and local approach that takes communities and individuals as it finds them. This is the long way but it is the only way round the problems.

The quite appalling system of 'consultation' must stop. We haven't the faintest idea of how Aborigines make decisions or how they want them made. At this stage of confusion, I don't believe Aborigines know either. But resort to a constant stream of meetings, in white venues and with white agendas and timetables always results in whites hearing what they want to hear. We can do better. Similarly, Aborigines should surrender the current practice, now habit, of saying that literally everything under the sun must 'go to the people' for consideration. Often there are no 'people'. And the idea, for example, that a matriculation syllabus on Aboriginal Studies—replete with aims, objectives, learning principles, pedagogies, assignments—must be scrutinized by *every* brother and sister in New South Wales is ludicrous.

The premise that each Aboriginal settlement is a *communitas* must be shaken. Often it is an aggregation of mixed clans, tribes and language groups, dumped or lumped there for good or bad, mostly bad, reasons.[19] Missionaries sought remoteness from 'Satanic influences' and vice, isolation for their evangelism; governments sought remoteness from genocidal white predators of various kinds. It cannot be assumed that people live where they want to live or where they have always lived. 'Community' tends to be a euphemism for what was, until very recently, a settlement, mission, reserve or pastoral property.

In the sphere of law making, governments should approach the

---

[19] Catherine de Mayo, 'Splendidly Secluded' (a study of the location of Aboriginal mission stations), M.A. thesis, Macquarie University, 1990.

issue of rights in the form of specific and positive statutes. There has been a history of negative law affecting Aborigines, establishing them as a special and inferior class of persons who have to be controlled by criminal sanction in relation to behaviour which is not criminal in the mainstream society. By contrast, and for the first time in 1976, the Aboriginal Land Rights (Northern Territory) Act was a piece of appropriately positive legislation. In an elaborate document, this Act spelled out meticulously and precisely just what the government wanted to give the Aborigines, how it was to be given, and how those who tried to subtract from the gift were to be treated. The Act gave Aborigines an instrument of power, a source of income, definite procedures of acquisition and a system of defence of their rights. This was far more than any abstract Bill of Rights could accomplish.

Governments can do many other things. They can, for instance, open up their police forces to inquiry by independent tribunals rather than perpetuating a view that they are beyond reproach in matters Aboriginal. Police forces may well be laws unto themselves. But governments show no signs of even trying to stop the wholesale arrest and imprisonment of Aborigines for trivia. This is not only a constant source of bitterness and hostility but also, as we have seen, of death.

From the Aboriginal side, they may care to try a number of avenues out of their powerlessness. First, they have yet to 'internationalize' their problems. Previous attempts to do so have been pathetic: reverse rowing boat landings at Dover, sardonic proclamations to the British by their Aboriginal 'invaders' during the 1988 bicentennial celebrations, a few desultory visits by small groups to Kenya, China, and the southern USA. In 1972 the Tent Embassy in front of Parliament House, Canberra, was a stroke of genius. It said to an uncomprehending world that we are foreigners in this country and as such we are entitled to an embassy in the capital; but since we can't afford a palace, we're erecting a tent and a flat on parliament's lawns. It was all too sophisticated for the white community and eventually Prime Minister McMahon unleashed police violence to remove 'the squatting rabble'. Michael Mansell's recent visits to Libya have also been misunderstood. Another stroke of genius, it says to an even more uncomprehending world that the world's number one bad guy, Colonel Gaddafi, cares about Aborigines while one of the world's self-styled altruists, then Prime Minister Bob Hawke, does not.

Since the founding of the United Nations in 1946, the international spotlight has focused on racism, particularly South Africa's variety.

Australia has escaped almost entirely. The first real international jibe came in 1975, not from Russia or Indonesia, but from New Zealand's Robert Muldoon. The international arena is waiting to be exploited.

Aborigines are slowly forging an element of coherence under the rubric of Aboriginality. It is perhaps a form of 'black consciousness', but one dismissed or disparaged by many whites and some Aboriginal groups. Australia, even more so than South Africa, has practised a system of race classification based on the 'skin visibility' test. The person who looks like an Aborigine is one; the one who doesn't look like a full-blood tribesman, head-banded, loin-clothed, spear in hand, peering mystically into the mysteries of the Dreamtime, is simply not Aboriginal. And so we have a real and tragic dichotomy in Aboriginal life—one fuelled by the media of two 'races', 'Kakadu Man', tribally rich, tribally pure, and the other of 'Redfern Man', urban, poor, pretending to be what—in the eyes of the beholder—he is not.

Coherence has to come from a powerful source or force. To date, the land rights phenomenon has not been worked or moulded into a coherent ideology. The idea of Aboriginal Australia remains stunted in the absence of an ideological movement that transcends the individual differences that have been stressed in this chapter.

It may be that Aborigines will have to resort to what Emanuel Marx calls 'coercive violence', what I call civil violence. This is a drawing of attention to problems by violence of the bricks and bottles variety. This is not mutiny, rebellion, insurrection or treason. American and British blacks have long seen the value, albeit the short-term value, of civil violence as a *legitimate* political weapon when all else— plea, prayer, pleading and protest—have failed. Like Shakespeare's Viola, I would rather go with Sir Priest than with Sir Knight. But there can be no doubt—in the indelible phrasing of Tom Hayden in the heady days of the Students for a Democratic Society in the United States—that a few rocks and bottles cause more attention in the corridors of Washington than all the reports, enquiries and task forces put together.

It is possible that Aborigines understand intuitively that the white response will be out of all proportion to any initial force used. This is, after all, a society with a genocidal impulse and a genocidal track record. It came as no surprise in the 1970s when a group of Aboriginal kids began throwing stones at passing tourist cars en route to Ayers Rock in Central Australia that the local police superintendent wired headquarters for the issue of barbed wire, tear gas and automatic weapons. In 1990 the New South Wales police raided Aboriginal homes in Redfern (suburban Sydney), in darkness before dawn, looking for 'criminals'. The force comprised 130 officers, members of the Tactical Response Group and others, but they managed to make only two arrests on the basis of outstanding warrants for minor offences.

I have often said that there is more hope for Aborigines in the legal than in the political arena. Their recent victories in the High Court attest to this. Overall there has been very little use of civil law, but where it has been used, the victories have been significant. Only now have Aborigines begun discovering legal procedure as a way of recovering legal rights.

One joint venture is vital as an exercise in which elements of both western and traditional Aboriginal culture are blended to form hybrid politico-legal institutions with forms and procedures recognizable to both 'sides'. The present land councils, composed of Aborigines, are not that. They are white creations, with white agendas and procedures. Putting blacks in a white structure does not make it a black structure. We have failed to devise such hybrid structures (which I first suggested some thirty years ago on the basis of what was then needed in Africa) because we are quintessential assimilationists who make all others accommodate to our systems. We continue to resist the notion that Aboriginal systems and institutions have any validity or efficacy. There is still some time left in some Aboriginal domains for this attempt to be made.

Finally, there is one more joint venture, though it is fraught with such difficulty that merely articulating the idea may cause misunderstanding. The project is what Ernest Hunter, a psychiatrist working in Aboriginal health, calls 'restructuring Aboriginal childhood'. In the violent context of suicide, homicide and self-mutilation discussed earlier, Hunter has shown that the victims tend to be young people who have been socialized to heavy drinking and violence in the present permissive era. These are the children of parents who themselves lived through the prohibition era, an administrative phase in which there were tight controls and brutal and authoritarian paternalism. There can be no nostalgia or return to this era of prohibition, censorship, control and curfew. But the structure has gone from these same communities, partly as a by-product of having to recognize human rights. Now, in this climate of freedom of an important kind, there is, literally, chaos. The centres cannot hold.

The idea of reconstructing childhood is based on the current experiments in the United States with parents who beat their children. The aim is not to stop the beating—for such attempts have failed—but to raise children in an atmosphere in which they are socialized not to beat *their* own children, something that would be 'normal' otherwise. How does one restructure Aboriginal childhood? I don't know and I don't believe anyone else does. I know that only Aborigines can stop doing what some of them do. When I see a gambling mother pour petrol on a blanket and then suffuse her crying infant's face to quieten it while she deals the cards, I know that calamity is taking place. Into such scenes we cannot rush doctors, nurses and social workers; nor enforcement officers to punish the mother for doing what she does not know she is doing. Somewhere, somehow, internally, Aborigines have to initiate and practise the controls that are essential not just to their survival but to the enjoyment of those characteristics which Turnbull says are the luxury of ordered societies.

POSTSCRIPT

The Royal Commission into the Aboriginal Deaths in Custody made over 300 recommendations. In 1992 the Australian government had called for a meeting of State and federal instrumentalities to work out ways of implementing these proposals. As at the end of 1991 the Australian government had pledged a mere $8 million towards these objectives, and the phenomenon of deaths in custody continues unabated. By 1996 the problem of deaths *outside* custody had reached another apogee. Now even the mainstream press has expressed concern about this matter, which has become a litmus test of the catastrophe now enveloping Aboriginal society. Yarrabah, near Cairns in North Queensland, has the highest rate of teenage male suicide ever recorded anywhere.

Legal Pluralism and the Indigenous Peoples of Australia

JAMES CRAWFORD[1]

I Introduction

The 'frontiers' of colonization, or of the imposition of central government on diverse peoples, have consistently been marked by conflict, initially of arms, in the longer term, of laws. The subjection of aboriginal peoples to state authority does not extinguish the traditions and ways of life of those peoples. Even in the long term, given at least some degree of tolerance, accommodation or just indifference by the introduced population and government, those ways of life are likely to survive, changing and adapting to the new circumstances but still retaining continuity with the past. Where ways of life survive, in recognizable form, so too will ways of law. Hence the issue arises whether the recognition—however qualified—of the right of such peoples to follow their way of life entails at least some recognition also of their law-ways.

Whether the question is asked by the members of the group themselves, by persons representing them or by members of the wider society (especially lawyers or other professionals confronted with issues of justice in dealing with conflicts between the two groups), it is usually posed from the point of view of the surrounding legal system. The question is thus concerned less with 'custom' as such, than with the response of the surrounding legal system to the custom of the people concerned. Of course any response must take into account the characteristics of what is recognized, however imperfect the match between the indigenous reality and the legal construct.[2] This

---

[1] Challis Professor of International Law, University of Sydney. My thanks to Garth Nettheim, Peter Hennessy, Mary Fisher and Tom Musgrave for their help at various stages with this review.

[2] The terms 'lawyers' and 'customary law' have been coined to describe the seemingly inevitable divergence between actual custom and the rule that is recognized or enforced: see G. R. Woodman, 'How State Courts Create Cus-

is no doubt a major reason why this topic—unusually for topics which lawyers profess—has generated interdisciplinary work (especially with anthropologists and sociologists) which is considerable both in quantity and quality.[3]

But there is another perspective on these issues. Customary law is part of a way of life, the province or domain of the people concerned. The recognition of that customary law has often meant its limitation or confinement. It has also been used, on occasions, as a smokescreen to avoid consideration of issues such as autonomy, including the autonomy to change or even to abandon customary ways. The spectre is that of the exhibited Aborigine, recognized as long as recognizably 'traditional'. The recognition of customary laws, an important issue in its own right and from the perspective of justice within the wider legal system, must not be allowed to obscure the issues arising from the claims of indigenous peoples for the recognition of their rights as such, not only in terms of the existing law but in terms of land, resources and control over their lives.

II THE RECOGNITION OF ABORIGINALITY IN AUSTRALIA

In 1788, the year of British settlement of Eastern Australia, the country was inhabited by indigenous peoples with their own established traditions, practices, social structures and laws. Aborigines are believed to have occupied Australia for over 40,000 years.[4] The Australian continent (including Tasmania) was divided into hundreds of tribal areas, with many different language units. There were possibly as many as 600 distinct dialects or languages.

In deciding how to respond to the situation which confronted them in 1788, the British authorities faced an initial question of method. Official British policy was to acquire new lands only with the consent

---

tomary Law in Ghana and Nigeria', in B. W. Morse and G. R. Woodman, *Indigenous Law and the State* (Dordrecht: Foris Publications, 1988).

[3] One of the earliest landmarks in this area was Maine's *Ancient Law* (1861). In this century the tradition has been continued by writers such as Bohannan, Gluckman and L. Nader. A good example of more recent legal-anthropological collaboration is J. L. Comaroff and S. Roberts, *Rules and Processes* (Chicago: University of Chicago Press, 1981).

[4] An Aboriginal site in eastern Australia has been dated at c.43–47,000 years BP. See further D. J. Mulvaney, *The Prehistory of Australia* (rev. edn, Ringwood: Penguin, 1975).

of their inhabitants, if that consent could be obtained. Land which was unoccupied, on the other hand, could simply be occupied by the settlers, on the basis of the prior proclamation of British sovereignty, which asserted the right to occupy the land as against other potential colonizers.

Both international law and English law thus drew a distinction between territory occupied by cession or conquest on the one hand (where rights were derived or seized from a previous holder) and territory acquired by settlement (where there was no previous holder). But the common derivation of this distinction in international law and English law, and its common terminology, has tended to obscure fundamental differences between the *function* of the distinction in the two systems. International law was concerned primarily to resolve disputes between states competing for control of particular territory, and to attribute responsibility for territory to the appropriate state in the context of claims for damage done to foreigners—a particular problem at the 'colonial frontier'.[5] At the relevant time it was not particularly concerned with the treatment of colonized peoples after colonization, or with changes in the legal regime in colonized territory, and not at all concerned with the distribution of governmental authority as between legislature and executive in a colony. By contrast English law was not concerned to adjudge the international propriety of the acquisition of a colony to the Crown—a matter covered by the act of state doctrine.[6] Its principal concerns were precisely the allocation of internal governmental powers between the Crown and Parliament, and the continuity of any pre-existing laws or property rights after colonization. Because of their different focus, it was entirely possible that territory which as a matter of international law was ceded or conquered would later be classified as a settled colony for the purposes of English law: this was the case, for example, with New Zealand.[7]

---

[5] Cf. J. Crawford, *The Creation of States in International Law* (Oxford: Clarendon Press, 1979) pp. 182–3. It is significant that the only modern international decision on these issues (the Western Sahara Opinion ICJ Rep 1975 p12) was an advisory opinion with strong undercurrents of a territorial dispute. See further R. Balkin, 'International Law and Sovereign Rights of Indigenous Peoples', in B. Hocking, *International Law and Aboriginal Rights* (Sydney: Law Book Co, 1988) p. 19.

[6] *Coe v Commonwealth* (1979) p. 24 ALR 118.

[7] See further Australian Law Reform Commission, Report 31, *The Recognition of Aboriginal Customary Laws* (AGPS, Canberra, 1986) (hereafter ALRC 31) vol. 1, chapter 5.

In the event, and despite an unsuccessful attempt to adopt a different policy in South Australia,[8] the Colonial Office treated Australia as previously uninhabited by a sovereign or sovereigns, or by people with recognizable institutions or law. No treaties were made with Aboriginal groups, as occurred in North America and New Zealand.[9] Aborigines were treated as British subjects, subject to British law—as individuals, not communities or nations—despite the fact that they had no understanding of the imported legal system and adhered to their own traditions and laws. British policy was stated, for example, by George Grey in 1837:

It is necessary from the moment the Aborigines of this Country are declared British subjects they should, as far as possible, be taught that the British Laws are to supersede their own, so that any native, who is suffering under their own customs, may have the power of an appeal to those of Great Britain, or, to put this in its true light, that all authorized persons should in all instances be required to protect a native from the violence of his fellows, even though they be in the execution of their own laws. So long as this is not the case, the older natives have at their disposal the means of effectually preventing the civilization of any individual of their own tribes, and those among them, who may be inclined to adapt themselves to the European habits and mode of life, will be deterred from so doing by their fear of the consequences that the displeasure of others may draw upon them.[10]

Consistent with this policy the entire body of English law was applied throughout Australia without regard to the existence of Aboriginal traditions and institutions. This non-recognition applied as much in civil as in criminal matters: it involved the denial of land rights[11] and the non-recognition of traditional marriages[12] as much as the refusal

[8] The history is informatively set out in H. Reynolds, *The Law of the Land* (Ringwood: Penguin, 1987) chapters 5–6. But Reynolds glosses over the crucial failure to amend the South Australia Act 1834 (UK), which was a major legal obstacle to the recognition by the Crown of aboriginal title: ibid, pp. 103–5, 124; cf. J. Bray, 'Underestimating the Fundamentals', *The Adelaide Review*, February 1988.

[9] Batman's 'treaty' (which would have been at best an unlawful attempt to acquire land other than through the Crown) is now thought to have been a forgery: A. H. Campbell, 'Was Batman's Treaty Authentic?' (1987) 79 *Arena*, p. 66.

[10] Report by Captain G. Grey on the Method for Promoting the Civilization of Aborigines, Enclosure, Lord John Russell to Sir George Gipps, 8 October 1840, *Historical Records of Australia Series* 1, vol. 21, p. 35.

[11] *Milirrpum v Nabalco Pty Ltd* (1971) 17 FLR 141.

[12] *R v Neddy Monkey* (1861) 1 W & W (CL) 40; *R v Cobby* (1883) 4 LR (NSW) 355, 356.

to recognize Aboriginal traditional laws as a defence to crimes defined by British law.[13]

The injustice of this policy was noted at the time. In 1837 the British House of Commons Select Committee on Aborigines stated that to require from Aborigines 'the observation of our laws would be absurd and to punish their non-observance of them by severe penalties would be palpably unjust'.[14] But these sentiments were not reflected in the actual recommendations of the Select Committee, or in any other action at the time or later. It became an axiom of British and then Australian law that Aborigines, whatever their actual lack of contact with or awareness of the law, were subject to it without qualification or exception.[15]

Under this regime, conflicts between settlers and Aborigines, and the devastation of introduced diseases and alcohol reduced the Aboriginal population during the first hundred years of settlement from an estimated 300,000 to 60,000. Many who survived had their traditional way of life destroyed or suppressed. In Tasmania the effects of British settlement were particularly devastating.[16] Growing awareness within Australia of the maltreatment of Aborigines by colonial settlers and criticism of such maltreatment in England led to a policy of 'protection'. Aboriginal protectors were appointed and there was an increased missionary influence. This preceded a more formal policy of protection, resulting in the segregation of Aborigines into reserves, restrictions on the contact of other Aboriginal people with settlers, prohibition on the use of alcohol and the removal of part Aboriginal children from their families.[17] Later, during the 1930s and 1940s, official policy began to favour the absorption or assimilation of all Aboriginal people into a 'white' Australia. Protectionism was phased out, to be replaced by health, education and housing programmes designed to ensure that all Aborigines achieved the same manner of living as white Australians.[18] Later still, in the 1960s and 1970s, such

---

[13] *R v Jack Congo Murrell* (1836) 1 Legge 72. See B Bridges, 'The Extension of English Law to the Aborigines for Offences Committed Inter Se, 1829–1842' (1973) 59 *JRAHS* 264.

[14] House of Commons Parliamentary Paper No. 425, 1837, 84.

[15] See ALRC 31, vol. 1, para 39–40.

[16] See eg G. Blainey, *A Land Half Won* (Adelaide: MacMillan, 1980); H. Reynolds, *The Other Side of the Frontier* (Ringwood: Penguin, 1982); L. Ryan, *The Aboriginal Tasmanians* (St Lucia: University of Queensland Press, 1981).

[17] See ALRC 31, vol. 1, para 25 & works there cited.

[18] Ibid., para 26 & works there cited.

policies of paternalism were challenged and were ultimately reformulated under the label of 'integration'. Loss of Aboriginal identity was no longer proclaimed as the ultimate goal. Instead Aboriginal people were, it was argued, to a certain extent at least, entitled to retain their racial identity, their languages, customs and distinct lifestyles, presumably including their customary laws.[19] Present Australian policy is variously described in terms of Aboriginal self-determination or self-management. It has involved the granting of Aboriginal land rights in parts of Australia, and the encouragement of Aboriginal self-management in programmes such as housing, education, health, child-care and the provision of legal services.[20]

The policy of non-recognition was tempered by the reluctance of law enforcement agencies to become involved in disputes between Aborigines, and by practices of non-prosecution and mitigation of sentence. During the 1920s matters were taken a little further, and a number of special institutions were established or proposed to deal with Aboriginal cases. In Western Australia a special court was created for Aboriginal cases.[21] In the Northern Territory an Aboriginal tribunal was proposed, though never established.[22] In Queensland Aboriginal courts and Aboriginal police were established in 1939, and in modified form these still operate.[23] In the Northern Territory juries for Aboriginal people were abolished except for capital offences. The Supreme Court of the Northern Territory was given a discretion not to apply the death penalty to Aborigines convicted of murder, and Aboriginal customary laws were to be taken into account in cases of sentence.[24] In Western Australia the death penalty for Aborigines was abolished and a maximum of ten years imprisonment was substituted: Aboriginal confessions and admissions were made inadmissible for any offence punishable by death.[25]

Few of these provisions remain today. Recognition instead is even more piecemeal and tends to take the form of the exercise of discretions in particular cases. For example, the courts have been prepared to take customary laws into account in determining a defendant's

[19] Ibid., para 27 & works there cited.
[20] Ibid., para 28, p. 107.
[21] ALRC 31, vol. 1, para 53.
[22] ALRC 31, vol. 1, para 52, 56.
[23] ALRC 31, vol. 1, para 55.
[24] ALRC 31, vol. 1, para 52.
[25] ALRC 31, vol. 1, para 53.

intent in criminal cases, in determining whether certain defences (e.g. provocation) are available and in passing sentence.[26] The courts have at times regarded the loss of traditional status and privilege as a compensable injury in motor vehicle accidents.[27] In one Northern Territory decision a traditional marriage was recognized for the purposes of adoption.[28] At the legislative level recognition has occurred through the granting of land to Aboriginal people on the basis of traditional association (in particular in the Northern Territory and South Australia),[29] recognition of traditional marriages for certain purposes (Commonwealth, Northern Territory and Victoria,[30] provisions recognizing Aboriginal child-care practices (Northern Territory, Victoria and New South Wales),[31] sacred sites legislation (which exists in some form at the federal level and in all states and the Northern Territory),[32] and exemptions from wildlife, conservation and fisheries laws to enable Aboriginal people to engage in traditional hunting and fishing (Commonwealth, Northern Territory, and all states except Victoria and Tasmania).[33] Thus recognition, whether judicial or legislative, has been particular rather than general.

III THE REVIVAL OF THE RECOGNITION DEBATE

But the question whether Aboriginality should be given some special or distinctive recognition in Australian law and public institutions has again become a live issue in the last fifteen years. The most important manifestation of this debate has been the recognition or conferral of

[26] On provocation, see eg *R v Muddarubba* [1956] NTJ 317; *Moffa v R* (1977) 13 ALR 225 (a case concerning a migrant). On sentencing, see e.g. *R v Moses Mamarika* (1982) 42 ALR 94.

[27] See e.g. *Napaluma v Baker* (SA Supreme Court, 5 March 1982) (1982) 4 *Aboriginal Law Bulletin* 9; *Dixon v Davies* (NT Supreme Court, 17 November 1982) (1983) 7 *Aboriginal Law Bulletin* 9; *Weston v Woodroffe* (1985) 36 NTR 34.

[28] ALRC 31, vol. 1, para 276.

[29] Aboriginal Land Rights (Northern Territory) Act 1976 (Cth); Pitjantjatjara Land Rights Act 1981 (SA); Maralinga Tjarutja Land Rights Act 1983 (SA).

[30] See ALRC 31, vol. 1, para 80, pp. 237–40 for details.

[31] See ALRC 31, vol. 1, para 81, pp. 359–64.

[32] E.g. Aboriginal and Torres Strait Islanders Heritage Act 1984 (Cth). See ALRC 31, vol. 1, para 78.

[33] See ALRC 31, vol. 1, para 79, pp. 906–69. See e.g. Fisheries Act 1905 (WA) s56(3); Aboriginal Land Rights Act 1983 (NSW) s4(1).

land rights over very substantial rural areas of the Northern Territory and South Australia, and to a much lesser degree in New South Wales, Victoria and Queensland.[34] Only Western Australia of the mainland states has not made some legislative provision for land rights—a major omission considering the number of Aboriginal groups with potential claims based on traditional affiliation.[35] Other forms of recognition of the 'Aboriginal legal heritage' have also occurred, and will be outlined below.

Despite these changes, the initial position remains that Aborigines are Australian citizens subject to Australian law in the same way as all other citizens.[36] Exceptions to that position tend to be challenged, either legally (as the Pitjantjatjara Land Rights Act 1981, SA, was challenged in the High Court in *Gerhardy v Brown*)[37] or politically (as the present New South Wales Government pledged to repeal the Aboriginal Land Rights Act 1983, NSW, a pledge which has not been met because the Government does not control the Upper House).[38] Justifications for such exceptions tend to imply that Aboriginality, or at least traditional Aboriginal culture, is transitional or temporary. For example, the decision in *Gerhardy v Brown*[39] that legislation recognizing traditional land rights was a 'special measure' under Article 1 paragraph 4 of the Racial Discrimination Convention of 1966 (as implemented in section 8(1) of the Racial Discrimination Act 1975 (Cth)) can be read as implying that such legislation is inherently 'temporary' in character: under Article 1, paragraph 4 of the Racial

[34] ALRC 31, vol. 1. para 77, 212; and see also Aboriginal Land (Lake Condah and Framlingham Forest) Act 1987 (Cth).

[35] Aboriginal Land Bill 1985 (WA); (1985) 12 ALB 6.

[36] It was disagreement about the implications of this proposition that led to a roll-call division on the first motion debated in the new federal Parliament House. A Government motion affirming 'the entitlement of Aborigines and Torres Strait Islanders to self-management and self-determination subject to the Constitution and the laws of the Commonwealth of Australia' was passed by majorities in both Houses, after an Opposition amendment to add, after 'self-determination', the words 'in common with all other Australians' had been rejected. Like the motion itself, the debate and the disagreement were symbolic rather than substantive: it was nonetheless significant. See *Parl Debs (H of R)* 23 August 1988, pp. 137–52; *Parl Debs (Senate)* 23 August 1988, pp. 56–72.

[37] (1985) 159 CLR 70.

[38] Administrative attempts to negate the 1983 Act were held ultra vires: *New South Wales Aboriginal Land Council v Minister Administering the Aboriginal Land Rights Act*, NSW Sup Ct (Bryson, J.), unreported, 13 May 1988.

[39] (1985) 159 CLR 70.

Discrimination Convention, special measures 'shall not be continued after the objectives for which they have been taken have been achieved'.[40] Thus the impression is given that what is required are 'special measures' of adjustment or advancement, rather than some more basic settlement of grievances.

On the other hand, the consciousness that something more is needed does exist. The then Prime Minister's commitment to some form of 'treaty' with Aboriginal representatives (discussed below) is one indication of this. A joint resolution of both Houses of federal Parliament of 23 August 1988 stated that:

the Commonwealth [should] further promote reconciliation with Aboriginal and Torres Strait Islander citizens providing recognition of their special place in the Commonwealth of Australia.[41]

In a similar vein, paragraphs 2–4 of the preamble to the Aboriginal and Torres Strait Islander Commission Bill 1988 states that:

. . . *whereas* the people whose descendants are now known as the Aboriginal and Torres Strait Islander peoples of Australia were the prior occupiers and original owners of this land;

And whereas they were dispossessed by subsequent European occupation and have no recognized rights over land yet recognized by the Courts other than those granted or recognized by the Crown;

And whereas that dispossession occurred without compensation and no serious attempt was made to reach a lasting and equitable agreement with them on the use of their land . . . [42]

---

[40] For the reasons stated in ALRC 31, vol. 1, paras 153–7, this is a misreading of both the decision and of the Convention. Cf. also *Mabo v Queensland* (1988) 83 ALR 14. But the public impression of land rights as 'special' or 'unequal' remains.

[41] *Parl Debs (H of R)* 23 August 1988, 137; *Parl Debs (Senate)* 23 August 1988, p. 56.

[42] In his second reading speech the Minister for Aboriginal Affairs stated that the third paragraph of the preamble was intended to have 'no legal consequences': *Parl Debs (H of R)* 24 August 1988, 251. Earlier versions of the Bill would have stated that the Aboriginal and Torres Strait Islander peoples 'have no recognized rights over [their land] other than those granted by the Crown', a strong endorsement of the *ratio decidendi* in *Milirrpum v Nabalco Pty Ltd* (1971) 17 FLR 141. For criticism, see e.g. G. Nettheim & J. Crawford, 'Preamble Perils' (1988) 30 ALB 15. Similarly the preamble to the Aboriginal Land (Lake Condah and Framlingham Forest Act 1987) (Cth) states that the Government of Victoria 'acknowledges that... Aboriginals residing on [the land in question] and other Aboriginals are considered to be the inheritors in title from Aboriginals who

The preamble goes on to refer to 'the intention of the people of Australia . . . to ensure for all time that the Aboriginal and Torres Strait Islander peoples receive that full recognition and status within the Australian nation to which history, their prior ownership and occupation of the land, and their rich and diverse culture, fully entitle them to aspire', and that 'there [should] be reached with the Aboriginal and Torres Strait Islander peoples a real and lasting reconciliation of these matters'. (With no apparent sense of incongruity, the bill goes on to establish an Aboriginal and Torres Strait Islander Commission as an elected representative body chaired by the minister's nominee, subject to the minister's general directions, and with the intention of vesting in it functions of the 'old Department' of Aboriginal Affairs.[43])

The need for special 'recognition of (Aboriginals' and Torres Strait Islanders') special place in the Commonwealth of Australia' has been acknowledged by other bodies. The Australian Law Reform Commission in 1986 recommended federal legislation to recognize Aboriginal customary laws in areas such as marriage, child care, property distribution, the criminal law, the law of evidence and procedure and hunting and fishing legislation.[44] A 1988 report of a visiting mission by the United Nations Working Group on Indigenous Peoples

---

owned, occupied, used and enjoyed the land from time immemorial' (para (a) (v) (b) (v) but that 'the Commonwealth of Australia does not acknowledge the matters acknowledged by the Government of Victoria'. Despite this remarkable admission, the Commonwealth passed the Act at the request of the Victorian Parliament (presumably under s51(xxxvii) of the Constitution), thereby making the legislation unrepealable by a later Victorian Parliament.

[43] Aboriginal and Torres Strait Islander Commission Bill 1988 (Cth) ss8, 11, 21(2), 223, 230.

[44] The proposed legislation is set out in ALRC 31, vol. 2, pp. 251–73. For exposition, comment and discussion of the Report, see: J. Crawford, P. Hennessy & M. Fisher, 'Aboriginal Customary Laws: Proposals for Recognition' in G. Woodman & B. Morse (eds.) *Indigenous Law and the State* (Dordrecht: Foris Publications, 1988) 27; G. Woodman, 'Towards Legal Pluralism in Australia' (1985), 23 *Jnl of Legal Pluralism* 225–30; Editorial (1986) 60 *ALJ* 655–6; Lancaster, [1987] 1 *Canadian Native Law Review* 1–9; W. Sanders, 'The Department of Social Security's Treatment of Aboriginal Polygyny and Tribal Marriage: A Saga of Administrative Debate' (1987) 46 *Aust J Pub Ad* 402; S. Poulter, 'Review Essay: Cultural Pluralism in Australia' (1988) 2 *Int J Law & Fam* 127; C. McLachlan, 'The Recognition of Aboriginal Customary Law: Pluralism beyond the Colonial Paradigm—A Review Article' (1988) 37 *ICLQ* 368; R. Chisholm, 'Aboriginal Law in Australia: The Law Reform Commission's Proposals for Recognition' (1988) 10 U Hawaii LR 47.

was highly critical of Australia's 'violation of her international human rights obligations relating to non-discrimination and unequal treatment in general and to the provision of certain minimum services in particular', and recommended, among other things, 'that the Aboriginal and Islander peoples be given self-government over their local and internal affairs . . . [with] powers sufficient for the protection of the groups, collective right to existence and for the preservation of their identities' and with 'a secure financial basis'.[45]

Whatever the strength of particular criticisms or the merits of particular proposals, these developments imply, first, that there is an Aboriginal legal heritage, and secondly, that it is not enough for the state merely to permit it to exist alongside other minority legal and cultural traditions in Australia—in other words, that something needs to be done to recognize it in a special or distinctive way. But it is remarkable that, despite extensive effort and expenditure over twenty years and more, comparatively little has been done, and that the legitimacy of that little is still under challenge from different perspectives.[46] It is important to ask why this is the case.

IV SOME ISSUES UNDERLYING THE RECOGNITION DEBATE

Arguments about recognition of customary laws tend to start with, and sometimes get no further than, definitional questions and the accumulation of general arguments for or against recognition. Many of the definitional problems, and some at least of the general arguments against recognition, can be avoided or minimized by adopting particular and specific rather than general measures of recognition. But something should be said about the more general issues.

[45] EIA Daes, Chairwoman-Rapporteur of the United Nations Working Group on Indigenous Populations, 'Report on Visit to Australia, 12 December–2 January and 7–22 January 1988' (mimeo, Athens, April 1988) 12, 26.

[46] The Liberal Party's apparent insistence that this recognition must occur 'in common with all other Australians' negatives the idea of recognition, since by definition we are taking about characteristics of Aboiginal and Torres Strait Islander people which are distinctive, and which are not shared by others, e.g. recent immigrant groups. For example, it has long been recognised in the United States that issues affecting the black population or immigrant groups are quite distinct from issues affecting American Indians. See ALRC 31 vol 1 para 118, 134, 163–5.

1. The Definition of 'Aborigine'

An issue which has been a source of considerable difficulty in the United States and Canada is the definition of 'Aborigine' or 'Indian', that is, the criteria for membership of an indigenous minority. In Australia there has been no build-up of restrictive, technical or bureaucratic definitions of what constitutes such a member, for example, by reference to membership in a 'tribe' of 'band'. Although there are examples of earlier legislation defining Aboriginality by reference to degrees of blood (with phrases such as octoroon, quadroon, half-caste), the accepted Commonwealth administrative definition, which is also adopted widely in the states and territories, is that an Aborigine is a person of Aboriginal descent, who identifies as an Aborigine and is accepted by other Aboriginal people as an Aborigine. The framers of this definition preferred flexibility and breadth to certainty or exclusiveness. What was unclear was whether this broad definition corresponded with the Constitutional definition of the 'Aboriginal race' for the purposes of s51(26) of the Constitution.[47] The High Court's decision in *Commonwealth v Tasmania*[48] indicates support for such a broad definition for Constitutional as well as administrative purposes. As Deane J expressed it:

by 'Australian Aboriginal' I mean, in accordance with what I understand to be the conventional meaning of that term, a person of Aboriginal descent, albeit mixed, who identifies himself as such and who is recognised by the aboriginal community as an Aboriginal.[49]

Experience under state and Commonwealth legislation does not suggest that a more restrictive definition is necessary.

---

[47] This is the basic source of federal legislative power over Aboriginal issues. In the original Constitution of 1900, s51(26) gave the Commonwealth Parliament power to enact special laws for the people of any race for whom special laws were deemed necessary, but excepted from this power 'the Aboriginal race in any State'. This exception was repealed in a referendum in 1967, thus enlarging the 'races' power to include special laws for Aborigines. Of course the Commonwealth Parliament can also pass laws specially concerned with Aboriginal people under its other legislative powers (eg over marriage and social security). In the absence of actual federal legislation on a topic the States remain free to deal with the topic: federal legislative power is concurrent, not (as in Canada) exclusive.

[48] (1983) 158 CLR 1; 46 ALR 625.

[49] Ibid, 817.

2. *The Definition of Aboriginal Customary Laws*

This is a more complex question. Aboriginal customs and laws are part of an oral culture. Indeed in terms of that culture it is usual to speak of 'the Law' rather than of laws. The emphasis is on unity and immutability rather than on plurality and change. But the traditional culture is an oral one, and there are no written codes or statements of customary laws such as are found in some other countries. There is a considerable amount of general anthropological discussion on Aboriginal traditions and practices, including especially marriage, kinship, hunting and fishing practices, relations to land and dispute resolution. There is however no agreement among anthropologists on important issues, such as, for example, whether in Aboriginal traditional communities there were institutional authority structures for dispute resolution. There is however agreement among anthropologists that traditional societies had and continue to have a definable body of rules, practices and traditions accepted by the community. In *Milirrpum v Nabalco Pty Ltd* (the *Gove Land Rights case*) in 1971,[50] Blackburn J had no hesitation in treating the system of land-holding and kinship rules of the North-East Arnhem Land people disclosed by the evidence as a system of laws. Blackburn J commented that a recognizable sovereign or a separate territorial community with well-defined boundaries were not prerequisites for 'law'. He preferred to place emphasis on the processes of dispute resolution in traditional societies and to avoid a precise and exclusive definition of what constitutes Aboriginal customary laws. This would be to distort the reality:

I do not think that the solution . . . is to be found in postulating a meaning for the word 'law' . . . What is shown by the evidence is, in my opinion, that the system of law was recognised as obligatory upon them by the members of the community which, in principle, is definable in that it is the community of Aboriginals which made ritual and economic use of the subject land. In my opinion it does not matter that the precise edges, as it were, of this community were left in a penumbra of partial obscurity.[51]

This view accords with the Australian experience, where the absence of a single all-purpose definition has not produced serious difficulties. Indeed it can be argued that in Canada, for example, the existence of rigid exclusionary definitions has caused problems.[52]

[50] (1971) 17 FLR 141.
[51] Ibid, 266–7.
[52] E.g. the controversy over band membership epitomized by *Attorney-General*

3. Why Recognize Aboriginal Customary Laws?

In its consideration of the recognition of Aboriginal customary laws, the Law Reform Commission was presented with a variety of arguments both for and against recognition. The principal arguments in favour of recognition, as outlined in the Report, may be summarized as follows:[53]

A. Non-recognition contributes to the continued undermining of traditional laws and authority structures. Aboriginal customary laws are a continuing reality in the lives of traditionally oriented people.

B. Non-recognition can lead to injustice. It is unfair, for example, for an Aboriginal person to be punished by the general law for taking action required by his or her customary laws.

C. Aboriginal people generally support recognition of their laws and, more specifically, have sought ways to enable the two laws, the general law and Aboriginal customary law, to work together. One concern, however, is their desire to maintain secret aspects of their law and to retain control over their law.

D. Aboriginal customary laws assist in maintaining law and order within Aboriginal communities. Non-Aboriginal law and order mechanisms are often seen as ineffective and based on alien value systems.

E. Recognition may also provide a way to compensate Aborigines for past wrongs, including the injustice of initial non-recognition.

F. Australia's international standing would benefit from appropriate forms of recognition.

On the other hand a number of arguments against recognition were also made:

A. Recognition would involve endorsement of unacceptable punishments which cannot be tolerated by the general legal system.

B. Recognition would involve endorsing a system which discriminates against Aboriginal women and leads to other violations of basic rights.

C. Recognition would entail the loss of Aboriginal control over their laws and their traditions.

D. Recognition requires reliable information about Aboriginal

---

for Canada v Lavell (1973) 38 DLR (3d) 481. The Constitution Act 1982 (Can) s35(2), however, takes a more flexible and inclusive approach.

[53] See further ALRC 31, vol. 1, Chapters 8–10.

traditions, including secret matters, and this information is usually lacking.

    E. Aboriginal customary laws have ceased to exist in any meaningful form.

    F. Aboriginal communities are undergoing such change and the variety of Aboriginal experience is such as to preclude recognition altogether.

    G. Recognition would create a form of legal pluralism which is discriminatory and divisive.

The Commission did not find the latter arguments persuasive as arguments against any form of recognition whatever.[54] However, some of these arguments raised issues which required careful consideration in framing proposals for recognition. One of the most important of these was the variety of Aboriginal lifestyles and the right of Aboriginal people to make their own choices about their lives. Two further matters, partly related to the first, were the often-raised questions about pluralism and equality before the law, and the need to take account of Australia's international obligations, especially in the field of human rights.

4. *The Diversity of Aboriginal Lifestyles*

There are among Aboriginal people enormous variations in experiences and circumstances. To some extent these variations must always have existed, but they also reflect the extent of European contact and the very different responses of different groups to European contact. It was therefore essential for the Commission's proposals to take account of differences between Aborigines living in remote and relatively inaccessible areas, whose life is still predominantly traditionally-oriented, and those Aborigines who have been living for some considerable time in or around cities or larger country towns and who have modified their social organization to a greater or lesser extent to reflect their changed circumstances and the new pressures upon them. These broad groups are commonly identified as: traditionally-oriented Aborigines, 'detribalized' or 'fringe-dwelling' Aborigines and urban Aborigines.[55] However, there are many difficulties in attempting to adopt classifications which do not take into account fluctuations in

---

[54] ALRC 31, vol 1 para 127, 165, 192, 194, 209.
[55] See ALRC 31, vol 1 para 33–36 for some demographic information.

the composition and nature of the different groups, or the extent to which groups converge. Nor can it be assumed that there is any inevitable, one-directional movement away from more traditional ways of life. The situation varies markedly in different areas, and is influenced by such developments as land rights (especially in the Northern Territory and South Australia), the outstation movement,[56] and the internal dynamics of particular communities.

On the other hand, many social, economic and legal difficulties are common to all Aboriginal people, regardless of where they live. Where the varying needs and demands of Aborigines in different areas called for care and flexibility in the development of the proposals for recognition, the available evidence does not support the view that Aboriginal customary laws and traditions are transitory. As the Commission concluded:

What the position will be in twenty-five years time is unnecessary (even if it were possible) to predict. There are good arguments for action to be taken now to recognize aspects of Aboriginal customary laws and traditions which do now exist, and which are likely to continue to exist in much the same form for the foreseeable future.[57]

Arguments based on the fact that Aboriginal customary laws are undergoing change are not arguments against recognition so much as arguments for care to be taken in the form of recognition proposed.

5. *Equality, Discrimination and Pluralism*

A common argument against legislative, and even administrative, recognition of indigenous minority rules and traditions is that such recognition would be discriminatory or unequal, or would violate the principle that all persons in a democratic society should be subject to 'one law'. These are powerful arguments, and, so far as basic standards of discrimination and equality are concerned, reflect fundamental values. However these standards are more difficult to apply than is commonly realized.

---

[56] 'Outstations' are smaller groups established in remoter areas by movement away from larger Aboriginal settlements. They usually focus on local groupings and on attachment to particular land. See H. C. Coombs, B. G. Dexter & L. R. Hiatt, 'The Outstation Movement in Aboriginal Australia' in E. Leacock & R Lee (eds) *Politics and History in Band Societies* (Cambridge: Cambridge University Press, 1982) 427.

[57] ALRC 31, vol 1 para 122.

Applying the standards of non-discrimination and equality in the light of the Racial Discrimination Convention and of other international and comparative experience in the field, the Law Reform Commission concluded that special measures for the recognition of Aboriginal customary laws would not be racially discriminatory, or involve a denial of equality before the law or of equal protection, if these measures were reasonable responses to the special needs of those Aboriginal people affected by the proposals, were generally accepted by those people, and did not deprive individual Aborigines of basic human rights or of access to the general legal system and its institutions.[58] Thus the Commission applied the following guidelines in making its recommendations:

A. Aborigines should, wherever possible, obtain rights under the general law (e.g. to enter into marriages or make wills under the general law).

B. Legislation should be no more restrictive than necessary to ensure fidelity to the customary laws or practices being recognized.

C. Measures of recognition should not unreasonably withdraw legal protection or support from individuals, whether Aboriginal or non-Aboriginal.

D. Where the most appropriate remedy to a problem revealed by the Commission's inquiries is not a recognition of Aboriginal customary laws as such but some more general provision, the question becomes whether that provision can legitimately be applied to some class of Aborigines only or whether the reasons for the provision apply equally to all members of the community.[59]

These guidelines were intended to ensure that any proposals made are not discriminatory or unequal as between Aboriginal and non-Aboriginal Australians generally, or in relation to specific groups, including immigrant groups.

It is interesting to note that in this context one of the undoubted pressures is the question of 'special treatment' for immigrant communities, their customs and traditions. In view of the size and diversity of Australia's immigrant communities, the question of legal pluralism as it affects migrant groups is a particularly sensitive one.[60]

---

[58] ALRC 31, vol 1 para 165.

[59] ALRC 31, vol 1 para 158–69.

[60] Indeed it has surfaced in a number of the Australian cases: eg *Moffa v R* (1977) 13 ALR 225 (provocation); *Re Qazag* (1984) 20 SSR 219 (entitlement to social security); *Yildiz v R* (1983) 11 A Crim R 115 (sentencing; admissibility of

Some at least of the Commission's proposals might be applicable to members of immigrant groups with their own customs and traditions. In view of its Terms of Reference the Commission made no recommendation to this effect: instead in two areas (child care payments and right to an interpreter) it refrained from making a recommendation for legislation partly on the basis that these provisions were equally necessary for immigrants as Aboriginal peoples.[61] However, the Commission did stress the special justification for the recognition of indigenous customary laws, and the distinction between indigenous and immigrant groups.[62] The Report clearly proceeds on the view that Aborigines are in a special position, and this quite apart from any special treatment due to those with continuing claims to land by virtue of prior occupation. The effects of European settlement have been devastating on Aboriginal people. Their traditional ways of life have undergone enormous changes. Criminal statistics demonstrate the difficulties Aborigines face with the legal system. Special measures to deal with this situation are not merely justifiable but necessary. In this context each of the proposals made in the Report, the Commission concluded, was justified in individual cases as necessary (and, if necessary, as 'special') measures.[63]

6. *The Protection of Basic Human Rights*

As the Commission's Terms of Reference made clear, certain aspects of the recognition of Aboriginal customary law raise problems of the application and the interpretation of basic human rights standards. It might be thought a sufficient reply to say that Aborigines themselves can determine and maintain adequate standards of human rights. The Commonwealth Parliament cannot abrogate its responsibility for ensuring the maintenance of the human rights of all Australians, including Aboriginal Australians, in the formulation and application of the law. But this does not dispose of the proposition that Aborigines

---

'expert' evidence of Turkish traditions and attitudes). The only official Australian report touching on these issues took a very restrictive and assimilationist approach: Australian Institute of Multicultural Affairs, *Multiculturalism for all Australians* (AGPS, Canberra, 1982).

[61] ALRC 31, vol 1 para 390, 600.

[62] Ibid, para 163–4.

[63] Ibid, para 165. See also J. Crawford, 'International Law and the Recognition of Aboriginal Customary Laws' in Hocking 43.

themselves should assume responsibilities for the maintenance of human rights in their own communities. There are obviously tensions between the values of self-determination or self-management and other human rights standards, and their detailed resolution is not a simple or straightforward matter.

What is true is that the International Covenant on Civil and Political Rights of 1966, which is a widely accepted formulation of basic civil and political rights, has to be interpreted and applied on a universal basis, in a wide variety of contexts and cultures. It is not to be assumed that its provisions are to be interpreted in the light of just one culture, however influential.[64] The Report concluded that the need for consistency with fundamental human rights did not preclude the recognition of Aboriginal customary laws. Whether human rights are preserved or infringed by a particular proposal, however, depended on the detailed proposal in question. The Commission concluded that its recommendations are consistent with basic human rights.[65]

7. The Commission's General Approach

The Law Reform Commission's Report is based on the premise that, whatever form of recognition is adopted, recognition should take place within the framework of the general law. The Commission also concluded that arguments for the recognition of Aboriginal customary laws through the re-examination of the status of Australia as a settled colony would not bring about appropriate forms of recognition of Aboriginal customary laws and traditions as these exist now.[66] But this left many questions unresolved. Recognition could be effected in a number of ways. Apart from recognition through common law rules and discretions (which, the Commission concluded, was limited and inadequate to deal with the questions raised by the Terms of Reference) the obvious method was legislative recognition. But legislative recognition of Aboriginal customary law can itself take several forms, including codification or specific enforcement of customary law; specific or general forms of 'incorporation' by reference; the exclusion

[64] See ALRC 31, vol 1, para 183–92 for the Commission's general discussion of this issue.

[65] Ibid, para 171–93.

[66] Ibid, para 67–8. For an attempt to litigate some of these issues in the context of the settled/conquered colony distinction see *Coe v Commonwealth* (1979) 24 ALR 118.

of the general law in areas to be covered by customary laws; the translation of institutions or rules for the purposes of giving them equivalent effect, and the accommodation of traditional customary ways through specific measures taken within the general legal system.[67] The Commission rejected codification and the general incorporation of Aboriginal customary law within the general legal system, on the ground that both involve the danger that Aboriginal people would lose control over their laws, and that there could be unwarranted intrusion into or disclosure of secret matters.[68] Aboriginal people repeatedly impressed these concerns upon the Commission. In general they sought incorporation only of specific customary laws, usually as a protection against outside invasion or interference (an example is the protection of sacred sites). For these reasons the Commission preferred specific rather than general forms of recognition, but saw no need to adopt only one approach to recognition. Some of the recommendations are for measures in the form of translation of customary institutions or rules for the purposes of giving them equivalent effect (e.g. the proposals for the recognition of traditional marriage, outlined below). Other proposals would be best implemented by legislation requiring that the general legal system take Aboriginal customary laws into account (for example the exercise of sentencing discretions). In other cases some specific exclusion of the general law may be an appropriate way to recognize the operation of Aboriginal customary laws (for example, exemptions to hunting or fishing legislation to recognize Aboriginal traditional hunting and fishing rights). This approach accorded with the Commission's view that problems of recognition would be minimized by approaching the Reference in a functional way, issue by issue. Wide-ranging categorical forms of recognition raise difficulties of definition, already referred to, and heighten problems of translation of the different concepts involved in the general legal system and under Aboriginal customary laws. Adopting a functional approach, the Commission found, had the advantage of maximizing the extent to which Aboriginal people would retain control over their laws. It also enabled specific proposals to be formulated to reflect the fact that Aboriginal customary laws continue to be subject to external pressures and to change, and that they vary from

[67] See ALRC 31, vol 1 para 199–207 for a review of these different forms of recognition.

[68] ALRC 31, vol 1 para 200–2.

community to community both in strength and content. The criticism that functional recognition involves the general legal system dictating the extent to which it is prepared to recognize customary laws, rather than allowing full recognition,[69] is a criticism that can be made of any form of recognition within the framework of the general law.

V AREAS FOR RECOGNITION

Against this background the Report examines, in Parts III–VII (Chapters 12–36), a series of areas of the law where recognition may be necessary. Some brief reference will be made to each of these.

1. Recognition of Traditional Marriage

Despite the longstanding failure to recognize them, patterns of traditional marriage continue to exist, and remain strong not only in the Northern Territory but also in parts of Western Australia, South Australia and Queensland. There has been a tendency to revert to patterns of traditional marriage even in communities which had previously been subject to strong missionary influence.[70] Responding to this situation is, however, another question. Traditional Aboriginal marriages are informal, non-ceremonial relationships, which can be entered into in a variety of ways, which are not infrequently polygynous and which do not conform to the model of 'marriage' under Australian law in other ways.[71] It is sometimes suggested that the best way to deal with traditional marriages is to recognize them as de facto relationships, which also lack ceremonies or documents marking their commencement and conclusion, but which are nonetheless recognized for certain purposes in most Australian states and territories. But this is very much a second class form of recognition, since the distinguishing feature of a de facto relationship in the wider society is that it is *not* a marriage. Aborigines do regard stable unions entered into within

---

[69] A criticism made, eg, by N. Rees, 'What Do we Expect?' (1983) 8 *Aboriginal Law Bulletin* 10.

[70] ALRC 31, vol 1 para 226–9.

[71] R.M. Berndt, 'Tribal Marriage in a Changing Social Order' (1961) 5 *UWAL Rev* 326, 338–9; P. Sutton, 'Aboriginal Customary Marriage—Determination and Definition' (1985) 12 *Aboriginal Law Bulletin* 13.

the appropriate kinship categories as marriages, rather than as de facto relationships.

On the other hand it is not appropriate to recognize such marriages as having all of the legal consequences of marriage under the Marriage Act. Most obviously, marriage under general Australian law is mono-gamous, requires a formal judicial termination and carries obligations of continuing maintenance after the termination of the relationship which have no direct analogue in Aboriginal tradition and which may well cut across other methods of providing for spouses. The Com-mission recommended the functional recognition of traditional mar-riages, that is, treating them as marriages under the general law for certain specified purposes. The aim was to avoid foisting on the parties to what is in most cases a rather informal relationship a set of rules and structures developed in a different culture and involving different assumptions about the status and consequences of marriage, while still offering appropriate forms of protection to traditional spouses consistent with Aboriginal marriage traditions. Thus it was recommended that parties to a traditional Aboriginal marriage should be regarded as married persons for the purposes of Australian law relating to such questions as the status of children; adoption, fostering and child welfare laws;[72] distribution of property on death (intestacy, family provision); accident compensation (including workers' com-pensation, compensation on death, criminal injuries compensation and repatriation benefits); statutory superannuation schemes (and private superannuation schemes established in the future); the Social Security Act 1947 (Cth), with special provision being made for separate payment to spouses; spousal compellability and marital com-munications in the law of evidence; unlawful carnal knowledge, provided both actual consent and traditional marriage are proved, and spouse rebates under the Income Tax Assessment Act 1936 (Cth) and related legislation. On the other hand, it recommended that traditional marriages should not be recognized for the following purposes: variation of maintenance and property rights during a relationship or on divorce; bigamy; rape in marriage and the Family

---

[72] This has been done in a number of jurisdictions: see ALRC 31, vol 1 para 80, 239; Community Welfare Act 1983 (NT); Adoption Act 1984 (Vic); Children (Care and Protection) Act 1987 (NSW) s87; Adoption of Children Act 1965 (NSW) s19 (1A) (c); R. Chisholm, 'Aboriginal Children and the Placement Principle' (1988) 31 ALB 4, 6–7.

Court's jurisdiction with respect to principal and ancillary relief (including its powers with respect to domestic violence).[73]

2. Traditional Distribution of Property[74]

The idea of 'property' in Aboriginal tradition is very different to that adopted by Australian law. This is so both for personal property and land, but especially for land. Traditional Aboriginal society was not materialistic and placed little importance on wealth or possessions. Much more important was the development, management and transfer of knowledge and skills, which involved the recognition of individual and collective 'ownership' of knowledge in a way not unlike Western legal doctrines of intellectual property.[75] Aborigines, even those living in remote areas, have in general accepted the cash economy and its rules. But conflicts can arise between Aboriginal ways of doing things and legal rules for transferring property, for example in the area of the distribution of property upon death, where there is potential conflict between the general rules for property distribution and claims upon death, based on the assumption of a nuclear family, and Aboriginal family structures and kinship obligations. Along with the recognition of traditional marriage for the purpose of distribution of property upon death, including family provision, the Commission recommended reform of the general law relating to the distribution of property on death in the following form:

A.   Traditional marriages should be recognized for the purpose of intestacy legislation.

B.   Aborigines should be able to apply to have an intestate estate distributed in accordance with the traditions or customary laws of the deceased's community.

C.   State and territory legislation for family provision (testator's family maintenance) should allow for applications for family provision by persons related by blood, kinship or marriage to a deceased member of an Aboriginal community and who could at the time of the deceased's death have reasonably expected support (including

---

[73] ALRC 31, vol 1 para 271–323.

[74] See ALRC 31, vol 1 para 326–43.

[75] Even here, however, the analogy is a distant one, since the concomitant of ownership was a responsibility to maintain the ritual information and practices. See Ibid, para 327–31.

material support) from the deceased in accordance with the customary laws of that community.

D.   Claims for family provision should prevail, in clear cases of need, over claims for traditional distribution on intestacy.[76]

3. Aboriginal Child Custody

It would be difficult to find an Aboriginal person above the age of thirty who has not had some experience of state intervention in Aboriginal families. This makes the issue an extremely sensitive one for many Aboriginal people. Like many other areas covered in the Report, this has so far been exclusively a matter of state administrative and legislative responsibility. The questions of which government should take responsibility for child welfare services, and to what extent the Commonwealth's involvement in certain areas of funding (e.g. in funding Aboriginal Child Care Agencies) should carry with it some share in the determination of policy are extremely sensitive ones. However it is important not to confuse federal issues with the substantive question of what should be done. The Report recommended that:

A.   There should be an Aboriginal child placement principle established by legislation, requiring preference to be given, in decisions affecting the care or custody of children, and in the absence of good cause to the contrary, to placements with a parent of the child; a member of the child's extended family; other members of the child's community (in particular, persons with responsibilities for the child under the customary laws of the community).

B.   Where such a placement is not possible, preference should be given to placement with families or in institutions for children approved of by members of the relevant Aboriginal communities having special responsibility for the child, or by an Aboriginal child care organization working in the area.

C.   In making these decisions account should be taken of the standards of child care and child welfare of the Aboriginal community to which the child belongs.

D.   Child welfare legislation should provide explicitly for consultation with the relevant Aboriginal custodians of a child and (unless they direct to the contrary) with the relevant Aboriginal child care

[76] Ibid, para 333–42.

agency, before placement decisions (except emergency decisions involving short-term placement) are made.

   E.   Careful attention should be given to the possibility of devolving child care responsibilities to regional or local child care agencies by agreement, and with appropriate resources.[77]

   In a number of cases these recommendations have been influential at the state level.[78]

4. *Criminal Law*

The application of the general criminal law to Aborigines raises the possibility of conflict between that law and Aboriginal customary rules adhered to by traditionally oriented Aborigines. While Aborigines are grossly over-represented in the criminal justice system, the relationship between particular offences and Aboriginal customary laws is not a direct one. Examination of the limited evidence available suggests that, even when traditionally oriented Aborigines are involved in criminal charges, the case will frequently involve non-traditional elements (especially alcohol) or a non-traditional offence. It is much more common, even for traditionally oriented Aborigines, that the act that resulted in the charge was a violation of both Aboriginal customary law and the general law, or was not specifically allowed or justified by Aboriginal customary law, than that it was so justified. For these and other reasons the explanation for the very high offence and imprisonment rates of Aborigines[79] is not simply a product of non-recognition of Aboriginal customary laws by the substantive criminal law. Nor are the problems reflected by those exorbitant rates likely to be solved by the recognition of Aboriginal customary laws within the substantive criminal law. Indeed, if (as appears to be the case) the characteristics of traditionally oriented Aboriginal offenders do not differ markedly from other Aborigines it may be that solutions will not be found directly through *any* form of recognition of Aboriginal customary laws.[80]

   Nonetheless, particular conflicts do occur, and so too (more often) do problems of the interaction of the two systems. Such conflicts can

[77] Ibid, para 365–71.

[78] ALRC 31, vol 1 para 81, 359–64. See also Children (Care and protection) Act 1987 (NSW) s87; Chisholm, 4–6.

[79] As to which see above, text to nn 24–5.

[80] See ALRC 31, vol 1 para 399–400 for discussion of these propositions.

to a certain extent be resolved by taking the operation of Aboriginal customary laws into account in determining criminal liability. The courts have on occasions taken the customary laws of the defendant's community into account in determining whether a defence of provocation or duress was established sufficient to reduce charges of murder to manslaughter.[81] To ensure that the law as represented by these decisions is applied fairly and consistently, the Report recommended legislation expressly providing that evidence of Aboriginal customary laws is admissible in such circumstances.[82] Existing defences do not however completely cover the situation where an act sanctioned by customary laws comes to be considered by the courts. The fact that a defendant was impelled to do the act in question under his or her customary laws does not as such constitute a defence. The Report considered whether a customary law defence exonerating the defendant from liability in such cases should be created. While such a defence would constitute the most direct way of dealing with such situations its introduction was rejected for several reasons. A customary law defence would involve endorsing tribal killings, and would deprive persons, including Aboriginal victims of offences, of legal protection. The defence therefore raised serious problems of equal protection under the law. The Commission concluded that evidence of Aboriginal customary laws can be taken into account sufficiently in the general criminal law through the exercise of sentencing and other procedural discretions, and that a customary law defence was neither necessary nor desirable.[83]

The Commission did however recommend the creation of a partial defence, similar to a defence of diminished responsibility, which would operate to reduce the level of liability in particular cases from murder to manslaughter. This defence was thought to have several advantages: it would not involve condoning or endorsing payback killings or woundings, nor would it deprive victims of legal protection or the right of redress. But it would nonetheless represent a direct acknowledgement of conflicts that can occur between the general legal system and Aboriginal customary laws, would allow the jury a role in mitigating the degree of culpability, and would operate as an adjunct to the sentencing discretion.[84]

[81] The cases are discussed in ALRC 31, vol 1 para 422–7, 430.
[82] Ibid, para 441.
[83] Ibid, para 442–50.
[84] Ibid, para 451–3.

5. Sentencing of Aboriginal Offenders

After examining numerous (mostly unreported) cases involving Aboriginal defendants, the Commission concluded that Aboriginal customary laws are already, and to a considerable extent, taken into account in sentencing. It is however necessary to strike the right balance between the requirement that the courts cannot incorporate or require traditional punishments or other customary law processes to occur as a condition to the release of offenders or in mitigation of punishment, and the need to take account of traditional Aboriginal dispute settlement procedures and customary laws. The Report drew on existing case law to establish certain principles which should guide the exercise of the sentencing discretion. For example, it was concluded that:

A. A defendant should not be sentenced to a longer term of imprisonment than would otherwise apply, merely to 'protect' the defendant from the application of customary laws including 'traditional punishment' (even if that punishment would or may be unlawful under the general law).

B. Similar principles apply to discretions with respect to bail. A court should not prevent a defendant from returning to the defendant's community (with the possibility or even likelihood that the defendant will face some form of traditional punishment) if the defendant applies for bail, and if the other conditions for release are met.

C. Aboriginal customary laws are a relevant factor in mitigation of sentence, both in cases where customary law processes have already occurred and where they are likely to occur in the future.

D. Aboriginal customary laws may also be relevant in aggravation of penalty, in some cases, but only within the generally applicable sentencing limits (what is commonly referred to as the 'tariff') applicable to the offence. Within certain limits the views of the local Aboriginal community about the seriousness of the offence and the offender are also relevant in sentencing. But the courts cannot disregard the values and views of the wider Australian community, which may have to be reflected in custodial or other sentences notwithstanding the mitigating force of Aboriginal customary laws or local community opinions.

E. Nor can the courts incorporate in sentencing orders Aboriginal customary law penalties or sanctions which are contrary to the general law.

F. In some circumstances, where the form of traditional settlement involved would not be illegal (e.g. community discussion and conciliation, supervision by parents or persons in loco parentis, exclusion from land) a court may incorporate such a proposal into its sentencing order (e.g. as a condition for conditional release or attached to a bond), provided that this is possible under the principles of the general law governing sentencing. Care is needed to ensure appropriate local consultation in making such orders, and flexibility in their formulation. In particular it is important that anyone into whose care the offender is to be entrusted, is an appropriate person, having regard to any applicable customary laws (e.g. is in a position of authority over the accused, and not subject to avoidance relationships), has been consulted and is prepared to undertake the responsibility.

G. An opportunity to attend a ceremony which is important both to the offender and the community may be a relevant factor to be taken into account on sentencing, especially where there is evidence that the ceremony and its associated incorporation within the life of the community may have a rehabilitative effect. However initiation or other ceremonial matters cannot and should not be incorporated in sentencing orders under the general law.[85]

6. Community Justice Mechanisms

The Commission's Terms of Reference specifically required it to consider to what extent Aboriginal communities should have the power to apply their customary law and practices in the punishment and rehabilitation of Aborigines. Requests, from the Yirrkala community in North Eastern Arnhem Land and from other Aboriginal communities in the Northern Territory, for assistance in handling law and order problems to a large extent prompted this aspect of the Terms of Reference. Previously a number of reports and inquiries had considered the question of Aboriginal involvement in law and order matters. While the question as framed in the Terms of Reference appeared to be limited to the empowering of Aboriginal communities to apply their customary laws, procedures and sanctions to offences defined by the general law, other matters such as the conferral of by-law making powers on Aboriginal communities, the establishment of Aboriginal courts and the use of Aboriginal personnel are relevant.

[85] Ibid, para 504–22.

Thus the Commission examined a broad range of issues, including the operation of Aboriginal courts in their various forms in Queensland, Western Australia and the Northern Territory.[86] It also considered the overseas experience, especially the village courts in Papua New Guinea and the United States Indian tribal courts.[87] In making its recommendations the Commission adopted certain criteria by which the suitability of local justice mechanisms for a particular community could be assessed. These included the acceptability of the proposals to the local community as a whole; the extent to which the Aboriginal courts or other official structures reinforce or detract from local authority structures; the administrative feasibility of the proposed scheme; and the need to maintain basic individual rights in the administration of justice.[88]

In many Aboriginal communities, unofficial methods of dispute resolution operate alongside the general legal system. While local resolution of disputes in these kinds of ways should be encouraged and supported, the Commission concluded that there should be no general scheme of Aboriginal courts established in Australia. Courts or similar bodies should only be set up in particular communities at the instigation of and after careful consideration by members of the community. Underlying this aspect of the Report was a certain scepticism at some of the existing 'Aboriginal local justice machinery', and at the claims for 'alternative dispute resolution machinery' made by some of its proponents.[89] But demands for such machinery seem unlikely to disappear, and the Report thus set out basic requirements for any special courts or similar official bodies, if these were to be continued or established in Aboriginal communities. These included the following:

A.   The Aboriginal group concerned should have power to draw up local by-laws, including by-laws incorporating or taking into account Aboriginal customs, rules and traditions.

B.   Appropriate safeguards need to be established to ensure that individual rights are protected, e.g. by way of appeal.

[86] Ibid, chapter 28–9.

[87] Ibid, chapter 30.

[88] Ibid, para 804–8.

[89] To some extent these demands reflect a trend towards establishing alternative methods of dispute resolution, e.g. in the form of community mediation centres. The Report surveyed the Australian and overseas experience in this field but concluded that systems so far established seemed to have limited relevance to Aboriginal people: ALRC 31, vol. 2 para 681–91.

C. By-laws should, in general, apply to all persons within the boundaries of the community.

D. If the court is to be run by local people, they should have power within broad limits to determine their own procedure, in accordance with what is seen to be procedurally fair by the community at large. In any event the community should have some voice in selecting the persons who will constitute the court, and appropriate training should be available to those selected.

E. In minor matters there need be no automatic right to legal counsel, though the defendant in such cases should have the right to have someone (e.g. a friend) speak on his or her behalf.

F. The court's powers should include powers of mediation and conciliation, as well as powers to order compensation to be made. A court which is receptive to the traditions, needs and views of the local people may be able to resolve some disputes before they escalate, perhaps avoiding more serious criminal charges.

G. There should be regular reviews of the operation of any such court, undertaken in conjunction with the local community.[90]

7. Traditional Hunting and Fishing Rights

One area of great significance to the recognition and acceptance of traditional ways of life and law in comparable countries has been the recognition of traditional rights to hunt, fish and forage. These have generated great concern and much litigation in countries such as New Zealand[91] and Canada.[92] The position in Australia, with certain exceptions, is less well developed, partly because of the absence of any treaty or constitutional guarantee of Aboriginal rights,[93] and of the lack of recognition so far of any common law on traditional rights in

---

[90] Ibid, para 880.

[91] See esp Waitangi Tribunal, *Report 22 on the Muriwhenua Fishing Claim* (Wellington, 1988); Law Commission, Preliminary Paper 9, *The Treaty of Waitangi and Maori Fisheries* (Wellington, 1989).

[92] Many of the aboriginal rights cases in Canada either focus on or involve hunting and fishing rights: see eg *R v Eninew* (1984) 10 DLR (4th) 137; *Sparrow v R* (1987) 36 DLR (4th) 246; *R v Agawa* [1988] 3 CNLR 55.

[93] It is perhaps significant that one of the most far-reaching cases of recognition of traditional rights to hunt or fish is in an international treaty, the Torres Strait Treaty of 1978, and that the method of internal implementation of the Treaty on the Australian side is open to criticism: see ALRC 31, vol 2 para 943–8.

these fields, although *Mabo v Queensland*,[94] where the claim is not merely to land rights but to rights over the sea, may change that.

In response to requests for recognition and protection of tradition-al hunting and fishing interests, and having regard to the extreme diversity of situations around Australia, the Report merely sought to spell out general principles by which an equitable balance could be struck between Aboriginal interests and other legitimate interests, including conservation, the effective management of natural resources, pastoral interests, commercial fishing and tourism. The multitude of conflicting interests, the need for unitary management of resources and the extensive activities at state and territory level combined led the Commission to conclude that it was not appropriate for comprehen-sive federal legislation to be enacted. Instead the Commission advo-cated a set of general principles to be adopted by the Commonwealth, State and Territory Governments.[95] In articulating these principles the Commission sought information from Aboriginal people, anthropo-logists, marine biologists, conservation and wildlife authorities and others to demonstrate the significance of bush and sea foods, in terms of diet and way of life and in terms of customary laws and practices. The provisions of some fifty federal, state and territory Acts and associated Regulations were examined, as well as their operation in practice. Recommendations were made along the following lines:

A.   The determination of whether any is traditional should focus on the purpose of the activity rather than the method, so that the incorporation of new materials and hunting methods would not as such prevent an activity being classed as 'traditional'.

B.   Traditional hunting should not be limited to indigenous species but may extend to introduced feral animals.

C.   Traditional hunting should not be limited to the taking of food for sustenance but may include ceremonial exchange within the community concerned and the satisfaction of kin obligations.

D.   Traditional hunting and fishing must be subject to legitimate conservation and other identifiable overriding interests. In particular in the case of rare and threatened species it may be necessary to prohibit hunting or fishing altogether or to restrict the numbers taken or the methods by which or the areas in which they are taken.

E.   As a matter of general principle Aboriginal traditional hunting

[94] (1988) 83 ALR 14.
[95] ALRC 31, vol. 2, para 970–3.

and fishing should take priority over non-traditional activities, including commercial and recreational activities, where the traditional activities are carried out for subsistence purposes.

F. Aborigines should be accorded access to traditional lands for the purposes of hunting, fishing and gathering, whether these lands are unalienated Crown lands or are subject to leasehold or other interests. In doing so it is necessary to take account of the interests of persons other than the Crown, whether by negotiated provisions or otherwise.

G. Areas of sea adjacent to Aboriginal land should be preserved for traditional fishing.

H. There is need for consultation with Aboriginal people affected before steps are taken to restrict traditional hunting and fishing, to ensure that the views of the Aborigines affected are taken into account in reaching any decision on the management of resources.[96]

8. *Other Issues*

It is not possible here to give a detailed account of all areas of the Commission's work. But one other area of the Commission's inquiry does need to be mentioned briefly, given its great practical importance. The Report includes a detailed discussion of questions of evidence and procedure as they affect traditional Aborigines coming before the courts. Aboriginal people experience particular difficulties in dealing with the police and in giving evidence in court. In this context, the Report proposes legislation to cover:

A. The procedures to be followed by the police when interrogating Aborigines and rules relating to the admissibility of evidence obtained during such interrogations.[97]

B. The right of certain Aborigines to make an unsworn statement.

C. The protection of secrecy and confidentiality of evidence given about Aboriginal customary laws.

D. Power in the courts to protect a witness against self-incrimination under Aboriginal customary laws.

E. The giving of group evidence by Aboriginal people and submissions from community members on sentencing.[98]

---

[96] Ibid, para 1001–3.

[97] See ibid, ch 22.

[98] Ibid, chapters 23, 25.

Amendments are also proposed to certain rules of evidence (for example, the hearsay, ultimate issue and expert evidence rules) where these present obstacles for the admission of evidence of Aboriginal customary laws.[99]

VI BEYOND RECOGNITION: ABORIGINAL PUBLIC LAW AND THE TREATY PROPOSAL

1. *Functionalism and Autonomy*

The Law Reform Commission's recommendations were framed from the point of view of the general legal system, with the aim of achieving justice in cases where Aboriginal customary laws are relevant. In seeking to achieve this aim the Commission adopted certain criteria. Proposals for the recognition of Aboriginal customary laws should be flexible enough to cope with change; should interfere as little as possible with the way Aborigines choose to live their lives, and should allow maximum control over their customary laws; should maintain basic rights, including basic individual rights, while avoiding, as far as possible, ethnocentric judgments about Aboriginal cultures and traditions.[100] Adherence to these principles underlay the Commission's rejection of codification and of direct enforcement of customary laws as principal forms of recognition. Instead the Commission adopted a piecemeal approach, which it described as 'a functional approach', to the issues.[101]

Implicit in this approach was a judgement that a single 'programme' is unlikely to be successful, even assuming that it would achieve sufficient political and public support to be adopted in the first place. But the approach also has its dangers, in particular the danger that decisions may be made about issues directly affecting Aboriginal people without their direct involvement in the decision-making. There is an important distinction to be made between the technical role of the Law Reform Commission, as a non-Aboriginal

[99] Ibid, para 677.

[100] ALRC 31, vol. 2, para 1033.

[101] Consistently with this avowed approach the Report argued that the Commission's proposals should be subject to continuing review, and that new demands for recognition of Aboriginal customary laws should also be dealt with on their merits: ibid, para 1032–4.

body advising government on changes to the general Australian law,[102] and the representative role of governments in making ultimate decisions on recommendations, decisions which (the Commission stressed)[103] would require further discussions with Aboriginal people affected by the recommendations, and an ultimate determination by government of the desirability of proceeding with them. It can be argued that ethnocentrism, or at least the preempting of Aboriginal views and options, can only be avoided if the recognition of Aboriginal customary laws is seen as part of a wider process of negotiations for autonomy conducted beween Aboriginal people and the government. The history of Australian indigenous policy to date has usually been regarded not as raising issues of local autonomy or self-determination so much as involving programmes for Aboriginal advancement, attempts at resolving problems of Aboriginal welfare and the delivery of services to Aboriginal people.

In Canada developments in the area of self-government suggest that the indigenous people of Canada no longer seek merely the provision of finance for particular projects or the provision of services from the Federal, Provincial or Territory Governments. Instead their claims are framed in terms of self-government or self-determination.[104] In Australia the language of 'self-government' is now quite widely used, but the perception of what is spoken about under that title is different, as the giving of a reference about Aboriginal customary laws to a statutory law reform body might suggest. The Commission's recommendations for the recognition of customary law were not part of a negotiated or independent settlement of Aboriginal claims for self-government or self-determination. Nor did the Commission claim to speak for Aboriginal people. The Commission's recommendations were presented as a response to a search for justice on the part

---

[102] There was a considerable degree of Aboriginal participation in various ways in the Commission's work (detailed in ALRC 31, vol. 1, chapter 2), but this was essentially 'consultation' rather than participation in decision-making.

[103] Ibid, para 1030–1.

[104] E.g. the Report of the House of Commons Special Committee on Indian Self Government; the introduction of the Indian Self Government Bill (Bill C 52 of 1984); the constitutional initiatives culminating in the Constitution Act 1982 (s 35), and the land claims experience (specially the James Bay and Northern Quebec Agreement, the Western Artic Claim and the Inuvialuit Final Agreement Entitlement). See also B. W. Morse, 'The Resolution of Land Claims' in B. W. Morse (ed) *Aboriginal Peoples and the Law: Metis and Inuit Rights in Canada* (Ottawa: Carleton University Press, 1985), 617.

of the legal system in its dealing with Aboriginal people. Their validity from that point of view is a matter for others to determine. But the adoption—necessary for the legitimacy of the Commission's task—of that point of view itself places the Report in a subordinate position, in terms of the basic issues of the relationship between Aboriginal people and other Australians.

2. *The Aboriginal Legal Heritage and Aboriginal Public Law*[105]

Thus it is necessary to return to those more basic issues. And the question that must be asked is why, compared with other similar countries, there has been so little in the way of a resolution, or even a framework for resolution of those basic issues, despite attempts at resolving them in various ways at various times? Why, in other words, is there such an apparent discrepancy between the protestations and the performance? Why is the preambular acknowledgement, for example in the Aboriginal and Torres Strait Islander Commission Bill 1988 (Cth), of the need for recognition not translated into law? Why is there such strong resistance to the recognition of the Aboriginal heritage,[106] so much so that to use the term 'Aboriginal legal heritage' sounds like a contradiction: heritage, yes; legal, no. I argue that the failure of recognition, historically and currently, is the result of a failure to recognize, on its own terms, the existence and characteristics of Aboriginal public law. This continuing failure—which contrasts with the position in the United States, Canada and New Zealand—needs first to be addressed, in particular because the failure to address that issue is likely to render the proposed Aboriginal treaty a mere exercise in public relations.

Throughout the last 200 years (as least after the 'frontier' had passed), there has been some willingness, and at some times, a considerable willingness, to recognize Aboriginality: examples of this have already been given. But the key feature has been the unwillingness to do so on the basis that many of the elements requiring recog-

---

[105] This section is a revised version of J. Crawford, 'The Aboriginal Legal Heritage: Aboriginal Public Law and the Treaty Proposal' (1988) 62 *Law Institute Journal* 1174.

[106] Throughout this paper I will concentrate on issues of Aboriginal heritage and recognition. In principle the recognition of the position of the Torres Strait Islanders, though it has its own chronological and legislative history, is not different. See ALRC 31, vol. 1, para 96.

nition fell within the domain of Aboriginal public law. For example, the apparent failure of the common law to recognize Aboriginal title to land was based on the absence of a recognizable form of land tenure.[107] By seeking an analogy within the field of private law, the point was ignored that for most purposes land-holding in Aboriginal communities is a public law institution.[108] Legislation recognizing traditional land rights has for the most part abandoned private law analogies and adopted a public and collective form of land-holding (e.g. the Pitjantjatjara Land Rights Act 1981 (SA). Where it has not done so (as with the identification of 'traditional owners' under the Aboriginal Land Rights (Northern Territory) Act 1976 (Cth)), the partial individualization of title or beneficial interest involved or implied has tended to cause distortion and, in some cases, injustice.[109]

3. An Aboriginal Treaty?

The absence of any treaties or agreements between Aboriginal groups and the British government was, as we have seen, the basis of the '1788 settlement'. A strongly held Aboriginal view has been that that very fact made the 1788 settlement a physical one only. In any event, over the last ten years there have been calls both from Aboriginal and non-Aboriginal sources for some comprehensive settlement of issues between Aboriginal and non-Aboriginal Australians, and these have usually taken the form of calls for a 'treaty'.[110] This development has

[107] *Milirrpum v Nabalco Pty Ltd* (1971) 17 FLR 141.

[108] The position is different in the Torres Strait Islands, where there is an elaborate individual tenure system both for land and sea. See B. Hocking, 'Torres Strait Islanders and Australian Law' (1987) 2 *Law & Anthropology* 359, 362–3.

[109] This is even more clearly true of the attempt to 'individualize' communal land holdings in Queensland under the Land Act (Aboriginal and Islander Land Grants) Amendment Act 1982 (Qld).

[110] On the Aboriginal Treaty Committee's work see S. Harris, *'It's Coming Yet . . .' An Aboriginal Treaty within Australia Between Australians* (Aboriginal Treaty Committee, Canberra, 1979); J. Wright, *We Call for a Treaty* (Collins, Sydney, 1985); J. Wright, 'What Became of that Treaty?' (1988/1) *Aust Ab Studies* 40. For the views of an Aboriginal leader who participated in the Barunga Statement see G. Yunupingu, 'An Aboriginal Treaty: Constitutional Guarantees' (1988) 7 *Social Alternatives* 25. See also Senate Standing Committee on Constitutional and Legal Affairs, *Two Hundred Years Later . . . Report on the Feasibility of a Compact, or 'Makarrata', between the Commonwealth and Aboriginal People* (AGPS, Canberra, 1983); B.D. Bailey, 'A Compact (Makarrata) with Australia's Aboriginals and Torres Strait Islanders. A Study of Treaty and Agree-

been spurred to some extent at least by developments at the international level and in other countries. At the international level the Working Group on Indigenous Populations has held a series of meetings attended by indigenous peoples' organizations, and has achieved at least some measure of visibility at the international level for these issues.[111] In both New Zealand and Canada, treaty rights have come to have much greater significance, in Canada through the affirmation in the Constitution Act 1982 (UK) of existing and future treaty rights,[112] and in New Zealand through the work of the Waitangi Tribunal under the Treaty of Waitangi Act 1975 (NZ).[113]

Despite many unresolved questions about the nature of a treaty, its terminology and its legal or other effect, the 'treaty settlement' issue was recognized as a national political question by the Prime Minister in what is known as the 'Barunga Statement', a statement of intent made by the Government on 12 June 1988 after discussions with Aboriginal representatives at Barunga in the Northern Territory. The Barunga Statement consists of two separate documents, one a statement made by a number of Aboriginal leaders on behalf of 'the indigenous owners and occupiers of Australia', the second a statement signed by the Prime Minister and by three Aboriginal leaders, which can best be described as a statement of intent. The Aboriginal statement is set out as an Appendix to this paper. The Prime Minister's statement, which was much shorter, reads as follows:

1. The government affirms that it is committed to work for a negotiated Treaty with Aboriginal people.
2. The government sees the next step as Aborigines deciding what they believe should be in the Treaty.
3. The government will provide the necessary support for Aboriginal people to carry out their own consultations and negotiations: this could include the

---

ment-making involving the Indian Nations of the United States of America: Lessons for Australia' (mimeo, Aboriginal Development Commission, Canberra, May 1988).

[111] M. Davies, 'International Developments in Indigenous Rights' (1987) 2 *Law and Anthropology* 29, 30–3; G. Nettheim,' "Peoples and Populations": Indigenous Peoples and the Rights of Peoples' in J. Crawford (ed), *The Rights of Peoples* (1988) 107, 114–15.

[112] Constitution Act 1982 (Can) ss25, 35.

[113] On the Treaty of Waitangi 1840 see also *New Zealand Maori Council v Attorney-General* (1987) 6 NZAR 353; Waitangi Tribunal, *Report on the Orakei Claim* (Wellington, 1987) 128–31. See also C. Orange, *The Treaty of Waitangi* (Wellington: Allen & Unwin, 1987).

formation of a committee of seven senior Aborigines to oversee the process and to call an Australia-wide meeting or Convention.

4. When the Aborigines present their proposals the government stands ready to negotiate about them.

5. The government hopes that these negotiations can commence before the end of 1988 and will lead to an agreed Treaty in the life of this Parliament.

Cynics might regard the statement merely as a form of words designed to compensate for the lack of substantial legislative progress in Aboriginal affairs under the Hawke Government. Neither the proposed national land rights legislation,[114] nor legislation recognizing Aboriginal customary laws (as recommended by the Law Reform Commission) has been introduced. In the bicentennial year, with considerable international attention focused on Australia, the pressures for some form of verbal reconciliation must have been real. But it is proper to assume that the statement is not merely an exercise of verbal bicentennialism, to be conveniently forgotten by the end of the year. Furthermore, the reality of the issue was underlined when the Leader of the Opposition's statement rejecting any notion of a treaty was itself severely criticized from within the Liberal Party, leading to an apparent modification in the Opposition's position.[115]

Nonetheless, the notion of an Aboriginal treaty raises fundamental questions not merely about the content of the document but about the assumptions which underlie it. No doubt the content of the document, and whether the parties to it in the end wish to conclude an agreement on the terms available, are essentially political and evaluative questions about which lawyers have no special authority to speak. But to the extent that the treaty will be a legal or para-legal document (if not having legal consequences itself, at least capable of generating them through subsequent action or implementation), the assumptions underlying the treaty are themselves legal or para-legal and do require examination.

An extended discussion of these assumptions is beyond the scope of this paper, but I would argue that, again, the failure so far to address the assumptions behind the treaty proposal is another example of the failure to treat Aboriginal issues as public law issues of a bilateral kind—in short, the failure to recognize an Aboriginal public law—and

---

[114] For the federal Government's abandonment of the proposed legislation see *Parl Debs (H of R)* 18 March 1986, 1475.

[115] See Sydney Morning Herald 13 June 1988, 1; 14 June 1988, 1, 12; 15 June 1988, 3; 17 June 1988, 13.

that this failure threatens to void the treaty proposal before negotiations have seriously commenced.

4. An Aboriginal Treaty: A Matter of Presentation or Representation?

Broadly, one can say that there are three categories of agreement (although this is obviously only one classification amongst many possible). The first category is that of agreements binding under a particular national legal system (i.e. contracts). The second is that of agreements binding under international law (i.e. treaties).[116] The third is that of agreements between two or more parties, whatever their status, which are not intended to be effective as such under any particular legal system, but which record an understanding or arrangement between the parties which, at the time of making it, they propose to honour or perform, but which they do not intend to subject to a particular legal system (national or international) as an agreement binding under that system.

Whatever the differences between them, contracts and treaties have a number of common features. In both cases the parties to the agreement must be recognized by the legal system in question as existing entities (e.g. not unincorporated associations or 'non-persons') and as having the capacity to enter into the agreement in question (not *ultra vires*, not illegitimately affecting the rights or obligations of others, etc). In both cases there is a clear understanding of who is committed by the agreement (in principle the parties themselves, and any person who they have the capacity to bind under the legal system in question, including any persons bound by virtue of their agency).

The third category of 'innominate agreements' (as I will call them) is a broad and residual one. It includes informal or domestic arrangements between individuals, but also non-binding agreements between the governments in a federation,[117] or between national governments

[116] The term treaty is used generically: in fact international treaties have all sorts of titles (convenant, character, agreement, exchange of letters, etc). See Vienna Convention on the Law of Treaties 1969, 1155 UNTS 331, Art 1(a).

[117] *South Australia v Commonwealth* (1962) 108 CLR 130. There is a difficulty here in that governments within a federation do not have the choice which national governments have of contracting under a non-national system of law (unless the view is accepted that international law binds governments within a federation *pro tanto*). Thus non-binding arrangements perform at the federal level many of the functions which treaties perform internationally.

at the international level.[118] I stress that I am not concerned here with the problem of illusory or apparent agreements, i.e. agreements which, though made in the form of contracts or treaties, on examination involve no obligation whatever. Innominate agreements, like contracts and treaties, may be illusory, but that is because the parties have chosen to adopt the form of agreement while withholding its substance. On the other hand the category of innominate agreements may, and often does, include agreements of the utmost seriousness, involving obligations which the parties intend to comply with and which have a clear and definable content.

Given the diversity of this third category, it would be wrong to try to force it into any straitjacket of rules or concepts, the more so since by definition the category is concerned with agreements which are not legally enforceable as such (although they may well constitute factual elements giving rise to rights or obligations under rules other than the law of contracts or treaties).[119] There is also the possibility that the parties to innominate arrangements will bring to them many of the assumptions which they make or employ in entering into legally binding agreements, and this is the more likely where the agreement in question is of a serious or substantial character. These assumptions include a clear understanding of each other's identity and capacities, including the entities or range of persons which the other party has the capacity to commit by its agreement. In cases where a party does not have the capacity or authority to commit others, the agreement is if it is anything at all, an agreement to use one's best efforts to encourage or persuade others to the relevant conduct or point of view.

Although assumptions applicable to legally binding instruments may be carried over in the making of innominate agreements, the key difference between them is that innominate agreements are not made against the background of a particular legal system. The answers which a developed legal system provides to such questions as 'who is bound by this agreement?' or 'who is the contracting party and what authority does that party have to act?' may well be lacking. The chances that the parties to the agreement will misunderstand each other's intentions, by bringing to the negotiation different assumptions as to the nature and status of the agreement, are greatly increased.

118 O. Schachter, 'The Twilight Existence of Non-Binding International Agreements' (1977), 71 *AJIL* 296.
119 Cf. *South Australia v Commonwealth* (1962) 108 CLR 130, 141 (Dixon CJ).

In the case of the proposed Aboriginal treaty there are already clear indications of such misunderstandings. One Aboriginal leader, at least, envisages 'a treaty which is recognized by International Convention . . . [and which] must lead to full legal recognition of our rights in the Australian Constitution'.[120] It is unlikely that the Prime Minister, his co-signatory of the Barunga Statement, would share this view of the proposed treaty.

It should be remembered that, whatever the status of Indian treaties or agreements in Canada and the United States (and in both countries they have some considerable status as public law instruments), those treaties were, for the most part at least, made at the local or regional level with recognized public law entities. In neither country would it be seriously suggested that a single national agreement could commit individual tribes or communities to specific obligations.[121] In New Zealand the Treaty of Waitangi 1840 was negotiated with a confederation of tribes and separately ratified or acceded to by different groups, but the Maori public law background to the Treaty was and is very different than would have been the case in Australia.

To summarize, there are serious and substantial unresolved questions about the basis of the proposed treaty, and about the foundations, as a matter of Aboriginal public law, of Aboriginal participation in it. It is not enough simply to ask unspecified Aboriginal leaders to negotiate among themselves in order to present a proposal, when the assumptions underlying that proposal are not merely not shared, but have not even been articulated. In the absence of any such articulation, it would not be surprising to find the proposed Aboriginal and Torres Strait Islander Commission pressed into service in the intensely difficult task of gaining Aboriginal agreement to a proposal. But that Commission is intended primarily as an advisory governmental body and to perform Departmental functions, a surrogate Department of Aboriginal Affairs. To give it the task of negotiating a treaty with the government would be a serious category mistake. Before steps are

---

[120] Yunupingu (1987), 26.

[121] There was an (unsuccessful) attempt in Canada to negotiate an 'umbrella' agreement on self-government to be included in the Constitution. With the failure to reach agreement on these issues at the 1987 First Ministers' Conference the focus has shifted back to settlements at local or regional level. See e.g. B Schwartz, *First Principles, Second Thoughts: Aboriginal Peoples, Constitutional Reform and Canadian Statecraft* (1986); B Slattery, 'Understanding Aboriginal Rights' (1987), 66 *Can BR* 727; Crawford (1988), 62–7.

taken to commence the substantive process of discussion on a treaty, the Government should make efforts to clarify from its perspective the assumptions that are to underlie any treaty eventually agreed on. Otherwise the treaty process risks being little more than an extended negotiation of Aboriginal groups with themselves, followed by a dialogue based on conflicting assumptions in which presentation will prevail over representation. The issues at stake are too important for that.

APPENDIX: THE BARUNGA STATEMENT

We, the indigenous owners and occupiers of Australia, call on the Australian Government and people to recognise our rights:
- To self-determination and self-management, including the freedom to pursue our own economic, social, religious and cultural development;
- To permanent control and enjoyment of our ancestral lands;
- To compensation for the loss of use of our lands, there having been no extinction of original title;
- To protection of and control of access to our sacred sites, sacred objects, artefacts, designs, knowledge and works of art;
- To the return of the remains of our ancestors for burial in accordance with our traditions.
- To respect for and promotion of our Aboriginal identity, including the cultural, linguistic, religious and historical aspects, and including the right to be educated in our own languages and in our own culture and history;
- In accordance with the Universal Declaration of Human Rights, the International Convenant on Economic, Social and Cultural Rights, the International Convenant on Civil and Political Rights, and the International Convention on the Elimination of All Forms of Racial Discrimination, rights to life, liberty, security of person, food, clothing, housing, medical care, education and employment opportunities, necessary social services and other basic rights.

We call on the Commonwealth to pass laws providing:
- A national elected Aboriginal and Islander organisation to oversee Aboriginal and Islander affairs;
- A national system of land rights;
- A police and justice system which recognises our customary

laws and frees us from discrimination and any activity which may threaten our identity or security, interfere with our freedom of expression or association, or otherwise prevent our full enjoyment and exercise of universally recognized human rights and fundamental freedoms.

We call on the Australian Government to support Aborigines in the development of an international declaration of principles for indigenous rights, leading to an international convenant.

And we call on the Commonwealth Parliament to negotiate with us a Treaty recognising our prior ownership, continued occupation and sovereignty and affirming our human rights and freedoms.

Barunga, 12 June 1988

Representing Aboriginal Women: Who Speaks for Whom?*

DIANE BELL

A child is gang raped. Is our understanding framed by the experience of race, age and kinship-relationship to the rapists' educational, employment and residential status? If the victim is Aboriginal, all are relevant, but as a general rule we pay little attention to gender. At one level it is non-problematic: it is after all women who are raped.[1] Feminists have engaged in major public-awareness campaigns, undertaken painstaking research, and published widely to bring to the threshold of public consciousness the aetiology of rape.[2] But the awkward relationship of Aboriginal women to the women's movement, the pursuit of Aboriginal self-determination as a distinctive category of rights, and the transformation of gender relations through the colonial and into the neo-colonial period have created a domain in which race is privileged over gender.[3] Speculation regarding intra-racial violence is deemed 'ideologically incorrect' by influential (but certainly not disinterested) parties, and a researcher who ventures into this fraught arena is likely to be 'white listed'. In short there is no discursive space in which to confront intra-racial rape.[4]

* I appreciate the assistance of Jocelynne Scutt, Jane Lloyd, and Renate Klein as I prepared this article.

[1] I do not deny that men are raped but I know of no example of a pack of women raping a young man. When we consider why this is improbable, we begin to unravel rape as a gendered crime. The asymmetry of the power relations which characterize rape are a microcosm of those which underwrite the wider society. (See Catherine A. Mackinnon, *Towards a Feminist Theory of State* (Cambridge: Harvard University Press, 1989), p. 243.

[2] Hester Eisenstein, *Contemporary Feminist Thought* (Sydney: Allen & Unwin, 1984), pp. 27–34.

[3] Diane Bell, 'Considering Gender: Are Human Rights for Women Too? An Australian Study', in A.A. An Na'in (ed.), *Human Rights in Cross-cultural Perspectives* (Philadelphia: University of Pennsylvania Press, 1992), pp. 329–62.

[4] In the 'Violence Today Series', published by the Australian Institute of Criminology, regarding the work of the National Committee on Violence there is no specific reference to women: National Committee on Violence, 'Racist

My title, 'Representing Aboriginal Women', is deliberately ambiguous. At law we have the notion of 'representation' in that the accused has the right to legal representation. Aboriginal Legal Aid is an important instrument of the policy of self-determination, but existing services reflect the interests of their founders and the conditions of their founding. They flourish or flounder in political climates over which they have little control. In defining 'Aboriginal' interests, it is often those of men which are on the political agenda and which are most energetically addressed.[5] The victim and accused cannot be represented by the same organization: that would constitute a conflict of interests. So I ask: who speaks for the interests of Aboriginal women?

In anthropology we seek ways of representing the experience of the peoples with whom we work. When we delve into the ethnographies and classical anthropological analyses which have informed policy and are the stuff of customary law defences, we find it is the interests of men which are foremost.[6] Of gender relations, and particularly of those within Aboriginal culture(s), we find the ideology of male dominance represented as an enduring, non-negotiable and timeless reality.[7] Here I would ask: how have anthropological representations of Aboriginal women and their relationship to men framed the practice of law and formulation of policy?

Violence', *Violence Today*, no. 8, 1959. Women are subsumed under domestic violence and no doubt make an appearance under other rubrics (e.g. ethnic background). The other current enquiry is one on Racial Violence and it is focussing on violence against, not violence within, racial groups. Atkinson suggests we acknowledge first the systematic nature of the violence: it is grounded in the experience of colonization, internalized and transmitted from one generation to the next so that a high level of 'domestic violence' has become normative. She cites an anecdote from an unpublished paper by Pat O'Shane who records the answer of a ten-year-old boy to 'What do you want to do when you grow up?' as 'Rape women'. Judy Atkinson, 'Violence in Aboriginal Australia', draft manuscript for National Committee on Violence in Australia.

[5] Diane Bell and Pam Ditton, *Law: The Old and the New Aboriginal History* (Canberra, 1980).

[6] See D. Bell, 'Aboriginal Women and Customary Law', in B.W. Morse and G.R. Woodman (eds.), *Indigenous Law and the State* (Holland, Foris, 1987), pp. 297–314.

[7] D. Bell, *Daughters of the Dreaming* (Melbourne: Allen and Unwin, 1983).

Contextualizing Issues of Race and Gender

The general condition of Aboriginal society is discussed by Colin Tatz in this volume. In the more densely settled south within Australia, Aborigines have been in contact with the colonisers for two centuries, but in the Northern Territory, where the population is 126,000, of whom about 22 per cent are Aboriginal, first contact is in the living memory of the older generation. Here Aboriginal people live on the fringes of the towns in town camps (some with a lease, some not); on cattle stations where the work is seasonal (sometimes they have title to a residential excision from the pastoral lease but mostly not); on old reserves now held as Aboriginal land under the *Aboriginal Land Rights (Northern Territory) Act, 1976)*. Some have secured title to traditional land by claim to 'Vacant Crown Land' brought under this Act; some have secured title to pastoral leases bought for them in earlier times but very few live *in* the towns; very, very few have professional jobs. The nature of interactions with the non-Aboriginal population varies across Australia, but for the most part Aborigines are positioned on the margins of Australian society. They endure appalling health, are inadequately sheltered, underemployed and educated, over-imprisoned and institutionalized.

In terms of addressing the special needs of women it has for the most part been where there has been collaboration between Aboriginal and non-Aboriginal women that substantial reports and recommendations addressing women's concerns have resulted. The reference on the question of recognition of customary law brought together Aboriginal women, lay and expert, non-Aboriginal women lawyers, anthropologists and bureaucrats. Working with a lawyer from Aboriginal Legal Aid and in consultation with Aboriginal women in Central Australia, we prepared a submission which addressed the issues those women thought critical.[8] On the subjects of marriage, divorce and social security payments women had a significantly different set of interests from those that their menfolk had articulated,[9] and intervention was

---

[8] See Bell and Ditton; Australian Law Reform Commission, *The Recognition of Aboriginal Customary Law* (Canberra: Australian Government Publishing Service, 1986), paras 11, 17 and 18.

[9] See D. Bell, 'Desert Politics: Choices in the "Marriage Market"', in M. Etienne and M. Leacock (eds.), *Women and Colonization: Anthropological Perspectives* (New York: Praeger, 1980), pp. 239–69.

necessary to create fora within which women's concerns might be raised.[10]

The inappropriate and inadequate nature of consultation with Aboriginal women has been demonstrated repeatedly. In the 1970s we reported that the Department of Aboriginal Affairs (DAA) had no women field officers or community advisers and officials openly acknowledged their ignorance of women's business.[11] But no policies or structures to facilitate women's views imprinted on the political agenda made it into policy. Staff ceilings, the lack of suitably trained senior Aboriginal women and the inappropriateness of non-Aboriginal women playing a role in Aboriginal affairs were cited as impediments. These arguments came from the bureaucracy and senior (non-Aboriginal) males in the DAA who saw no contradiction in their collaboration with Aboriginal men in the bureaucracy. These relations of power were not subject to scrutiny.

The Aboriginal Task Force, which was able to address many of the issues raised in the 70s and early 80s, is another example of a co-operative endeavour.[12] Marion Sawer gives a fine-grained history of the thwarting by ministers, bureaucrats and various organizations that routinely frustrated plans to establish a body to deal with the issues women were raising.[13] The Task Force would almost certainly have continued to languish had it not been for persistent lobbying by the Office of Status of Women, and the determination of key Aboriginal women in Canberra to see established a forum in which women's views might be made known. Here it is important to underline that it is a very different matter to work with Aboriginal women in terms of getting their interests on the political and legal agenda, on the one hand, and, on the other, to assume that because women (black and white) are vulnerable, Aboriginal women will wish to establish the same priorities or pursue the same strategies as non-Aboriginal women. However, the failure to implement the major recommendations of the Law Reform Commission and those of the Task Force indicates that sound research, responsible consultation and co-opera-

[10] See Bell and Ditton.
[11] Ibid., pp. 6–7.
[12] Phylis Daylight and M. Johnstone, *Women's Business: Report of the Aboriginal Women's Task Force* (Canberra: Australian Government Publishing Service, 1986).
[13] Marion Sawer, *Sisters in Suits: Women and Public Policy in Australia* (Sydney: Allen & Unwin, 1990), pp. 164–71.

tion are not sufficient: Aborigines, and Aboriginal women in particular, need a voice in the policy and executive arms of government.

To be Aboriginal puts one at risk in any encounter with the legal system; to be a woman exacerbates the situation. Gender and race intersect in ways which permit the abuse of Aboriginal women to be rendered almost invisible. Violence against women accounts for more deaths than those in custody, but it is under-reported and does not have the political profile of matters investigated by the Royal Commission.[14] Many of the worst abuses occur in areas of women's experience which are deemed personal or culturally sensitive—areas where the state is loath to interfere. Add race to gender and you have created an extremely marginal voice. Who will/can/may/should/ought to speak of violence against Aboriginal women? Aborigines? Men or women? The law? The state? The social scientist?

Until recently this topic was taboo for those who advocate self-determination and self-management; it places radical feminists at loggerheads with both socialist feminists and the broad left; it generates charges of giving sexism priority over racism from black activists, of opportunistic whites creating new divisions within the Aboriginal community. Two recent cases, plus conversations and correspondence with Aboriginal women, convinced me that my own continuing silence was tantamount to complicity. One case involved the prosecution of an Aboriginal male in a rape case where the defence relied on 'customary considerations'. The other case, not yet reported, and most unlikely to ever come to court, involved the gang rape by Aboriginal youths of Aboriginal girls who were 'surprised' in the act of house breaking. There are dedicated Aboriginal women working to bring the dimensions of violence against women to the attention of enquiries such as the National Committee on Violence in Australia, but they find that they are not always consulted when the Commission visits their communities.[15] Self-determination provides a rationale for not dealing with intra-community problems.

I am suggesting that the most productive framing of the issue of

[14] Judy Atkinson, an Aboriginal woman working within her own community, found that the National Committee on Violence 'had not thought to talk to us' (*Personal Communication*). Her submission in 1989 represents an important attempt to create the discursive space within which violence may be addressed.

[15] See J. Atkinson, 'Violence in Aboriginal Australia: Colonisation and Gender', Parts I and II, in *The Aboriginal and Islander Health Worker*, vol. 14, nos. 2 & 3; and Pat O'Shane, 'Report on Aboriginal Women and Domestic Violence', unpublished ms, 1988.

intra-racial violence is to see the experience of Aboriginal women as refracted through the twin prisms of gender and race. It is at the points of intersection of these two analytical beams of light that we can begin to interrogate the representations of Aboriginal women. This necessarily takes us into matters which are not generated by Aborigines per se but requires an analysis of the ways in which Aboriginal societies are enmeshed within the wider Australian polity. On the one hand, Aboriginal women are disadvantaged in their dealings with the state: as women they constitute a different kind of citizen from men, or, put in another way, women experience the state differently from men and enjoy different access to its resources.[16] On the other hand, as colonized persons, their traditional modes of decision-making, exercise and legitimation of power and authority, economic independence and politico-religious standing have been fundamentally transformed.[17] As women they are disproportionately vulnerable to violence, and the law has only recently acknowledged women's right to self determination as persons, i.e. a woman's body is not to be treated as property, nor does marriage entail automatic sexual access.[18] As Aborigines they are marginal to the political process, and it is only within the context of special policies such as self-determination and self-management that they may raise an agenda of rights as an Aboriginal concern. But the self-determination movements of indigenous peoples necessarily privilege race over gender. Their survival as a people is paramount and gender inequalities within embattled minority groups (traditional or recent in origin) are not up for scrutiny. The consequences for persons who are both Aboriginal and female are significant. The impaired enjoyment of their human rights and constraints in the pursuit of their rights within neo-colonial modes of the delivery of justice are two obvious examples.[19]

At the international level, yet again, we can see that indigenous women constitute a special case, and it is one that allows them to slip through the cracks between the apparently inclusive language of hu-

[16] I am relying on a broad, inclusive definition of the state, i.e. law, bureaucracy and enforcement agencies (local, provincial and national), all of which act in the name of the state. The different impact on men and women is apparent in tax structures and child care, in family law reform and the feminization of poverty, in reproductive rights and public health funding.

[17] See Bell, *Daughters of the Dreaming.*

[18] See Jocelyn Scutt, *Even in the Best Homes: Violence in the Family* (Ringwood: Penguin, 1983).

[19] See Bell, 'Considering Gender..', pp. 343ff.

man rights instruments at the international level, and the sensitivity to local conditions in implementation by particular nations.[20] To locate the instruments which purport to afford indigenous women protection, we must explore the interweavings of the Conventions dealing with the Elimination of Sex Discrimination, Race Discrimination and the Protection of Indigenous Peoples. However, despite the numerous clauses in these conventions, Aboriginal women are still vulnerable. There is much celebration of the soundness of government policy in the *Report of Australia* regarding the operation of the Convention on the Elimination of all Discrimination Against Women, but it does not sit well with the reality of most Aboriginal women's lives. Indeed most are unaware of the bright picture painted of their futures in these international documents.[21] They would, I think, be quick to hold the government up to ridicule if, like their menfolk, they had access to the arena in which policy is forged and enjoyed long established links with the national media. To understand the failure of international regimes to enfranchise women we need to look at the ways in which seemingly enlightened provisions are interpreted, and by whom they are implemented. At the domestic level, we see that reforms which accompany self-determination policies may also create barriers for women's participation in the emerging political structures which purport to represent indigenes.[22] It is this phenomenon I am styling 'neo-colonial'.

Empirical research regarding the inter-relations of race and gender —not to mention class, generation, sexual preference—is difficult to undertake. I am only too aware of the multiple hurdles put in the path of a female social scientist who takes women's rights seriously.[23] With reference to the land claim process, I have detailed this dilemma and noted the persuasive nature of the opposition to acknowledging

[20] Ibid., pp. 345–9.

[21] Commonwealth of Australia, *Report of Australia*, Convention on the Elimination of all Discrimination against Women, June 1986, Department of Prime Minister and Cabinet, Office of Status of Women (Canberra: Australian Government Publishing Service, 1986), pp. 6–7.

[22] See Bell and Ditton, pp. 11–5; D.Bell, 'Aboriginal Women and Land: Learning from the Northern Territory Experience', *Anthropological Forum*, vol. 5, no. 3, pp. 353–63.

[23] See D.Bell, 'Exercising Discretion: Sentencing Aborigines for Murder in Norther Territory', in Morse and Woodman, ibid., pp. 367–94; and D. Bell, 'A Reply to the "Politics of Representation"', *Anthropological Forum*, vol. 6, no. 2, pp. 158–65.

women's land rights: at the level of research, evidence, report, implementation, there are procedural, ethical, resource, political and cultural constraints.[24] There has, I think, been a significant shift in the way in which women's rights in land are now treated. Indeed, in the revised legislation regarding protection of sacred sites in the Northern Territory, the composition of the authority which has oversight of the legislation now is fifty per cent female. That is quite an advance on the situation of a decade earlier when it was commonplace to assume that only men could speak of sacred matters and that women did not have sacred sites.[25]

The victories are few and fragile: significant resistance is still evident. This resistance will, I think, assume a different shape in the 1990s from the 70s and 80s and the forces shaping the forum in which the rights of indigenes and women are negotiated will not be of their making. With the shrinking of the welfare state and 'economic rationalism' displacing social justice and equity programmes, the rolling back of civil liberties is hardly noted. The 'social contract of the multicultural welfare state is ruptured',[26] and in hard times the shrinking quotient of tolerance for the cost of programmes that promote and support difference will be far-reaching on indigenes and women. The events of 1984–5 are a good example of the way in which public opinion can be manipulated and misrepresented to legitimize non-action by governments in terms of implementing their platform on Aborigines.[27] While there is heavy reliance on state support (especially fiscal and legislative), the advances of both women and indigenes will continue to be fragile, always in jeopardy of being hijacked or defused

[24] Ibid.

[25] See D. Bell, 'Sacred Sites: The Politics of Protection', in Nicolas Peterson and M. Langton (eds.), *Aborigines and Land Rights* (Canberra, Australian Institute of Aboriginal Studies, 1983), pp. 278–93.

[26] Douglas Daniels, 'The Coming Crisis in the Aboriginal Land Rights Movement: From Colonialism to Neo-colonialism to Renaissance', *Native Studies Review*, vol. 2, no. 2, p. 112.

[27] A campaign by the Western Australian Chamber of Mines convinced the WA Labour Government that land rights legislation was electoral suicide. They rejected the recommendations of Mr Paul Seaman QC, who had conducted a state backed enquiry, and further were able to convince the Federal Labour Government to step back from its commitment to national land rights legislation. Prime Minister Hawke cited the lack of community support for Aboriginal land rights as critical. The findings of the Australian National Opinion Poll which ran counter to this view were not made public until the next year. See Eve Fesl and A. Markus, 'Land Rights: the Wrong Numbers', *Australian Society*, 3 May 1986.

by the state: be it by way of incorporation or creation of a special status. The shift to the Right, which is currently apparent in the USA (especially in the recent decisions of the Supreme Court regarding women's rights and civil liberties), will no doubt influence Australian social reform and fuel the resistance to acknowledging women's rights.[28] Already we have media coverage of the so called 'post-feminist' era.[29]

In certain areas Aboriginal women are now in a position to pursue their issues through existing organizations, and may be able to withstand the onslaught of the Right on the projects with which they are involved. One of the major objections raised by the Department of Aboriginal Affairs and Ministers for Aboriginal Affairs against women's representative bodies was that there were no Aboriginal women of sufficiently senior standing in the bureaucracy to staff such organizations, and it wouldn't be democratic to insist that women be elected to positions within existing ones. (A variation on this theme was that there were not enough women willing or competent to be elected to these positions.) Women have shown themselves to be both capable and eager to take on positions of responsibility, but the same barriers which inhibit white women from holding political office also apply to Aboriginal women.

Women's predominance in organizations which concern education, health and shelter, are all, we might observe, essential but non-valorized occupations. Citing a Commonwealth Department of Education survey of 1981, Sawer points out that 63.5 per cent in receipt of Abstudy grants for tertiary education were women.[30] She goes on to enumerate the positions of responsibility held by Aboriginal women.[31]

---

[28] See *Webster v Reproductive Health Services*, U.S. Supreme Court case (July 3 1989).

[29] See Susan Faludi, *Backlash: The Undeclared War Against Women* (New York: Crown Publishers, 1992).

[30] Ibid., p. 162.

[31] In 1985 the National Convenor, Secretary and Chairperson of NAIHO (National Aboriginal and Islander Health Organization) were all women. Ten of the 20 members of the National Aboriginal Educational Committee and 6 of the 7 members of the National Committee of the National Secretariat for Aboriginal and Islander Childcare were women: Daylight and Johnstone, p. 24. A number of Aboriginal women have held important administrative posts. They are now well positioned in terms of education and service and they are free of the taint of corruption which has damaged the careers of male colleagues. But, from a cynical perspective, it may also be that Aboriginal Affairs are no longer a priority for the

Despite these obvious signs of competence, talent and commitment to the furthering of 'Aboriginal interests', these women do not have a significant profile in policy formation and governmental decision-making. These matters continue to be negotiated between white male politicians/bureaucrats/experts and their Aboriginal male counterparts.

THE CHANGING NATURE OF GENDER RELATIONS IN ABORIGINAL SOCIETY

In writing of the scope of women's relationship to land; the wide ranging changes in marriage, ceremonial practice and gender relations wrought by the colonization of desert lands; the political problems women confront in their dealings with established bureaucracies and the more recently formed Aboriginal organizations, I have argued that the cash economy has offered little to women.[32] In traditional society women had a power base underwritten by their economic independence as the producers of up to 80 per cent of the reliable diet and their ritual autonomy as the direct descendants of the formative era, the *jukurrpa* (dreamtime). Relations between men and women were characterized by a high degree of flexibility wherein each had sanctions that could curb the political ambitions of the other: each had room to manoeuvre; women could withdraw to the *jilimi* (the single women's camp) without suffering economic or social deprivation. For women, this residential structure and their separation from men in daily and ritual activity was a source of strength. However, with the loss of traditional lands and the concomitant skewing of the checks and balances of customary law, women found their power base undermined. They became dependants, members of households which in the view of the major service organizations have a male breadwinner.

Initial contact with those who 'opened' the territory to white settlement was made to males. For women to join in these meetings of males would have been inappropriate, even dangerous. It was men, through their contacts with the representatives of dominant society, who were groomed as community spokespersons. It is their power

---

government, and one way of reducing the standing of representative organizations is to support women candidates.

[32] See, for example, D. Bell, 'The Politics of Separation', in Marilyn Strathern (ed.), *Dealing with Inequality* (Cambridge: Cambridge University Press, 1988).

base which has been legitimized and deemed the negotiating forum, not women's. The subtleties of traditional gender arrangements have been conveniently ignored and, in the shift from reliance on a hunter-gatherer mode of subsistence to welfare colonialism, men have found a more accommodating niche in the male-oriented political institutions of colonial and neo-colonial society than have women. With men recognized as authoritative representatives of communities, women, for the most part, were locked out of the new decision-making arenas. In short, they have been forced to rely on others to represent their interests, be it with respect to land, law reform or resource development. Their political autonomy has been eroded and their economic independence undermined. Aboriginal women now share the marginality of women in Australian society and the powerlessness of an economic underclass.

THE RESOUNDING SILENCE OF SOCIAL SCIENTISTS

Feminists seeking to reform the law have had to confront 'the woman as property' concept. Socio-biologists gave us 'man the aggressor' and all but rendered violence against women 'natural'.[33] In the general anthropological literature on sex relations in Aboriginal society, it is commonplace to find references which evoke images of women as property: man the hunter partakes of sex after a successful kill; an aggrieved man may be appeased by access to the wife of the offender; sexual licence at times of male ritual gives men access to otherwise prohibited women; a young girl is made a woman by multiple penetrations by men other than her husband.[34] None of these practices appear to require a woman's consent, but, by adopting the stance of the cultural relativist, anthropologists have been able to write of these abuses in 'non-judgemental' terms.

Those anthropologists and historians who have been prepared to address difficult cross-cultural questions have done so within very narrow confines. It has been acceptable to write of the rape of Aboriginal women by white men—in fact for some it was obligatory. But I would suggest that this and characterizations of women as

[33] See Robin Fox and L. Tiger, *The Imperial Animal* (New York: Holt Rinehart and Wilson, 1971).
[34] See for example, Ronald M. and C.H. Berndt, *The World of the First Australians* (Sydney: Ure Smith, 1964).

prostitutes and men as pimps is simplistic and does not accord with women's accounts of first contacts. To be sure, inter-racial sexual relations mirrored the brutality of frontier society, but to argue that 'all black woman/white man unions were transient, demeaning and violent', or that women were 'sexual objects' which their men traded with white men for tobacco, sugar and tea denies women agency.[35] Women's sexuality, I have argued, was theirs to bestow as they wished, but their forthright behaviour was misread and interpreted as promiscuous.[36] In my reading of the evidence I would allow that both women and men politicked with sex, but that women quickly were out- manoeuvred and that it is this state of affairs that became the received wisdom of sex relations on the frontier. I have suggested that because women's relations with white men threatened Aboriginal men by making new resources available to women and thus diminishing the male powerbase, men responded by attempting to bring the white intruders within their scheme of male-to-male reciprocity. When that strategy failed, violence ensued. It was not so much a matter of men seeking to protect their womenfolk from abuse as men attempting to maintain their negotiating position *vis-a-vis* their women.

It has also been acceptable to write of the loss of self esteem that this theft and abuse of women constituted for Aboriginal men. Women, it was argued, enjoyed access to the hearth and home of the white man while her Aboriginal mate was demeaned, denied his woman by another male with more resources. Of course, these analyses fail to acknowledge that women are not objects, passed from man to man; that they did make choices, but that they did so on the basis of incomplete information regarding male-female relations in white so- ciety. As to their privileged access to the dwellings of the conqueror, their contact with the home and hearth rendered them familiar with domestic routines, but little else.[37] Their standing within restructured extended family-groupings may have been enhanced cross-culturally, but they were firmly locked out of emerging relations and institutions where political decisions are made.

When we look to the legal arena we find that these male- oriented representations of women resonate cross-culturally for lawyers, and once again male/male constructs predominate. In giving evidence in cases where an Aboriginal man is accused of rape, defence counsel

[35] Bell, *Daughters of the Dreaming*, p. 98.
[36] Ibid., pp. 100–1.
[37] See Berndt and Berndt, ibid., pp. 441–2.

have consistently argued that rape is a light matter in Aboriginal society. Male anthropologists give expert evidence to the effect that 'pack rape' was a traditional punishment for a woman who transgressed, for example, by stumbling, be it unwittingly, on a male secret ceremony, or seeing a male secret object. However, few cases that come to the attention of non-Aboriginal authorities are of this nature. Most entail conflicts/tensions/disputes engendered by non-religious, indeed profane considerations such as money, alcohol and relationships with persons outside the kin system. Many of the violent encounters leave women maimed and destitute of assistance they could have expected from supportive kin who are often intimidated or restrained from coming to the victim's defence.'[38]

Those brutal rapes and assaults that find their way into the Supreme Court in the Northern Territory, with notable exceptions, have not drawn sympathy from judges for rapists. Rather the record shows that superior court judges have been anxious to afford protection to Aboriginal women. Mr Justice Muirhead in sentencing in *R.v. Pat Edwards*, said:

Sitting as a judge of this court, I am not just prepared to regard assaults of Aboriginal women as a lesser evil to assaults committed on other Australian women, because of customary practices or lifestyles, or because of what at times appears to be the almost hopeless tolerance or acceptance by some Aboriginal people to drunken assaults of this nature . . . [39]

It helps to give these statements some context. The behaviour of Aboriginal women certainly 'shocked' many early observers. Their language was direct and graphic, their interest in matters sexual not disguised, their enjoyment obvious, their approaches unmistakable. The writing of anthropologists exudes the same mistrust and fear of women's sexuality manifest in white society; a questioning of their previous sexual activity; their inability to say no and mean it. But they did and could say no. If a woman was not interested in sex, then she merely stayed in the *jilimi*, the single women's camp, an area taboo to men; she did not walk alone. If a man attempted to force himself, there were always plenty of able-bodied women to deter him; there was the woman's family to deal with if it was a wife; there were ritual

[38] See D.Bell, 'Intra-racial Rape Revisited: On Forging a Feminist Future Beyond Factions and Frightening Politics', *Women's Studies International Forum*, vol. 14, no. 5.

[39] SCC, nos. 155 and 156 of 1981, 16 October 1981, unreported.

deterrents employed by women to ensure that the activities of over-active men and rapists were curtailed. Enraged female kin wielding digging sticks (today metal crowbars) could leave a rapist incapable of offending again. The force of these strategies, preventive and defensive, has been reduced as women have lost their power to participate in decision-making arenas and become dependants, be it on the state, a husband or father. Again, women's ability to pursue remedies is constrained. I am not minimizing the ethical and human-rights issues here, merely pointing out the asymmetry in perceptions of who needs protecting from whom.

FEMINISTS AND THE AETIOLOGY OF RAPE

In 1971 Susan Griffin wrote of rape as 'the all American crime'.[40] In 1974, *Against Rape*, Andra Medea and Kathleen Thompson's survival manual for women was published.[41] But it was undoubtedly Susan Brownmiller's *Against Our Will: Men, Women and Rape* (1975) which placed rape on the feminist agenda internationally.[42] Echoing the theme of earlier analysts, she wrote, 'rape is nothing more or less than a conscious process of intimidation by which *all men* keep *all women* in a state of fear.[43] For Brownmiller the 'ideology of rape' was the superstructure built on the biological base (humans unlike other primates could mate 365 days of the year). In her analysis, it was not necessary for all men to rape to sustain the ideology. Having identified 'the secret of patriarchy', the task was then to demystify rape.

Radical feminists such as Susan Brownmiller and Susan Griffin accorded gender primacy in their analyses of women's oppression. In patriarchal relations they located the forces which sustain and perpetuate the social conditions under which the culture of rape is produced and reproduced. Claiming it was class not gender that accounts for women's oppression, socialist feminists charged Brownmiller with false universalism. More recently Catharine MacKinnon has argued

[40] Susan Griffin, 'Rape: The All-American Crime', in J. Freeman (ed.), *Women: A Feminist Perspective* (Stanford: Mayfield), pp. 3–22.

[41] Andra Medea and K.Thompson, *Against Rape* (New York: Frarrar, Straus and Giroux, 1974).

[42] Susan Brownmiller, *Against our Will: Men, Women and Rape* (Penguin, 1975), p. 15.

[43] Ibid., p. 15.

that taking rape from the realm of the 'sexual' and placing it within the realm of the 'violent' removes force, as part of heterosexual relations, from the legal definitions of rape.[44] This she takes to be a retrograde step and one that mystifies the power relations between men and women. How, MacKinnon asks, may one distinguish sex as intercourse from sex as rape, under the conditions of male dominance?[45] There is also the question of the relationship between pornography and violence, which Topsy Nelson[46] and other researchers have raised,[47] and which Catharine MacKinnon and Andrea Dworkin locate as central to any analysis of rape.[48]

What I want to emphasize here is the consequences for strategy these theoretical differences represent. Radical feminists are more inclined to promote women's-only services, refuges and crisis centres, than are those who look to transforming the relations of production. To black women neither the radical nor socialist feminists were sufficiently cognizant of race and racism. Angela Davis in *Women, Race and Class* charged Brownmiller with having 'resuscitated the old racist myth of the Black rapists' and 'the image of the Black woman as chronically promiscuous.'[49] Having demonstrated the vulnerability of black women, Davis says little of rape within black society, and when she admits the possibility, she subsumes the black man under the working-class rubric. Davis writes:

Working class men, whatever their colour, can be motivated to rape by the belief that their maleness accords them the privilege to dominate women ....When working class men accept the invitation to rape extended by the ideology of male supremacy, they are accepting a bribe, an illusory compensation for their powerlessness.[50]

In terms of the conceptual framing of rape as a feminist issue, I think there is more to be done in exploring the differences in emphasis between Brownmiller and MacKinnon on dominance and sexuality;[51]

---

[44] Op. cit., pp. 135, 173, 211.

[45] Ibid., p. 174.

[46] D. Bell and T.N. Nelson, 'Speaking About Rape is Everyone's Business', *Women's Studies International Forum*, vol. 12, no. 4, p. 413.

[47] See Atkinson, 1989, pp. 11–4.

[48] Catharine A. MacKinnon, *Feminism Unmodified: Discourses on Life and Law* (Cambridge: Harvard University Press), pp. 127–33.

[49] (New York: Random House, 1981), pp. 178ff.

[50] Ibid., p. 200.

[51] *Feminism Unmodified*, p. 92; *Towards a Feminist Theory*, pp. 56, 173, 178.

and the insistence of Angela Davis[52] and bell hooks[53] that Brownmiller take into account the legacy of slavery and the 'systematic devaluation of black womanhood'.[54] If these writers are read chronologically an argument can be made for seeing their theorizing as deepening our appreciations of rape, in terms of race, culture, class, power, history and so on, rather than casting their critiques as oppositional.

Until quite recently the ramifications of women's 'powerlessness' has been the stuff of novels rather than scholarly debate. Hester Eisenstein, for instance, in *Contemporary Feminist Thought*, quotes from *Vida* by Marge Piercy in which the heroine challenges her sister with: 'I hope you don't go around saying in your women's group that a Black man raped you. . . . He was probably terribly oppressed.'[55] The white woman working in black organizations charged with being racist, not 'cool' if she won't sleep with black men, has remained part of personal experience. Aickin-Rothschild was prepared to draw on these experiences in the writing of 'White women volunteers in their freedom summers: their life and work in a movement for social change', but this is an exception.[56]

Eisenstein traces the implications, both theoretical and practical, of Brownmiller's thesis; she touches on the critique of black women but does not venture into the Australian field. This is not surprising: the literature is sparse. Neither the fear of the black male rapist evident in the lynching mobs described so dramatically by Davis, nor the sexual anxiety manifest in the White Women's Protection Ordinance of 1926 in colonial Papua, are part of the Australian experience.[57] Why it is that the Aboriginal male did not constitute the 'Black Peril' of the islands or the 'Black Buck' of the American south is another question worthy of future consideration.

It seems, once again, that it is in fiction that the power relations of rape are explored. When Alice Walker wrote *The Color Purple* the responses polarized along the following lines: she had no right to say such things, a traitor to her own; it was a relief to be able to confront these issues; it was only fiction.[58] The film didn't help the discussion

52 Op.cit, pp. 178ff.
53 Bell Hooks, *Ain't I a Woman: Black Women and Feminism* (Boston: South End Press, 1981), pp. 51–9.
54 Ibid., p. 60.
55 Op.cit., p. 33.
56 M. Aickin-Rothschild, *Feminist Studies*, vol. 5, no. 3, pp. 466–95.
57 See A. Inglis, *Not a White Woman Safe* (Canberra: ANU Press, 1974).
58 London: The Women's Press, 1983.

as it obliterated the nature of the relationship between the two women. There is, it seems, a taboo beyond rape.

In Australia the best known research on rape is that of Jocelynne Scutt. In her study of domestic violence in *Even in the Best of Homes*, Scutt successfully debunks the rape stranger paradigm.[59] In unmasking the rapists, we discover not a deranged individual but someone known to the victim, often in a position of trust. Further, rape cuts across class lines.[60] Scutt provides a critique of the power relations within the family and between men and women. Women victims become the accused, the shamed, the guilty, and this she suggests is in the interests of men. Mapping the extent of rape entailed the 'coming out' of rape victims, and it was feminist consciousness raising which provided a forum where experience was shared and catalogued, where the blaming of the victim was exposed.

Men, Scutt argues, are well served by the silence on rape. Women had not 'asked for it': they had been treated as male property and the law protected property. The origins of rape laws Scutt terms akin to those of robbery and theft. They involve 'the taking, without consent, of goods from the lawful owner with the felonious intent of converting them to the taker's use . . . ravishment of another's property', the other being male.[61] In Scutt's analysis, rape is the ultimate act of sexism, of domination, of objectification, of powerlessness, of owning nothing, not even one's body.[62]

The practical strategies—reforming the law to include marital rape, sensitizing law-enforcement agencies to the needs of the raped, educating women regarding their rights, establishing rape crisis centres and counselling services—for a time moved in tandem with the theoretical explorations of Brownmiller's hypothesis. Of necessity Brownmiller had raised more questions than she answered but, as Eisenstein points out, it was feminists, not criminologists, who held up to scrutiny the aetiology of rape, who exposed the deep mistrust of women and fear of their sexuality that was embedded in the law. Speaking of rape in Aboriginal society, however, raises a host of cross-cultural questions that too often have obscured the substantive issue: Aboriginal women and girls are being brutalized and two of the

---

[59] Op.cit. p. 69.
[60] Ibid., p. 70.
[61] Ibid., p. 141.
[62] Ibid., p. 172.

most obvious advocacy groups, feminists and Aboriginal Legal Aid, are reluctant to engage.[63]

ABORIGINAL WOMEN'S PERSPECTIVES

Many of the specific concerns of the women's movement have been irrelevant, and in some cases antithetical, to the needs of Aboriginal women. Aboriginal women in remote areas of Australia have had little opportunity to speculate on their lives as Aborigines and Australians from a feminist perspective. The daily round of survival and the concerns of kin and country dominate. It has been Aboriginal women in the bureaucracy, Aboriginal organizations and the academy who have issued challenges to the women's movement. In 1975 certain prominent Aboriginal women decided not to participate in the activities of International Women's Year and their reasons demonstrate the nature of their alienation from the movement, but also underscore their need for representation as women. The issues they identified as important—high infant-mortality rates, forced sterilization, poor maternal health—stood in stark contrast to those concerning white women—child care and reproductive rights. Accused of being racist, divisive and irrelevant, the members of the movement responded by attempting to include Aboriginal women within existing structures, only to find themselves rebuffed.[64]

Until the pioneering research of Judy Atkinson[65] and Audrey Bolger,[66] the literature on rape rarely recorded the views of Aboriginal women. The exceptions are the comments from urban activists and they have been advanced in the context of their comments on the white women's movement. In the seventies, black women activists such as

[63] See Bell, 'A Reply to the "Politics of Representation"'; Bell, 'Intra-Racial Rape Revisited'; and Bell, 'Letter to the Editor'.

[64] At the Women and Labour Conference in Brisbane, 1984, Aboriginal women activists insisted that only Aboriginal women could speak about their experience and demanded the removal of papers written by White women. There are multiple narratives of this encounter: see Huggins *et al.*, 'Letter to the Editor', *Women's Studies International Forum*, vol. 14, no. 5, 1991; and Bell in *Women's Studies International Forum*, 1991.

[65] See footnote 14.

[66] Audrey Bolger, *Aboriginal Women and Violence: A Report for the Criminal Research Council and the Northern Territory Commissioner of Police* (Darwin, A.N.U. North Australia Research Unit, 1990).

Bobbi Sykes tended to argue that the experience of Aboriginal women was not addressed by feminists. Accusing white women of not paying attention to the facts of rape of Aboriginal women and not challenging the myth of the over-sexed woman, Sykes cited a leaflet put together by the Canberra-based Joint Women's Action: 'If you are black and a woman and in your early teens, you have probably been raped at least once. If you are black and a woman and in your early twenties, then you have been raped two or three times'.[67] Sykes of course is speaking of rape by White men, like policemen who abused positions of trust. Although she is intent on castigating feminists, the proposition that it is rape, literal or metaphorical, which is the shared experience of black women, allied her analysis with Brownmiller in a way she probably did not intend. While stating she has never been involved in the women's movement, Sykes questions whether her contacts with feminists are patronising of her or them, but she is certain about the power differentials: she is the helped and they the helper. The women's movement concerns a power struggle within white society and she has little faith that the changes will 'trickle down' to black women.[68] Similarly, Eve Fesl has little time for white women's politics.[69] She argues that outsiders should not interfere in Aboriginal matters, but berates those women who prevented both black and white from using the women's refuge in Alice Springs. By way of contrast, Lilla Watson writing of her experience of growing up black and female, acknowledges the specificity of her experience, but writes: 'There was and is no question that I support in strongest terms women's liberation, whether it be for black or white women.'[70]

By the eighties, Aboriginal women working in bureaucracies, such as Pat Eatock, Marcia Langton and Elizabeth Williams, began to acknowledge the myriad positions adopted by feminists. Responses became more pragmatic. Eatock tells how her daughter, pack-raped at 17 learnt to read through her contact with women and their writing

---

[67] Bobbi Sykes, 'Black Women in Australia: A History', in Jan Mercer (ed.), *The Other Half* (Penguin, 1975), p. 319.

[68] Bobbi Sykes in R.Rowland (ed.), *Women Who Do and Women Who Don't Join the Women's Movement* (Melbourne: Routledge and Kegan Paul, 1984), pp. 66–7.

[69] Eve Fesl, in Rowland (ed.), ibid., pp. 109–15.

[70] Lilla Watson, 'Sister, Black is the Colour of My Soul', in Jocelynne Scutt (ed.), *Different Lives* (Melbourne: Penguin, 1987), p. 51.

in the Crisis Centre.[71] Williams explores some of the subtleties of her involvement with the women's movement which she depicts as being of mutual advantage. 'I appreciated the support of feminists . . . [and] it helps . . . to have me to promote to the position.'[72]

Marcia Langton, as research director of Central Land Council, Alice Springs, daily confronted racism and sexism.[73] She writes of women as the inclusive 'we', of the enduring nature of their lack of power in Australian society, and makes a case for giving 'credit where credit is due'; but it is the Aboriginal agenda for self-determination for which she seeks support from feminists. She looks to fora, such as the Broad Left Conference and the Socialist Feminist Conference; while these are appropriate arenas in which to pursue Aboriginal political demands, they are not ones in which the issue of rape is given priority.

Vivian Bligh,[74] Pat O'Shane[75] and Judy Atkinson[76] have directly addressed, in published form, the needs of women who have been raped. Bligh set out to establish why Aboriginal women were not using the Rape Crisis Centre (Adelaide). Her initial attempts to contact women through existing organizations proved fruitless. It was through direct exchanges that information was forthcoming. Her findings confirm those of Scutt's. Bligh found that the incidence of rape was high; that the age of victims ranged widely (4 to 58); that both white and black men were involved but women talked more readily about the former than the latter; that a pack rape by seven men had occurred; that there was an extremely low level of reporting to non-Aboriginal agencies, including women's organizations.[77] The one girl who had sought help from an Aboriginal organization found that their informal procedures did not give confidentiality a high priority. Her story was

[71] Pat Eatock, 'There's a Snake in My Caravan', in Scutt (ed.), *Different Lives*, p. 28.

[72] Elizabeth Williams, 'Aboriginal First, Woman Second', in *Different Lives*, p. 72.

[73] Marcia Langton, 'The Getting of Power', *Australian Feminist Review*, no. 6; Langton, 'Feminism: What Do Aboriginal Women Gain?', *Broadside*, National Federation of Australian Women's Newsletter, December 1989.

[74] Vivian Bligh, 'Study into the Needs of Aboriginal Women Who Have Been Raped or Sexually Assaulted', in F. Gale (ed.), *We Are Bosses Ourselves* (Canberra: AIAS, 1983), pp. 100–4.

[75] Op.cit.

[76] Op.cit.

[77] Ibid., p. 101.

soon common knowledge in the entire Aboriginal community. Few cases resulted in convictions. Alcohol played an important part for most of the women, and there was little sympathy for Aboriginal women raped when drunk. Most thought an Aboriginal worker at the Centre would alleviate the situation of having no-one to offer sympathy to rape victims. In the discussion following Bligh's paper, further experience of rape was recorded. It was said that in the case where the seven men were accused of a pack rape, they had the 'best top-notch lawyers in the state'. They got off but the woman had then to leave the city and 'go back home', where the stigma is still at the back of her mind.[78]

Bligh's findings are supported by the frighteningly brutal and brutalizing cases of violence cited by Judy Atkinson. With reference to her work in Northern Queensland, she notes that rape 'is a daily occurrence but 88 per cent go unreported, only pack rapes are reported', but even these may go unreported.[79] Under-reporting is a problem in all rape cases, but there are particular reasons why, in small kin-based communities, crimes go unreported. Victims fear retribution, learn to protect themselves from further abuse by keeping quiet, and the power to intimidate is known to boys and men; police are not always interested and may even be part of the abuse patterns; people are reluctant to see offenders go to jails in distant cities.[80] Separate statistics are not kept for Aborigines, and deaths due to violence are often subsumed under natural causes such as pneumonia.[81] Violence is not always prosecuted.

Pat O'Shane traces the way violence has become so routine that it has been incorporated into a range of acceptable affective responses: 'I gave her a bit of 'Black fellow's love last night' (i.e. bashing) is a 'common expression around here'. Young women, having known nothing else, ask: 'It's part of being black isn't it?'[82] This echoes the comment recorded by Atkinson that 'women do not think their bloke loves them unless he belts them'.[83] The folk explanations include accounts of men treating women as property, of appalling living conditions, alienation, jealousy and despair: 'The men feel rejected

[78] Ibid., pp. 102–3.
[79] *Violence in Aboriginal Australia*, p. 11.
[80] Ibid., p. 21; O'Shane, p. 112.
[81] Ibid., p. 100.
[82] Ibid., p. 102ff.
[83] Atkinson, p. 7.

and depressed and they take it out on their women', O'Shane was told.[84] Again I ask: who speaks of the interests of women? To whom do they turn for a model which will give them a future? Male oppression has a model which addresses loss of self-esteem, but we cannot condone violence because women are the only category left through whom men may be made to feel better about themselves. What we have here is a crisis in masculinity and it is here that we need acknowledgement from men that they are responsible for the carnage. 'Aggression against those with less power', MacKinnon argues, 'is experienced as sexual pleasure, an entitlement of masculinity', and that is what is revealed in the expectation of Aboriginal women, that being bashed is being loved.[85] Subordination has been sexualized and sexuality is private: feminist researchers beware.

Although the literature is sparse and much is anecdotal, it does appear that many of the features of rape documented by Scutt are relevant to Aboriginal women's experience. What is not present in Australia (unlike the USA) is participation in the theoretical debates. I would suggest that the initial rejection by influential articulate Aboriginal women of white feminist analyses of gender relations reflects the influence of the socialist left on Aboriginal activists, and it has taken time for Aboriginal women to recognize that there are many types of feminism, some of which may be more relevant than others. The underlying dilemma in the theoretical positioning of the topic of rape which polarized feminists in the seventies is now entering the writing of Aboriginal women. What is probably most tragic is that the provision of safe places to which women might retreat, places which provide an alternative to a violent relationship, have a traditional analogue in the *jijimi*, the single women's camp.[86] It was in this area, separate from the main camp, that ritually important women lived, that others gathered to socialize during the day. It was where the secret women's objects were stored. Above all in terms of safety, it was an area where men feared to tread.

Two Recent Cases

The first case was brought before the Supreme Court of the Northern

[84] O'Shane, pp. 104–5.
[85] *Feminism Unmodified*, pp. 6–7.
[86] See Bell, *The Politics of Separation*.

Territory: Dennis Narjic of Port Keats, Northern Territory, pleaded guilty to four counts of rape of one Aboriginal girl and to two of another in 1986. Defence counsel indicated that the pre-sentence report would canvass the customary elements of the case, viz. the 'tribal elders indicated that there is little likelihood of any payback'. Mr Justice Maurice asked:

Are you telling me it's normal behaviour to have forcible sexual intercourse with your wife's younger sisters . . . never once have I had a glimmer that it's a normal part of cultural life for Aboriginal people to treat women in this way . . . for the kind of sadistic behaviour involved . . . [87]

Recognizing that this may be an important man and that the court would no doubt have the views of the 'tribal elders', Mr Justice Maurice asked, 'Why should we only hear from men?' In his view there was a need for somebody with 'fair dinkum anthropological qualifications' and knowledge of the Port Keats area to do an assessment.[88]

If we're going to go into this question of what's culturally acceptable behaviour, why shouldn't we hear from some female, some female leaders of the female community of Port Keats? Why should it be men who are the arbiters of what's acceptable conduct according to the social and cultural values of Port Keats?

But, protested the defence, we may not be able to get women to speak. 'It's just that historically no one ever asks them', the judge observed.[89] The charges took a considerable time to be resolved and by the time the rulings were made another judge was hearing the case. Ultimately the judge's requirement that he hear from a woman of women's interests was neglected. Because of a procedural error in the lower court, the charges were dropped and it was unreasonable to expect that two young girls could continue to testify against a violent adult male.[90]

[87] Transcript of R v Denis Narjic, SCC nos. 108, 109, 110 of 1988 (facts and submissions), pp. 17–8.

[88] Ibid., p. 24.

[89] Ibid., p. 25. Maurice, J., as the Aboriginal Land Commissioner, heard extensive evidence on customary law regarding land from Aboriginal women and feminist anthropologists. Prior to that he had represented the Aboriginal claimants in the Daly River claim and tendered a submission (restricted to women) which I had prepared on behalf of the women claimants: see Bell, 'Aboriginal Women and Land'.

[90] In the lower court the proceedings had been by way of hand-up of documents,

The second case involves allegations of a gang rape in a town apartment during the absence of the resident. What happened is not clear. The woman returned to find her place had been turned over, that food and clothes were missing but that her books were untouched. She was undertaking research in this area and, after cleaning up the worst of the mess, washing the clothes strewn about, and after reporting the break-in to the police, sought information from local Aboriginal women. The girls, it appears, had entered by forcing a bathroom window, and had spent some time in the flat before being surprised by a gang of youths. The extent of the violence which then ensued is not fully known.

Reasons for the incident range from simple theft explained by 'if you work with blacks you invite theft', through dismissing the blood stains as menstrual, to brutal gang rape. If the latter is true why have the girls, their mothers, and local organizations not acted? One story runs that the girls have been intimidated: told that if they report the rape, they will be charged with theft, much easier to prove than rape. Another says women in this town are expected to tolerate such behaviour from black men and that is even what white women do. There is a white woman living in one of the town camps who invites multiple partners and violence nightly. There is a local woman doctor who is sympathetic to the needs of Aboriginal women but there are a number of obstacles to be overcome in consulting with her. Some of the local organizations do have Aboriginal women on their representative boards, but the most influential of these resists acting on information from white women. Indeed, the attempts of the woman to approach the community health centre, to ensure the girl had medical assistance, ended in her being refused entry to the premises. It now appears the girls have venereal diseases which could have been treated had they received medical attention promptly.

Recently there have been a number of violent attacks on Aboriginal women. It is hard to be certain that the number is increasing but on the basis of a range of evidence it is my opinion that it is, and evidence from Atkinson and Bolger supports this. I have been in

---

and thus the accused had not been cross-examined. Although all the officers of the court were at pains to point out that, regardless of what Narjic thought, he could not use his wife and her sisters as he wished and then claim it was a domestic matter in which no one had the right to interfere, the message received in the remote community where the crime had occurred was that 'might was right': see Bell, 'Intra-Racial Rape Revisited'.

communities when rapes have occurred and seen the way in which various persons react. Aboriginal women have been prepared to administer their own justice, i.e. women's customary law, to the rapists. But, the local police, assisted by local Aboriginal police aids, have placed the accused into protective custody. In this way women's power to respond has been thwarted. The adversarial mode is, in fact, ill suited to dealing with disputes in Aboriginal societies. Traditionally the emphasis would have been on the resolution of the conflict and restoration of harmony, not the apportioning of blame and punishment inflicted by a third party.

The existing Aboriginal organizations are heavily male oriented and, in the case of rape, legal aid is usually for the defence. In this regard it is interesting to note that where Aboriginal women as victims have sought compensation under the Northern Territory Crimes Compensation Act, they have done so through private solicitors, not Aboriginal Legal Aid. The limit of claim is $15,000, but it is being used by Aboriginal women. Now it appears Aboriginal women victims may have found an ally in the Crown. As I have already pointed out, the organization which in theory should be their ally, Aboriginal Legal Aid, is usually appearing for the accused. The reasons for the eagerness of the Crown to prosecute must, however, give cause for concern. It is rare indeed that Aboriginal women victims get as far as a court hearing and each case counts. But are prosecutors acting out of compassion for the woman? And does it matter? There has been a strong push in the Northern Territory administration to 'stamp out this customary law nonsense'.[91]

While I would certainly agree that the male orientation of legal services needs to be redressed, I would not wish to see this critically important organization dismantled. While I have seen numerous abuses of customary law by defence lawyers, I would not wish to trammel the tentative steps evident in a number of jurisdictions to take account of the existence of Aboriginal law. Given that Aboriginal Legal Aid is usually defending the Aboriginal man, they would not be calling anthropological evidence hostile to their case. In the absence of research with Aboriginal women on the issue of rape in Aboriginal communities, very partial representations of Aboriginal women are presented in the courts, and the precedents established are not ones which empower women.

[91] ABC Radio, Midday News, 23 March 1988.

In one case in the Magistrates court in Tennant Creek, working with a woman lawyer, I was able to explain the role of Aboriginal women in resolving marital disputes.[92] Several important local women gave evidence as to the existence and content of the relevant Warumungu law. They gave evidence as a group, a practice pioneered with great success in the land claim forum. (It is improper to speak of grave matters without an appropriate 'witness' present to verify your pronouncement and no one person can speak on all matters.) I gave evidence as to the kinship aspects—the magistrate was accommodating but admitted that the finer points of 'cross' and 'parallel' cousins needed some clarification—and the principles which might be distilled from the evidence. I had discussed the issue at some length with the women and had ascertained that which was for public presentation and that which was restricted to women. This, of course, raises tantalizing questions regarding confidentiality and privilege.

In most cases involving claims to customary law, a little intelligent anthropological research in the community can clarify that which is 'tradition' and that which is local politics. I would put the statement that it is 'customary to beat women' in the latter category. It is a reflection of the history of the particular settlement and the 'representative structures' through which tradition is articulated. As the judge has already noted, mostly we don't know because we haven't asked women. Of course finding ways of bringing women's evidence to court raises many problems but here again the experience of land claims is most helpful.

WHITHER?

Not to engage with the questions that intra-racial rape cases raise is to leave rape shrouded in myth, the subject of spirited legal defences based on spurious anthropological evidence by lawyers or the stuff of repressive law and order campaigns. Although it could be said this is 'not my business', it is very much my business. I hold to the position that, no matter how unpleasant, feminist social scientists do have a responsibility to identify and analyze those factors which render women vulnerable to violence. The fact that this is happening to women of another ethnic or racial group cannot be a reason for

[92] See 'Intra-Racial Rape Revisited'.

ignoring the abuse; it is cause to look carefully to the cultural context, to heed the silences. Thus, my tack in addressing this extremely sensitive topic has been to look again at the received wisdom regarding intra-racial rape; to interrogate anew the theoretical and practical pronouncements and, hopefully, in so doing, to map out terrain on which informed discussion may occur; to locate issues of gender and race within a wider perspective, one outside the experience of any individual; to provide an analysis of social change; to formulate a critique for the wider society.

We have put behind us, I hope, the theories of innate male aggression and rape. In the 1970s buying into the 'man-the-hunter' argument with male colleagues was a matter of being dismissed as a hopeless case of 'women's libbers' bias. Speaking in feminist gatherings one was caught in a pincer movement between the radical and the socialist feminists and confronted by accusations of racism by Aboriginal activists. However, the topic is now in the open in Aboriginal communities; some twenty years have elapsed since the first women's shelters, and Aboriginal women are now seeking theirs. The stories are beginning to be told. Feminists need to reopen the theoretical debates, to create the space within which a critique of rape may emerge, to allow the courts to set aside their assumptions regarding the abuse of Aboriginal women, to give protection to the women. Aboriginal women are beginning to speak out. The courts are prepared to listen.

Of course the problems confronting Aboriginal women rape victims are shared by other women, and one hopes ultimately all citizens will acknowledge that this is not an issue that only women must address: it is after all men who rape. The broader human rights issues have been recognized. Peter Bush, a police surgeon of twenty-eight years' experience, writes of the crime which concerns us all, of the law of rape 'not made with a woman's pride or passion in mind', of the willingness of defence counsel to exploit the situation so the victim is on trial, and of police procedures.[93] These insights now need to illuminate the rape of Aboriginal women by Aboriginal men.

Understanding the representations of Aboriginal women in both scholarly and popular fora requires sensitivity to cultural difference, the historical specificity of particular groups, the interaction of social, political and economic factors. This is critical in finding answers. The

[93] Peter Bush, *Rape in Australia: An Appraisal of Attitudes, Victims, Assailants, Medicine and the Law* (Melbourne: Sun Books, 1977).

Law Reform Commission has struggled with the tension between customary law and individual rights. Paradoxically, in view of the rejection of separatist tactics as divisive, it is the radical feminist strategies which emphasize the universality of key experiences of women and the need for separate institutions, and it is this which offers Aboriginal women the most likely strategy for success. But it will only succeed if it has full, ongoing support. The nature of the opposition is strong and comes from many directions. There are some unholy alliances in the campaigns against refuges for Aboriginal women and there may well be some unexpected ones in ensuring their success. Aboriginal women need to know their rights. Lawyers and courts need to be made aware of the plight of Aboriginal women. Deaths in cells now has a public profile, the violence which women endure should also be confronted.

In summary, then, I suggest we need to acknowledge the facts: Aboriginal women are being raped by Aboriginal men. We need to look at the complex of forces which keep this fact off the agenda and be prepared to range widely in setting the context for our analyses. Reference to a woman's unseemly behaviour (e.g. drunk, promiscuous) needs to be recognized as a form of blaming the victim, not cultural differences which explain the high incidence of violence. Analyses of rape need to focus on the intersection of gender, race and class. Rape concerns power, lawyers with an interest in customary law need to be educated regarding aspects of Aboriginal women's law and the subtle interweaving of sexual politics and social change. There is a delicate balance to be achieved by those striving for self-determination, and therefore not wishing to create divisions within Aboriginal communities, and the needs of women whose voices have no forum. The Right as well as institutions and individuals with an interest in outcomes will exploit these factions. The needs of women must be addressed within the broad agenda of reform, not as a matter of personal conflict. At present, Aboriginal men are better positioned to take advantage of existing organizations which represent Aborigines than are women. And finally, Refuges/Rape Crisis Centres do work for white women, and where Aboriginal women have been properly resourced they too have shown that separate institutions are a successful strategy. Furthermore as it is one which builds on a traditional practice, it returns a level of power to decide to women. In so doing it constitutes a threat for those who have found a comfortable niche in the patriarchal power structures of Australian society.

POSTSCRIPT

Throughout this paper I have indicated that speaking of intra-racial rape is a fraught task for a white feminist, and my engagement with this question sparked something of a furore in Australia which can be traced through a series of publications. In revising this paper for publication I have updated the substantive material. In order to update the debates on raising the issue of intra-racial rape, let me here briefly sketch the history of this paper. The decision to speak about rape at the colloquium on the 'Rights of Subordinate Peoples' at La Trobe University in 1988 was taken in consultation with Topsy Napurrula Nelson, an Aboriginal woman with whom I had worked in the field in Central Australia and had given joint presentations over the past fifteen years. She was concerned about the rise in violence in her home community in Tennant Creek, Northern Territory and asked me why no one cared. I had responded that they did but, when I set about explaining why, we began a dialogue which grew into our joint presentation at the colloquium. At that time we were made aware that raising the issue of intra-racial rape was going to be contentious, but we both felt that the incidence of violence against women was increasing and that the matter was one that should have an international profile.

On the basis of our ongoing conversations on the topic of violence, past and present, we published a paper in which we engaged in an exchange regarding the dimensions of intra-racial rape,[94] and were promptly attacked by a group of well educated Aboriginal women who accused me of exploiting Topsy Nelson who, as an older Aboriginal woman for whom English was a second language, could not have grasped the theoretical argument I advanced.[95] I took this to be an example of the very racism that those objecting to my raising issues sought to eradicate. The dispute spilled over into the popular media and was the subject of learned presentations at various conferences and journal articles.[96] A major challenge from Huggins et al. regarded the right of non-Aborigines to write, research, and speak on matters Aboriginal, and the nature of my relationship with my co-author.

[94] See Bell and Nelson, 'Speaking About Rape is Everyone's Business'.
[95] See Huggins et al.
[96] See my own publications in 1990 and 1991; Jan Larbalestier, 'The Politics of Representation: Australian Aboriginal Women and Feminism', *Anthropological Forum*, vol. 6, no. 2; and in Huggins *et al.*, T.N. Nelson, 'Letter to the Editor', *Women's Studies International Forum*, vol. 14, no. 5, 1991.

Conspicuously absent from the deliberations was any consideration of the substantive issue: women are being raped. Both Topsy Nelson and I responded to the challenges. Our letters plus a more extensive article in which I develop some of the themes raised in this paper and those raised by the angered activists have been published in *Women's Studies International Forum* throughout 1991.

The dynamics of the dispute reveal that there is a great deal yet to be written on this topic. Tragically, research undertaken since Topsy Nelson and I raised these issues indicates that the abuse of Aboriginal women is extensive, systemic and not a topic to which the instruments of self-determination are prepared to grant priority. Rape is occurring at a rate that qualifies as an abuse of human rights and on a scale that constitutes a crisis. I invite you, the reader, to become familiar with the facts and to reflect on the power relations underpinning the furore.

Strategies of Women and Women's Movements in the Muslim World *vis-à-vis* Fundamentalisms: From Entryism to Internationalism

MARIE-AIMEE HELIE-LUCAS

It is important to use the plural when speaking of fundamentalisms. There are significant differences between these movements, in relation to the political conditions of their emergence and growth and the dialectical relations which link them to national powers and international finance. There are also, of course, differences in their forms of expression. But beneath these differences we are witnessing the spread and generalization of the fundamentalist phenomenon in the world.[1] Here we are concerned specifically with fundamentalisms in Muslim countries and communities and the ways in which women are affected and respond.

We are not trying—others have done it[2]—to define fundamentalisms as totalitarianism, fascism, revivalism, traditionalism or Islamism. Neither are we analysing their links with specific political formations. Rather, we are concerned with what fundamentalisms have in common beneath the varied forms they have taken in different geographical and historical situations since World War II. We are concerned in short with their attempt to elaborate a general discourse. Within this discourse we will confine ourselves to those concepts which specifically affect women, and consider the way in which they

---

[1] In these times of exacerbated racism perhaps it needs to be said that Jews, Christians, Muslims, Buddhists and Hindus (and certainly others whom we do not hear from), are equally affected by the growth of their respective fundamentalist groups. We know this on the basis of what women's groups from country to country and continent to continent, tell us.

[2] See Oliver Roy, 'Fundamentalism, Traditionalism and Islam', *Telos*, no. 65, 1985, pp. 122–7; also Hassan Hanafi, 'The Origins of Violence in Contemporary Islam', in *Development*, 1987, no. 1 (special issue on Culture & Ethnicity), pp. 56–61; and also Bassam Tibi, 'Neo-Islamic Fundamentalism', ibid., pp. 62–6.

are internalized—or called into question—by women and women's movements, and how their responses to situations which they must survive are shaped by this discourse.

There are about 450 million women living in Muslim countries or communities. They are spread throughout the continents, but the majority live in Asia, with Africa next. The Arab world, where Islam has its origins and which till today claims to represent Islamic legitimacy, is already reduced to a minority in the Muslim world. At the moment, and except in the West where a civil code generally governs all citizens, most Muslim communities have specific laws allegedly transposed from Shariat. These laws, and also the influence of Muslim fundamentalists over the evolution and application of these laws, are increasingly affecting women's lives. Legal rights and traditional practices have been eroded, and the struggles and strategies of women's movements tightly circumscribed.

Among the points common to fundamentalist discourse which directly affect women, we will be especially concerned with the following:

(1) The quest for identity, for a transcultural and ahistorical 'Muslim identity', conceived on the one hand preeminently as a threatened identity defined in opposition to an external entity, and on the other hand as a 'return' to a mythical past.

(2) Women as repositories of this identity, an idea that legitimizes women's control.

(3) The deliberate confusion of the concepts of nation/community, religion, and race/ethnicity.

(4) The selective uses of traditions, as well as religious interpretations, in order to structure an image of women which conforms to their reconstructed identity.

(5) The failure to set up a 'Muslim society' and the transfer to the private sphere of all this society's legitimacy, expressed through personal laws and family codes.

We will first examine these matters as a general phenomenon and then turn to their more specific effects on the situation of women.

The Quest for Identity

In all Muslim societies today (and by this I mean both Muslim countries where laws are inspired by interpretations of the Koran and

Muslim communities which have a minority status and thus benefit from 'Koranic laws'), fundamentalists stress the quest for identity. There is a similarity in the arguments they put forward, despite their totally different historical and political situations.

The arguments can be seen in Pakistan, for example, where the state is Muslim and was specifically created as such in 1947 to protect the Muslims who today form more than 90 per cent of the population. But the very same arguments are also encountered in India, Sri Lanka or Nigeria, where Muslims enjoy separate laws on the basis of their minority status.

The same issues arise in 'socialist' Algeria; capitalist and cosmopolitan Tunisia; and in Saudi Arabia, whose royal capital swamps the international activities of fundamentalist groups with its resources. They appear in Morocco under its monarchical regime but also in theocratic Iran and the comparatively democratic Senegal, where the Muslim majority is demanding the repeal of the civil code and the adoption of Shariat law.

The same propositions are advanced in the Middle East or North Africa, long since Islamized, and in other African countries where Islam has spread recently and rapidly as a symbol of decolonization. (Islam has been promoted as an 'indigenous' religion, as distinct from the religion of the colonizers, despite its connection with Arabs and the slave trade.) Under all these different political regimes and irrespective of majority or minority status, Muslim identity is described and perceived as under threat.

This threat to religious and cultural integrity may have its origins in historical experience: in Algeria or Egypt, for example, colonization is seen as the root of all evil. Algeria is a particularly good example, because it represents the extreme case of cultural alienation in a colonized people. But in countries where the effects of colonization were far less severe, the colonial argument is still used many decades after independence. In other words, colonization is mythified in order to explain, justify and bear responsibility for current behaviour. We must then take into account the role of the state in exploiting the discourse of threatened identity to construct nationalism and communalism.[3]

---

[3] Feminist works analysing the role of the state and national construction projects, and the use of religion in the subordination of women, are increasing. See particularly the work of Deniz Kandiyoti (Turkey), Haleh Afshar (Iran),

It is true that French colonization in Algeria made systematic attempts to destroy Algerian culture and that this was violently resented by the population. Education was in French: there were only two *medersa* or bilingual Arab-French teaching establishments in the whole of Algeria in 1960–1. This policy was a repetition of Jules Ferry's linguistic unification effort in France; to speak Arabic or Berber at school, even during recreation, was a punishable offence. In this context, education of Algerian girls became the spearhead of acculturation: the French language was the crucial vehicle for transmitting the norms by which Algerian society would be transformed according to the French model. Interviews with French primary school teachers in Algeria show their devotion to the cause of education and the training of young Algerian girls, as well as the complete absence of critical thought about what that training might come to represent within the colonial situation or about the hierarchy of values implicitly or explicitly made between Algerian and French culture.[4]

In this education project aiming at the transformation of a society through its women, the importance ascribed to the unveiling of women takes its full symbolic importance. Although the vast majority of Algerian women were not veiled because they were peasants and Berbers, the veil became the concern not only of the colonial educators but also of the colonial army (persuasion or violence). On 13 May 1958 the 'fraternization' organized by the putsch of the French army generals made the public unveiling of a hundred unfortunate women the symbol of the renunciation of a backward society and of the adoption of the norms of civilization (French, of course). Colonial discourse on the question of women expresses naively and brutally the importance of the role of women as cultural repositories in the unconscious both of colonized and colonizers. We will inevitably return to this role in our discussion of the problems women face in

---

Kumari Jawardena (Sri Lanka), Amrita Chhachhi (India), Naila Kabeer (Bangla Desh), Ayesha Jalal (Pakistan), Farida Shaheed (Pakistan), Afsaneh Najmabadi (Iran), Margot Badran (Egypt), as well as those of Nawal El Saadawi (Egypt) and Fatima Mernissi (Morocco), even though these two writers less directly address the question of the state and national construction.

[4] Anissa Helie, 'French Women Teachers in Algeria During the Colonial Era', M. Phil. dissertation, University of Provence, 1988 (History Department); same author and theme, Ph.D. dissertation in I'Ecole des Hautes Etudes, Paris 1992. She analyses the contradiction whereby women enjoying autonomy in a work sphere newly opened to them have participated in the enterprise of alienating other women, within the historical context of colonialism.

liberating themselves, as well as the use made of it by states in the construction of nationalism and communalism, and by fundamentalists.[5]

Direct experience of colonization is not the only threat to Muslim identity. For Ataturk's Turkey and the Shah's Iran, the threat was perceived to be the West and Westernization as a whole. But the strategy of altering the society through its women was adopted in these cases too. The liberal laws concerning women in Turkey date from 1926: the Turkish Civil Code forbids polygamy and gives women equal rights with men in matters of divorce and child custody. Total female equality was enacted in 1934. The Kemalist strategies for women's advancement are well known and form the cornerstone of Turkish Westernization, symbolizing the country's separation from Islamic culture.[6] Here again we find the theme of unveiling of women, not as the result of their own struggle for emancipation but as a sign of apostasy. And this strategy is inextricably tied to that of the construction of a new political order and a new state.[7]

In the case of Iran, wearing of the veil was forbidden in 1936 and other legislative measures were taken to benefit women.[8] These measures had relevance mainly to women of the elite but despite this, they constituted in the eyes of the popular classes nothing less than state

[5] Amrita Chhachhi, 'Forced Identities: Communalism, Fundamentalism and Women in India', in Deniz Kandiyoti (ed.), *Women, Religion and the State* (London, 1989). A previous version of this paper appeared in Dossiers, Women Living Under Muslim Laws, no. 4, p. 20. She notes that colonial discourse too used the 'woman's question' as a crucial tool in asserting its moral superiority over the subject population. Thus in 1927 Katherine Mayo published *Mother India*, in which the source for India's subordination was located in the abuse of women by Indian men and a resultant weakening of the 'Indian stock'. Child marriage, widow practices, premature consummation and pregnancy, female infanticide, purdah and sati were the cause of India's plight. In its assertion of a biological basis for Indian unfitness for independence, this book simultaneously asserted Western cultural superiority.

[6] Farida Shaheed, 'Women, Religion and Social Change in Pakistan: A Framework for Research', Dossiers, Women Living Under Muslim Laws, nos. 5 & 6, 1988, p. 40. This research project concerned India, Pakistan and Sri Lanka.

[7] Deniz Kandiyoti, 'Women and Islam: What are the Missing terms?', in D. Kandiyoti (ed.), *Women, Religion and the State*. An earlier version of this paper was published in Dossiers Women Living Under Muslim Laws, nos 5 & 6, p. 5.

[8] See the numerous writings of Haleh Afshar, in particular the chapter, 'Women, Marriage and the State in Iran', in her *Women, State and Ideology* (London: Macmillan, 1987).

collusion with Western imperialism. This discontent was the basis for the fundamentalists' popularity in Iran. A similar process took place in Egypt where, during Sadat's time, some meagre rights were granted to women (including the requirement of consent of the first wife in cases of polygamous marriages, and the right of the wife and children to stay in the marital home after repudiation, i.e. unilateral divorce, by the husband, though no such right was enacted for a childless wife). These were called Jihan Sadat laws, after the name of the president's wife; her public image possesses some similarities with that of the Shah's spouse, Farah Dibah. The laws bearing her name did not long outlast her husband.

Muslim minorities have also felt their identity threatened by dominant majorities in their own nations, aside from and in addition to the threats posed by the colonial authorities or the West more generally. The Shah Bano case crystallized such feeling in India and was the occasion for much ink and also some blood to be spilt. In 1985 the Indian Supreme Court dismissed an appeal against a lower court judgment granting a seventy-three-year-old woman, Shah Bano, the meagre maintenance of Rs 179.20 a month after her husband had repudiated her, and thrown her out of their house, after forty-three years of marriage. The husband's grounds of objection were that under Muslim Personal Law he was not obliged to maintain his wife after divorce, and that the procedure under the Criminal Procedure Code could not be extended to such a case. Rejection of this argument led to mass action by hundreds of thousands of Muslim men calling for a reversal of the judgment as a violation of Muslim Personal Law. Eventually the government pushed through the Muslim Women's Protection of the Right to Divorce Act 1986, withdrawing the right of Muslim women to appeal for maintenance under the Criminal Procedure Code.[9]

The case engaged not only Muslim activists but also Hindu fundamentalists and the women's movement. Hindu fundamentalists championed the cause of a single civil code and thus the repeal of personal laws, while Muslim leaders accused Hindus of imposing their laws and values on the Muslim minority. Liberal Muslims and Indian feminists of all religions who had pleaded for the repealing of all minority laws and for the adoption of a single civil code found themselves in an impossible position. It was difficult for them to avoid the

[9] Amrita Chhachhi, op.cit.

trap of their view appearing indistinguishable from the opportunistic anti-Muslim attacks of Hindu fundamentalists.[10] Before them, Algerian women who unveiled under the impact of colonization or Iranian women emancipated under the Shah's dictatorship were trapped in substantially the same contradictions.

In fact, the quest for identity is not an ideological creation of fundamentalists. It has its origins—and its legitimacy—in national and communal demands for independence, liberty or equality, but these have been hijacked by states and political powers, whether in colonial situations (Algeria), under the weight of imperialism (Iran), or among national minorities (India, Sri Lanka and numerous African countries). Consequently it is very difficult to call into question any aspect of this identity once fully constructed and imposed on the people, without being accused of joining the forces threatening the community with destruction. This inviolability is reinforced by the deliberate confusion maintained between the concepts of race (or ethnicity), religion and nationality (or community).

Several decades before the start of the war for national liberation in Algeria, the Ulemas (Islamic scholars) played an important role both in the training of cadres who were responsible for starting the armed struggle and in the elaboration of a syncretism whose effects are still being felt today. Sheikh Ben Badis preached an identity based on difference from the colonizers with the slogan 'Arabic is my language, Islam is my religion, Algeria is my country'. In other words, Algerian identity was defined as non-French. On the other hand, to be Algerian, Muslim and Arab became synonymous.

In fact 85 per cent of the Algerian population is of Berber origin and often still Berber speaking, despite an education policy which has for twenty-five years since independence tried and failed to supplant indigenous languages with Arabic. So it must have been the second part of Ben Badis' slogan which cemented national unity and identity, namely religion. However, apart from Berber nationalists, an important section of the population (at least in the towns) did not define themselves through a religious identity and some even declared their atheism. Nonetheless, all submitted to what was considered a tactical

[10] Ibid. Also see, Rohini Hensman, 'Oppression within Oppression: The Dilemma of Muslim women in India', in Women Living Under Muslim Laws, Working Papers, no. 1, October 1987; and Ammu Krishnaswamy, 'Shah Bano and After', 3rd National Conference on Women's Studies, University of Punjab, Chandigarh, 1986.

necessity to create national unity and to drive out colonial power. The founding document of independent Algeria—the text of the Soumam Congress drawn up by Abane Ramdane—affirmed in its first sentence that 'Algeria will be a democratic, secular and socialist country'. This position on secularism was to be omitted from editions of this document printed after independence, but none of us who held copies of the clandestine publication will ever allow it to be forgotten. The first Constitution of the Algerian Republic, passed at the end of the summer of 1962 (just after independence), affirmed on the contrary the non-secularism of the state and officially made Algeria a Muslim country. During the war of liberation and after independence Ben Badis' formula triumphed. All questioning of Arabo-Islamic identity was condemned as anti-nationalist: one could not be Algerian without also being Arab and Muslim. Moreover since Algeria was also declared to be a socialist state, to be Algerian was to be revolutionary and so any criticism of religious or linguistic politics was viewed as a counter-revolutionary act.

As far as women are concerned, the consequences of all this have been incalculable. All criticisms of the repressive measures which little by little were curtailing the rights of Algerian women, up to the final codification in the Family Code of 1984, were judged anti-revolutionary, westernist and thus threatening to Arabo-Muslim identity.[11] In other words, women have been caught between two sets of legitimacy: they cannot serve their cause as women and at the same time belong to the nation for whose very existence they have struggled.

This scheme can be found throughout the Middle East where, despite the existence of several religious minorities, among whom are the Christians (an important minority, sure of its historical legitimacy and mythical basis since it lives in the very same place as its founder), the equation of Arab with Muslim is everywhere in force. But a similar equation is also to be found in Pakistan, where nation and religion are merged—the latter was the sole basis for the former. In African countries too, Muslims seek to achieve this synthesis between religion and nation, as soon as the Muslim minority attains the fateful 50 per cent of population. Even though their number effectively guarantees the liberty to practise their religion in the context of secular states

[11] The writings of Fadela M'Rabet remain indisputably realistic. See *Algerian Women*, fortunately republished by Maspero, Cahiers Libres, pp. 141–142, Paris, 1983. This edition holds in a single volume M'Rabet's writings previously published by Maspero in 1965, 1967 and 1969.

generally inherited from colonization,[12] the fundamentalist groups are active—in Senegal or in Nigeria—trying to impose Islam as the state religion. Even when religion is recently imported, it cements the process of nation-building, draws on rather than antagonizes local practices, and gives coherence and legitimacy to the concept of nation.

This geographical expansion of Islam explains the extreme diversity of custom incorporated into religious practice, even if theologians point to their anti-Islamic character. Hence, the sexual mutilation of women takes place in Sudan, Egypt or Somalia, within Muslim communities, while this is unknown elsewhere; adoption is banned in Algeria or in Sri Lanka, but allowed elsewhere; Muslim Indians are subjected to the caste system, unknown outside the subcontinent; veiling or seclusion is imposed on women here but not there. The cultures which Islam has absorbed persist and their traditions have become a part of the religio-customary ground on which political powers build national or communal identity. So it is irrelevant to look into the Koran to check whether the caste system does or does not contradict the Islamic ideal of justice and equity, or whether the sexual mutilations of women are anti-Islamic.

Deniz Kandiyoti reminds us that 'we should thus not assume that the action of modern state necessarily results in greater secularization of the personal status sphere or undercuts the power of religious authorities. This clearly depends on the nature of the state and the representation of clerical and other sectoral interests within it'.[13]

In fact identity is always defined as threatened by an external entity, be it colonial power, western imperialism or a dominant national group. This external entity is perceived as monolithic and devoid of internal contradictions, and therefore of potential allies within it. Thus on the one hand, whatever emanates from the exterior will be bad and threatening and is to be rejected; on the other hand the internal

---

[12] We face a double contradiction: the concept of secularism is part and parcel of the colonial frame and is therefore rejected as alien. And clearly it would be a mistake to consider colonial 'secular' laws as culturally neutral. For example, monogamous marriage is obviously perceived as 'Christian' in origin by Algerian Muslims and of 'British' (then 'Hindu') origin, by Muslim Indians; the official 'secularism' of the Indian state is very often taken at other than face value. In 1987 Le Monde published articles by migrant Algerian readers, who demanded a separate Personal Status Code and questioned the secularism of the laws of the French state in view of the historical heritage of the 'elder daughter of the Church'. The controversy was essentially about monogamy.

[13] Deniz Kandiyoti, op. cit.

contradictions of society are minimized, and their resolution deferred until after the defeat of the external enemy. But the immediate enemies are the ones within, those who can be seen to collude with the external enemy. In the classless society of the fundamentalists, these internal enemies can be drawn from the westernized elites, religious reformers and women who seek to improve their status.

Religion, understood as the symbol of the nation or community's identity, becomes the means of protest of the popular classes, and the public demonstration of their break with the ruling classes. Priority is thus eternally accorded to issues which continuously demand the temporary sacrifice of popular demands, and those of women in particular. It is never the right moment to raise certain questions: one must wait for the end of the liberation struggle, for national construction to get under way, and so on; any other attempt will destroy the unity of the threatened group.

The representation of society as atomized masses or interchangeable individuals has been familiar to us since Marx's critique of classical economists; nevertheless, that representation functions effectively to prohibit women's struggle, which is seen as premature. Identity, then, is essentially constituted as closed and defensive: to seek alliances with other communities, nations, and worse still the West, becomes structurally impossible. Women thus analyse their oppression by and in their internal national/communal contexts, with all the limitations this imposes. Within this context of closure, identity is defined as a 'return to origins', a 'return to our roots', a 'return to authentic national values', a 'return to our Arabo Islamic values', the precise formula varying according to time and place.[14] It is particularly striking that the vocabulary makes such explicit reference to the notion of going backwards, to rediscovery of a lost mythological past, uprooted or alienated by the external entity. One wonders how a future can be realized when it is so exclusively confined to the past—and a past which has not grown and changed, which remains frozen at a given historical moment; ahistorical, sacrosanct, unchangeable, dead.

The prohibition on developing external contacts which will destroy identity serves to imprison in a past which has been defined so as to be dead. Those in power are trapped in the following contradiction: how to breathe new life into something which is not, and should not be, living?

---

[14] Deniz Kandiyoti, ibid.; Farida Shaheed, op. cit.; Amrita Chhachhi, op. cit.

Both religion and traditions are involved in this process. Drastic choices are made among those traditions, religious practices and Koranic interpretations best suited to controlling the population. Some are authenticated, others completely eradicated. The importance of the control of women in the construction of identity is so great that in many instances only those traditions most unfavourable to women's autonomy are selected and brought up to date. The search for a transcultural and transhistorical Muslim identity which characterizes Muslim countries and communities today completely negates the cultural differences previously mentioned and the way in which Islam absorbs indigenous cultures and assimilates their practices.[15] What remains constant is the choice of reinforcing the subordination of women and of the popular classes. It is not surprising, then, to find that customs specifically associated with wage-earning or monogamous marriage in the West in the twentieth century are also incorporated into Muslim identity when required. Here are three examples.

The Algerian Family Code adopted in 1984 forbids adoption as contrary to Islam; traditionally, before state intervention, adoption took place as follows: a man would declare in front of two witnesses that he was taking responsibility for this child and that he would bring it up as his own; this was a private affair and no legalization was ever sought. Prophet Mohamed, himself an adoptive father, advised that the adopted child should not assume the name of the adoptive father nor inherit from him at par with the legitimate children. This traditional adoption is quite different from the adoption in use in the West nowadays, but it was a functioning system. Now we find that on the basis of the Koranic restrictions, the Algerian Family Code (among others) completely forbids adoption while the Tunisian Code (based on the same Koranic texts) permits it.

In Algeria 30,000 children were officially declared abandoned in state hospitals within ten years (1970–80) and innumerable women were repudiated on the grounds of infertility (even when it was the husband who was infertile), while all the time adoption could have resolved these problems, as it had done traditionally. But the state would not relinquish any of its control over the private lives of its citizens. After independence it made further inroads, particularly in the area of sexuality and its consequences, forbidding all contraception and adoption for more than ten years.[16]

[15] Deniz Kandiyoti, op. cit.; Amrita Chhachhi, op. cit.

[16] M.A. Helie-Lucas, 'The Veiled Production: A Political and Feminist Ap-

As for Sri Lanka, where the minority personal law also forbids Sri Lankan Muslims to adopt, the problem of abandoned children is regulated by international adoption—a practice which is much criticized. It is Sri Lanka, however, which exports women on a massive scale, heavily from the Muslim community. They go as domestic servants to the Gulf countries and to Pakistan.[17] No question of discretion arises: state agencies recruit women in an official capacity, while the ministries of labour and foreign affairs negotiate employment contracts for migrant workers, who are underpaid drudges without fixed hours of employment, holidays or social security. Their contract binds them for two or three years while a significant proportion of their salaries is sent straight home to their families (generally to their husbands, who in many instances use it to take another wife). They are totally—including sexually—exploited by their employers. As the crime of zina (sex outside marriage) is punishable in most of the Gulf countries and in Pakistan with death by stoning, these women fill the prisons of these countries, while the employers who raped them go free. This state of affairs is well known among the authorities and the public in Sri Lanka, yet Sri Lankan Muslim identity does not seem to suffer as a result. The theme of honour, the family, the man's authority over his wife-and-mother-of-their-children is not weakened, but simply put aside in the specific circumstances. As a part of this convenient adaptation, significant numbers among the female Muslim population travel, have a passport in their own name, leave their homes and even their families—all forbidden to women in other Muslim countries and communities.

The last example is that of the naming of women in Arab countries: traditionally, women were born, lived and died with their father's names. Thus Fatima Bent Mohamed (daughter of Mohamed) kept this name as a single woman and throughout her marriages, sometimes becoming Fatima Um Mohamed (mother of Mohamed) after the birth of her first son, although this second name never took precedence over

---

proach to Women and Reproduction in Algeria after Independence 1961–1982', in Sarec and Sida (eds.), *Women and Reproduction* (Stockholm, October 1983).

[17] It goes without saying that numerous Islamic authorities have issued fatwas authorizing contraception. Bangladesh adopted an aggressive population policy (and trials of dangerous methods of contraception); abortion and sterilization of both men and women are carried out with, or more often without, the consent of the individuals concerned: Farida Akhter, 'Depopulating Bangladesh', Ubinig Occasional Paper, Dhaka, 1986.

the first. At present, with the widespread introduction of identity cards, birth and marriage registers, the states throughout the Middle East and North Africa require the husband's name to be written on women's identity cards and passports. Meanwhile, with the high rate of repudiation and divorce, women may have three, four or five husbands in their lifetime and will accordingly change name each time. They therefore lose even the identity that is guaranteed by one's own name, an identity which till recently was guaranteed by lifetime retention of the father's name.

These three examples show that numerous transgressions against custom take place in ways unfavourable to women of Muslim countries and communities; both the scientific literature and novels describe this phenomenon.

At the same time one witnesses recent changes in personal status laws, together with the adoption of forms of Shariat which require careful scrutiny. Basically, these laws are identical and form the common terrain, despite the diversity of cultures, of women living in Muslim countries and Muslim communities. Laws deprive women of the right to marry by themselves, through submitting them to the authority of a 'marriage guardian' or 'matrimonial tutor' (*wali*); laws deprive them of free access to divorce, which remains the privilege of husbands, and confirm the latter's right to several wives (polygamy) and repudiation (*talaq*); laws confirm the inequalities in matters of inheritance. Women are also deprived of the right to guardianship and child custody in case of divorce: in these matters there are different modalities from one country to another. Mothers are granted the right to serve as nurses and maids till their sons are between two and ten years of age, and their daughters between eight years and puberty (or marriage). After this time fathers reclaim their property.

Muslim laws to a large extent render women's mobility and access to waged employment dependent on their husband's or father's permission. Specific activities like driving a car are sometimes, though admittedly not often, forbidden to women. In all cases but in varying degree, women's sexual life is the object of legislation. Sex outside marriage is punished: some countries punish it by death, as in the case of several Arab emirates and Pakistan. In the latter case the Hudood Ordinance presents particularly grotesque dangers to the woman who lays a charge of rape or who falls pregnant after a rape. This woman will be taken to have explicitly or implicitly admitted to having had sexual relations outside marriage (*zina*), and unless the rape is proven she herself faces punishment under the ordinance. Given the notoriously difficult nature of rape trials the world over, such danger is all too real.[18] In most Muslim countries, and certainly in the non-Muslim countries which grant personal status laws to Muslim minorities, these measures contradict constitutions which proclaim the legal equality of all citizens.

But what is particularly astounding is that these laws are usually the fruit of recent amendments, either through suppression of colonially inspired laws which were already in abeyance (Algeria, 1984), or by the hardening of existing laws inspired by the Koran, in ways which curtail women's freedom still further and increase control over their lives. Thus in 1984 an already mentioned amendment took place in Egypt; in 1984, too, the Muslim Senegalese demanded the adoption of the Shariat and the abolition of the Civil Code. In 1985 India passed the Muslim Women Protection of the Right to Divorce Act which had the effect of making women born in Muslim communities second-class citizens by denying them rights accorded to all other citizens—including women of other national minorities, who can still make use of the secular laws of the central state to escape the restrictions of personal status codes.[19] In 1986 Sri Lanka named a commmission to study the hardening of the Muslim Personal Status law, which feminists managed to counter by publishing a memorandum refuting the arguments of fundamentalists who initiated the project.[20] In 1987 a socialist government in Mauritius gave in to Muslim fundamentalist pressure to reintroduce the shariat for the Muslim minority, while there was simultaneously a secular civil code for all citizens. There too feminists managed to stop the project.[21] Let us also not forget the recent legal repression of women in the name of Islam in Khomeini's Iran and Zia-ul-Haq's Pakistan. Even Tunisia, the only example in the Muslim world to give full legal equality to women, is now under pressure to align with other Muslim countries. And a commission to bring about

[18] Deniz Kandiyoti, op. cit.

[19] Faizun Zackariya, 'The Situation of Muslim Women in Sri Lanka', Minutes of the Aramon Meeting, special dossier, Women Living Under Muslim Laws, 1986.

[20] Farida Shaheed, ibid. Also see Sabiha Sumar and Khalid Nadvi, 'Zina: The Hudood Ordinance and its Implications for Women', Dossier 3 of Women Under Muslim Laws, 1988.

[21] Thus, a civil marriage may permit escape from a marriage entered into under personal law during minority; but all marriages contracted under Muslim codes must be dissolved under the same law.

uniformity between the various family codes in the Arab countries has worked for several years, gathering ministers of justice and scholars of Islam well-versed in interpretations of the Koran. A similar commission exists in relation to Muslim minorities in South Asian countries.

The topicality of these events, long after national independence, demonstrates the fundamentalist power within state structures, even when they are officially excluded and overtly combatted. The fundamentalists claim not to limit their quest for Islamic identity to a rejection of Western values but rather purport to be restoring identity by an alternative model which should innovate in all domains—economic, political and social relations. In fact their activities directly and overwhelmingly affect women and the private sphere. We do not know of examples of Muslim specificity in the political or economic domains.[22] But family codes or personal status laws which rule personal life, in matters of marriage, divorce, guardianship and child custody, polygamy, inheritance, standards of behaviour, clothing and so on, constitute the sphere of fundamentalist preoccupation. And certainly this is their only field of action. Deniz Kandiyoti remarks:

It is very hard to escape the notion that the control of women and the representation of this control at the level of state ideology is a more pressing and enduring concern in Muslim societies than elsewhere . . . (Part of the reason) resides not in Islam per se but in the relationship in which Islamic societies have found themselves vis-a-vis the West.[23]

If the role of women as repositories of culture and identity and as symbols of indigenous forms undergoes such distortion, and if the fundamentalist obsession with women is so pathological,[24] one should undoubtedly see it as compensation for and proof of the incapacity of states to set up democratic regimes and to face the fair demands of people. Even though the recruitment to fundamentalist organizations is far from limited to classic groups of the extreme right, fundamentalists have clearly played the role of political counterweight to leftist

[22] Muslim Women's Research and Action Front (MWRAF), 'Memorandum submitted to the Committee on Proposed Reforms to Muslim Personal Law', Colombo, Sri Lanka, 1987. Published in Dossier 3 of Women Living Under Muslim Laws, 1988.

[23] 'Muvman Liberasyon Fam campaign for One Law for All Women' and 'Muvman Liberasyon Fam Women's Minimum Programme', ibid.

[24] See Charles Issawi, cited by Anwar H. Syed, 'Revitalising the Muslim Community', Race and Class, no. 3, vol. XXVIII, 1987.

groups, and the authorities have allowed them to grow so as to pit one group against the other, while pretending to play the role of a just arbiter between the extremes. In doing so they have effectively contributed to the creation of an extreme right nurtured under religious pretext. It is not the nature of Islam that is in question here; all religions have been repressively used, as well as sometimes to promote human and social values. What is at issue is both the use of religion as national or communal cement and the control over women in the name of religion, as substitutes for real power. It is in this context that women and women's movements (in so far as they are allowed to organize) will manoeuvre.

THE RESPONSES OF WOMEN

How does the fundamentalist argument revolving around an identity threatened by an external entity affect women's reactions? The answer is that they are bound to internalize the confusion between nation/religion/culture, the myth of a threatened identity and the role of Islam as a national/communal cement. It follows that women and women's movements have been divided into two groups. The first cleaves to the need to remain within the religious frame, and the second group is constituted by those who fear betraying nation or community.

The first reaction is seen in the fact that even secular feminists and communist feminists feel the need to refer to the Koran in order to justify their stands by quoting holy text; in other words without the church there is no salvation. Nawal El Saadawi initially followed this direction, as Fatima Mernissi still does. Feminists from Muslim countries are often very well-versed in Koranic exegesis and capable of challenging fundamentalists in the latters' own fields. Feminists learn the holy texts and their interpretations so as to re-establish the 'truth of the revealed texts', while denouncing the human and historical input; the latter is thereby established as debatable and can be depicted as responsible for the discrimination against women. These feminists are thereby joining a long tradition of progressive interpreters of the Koran who have generally paid with their life for opposition to political interests which use religion to assert their domination.[25] They

[25] Deniz Kanidyoti, op. cit. See also Amrita Chhachhi, op. cit.; and Fatima Mernissi, *The Fundamentalists' Obsession with Women* (Lahore: Simorgh Publications, 1986). It is striking that many fundamentalist publications are obviously

attribute to Islam a cultural role and counterpose this authentic identity to the adoption of 'Western values'.[26]

Researchers from within this grouping have emphasized the weakness of factual material on the role of religion, and research projects have been set up to explore this shadowy zone.[27] In so doing women recover an important part of thought until recently in the hands of men and men alone. They act as pioneers. It goes without saying that they are tolerated as long as they cannot reach a wide audience.

There are two important currents in this first group: the believers, for whom Islam must constitute its own theology of liberation, and the unbelievers who operate at the level of strategic alliances. All shades of religiosity are observable between the two groups.

The second group expresses the difficulty, even the impossibility, of freely choosing possible alliances outside the nation/community. The group encompasses a variety of standpoints, including refusal to communicate with other feminists from a different religion, yet within the same nation; declining to look for alliances within the region; and even shutting out any contact with western feminists.[28]

---

addressed to a Western audience: 'They have as an aim', writes Yvonne Yazbeck Haddad, 'to explain Islam to the Western public as a system of values and laws, as civilisation . . . ': 'The Critic of The Islamic Impact', by Yvonne Yazbeck Haddad, in Byron, Haines and Ellison Findlay (N.Y.: Syracuse University Press, 1984).

[26] Whoever needs to be convinced of the pathological character of such a control over private life (especially lives of women), should read Khomeini's writings. Each circumstance in life and each incident of a day are envisaged in his writings. Incredibly, this thought can rule not a group of nuns but an entire nation, with pretensions to rule other countries too.

[27] Tahar Haddad in Tunisia is one such example. Another is Nour Mohamed Tahi, who was killed in Sudan as late as in 1984. His books were publicly burned and his body buried in a place to avoid making it an area of pilgrimage; the possession of a copy of his works is punishable. Nawal El Saadawi spent several months in prison in 1981 for having written feminist works; she owes her freedom to the fact that she is a well-known writer in the Arab world, as well as more generally. Her books are banned in her own country, Egypt. For years her life has been threatened by Egyptian fundamentalists; since the Egyptian government would be embarrassed by such a martyr, she is constantly guarded in Cairo.

[28] Mernissi's works are a good example. There are other historical works too which attempt to locate early feminism in a past when identity was not yet threatened. This is a form of defence against accusations about resort to imported ideologies, and is comparable to efforts to recover subordinated history during national liberation struggles: see Margot Badran's writings on feminists in Egypt. This type of research is widely welcomed by feminist activists concerned to protect themselves.

As in national liberation struggles, primary allegiance goes to the group (always threatened, we must remember, whatever the circumstances) and women implicitly give up their own priority in favour of other priorities. To give only one example, Indian and Pakistani women have recently started to come together after years of broken relations;[29] one consequence is that Indian Muslim women have left interreligious feminist groups to set up their own groups. The false concept of 'Western feminism', and the false dichotomy between Western and Third World feminism work to prevent women from benefiting from each other's experiences: even reading Western feminists' work is seen as unsuitable and untimely, so great is the fear of contamination and so deeply rooted the notion of external evil. One finds in much feminist discourse within the Muslim world—and in an unconscious way—arguments which derive from the fundamentalists, who have managed to create the conditions for self-censorship and deadly isolation of women.[30]

Xenophobia and the impossibility of thinking about one's own situation from an angle other than that assigned are two major obstacles to the development of feminist movements in the Muslim

[29] In recent years, lecturers and activists have organized important meetings where theoretical questions and intercultural comparisons have been discussed. The following are some of the conferences: 'Muslim Women Speak', Lahore, Pakistan, 1986; Women Living Under Muslim Laws meeting, Aramon, 1986; 'Challenges facing Arab Women in the Next Decade', Cairo, 1986; 'Women, Islam and the State', London, 1987; 'Women, Religion and Family Laws', Bombay, 1987; 'Challenge for Change: A Workshop on the State of Muslim Society', Colombo, Sri Lanka, 1987. 'Women Living Under Muslim Laws' exchange program, 1988; 'Women and Fundamentalism', India, 1989. The International Union of Anthropological and Ethnological Sciences devoted a full workshop of its last congress in June 1988 to religious fundamentalist movements and to the situation of women, with themes such as: 'Revivalism and Fundamentalism: Religious, Ethnic and National Movements', 'The Plural Meanings of Feminism: Cross-cultural Perspectives', and 'Religious Movements in Social Contexts'. This proliferation of meetings shows the importance given to these themes by feminists.

[30] One recalls the poignant attempt of Kate Millett to speak to Iranian women upon Khomeini's coming into power; some feminists in the Muslim world ridiculed her, and many more did so in the West. Her intervention was seen as conceited Western meddling in foreign affairs, as disrespect for the particularities of non-Western cultures. All this reminds us of the fearful attitude and colonial guilt complex of those women who even today do not dare condemn female circumcision under the pretext that this forms part of African culture, even though African groups are fighting these customs from within. Rather, Kate Millett's courage and her internationalist concern deserve admiration.

world. It is the imprisonment in this ideological cage, or the effort to come out of it, that determines the form of women's struggles, and their strategies, from entryism to internationalism. In 'entryism' we include both feminist believers who are deeply involved in the study of the Koran to reinvent a new theology which they think is closer to divine truth, as well as all those who tactically, at different levels, either subscribe to religion itself or to 'sociological religion' (that is to say, the necessity of struggling from within the community). This latter approach is certainly that of the majority of feminists in the Muslim world who do not want to risk being cut off from their base. I also include in the entryist category women who join the fundamentalist movements.

By 'internationalists' I mean feminists who deliberately seek information and alliances beyond the frontiers of race, nation and religion. This tendency is the newest and is rapidly developing. Though it is premature to judge, its beneficial effects have already been felt over the past few years.

Let us take examples for each category. Thus the writings of Riffat Hassan, a Pakistani feminist theologian, analyse the Koran (i.e. the word of the Prophet, a sacred and intangible text), along with the *Sunna* (i.e. the interpretations which were later written down and codified), as well as the *Fiq* (i.e. the corpus of legal and judicial texts of the mediaeval period). She demonstrates that the verses most often used against women tend to be either remnants of pre-Islamic discriminatory practices, or erroneous interpretations which should be criticized from a historical point of view. The argument is that if one only examines the original text and puts it into the historical context of the Prophet, the literal words can be read in the light of this spirit and the progressive message adapted to present circumstances.

I would like for the feminist movement in Islam to be religiously rooted and for it to be religiously rooted we have to present the positive content of the Quran which has been lost because of centuries of male chauvinist interpretation of it . . . . All in all, it's a very difficult time for Muslim women because Muslims on the one hand want things that are modern, such as technology, science, industry; on the other hand, they're very jealous of their own traditions and are very conservative in many ways. So that there is tremendous tension between this desire to be modern and the desire to be traditional. And women are caught up in the struggle in all kinds of ways because the Muslim home is really the last citadel for the Muslim man and they are very reluctant to permit any changes in the home. That's where I believe the main struggle is in the situation of the Muslim woman, in the home.[31]

Riffat Hassan establishes the basis for a women's liberation movement rooted in religion, while maintaining links with women from other religions in the hope of developing a liberation theology in Islam. She is one of a number of feminist theologians who already constitute an international group of researchers of religious issues. And it goes without saying that this approach has an appeal to women, because they are reassured that they are not betraying their religious community. On the contrary, they can believe that they are helping to re-establish a lost truth. The fact that they are nonetheless prey to repression and marginalization reinforces their conviction that it is the men who are the lost ones of Islam. But the limits on their field of action should soon become clear to them: if they really have an impact on the population, they will be forced to disappear. They will come to see that what they oppose is not merely a version of religious doctrine but an immensely powerful social force acting in the name of Islam. But at present these women play a very important role in raising feminist consciousness by differentiating between its God and its clergy, between theology and politics. They are not only entryists but also internationalists, at two levels: they are in touch with women theologians from other religions who are also active in the historical critique of religions, and they remain permanently in contact with feminist activists who are not necessarily believers.

In a more secular sense, other feminists revisit the field of Islamic law and attempt to reform it from within. Let us again take up the two Indian cases of Shenaz Sheikh and Shah Bano. Both these women questioned the validity of Muslim personal law in relation to the Indian Constitution and have thus highlighted the contradictions between these two jurisdictions. But in both cases the use made by Hindu fundamentalists of their writ petitions led them to withdraw their complaint. In fact their community threatened to exclude them totally and to punish them by 'social death'. For old Shah Bano the affair ended with this defeat. But for Shenaz the return to her community

---

[31] Similarities with the Rushdie affair are striking. His book was burned not only by immigrants in London, New York and Paris, but also in India and Pakistan, usually by people who had not read it (it was banned in the latter two countries) but who were told that Rushdie had sold out to the West. The progressive Indian Muslim, Ashgar Ali Engineer, has analysed this process in courageous articles.

held a different meaning: if she did not want to pay the price of her betrayal, she had to elaborate her case further and to pass her experience on to other Indian Muslim women. She studied Muslim law and set up a group to help women through the medium of lawyers who are also Muslim scholars and activists.[32]

Here too was a solution which avoided posing the question of betrayal of the community; the fact of having set up a separate movement for Muslim Indian women and also the contacts maintained with multi-religious feminist groups place Shenaz too at the crossroad between entryism and internationalism. This is the same strategy followed by Fatima Mernissi; in order to pass on a feminist message concerning the whole position of Moroccan women, she has tried to get together with the progressive fraction of the clergy and also women believers. She thus shows a double concern to 'stick with the masses' and to confront fundamentalists on their own terrain. Given the evolution of the author's thought and the theme of 'return to tradition' evident in her latest books, her alliances can be seen as strategic. By contrast, Nawal El Saadawi followed an opposite direction which took her from a critique of the 'hard' interpretations of the Koran to an essentially secular approach based on human rights.

These approaches are not essentially different from those of women who enter fundamentalist groups; they only differ in appearance and we cannot ignore the tactical aspect of their choice. More and more women in every Muslim country and community are joining these groups, a phenomenon that seems to symbolize sexual repression. The development seems frightening and incomprehensible as long as one does not ask practical questions regarding the real or symbolic benefits women hope to or actually get from joining these groups, and as long as one denies logic to their processes. It is slightly premature to draw conclusions, but we could formulate a hypothesis based on the accounts which come to us (mainly from African and Arab countries).

First of all, one should know that fundamentalist groups benefit from funds which one cannot even approximately estimate. Where these funds come from and through which channels they transit is a research theme which is not without risk. But whoever works on this

---

[32] M.A. Helie-Lucas, 'Women's Struggle in Algeria During the War for Independence and After', in the papers of the symposium 'Images of Third World Women', Amsterdam, Transnational Institute. Also see Women Living Under Muslim Laws, Plan of Action (Aramon, 1986).

problem will render a real service to the women of Muslim countries and communities.

It is beyond doubt that these groups function on an international scale, and that certain groups have branches in countries as different as Malaysia or Australia.[33] They have in common that they provide their members clothes ('Islamic' for women and traditional for men), space (to work, pray, sleep in countries where the majority of the families are cooped up in overcrowded and noisy quarters); services, like free hospital treatment in countries where competent medicine is rare and expensive; scholarships for secondary and higher education, also for women, in countries where education is by no means 'free, secular and compulsory', but rather private, sectarian and dreadfully expensive; and even straight-out money (through devices like setting up Islamic banks to provide loans without interest).

Women who join these groups benefit from all these advantages, as do their families. Moreover they claim that they are protected from men's lust behind the 'Islamic dress';[34] that they can move freely with their families' consent and neighbours' respect, at least when they go out of their homes in order to work with the group—a highly respectable motivation; that they are encouraged to study and use their intellectual capacity; and finally, that they have opportunities when it comes to choosing their husband, as long as they choose him from within the group. (It seems that fathers hesitate to impose their own choice of husband in the face of an internal marriage which has the support of the group.) Limited facilities will also be made available to qualified women who seek to travel, since the fundamentalist groups act both as a freemasonry and pressure group in favour of their members.[35]

Such benefits are greater than have ever been offered, either by governments or by political parties of the left. Clearly, it is simplistic to see the entry of women into the fundamentalist movements as being merely to satisfy their moral and material needs: the 'obvious' reasons they themselves give tend to be illusory. But equally, it is ridiculous

[33] An interview titled 'Feminist Theology and Women in the Muslim World', published in the *Bulletin of the Committee Over the Women in the South of Asia*, vol. 4 (4), 1986.

[34] 'Awaaz e Niswaan', Bombay, India.

[35] An example is the Arkam group. The case of Australia is notable for its Syrio-Lebanese minority, which shows the same defensive behaviour as do Arab migrants in Europe. This is true despite a relatively low level of racist pressure.

not to listen to their discourse at all. Many of these women believe that the changes resulting from their participation in the fundamentalist movements are irreversible and form part of the social advancement of women, and that above all their participation aids in the evolution of these movements in a favourable way to women—an 'entryist' position, if anything. The existence and scope of this whole phenomenon demands more international attention than it has received thus far.

Meanwhile women's movements in Muslim countries and communities are throwing up new trends which are distancing themselves from entryist positions and which are not limited to struggle within the religious frame. These movements draw their force from a desire to communicate beyond communal or national frontiers which enforce isolation and permit analysis only within their own national political context. These movements are now discovering the similarities that exist among countries and different communities. Building up support networks and exchange of information within the Muslim world at least allows women to defend their rights without questioning their identity and their belonging to their community. How could one now convince Sudanese and Somalian women of Muslim communities that circumcision is Islamic, if they have known and seen that it is not practised amongst Muslims in North Africa or South Asia? How could one convince Iranian women that the veil and seclusion are Islamic, if they have seen that numerous other African or Asian Muslim women are neither veiled nor secluded? Such examples can be multiplied. Exchange of information allows women to identify traditional cultural elements incorporated into Muslim practices and unfairly presented as part of religion in a specific region.

As for Muslim law, it becomes easy to discover that it incorporates interesting variations that women can use to their benefit. In one place women are secluded, forcibly married, live as eternal minors in the shadow of a 'guardian', unable to divorce, subject to repudiation and polygamy, punishable by death for adultery, lose their children if the husband throws them out, unable to work without permission, unfavourably treated in matters of inheritance, and so on. In another place women move freely, work, can marry and divorce, benefit from maintenance and the custody of their children, can control their fecundity, refuse polygamy, and so on.

The myth of one homogeneous Muslim world explodes, and the differences appear. If all these different countries claim to be Muslim, why not benefit from the better conditions afforded to women in one particular place? The eventual submission of religious authorities to political powers is clearly revealed in the case of contraception. How many Muslim countries encouraged it with the blessing of the mullahs (Tunisia, Bangla Desh), how many tolerate it (Egypt, Pakistan), how many forbid it (Algeria) depending on the demographic requirements of the time? And how many Muslim countries will totally reverse their policies if need be (Algeria)? And if Islam is so flexible as to integrate such varied and contradictory traditions, should one refer to it as a unity when one demands one's rights? If so, which version of Islam should be referred to?

In these past few years women from the Muslim countries have organized many meetings and conferences for the purpose of exchanging information, and creating active forms of solidarity. For example, in 1985, AWSA (Arab Women Solidarity Association) assembled women from the Arab world in Egypt; in 1986 the Simorgh Association gathered together in Lahore, Pakistan, a group of fifteen women from the Muslim communities in Asia and the Arab world ('Muslim Women Speak'). Also in 1986, the 'Women Living Under Muslim Laws' network brought together ten women from Muslim communities within the Arab world, Africa and Asia and set down the basis of its first Plan of Action; in 1987 a conference was held in Bombay gathering several hundreds of women from various religious tendencies, under the theme 'Women, Religion and Personal Laws'. These are only some of many initiatives, and they are now increasing in number. Comparative analysis of laws most unfavourable to women is proceeding. Appeals for solidarity are also increasing: to liberate imprisoned women, to save from death sentence a supposed adulteress, to participate in a national campaign against the introduction of severe forms of Shariat, and so on. For a long time solidarity came from Western feminists only and was thus double-edged, since it supplied ammunition ('sold to the West', 'traitors of the community'). Now this external solidarity is balanced by the internal support coming from within Muslim countries themselves.

Women not only compare their situations but also inform each other about their struggles and draw inspiration from knowing each others' strategies. Sometimes alienation still emerges: in 1986, in Lahore, no exiled Iranians were invited on the ground that they defamed Islam in the West by exposing the vagaries of the Khomeini regime; in 1987, in Bombay, Pakistan women did not agree to speak freely of their situation in the presence of Indian women. Neverthless more and more groups feel the need and understand the value of these exchanges and try to link up their struggles, even if for only one action at a time. Little by little, the necessary conditions for the expansion of an internationalist approach are defined. The structure of networks seems to ensure maximum autonomy to local groups to define their own analysis, priorities and strategies; no central organization exists which could dictate a policy. Associations and exchanges are made and unmade freely, helped by coordination which does not seek to provide more than this simple service. Fluid, maybe precarious, but certainly invigorating, the network fits our need for the moment.

The difficulties to be overcome, as well as the force of nationalist and fundamentalist lies, invite us to respect the rhythm of the ideological liberation of each of us. The forces we confront are so powerful and so dangerous that we must gather all our strength and not exclude anyone who works for changes which are favourable to us.

Fundamentalism and Women in Iran

HALEH AFSHAR

As it has developed in Iran, Islamic fundamentalism has undoubtedly worked to produce concepts and laws that oppress women. At the same time there can be no doubt that many Iranian women, including an intelligentsia, have embraced fundamentalism apparently freely. This seeming paradox is the starting point for this paper. We first need to identify the arguments employed by female proponents of fundamentalism in Iran and to counterpose these to the arguments of some of the central (and therefore male) ideologues of the regime. Perhaps then we may be in a better position to understand the behaviour of many women who embrace an ideology and way of life that seem to the outsider to be a kind of prison.

This paper is concerned with a discussion of doctrine rather than a sociological or psycho-social exploration of why Iranian women have been receptive to Islamic fundamentalism. Such discussion cannot produce a complete explanation of individual female behaviour in Iran; it ignores, for example, the likelihood that some of this behaviour is an aspect of a tendency we know from elsewhere, whereby the oppressed sometimes embrace the teachings of their oppressors. This tendency may arise from a variety of non-rational motivations, including fear and isolation. But even if these forces are at work in Iran today, they are unlikely to represent anything like the whole explanation for the apparently widespread female acceptance of fundamentalist Islam. In the end, I must confess myself to be at a loss to account for this acceptance. But my own perspective, as an Iranian woman living in the West, is the operative one.

In recent times Western thinking about the women's question has worked to reinforce traditional European hostility to Islam. The image of Islamic societies is one of ruthless subordination of women, in implicit counterposition to the more liberated character of women in the West. And yet it is possible to see something of a convergence of some feminist analysis of Western society with the formulations of Islamic fundamentalism. What they share is a distaste for the use of women as sex objects by men. If mainstream fundamentalism can be doubted as a positive force for Iranian women, Western feminism too can be said to have had little to offer. More promising are the still fledgling analyses of Muslim women thinkers seeking to return to what they describe as a purer original Quran, discarding the traditions which have hardened into a profoundly anti-female ideology. In this enterprise it is possible to see important distinctions between the approach of male and female Muslim thinkers of the contemporary period. Female fundamentalists have made their own compromises with ideologues of the present regime in Iran, but their thinking has the merit of seeking to fashion an order in which Iranian and comparable women will feel comfortable.

In the hundred years that preceded the Islamic revolution women slowly and painfully struggled for and gained access to formal education (beginning in 1910), abolition of the veil (1936) and the vote (1962). During the last decade of the Shah's rule even the domain of personal laws was eroded, with a curb on the unequivocal male right to divorce and custody of children (1973), a ban on polygamy, the right to alimony after divorce (1976) as well as legal abortion on demand (1974). But many women remained critical of what they saw as an enforced liberation. The unveiling of women, though rooted in more than a hundred years of struggle, had been forced on them by royal decree.

It is true that the first recorded attempt at liberation from the veil was staged by the famous feminist Qoratolayn in the 1840s.[1] Nevertheless, there was some reluctance on the part of many women to abandon the decency of the hijab for what they saw as the nakedness of unveiling. The extension of capitalism in Iran and the gradual inclusion of women in the labour market did not bring the hoped for equality but rather created a double burden, shared by women everywhere, of paid and unpaid labour. The process of modernization in Iran sharply increased the gap between the wealthy and the poor and between urban and rural areas.[2] For many, particularly among the

[1] For further discussions see H. Mahmoudian, 'Tahira: An Early Feminist,' in H. Fathi, (ed.), *Women and Family in Iran* (Leiden: E.J. Brill, 1985), H. Afshar, 'The Emancipation Struggles in Iran, Past Expectations and Future Hopes', in H. Afshar (ed.), *Women Development and Survival in the Third World* (Longmans, forthcoming).

[2] Kamran Afshar, 'The Impact of the Urban Income per capita on Agricultural Output', in H. Afshar (ed.), *Iran: A Revolution in Turmoil* (London: Macmillan, 1985; reprinted 1989), pp. 51–7.

young intelligentsia, the process of modernization was seen as detrimental to the country as a whole and to the poorest groups in particular. Echoing the ideas of Islamic revivalists across the Middle East, the Iranian fundamentalists[3] sought a return to an Islamic idyll.[4] These disparate groups, including the ulema, university students, and a lumpen proletariat, rejected both socialism and capitalism in favour of their own alternative. They sought an Islamic solution for what they described as a country wrecked by moral and spiritual bankruptcy, subjugated to the worst that the West had to offer, and gaining little for its materialistic 'westoxfication'. Islam was to provide the correct path and its advocates were to lead lost souls back to the straight and narrow. What was on offer was not more income or higher standards of living. What fundamentalism promised was a high level of morality, austerity and spiritual freedom. In this context some of the criticisms of Muslim fundamentalists concerning the involvement of women in work and the public domain remain pertinent.

THE CRITIQUE

Adopting the language of feminist discourse and sometimes the terminologies of Marxism, young educated Iranian women had frequently focused on the failures of the labour market. Like many Western feminists, their view was that participation in the labour market had not resulted in the undisputed liberation of women. Their claim was that so long as they remained bearers of inferior labour women would be poorly paid and undervalued. Similarly, so long as the reproductive activities of women and the burden of child raising remain in the private and feminine domain of unpaid labour, this double or triple

---

[3] This paper will use the general term 'fundamentalism' to include authors and intellectuals who joined the Islamic revivalist movement in Iran in the 1960s and 1970s. I am well aware that there is no Persian or Arabic equivalent of the word 'fundamentalism', and that Muslims prefer adjectives such as 'revivalist' or 'radical', which they deem more appropriate. However, I prefer to use the term fundamentalist because of its echoes in Western and other religions, and to indicate that although the question under discussion is an Islamic aspect of this experience, it is part and parcel of the wider religious fundmentalism experienced across the world.

[4] For discussion of a similar experience with Hinduism, see Amrita Chhachhi's chapter in Deniz Kandiyoti (ed.), *Women and State* (London: Macmillan, 1989).

burden would prevent women from breaking out of their subordinate position.[5]

Prominent Iranian ideologues, including Ali Shariati (a teacher from the northern provinces who rejected Marxism but sought to forge an Islamic socialism) and Ayatollah Mottahari (an influential religious leader), as well as many women writers, have concurred in this analysis. They argue that the penetration of capitalism and its values has failed women totally and left them bereft of honour and dignity. One of the best-known Iranian exponents of this view is Zahra Rahnavard. One of the earliest converts to fundamentalism, Rahnavard abandoned her Persian name Zohreh, as well as the miniskirt, for an Islamic name and the veil. Rejecting both the 'left' and the 'right', she considers Marxism and labour anlysis to be as oppressive to women as capitalism and its associated cult of female beauty:

Imperialism declares that woman is a beautiful female species, who has the right and the duty to show off her looks and in the process by exhibiting this beauty enrich the capitalist.

The factory owners are of the view that her adaptable muscular force is useful for mobilizing the production process . . .

These depraved ideologies prefer to push women out of their nests and their homes and make them abandon their children to nurseries and boarding schools and line up to serve in the offices, factories, shops and up streets and down alleys.

On the other hand, the Marxists see women's liberation in terms of:

1. The necessity for the destruction of private property;
2. The destruction of family and its pattern of private ownership;
3. The liberation of women from the constraints of their family dependence on husbands and responsibility for children. They support the availability of publicly funded creches and nurseries to provide childcare and freedom of women from the menial drudgery of housework and irrelevant constraints such as virginity and adultery and freedom of young women to choose to sleep with whomsoever they wish.

[5] There is an extensive literature on both these points. These include, among many others, D. Elson and R. Pearson, in L. Sargent (ed.), *Women and Revolution: A Discussion of the Unhappy Marriage of Marxism and Feminism* (London: Pluto Press, 1981), pp. 1–42; V. Beechey, *Unequal Work* (London: Verso, 1987); S. Mitter, *Common Faith and Common Bond* (London: Pluto, 1987); H. Afshar (ed.) *Women, Work and Ideology in the Third World* (London: Tavistock, 1987); F. Frobel, *et al., The New International Division of Labour* (Cambridge: Cambridge University Press, 1980).

4. Enabling women to participate fully in the process of production.[6]

Rahnavard argues that in the unequal struggle in the labour market, women lose out physically and psychologically. They are exploited by the market and degraded in every sense:

> They exploit her labour in the fields and factories and offices so that in no time at all they turn her into an old hag, a broken woman who has nothing left . . . this is the disaster that has befallen the Russian woman so that in the Communist bloc, with very few exceptions, we do not see any remarkable women emerging in the public arena.[7]

Thus employment proves unrewarding. Furthermore, Rahnavard shares the views of some Western feminists that, on the whole, neither communism nor capitalism has effectively solved the dilemma of paid and unpaid employment of women. Both have failed to accommodate motherhood and social reproduction:

> The Marxists say women are equal to men in every respect. The only exception is the specific requirements of maternity such as giving birth and suckling new born babies, but these only last 1-3 months. Otherwise women are no different and must, like the men, the youths and the children serve the production process . . . The only road to freedom for women is by cutting the classical familial bonds and joining the great process of industrial production . . .
>
> These steps lead to the same ends as capitalism. What this process denies is the contradictions between the very existence of women and the survival of corrupt orders, the contradiction between womanhood and the supremacy of the processes of production . . .
>
> The Marxist solution on the one hand shatters the familial bonds, tears the children away from the warm embrace of their mothers and throws them to the mercy of nurseries, at the same time as it deprives mothers from their purest sentiments, the devotion for their children; on the one hand it encourages them to move towards prostitution and adultery . . . [8]

The view that state childcare inevitably leads to alienation and the emergence of a dislocated social order is shared by Rahnavard and Khomeini, but scarcely by Western feminists. On the other hand, we can find an example of a convergence of feminists and fundamentalists

[6] Zahra Rahnavard, *Toloueh Zaneh Mosalman* (Tehran: Mahboubeh Publication, n.d.), pp. 52–3.

[7] Ibid., p. 82.

[8] Ibid., pp. 52–3, 27–36.

in the view that both capitalism and socialism have come to exploit women as sex objects.

Now under this universal imperialist control . . . she too has become one of the many sources of exploitation, of disempowerment and of paralysis, of stealing and hoarding from all . . . the very essence of her life is sucked out.

How?

From her, now with the help of sociologists and psychologists they have built a scented, arousing, undulating, naked doll who wriggles through beauty and fashion journals to make herself ever prettier.

But why?

To improve the sale of their useless surplus products, old stocks which if left much longer on the shelves would bring about their total ruination and the downfall of their filthy order. So she advertises for them and sells for them. They have made her into a common doll.

. . . The values and standards of dependence on imperialism and capitalism make of woman the object of lust, a most desirable object that must beautify and expose herself.[9]

Similarly, Ayatollah Morteza Mottahari is of the view that capitalism has made women mere mannequins:

If you wish to see the rented woman then you must drop in at the cafes and night clubs and see how . . . for an insignificant wage . . . women have to surrender their body, soul and honour to men . . .

· The rented woman is the one who for the benefit of a commercial concern has to contort herself in a thousand different forms so as to lure a client for the goods. She has to appear in indescribable ways on our television screens to advertise their products.[10]

The language may be somewhat less puritanical, but of course there are feminists in the West who deplore the reduction of women to the status of sex objects and mindless pursuers of manufactured images of femininity, fashion and beauty.

Despite such similarities of analysis, the convergence between Islamic fundamentalism and Western feminism is obviously only partial. Certainly, the overall goals and strategies of the movements are quite dissimilar. In part, these are based on differing views of women and femininity, and in part on too optimistic a view of Islam. In the classic mould of revivalism, fundamentalists chose an idealized,

9 Ibid., pp. 11–12, 27.

10 Ayatollah Morteza Mottahari, *Nezameh Hoquqeh Zan Dar Islam* (Qum: Islamic Publication, 1980), p. 49.

timeless, static interpretation of Islam and its benefits for women in their writings.[11] In Iran, young disillusioned women responded to the call of Islam as a reaction against the anomie and alienation that helter-skelter models of dependent development had created. The ostentatious wealth of the new bourgeoisie had little perceptible impact on the lives of the mass of the people and provided little but envy for the growing numbers of the poor and destitute. The ever larger numbers of migrants and idealistic youth who had begun to gain access to education joined in their aspiration for a world in which women could occupy the sacred place allocated them by the holy text of the Quran. The problem is that, in practice, the world they live in is organized by men who for centuries have interpreted and implemented Islamic laws. These interpretations have always been detrimental to women and are backed by man-made laws.[12] Fundamentalist women have decided to return to the text and begin again.[13] But in their bargain with patriarchy, fundamentalist women have lost sight of the dynamics of economics and political reality.[14] Hence their different reasons for endorsing the veil and their Islamic views of motherhood and domesticity.

WOMEN AND ISLAM

Intellectually, women Muslim scholars have a great advantage in their current efforts to reinterpret Islam in favourable terms: this stems in part from the undoubted love and admiration that the Prophet of Islam had for his first wife, Khadijah, and for women in general. If we accept the proposition that all religions have endorsed a patriarchal structure and have discriminated against women, we may be able to argue that Islam has oppressed women less than some other faiths. At the very least, it should be possible to argue that there is no inherently greater

[11] I am indebted to Ruth Pearson for referring me to Amrita Chhachhi's chapter in D. Kandiyoti (ed.), op. cit., where this point has been discussed at length.

[12] H. Afshar, 'Khomeini's Teachings and Their Implications for Women in Iran', in Tabari, Azar and Yeganeh, Nahid (compilers), *In the Shadow of Islam* (London: Zed Press, 1983).

[13] There was a conference on this very issue, held in Pakistan in the summer of 1990, where participants included Riffat Hassan, who has been working extensively in this field.

[14] Deniz Kandiyoti, 'Bargaining with Patriarchy', *Gender and Society* 2(3), September 1988, pp. 274–90.

propensity for female oppression through Islam than through the other major faiths. This central proposition tends to be denied, implicitly as much as explicitly, in the contemporary discourse of international politics.

Female Muslim scholars have developed their favourable view of Islam by returning to the origins of the faith and disregarding both its current practices and the evolution of its views and ideas about women. Thus they denounce the well-known *hadith* that women were created from the left rib of Adam, which happened to have been bent. They argue that such views go against the very text of the Quran, the sacred word of God. There it is revealed that man and woman were created by God from the same essence.

Men, have fear of your Lord, who created you from a single soul. From that soul He created its mate, and through them He bestowed the earth with countless men and women. 4:1

Hassan and Rahnavard point out that in Arabic this single soul is a feminine noun and conclude that obviously it is man who has been created from the rib of woman.[15] Thus they argue that at least at the point of creation, Islam seems to do better than most other world religions in terms of equality of gender.

Islam also accords considerable economic autonomy to women and curtails the power of parents and spouses in disinheriting them or abusing their property rights. Thus Muslims point out that although women obtain half as much as men in terms of inheritance, their entitlement is inalienable, as is their independent rights of ownership:

Men shall have a share in what their parents and kinsmen have, and women shall have a share in what their parents and kinsmen leave: whether it be little or much, they are legally entitled to their share. 4:7

Those women who participate in the current Islamic resurgence have much to support their cause.

WOMEN AND MARRIAGE

It is undeniable that Muslim women do not have rights equal to those of men in marriage, but to jump from that situation to a wholesale

---

[15] Riffat Hassan, 'Made from Adam's Rib', *Al-Mushir*, vol. XXVII, no. 3, Autumn 1985, pp. 124–55; and Rahnvard.

denunciation of Islam relative to all other prevailing structures, religions and ideologies is to ignore aspects of Islam that are favourable to women. Women do not lose their identity or their wealth at marriage. In Quranic terms marriage is a flexible arrangement, arrived at by mutual consent, where women are expected to be 'obedient', but in return can expect to be kept in the style to which they were accustomed before marriage.[16] Marriage is negotiated as a contract binding on both parties, and for the consummation of marriage the contract includes an obligatory payment, *mahre*, by the husband to the wife (4:4 and 4:24). Even if the marriage is not consummated and the husband divorces his wife, he is still expected to pay half the mahre (2:238). Within marriage men are expected both to maintain their wives (4:34 and 2:236) and also treat them with kindness (2:238). Furthermore, they must pay an additional fee for mothers who agree to suckle their babies (2:233).

Thus, marriage is seen as a refuge of love and kindness for both men and women, a domain of mutual intimacy, comfort and protection. Women commentators tend to underline the importance of both partners in securing this haven of happiness:

They are expected to find tranquillity in each other's company and be bound together not only by sexual relationship, but by 'love and mercy'. Such a description comprises mutual care, consideration, comfort and protection.[17]

Given this analysis it is not surprising to see that a number of women fundamentalists argue forcefully for the separation of gender spheres and for women locating their work and energy in the domestic sphere. To them such a choice is not an indication of subordination but rather one of complementarity of genders, each with its own equally important domain of obligation. Proponents of Islam remain convinced that its great appeal to women arises from a recognition of the marital and reproductive obligations of women and the allocation of earthly and heavenly rewards for discharging these obligations. It is a heavenly duty—Islam abhors celibacy and celebrates married life. For all its differing facets and concepts of mutual obligation, marriage is not seen necessarily as a once-and-for-all event. It is an institution that

---

[16] There is much controversy among women Muslim scholars about the meaning of obedience, and whether or not it is a requirement for good behaviour rather than submission.

[17] Aisha Lemu and Fatima Hareen, *Women in Islam* (Islamic Council of Europe Publication, 1978), p. 17.

can change; men and women alike are allowed to choose different partners at different times of their lives. Divorce is extremely easy for men, and possible for those women who have the necessary foresight to include a right of divorce for themselves in their marriage contract. Failing that, women are allowed by the Quran to negotiate (4:128) or 'ransom themselves out of the relationship' (2:229). Although the Quran advises believers to seek reconciliation within marriage whenever possible (4:35, 2:28), when such efforts fail it requires that Muslim men should make reasonable provisions for their divorced wives (2:342), retain them in honour, or let them go in kindness (2:229). There is no shame attached to divorce and divorced men and women can meet and remarry (2:235). At no time are they permitted to take back the mahre.

Do not take from her the dowry you have given her even it be a talent of gold. 4:21

Thus Muslim scholars have long argued that Islam does not shackle women within marriage, and by allowing them a separate property entitlement makes them economically independent of their husbands, and therefore well able to fend for themselves. Much of this relatively progressive doctrine owed to Khadijah the Prophet's first and most remarkable wife. A rich widow who was considerably older than Muhammad, Khadijah initially appointed him as her trade representative, and he travelled the world on her behalf. Subsequently, she asked him to marry her. When Muhammad refused she referred him to his uncle, who was more or less commanded to marry off his nephew to Khadijah. The marriage was a success. Khadijah was the first convert to Islam and it was the protection of her powerful tribe that enabled Muhammad to survive the early turbulent years of Islam, when he was hunted out by the people of Mecca. So long as Khadijah was alive, Muhammad took no other wife and the verses of the Quran advocating polygamy (4:3), and the need for the relatives of the Prophet to cover their finery zinat (33:33) all came to the Prophet after her death.

POLYGAMY

But even the most submissive of converts has difficulties in accommodating the question of polygamy. The new emerging school of revivalist feminist Muslims, assisted by scholars such as Iqbal in Pakistan and Ali Shariati in Iran, all emphasize the positive aspects of Islam sketched above and explain away the negative ones. Hence the verse about polygamy is read in its totality, whereby it states:

But if you fear that you cannot maintain equality among them, marry one only or any slave girls you may own. This will make it easier for you to avoid injustice. 4:4

Rahnavard argues that polygamy is only permitted as a means to protect orphans and is a fallback position when, for reasons such as war, large numbers of men have been killed, and when women and particularly children are left unprotected. Lemu sees it as a way of dealing with 'the surplus of unattached women in the society'.[18]

Mahboubeh Rezayi, another of the pre-revolutionary young women fundamentalists writing in the 1970s in Iran, has a similar view. Rezayi emphasizes the fact that the Quran indicates that God viewed monogamy to be the norm and polygamy the exception, and that this respect for monogamy under normal circumstances is one of the firm pillars of women's rights within Islam.[19]

Lemu is of the view that in times of war and shortage of men, women should agree to polygamy: 'under these circumstances . . . if given the alternative many of them would rather share a husband than to have none at all'.[20] But one of the leading (of course, male) ideologues of the Islamic revolution in Iran, Ayatollah Mottahari, applauds temporary marriages whereby a man may marry a woman for as long or short a period as he wishes. Furthermore, he recommends polygamy as a 'social'necessity' to deal with depravity as well as (an assumed) gender imbalance. Hence he argues that men should approach polygamy 'as a necessary duty . . . just like the duty to do one's military service . . . '.[21] Thus the scholarly interpretations of women thinkers within Islam and their conditional support of polygamy is dismissed by a leading religious expert whose views echo those of contemporary lawmakers in Iran. In this way a crucial intellectual debate loses relevance in the context of insensitive fundamentalist laws and their purveyors.

[18] Ibid., p. 24.

[19] Mahboubeh Rezayi, *Horiat va Hoquqeh Zan dar Islam* (Milad Publication, 3rd reprint, 1979, Shahrivar 1358), p. 94.

[20] Lemu, p. 28.

[21] Mottahari, p. 348.

DOMESTICITY AND MOTHERHOOD

It is not so much marriage as motherhood that is seen by the devout as the particular privilege of women. It is argued that there has been a divine division of labour and that women, being made for domesticity and motherhood, should adopt this role willingly.

That motherhood is a sacred duty and that 'mothers of believers' have a special corner of heaven designed specially for them is not contested by any of the fundamentalist theorists. Islam ratifies a division of labour with women as guardians of the cradle and men as breadwinners. It is, however, the causes, the rewards and the length of time devoted to such division of labour which is open to discussion. For some, such as Ali Shariati, women can only achieve success in terms of their menfolk, be it through marriage, motherhood or daughterhood.

So, fundamentalism sees itself as a ratification of motherhood as a paid and respectable role for women, to be performed within the domestic sphere; and certainly part of its appeal is rooted in the validation of this role. Much of the writings of the fundamentalists is directed against what is seen as the feminist, Marxist or capitalist tendency to destroy the centrality of motherhood and to denounce domesticity as a restraining chain for women.

Rahnavard asks:

Does motherhood, wifehood, lack of responsibility for earning a family income . . . imprison the Muslim woman in her home, tie her down with familiar ties?

Never! Never . . .

This is the road to freedom, to the liberation of women, to her growth and achievement . . . She has the revolutionary responsibility of showing the right path and prohibiting the wrong deed, decrying the false and teaching the right . . . It is women who teach the future generations and it is women who must endorse or reject any political agenda.[22]

But of course such a sanguine view of motherhood, rooted as it is in biological essences, denies choice to women. Eternally they are to confine themselves to reproduction and any deviation from such a path would prove fatal to both the particular woman and the whole society. Mottahari explains:

[22] Rahnavard, op. cit., pp. 103–10.

The replacement of the father by the government, which is the current trend in the West, will undermine maternal sentiments, alter the very nature of motherhood from an emotional tie into a form of waged employment with money as an intermediary between mother and her love. Motherhood then is no longer a bond, but a paid employment. It is obvious that this process would lead to the destruction of the family and the unavoidable and total annihilation of womankind.[23]

FORMAL EMPLOYMENT

If women are the bastions of the family and if their failure to remain good mothers is perilous to the whole social well being, then of necessity they will become dependent on men for their livelihood. This is accepted by all believers who refer to the Quranic verse, stating:

Men have authority over women because Allah has made the one superior to the other, and because they spend their wealth to maintain them. 4:34

Using the quite diverse meaning of each word, Hassan argues that the interpreters of this verse have simply chosen the wrong meaning. What is implied here is merely a permission granted to men to spend their wealth on women for the short period of childbearing. Authority here is not given to men absolutely and forever, but is accorded to them for a specific purpose and a limited period. It is even possible to interpret the verse to mean that at the time of childbearing men have the responsibility to spend their wealth on the superior women who are capable of reproduction and must be provided for at this time.[24] Like Hassan, Rahnavard interprets the verse to mean that men are given a duty rather than an authority, and the notion that one is superior to the other is intended to convey that each is superior to the other in their own different spheres.[25]

But different scholars make different judgments on the implications of this responsibility. Riffat Hassan, a leading woman theologian of Pakistani origin who has embarked on an ambitious project of reinterpreting the Quran with women in mind, argues that this is a very temporary obligation. Hassan sees the episode of economic de-

---

[23] Mottahari, op. cit., p. 214.

[24] Riffat Hassan, discussion paper at the ISIS WICE meeting, Chapelle d'-Abondance, August 1988.

[25] Rahnavard, op. cit., pp. 79–82.

pendence as short term, and possibly lasting only while the mother is caring for the baby. It is a means of avoiding the terrible problems of being an impecunious single mother, or having to combine full-time work with childcare. But Hassan emphasizes that the bounties abundantly bestowed by God are not merely bestowed on men. Nor are they gender specific in kind, in terms of intellectual ability or artistic talents. There is no impediment on the formal employment of women in any field and they may have the same or greater abilities than men.

SEXUALITY AND THE VEIL

It is on female sexuality that male and female Muslim fundamentalists are most sharply divided in their analysis of women's role in society. Women thinkers have returned to the Quran in order to create a vision of the future that is based on the best that Islam can offer, in counterposition to laws made by men fearful of female sexuality and unable to come to terms with the degree of independence that the prophet of Islam can be seen to have conceded to women.

Sexuality in general and female sexuality in particular are major concerns among Muslim theologians. According to the scholar, Nabia Abbott, this dates back to the time of the Prophet: 'Sex was nearly an obsession with the entire population, and sex talk, frank among the better element tended to be indecent and lewd among the worst sort'.[26]

Islam, like other religions, decries overt female sexuality, but in common with Hinduism it also celebrates sexual union and does not ascribe a high religious value to celibacy and sexual abstinence. The problem is framed as one of men driven by ever-present desire, and thus extremely vulnerable to woman the temptress, forever hunting for male sexual prey.

In her fascinating study, *Woman in the Muslim Unconscious*, Fatna A. Sabba argues that there is a deep-seated fear of the omnisexual woman among Muslim men who are convinced that she

can hardly be a good believer, a pious Muslim bound by the faith to be content with one-quarter of a man . . . The unreasonable demands of her voracious vagina are going to compel her to launch an attack on all the rules that govern sexuality in Muslim civilization and especially those relating to hetero-

[26] Nadia Abbot, *Aisha the Beloved of Muhammad* (London: al Saqi Books, 1985), p. 22.

sexuality, fidelity, social hegemony . . . virtue (prostitution is condemned as the worst possible degradation). And finally these demands will push her to a lack of respect for sex roles . . .

Her desire is a force so irresistible, so biological, so animal, that she is fatally impelled to rebel against the constraints, the barriers that are supported to try to impair her capacity for sexual pleasure. She is by definition in rebellion against all the care taken for hierarchization and classification as the foundation of the spiritual Islam, which is based on the control of biological forces and their subordination to an order designed by and for man and his glorification in the male god Allah.[27]

Hence the need to hide women, to protect men against potentially omnisexual woman. The perspective of the Muslim unconscious makes it considerably easier to understand much of the writings of many male Muslim leaders, which would otherwise seem too full of hatred for women to be rational.

This surely is the reason for the introduction of the veil and polygamy. Today the obsession with sexuality remains as prevalent as it ever was, but there are strong differences between male and female accounts of the process. Men prefer to hide their fears behind the construct of woman the temptress. According to Mottahari:

Woman with her natural cleverness . . . has noticed the weak point that nature has given to men and has made him the seeker of love and the pursuer and has made woman the sought one and the pursued. . . . when woman realized this situation and her position where men are concerned and recognized his weak point, she resorted to make up and wear ornaments and luxury to help her capture the man's heart and at the same time she distanced herself from man in the knowledge that she must not give herself for nothing, but must inflame his desire and passion and thus raise her own status.[28]

Slowly and cleverly, Mottahari is doing away with any Islamic denial of the sinfulness of women, and once more we find woman the temptress enticingly luring the mind of this leading Shia ideologue. It is all well and good for women such as Mahboubeh Rezayi to warn us against 'these seemingly religious leaders who have pretension to understanding Islam but who in the guise of Islam knowingly or unintentionally interpret Islam according to their own wishes and

[27] Fatna A. Sabba, Rahnavard, *Women in the Muslim Unconscious* (London: Pergamon Press, 1984), p. 32.

[28] Ayatollah Morteza Motthari, *Massaleyeh Hejab* (Qum: Islamic Publication, 1984), p. 52.

interests and seek to enrich themselves from such misleading interpretations'.[29]

But it is Mottahari, and not Reyazi, who influenced decision-making, and who formulated the public ideology of the Islamic republic. Rezayi's role was at best to be no more than an apologist for the regime.

In the context of Islamic fundamentalist discourse, women thinkers see marriage as a partnership between equals and the men tend to see it more as a financial transaction between the body of the female believer and the purse of the male. The transaction must produce exclusive property for the man. So it is not the mini-skirts and see-through blouses per se that are objectionable, but the wearing thereof in public that is seen as problematic. Mottahari explains why: 'To drag out sexual urges and satiate them in public away from the home environment weakens society, undermines its labour power and reduces its production capacity'.[30]

But whether women themselves are willing participants or have been socialized into being so is in dispute. Whereas Rahnavard, a woman, is clearly of the view that it is the socialization process that has created such disgrace, Ayatollah Morteza Mottahari argues that capitalism has merely facilitated the expansion of women's 'natural' tendencies: 'The women's instinct for beautification and luring of men, is a terrible instinct. Beware of the day when men applaud this instinct and designer and fashion makes facilitate the process'.[31]

Oddly enough there is no discussion of why the corrupt West ends up with higher levels of productivity, and a male population that is not obviously traumatized. It may be true to say that Muslim men are caught in the trap of their own sexual fantasies. They have created this myth of the potent man in need of a harem full of women to satisfy his eternal lust, but they are then faced with women who are feared to be more sexually active and demanding (to the point of being voracious) than men. It thus becomes necessary to hide and cover women, to confine them to living in seclusion under the 'authority' of one man in order to confine their sexual demands and to protect other men from their allure. At the same time, all this hiding of women makes them appear even more desirable to Muslim men, who remain eternally obsessed with sexuality and unable to decode it.

[29] Rezayi, op. cit., p. 96.
[30] Motthari, op. cit., p. 77.
[31] Ibid., p.94.

CONCLUSION

As I noted earlier, I find it difficult to understand why women choose to accept the veil. Of course, by now standard accounts of the behaviour of the oppressed tell us that those who are subordinated sometimes espouse the teaching of the oppressor and adopt it unquestioningly. Undoubtedly, this has been a factor in regimes such as in Iran. But so has the need for women to have a clear identity, consistent with their own culture and separate from unattractive models fashioned on a Hollywood idea of womanhood. Just as Western feminists began rejecting make up, pretty dresses, etc., Islamic women merely covered it all up; or, in the case of the resistance groups, rejected the ornaments and accepted the garments of submission to the will of Allah.

Perhaps the most important factor of all is the inability of capitalism and the process of development to lighten the double burden of those women who take an active part in the formal employment sector. The ideology of patriarchy and its dictates demand that all women, whether employed or not, should remain the guardians of the home fire, the cradle and the grave. But they are expected to fulfil these roles free of charge for the doubtful joys of femininity and fulfilment. For Muslim women the burden is all the heavier since the belief in gender-specific familial demands is part and parcel of their stated religious duties. Furthermore, in practice, they have considerably less public provision for the care of the very young and the very old. Those women who do work do so thanks to the availability of unpaid familial support, often provided by their children.

Nor are women ever paid as well as men, and the segregation of the labour market firmly discriminates against all the work done and the skills acquired by women, who are everywhere considered secondary wage earners. Given this reality it is not surprising that Rahnavard points an accusing finger at both socialism and capitalism. The fragmentation of the family, the increasing alienation of the young, and the impoverishment and dependence of the old on ever-decreasing public resources make life in the advanced industrial societies appear less than alluring to many women who choose to convert or return to Islam for eternal solutions. There is of course the additional social pressure of what Helie-Lucas calls 'entryism'.[32] To gain peer approval

[32] See her essay in this volume.

and benefit from the practical and emotional support offered by fundamentalists, many chose the easier option of entering into this group rather than fighting for what, in the long run, may prove to be illusory benefits.

There is little evidence to suggest that any religious system has ever succeeded in protecting old cultures, traditions and familial values from the advent of industrialization, though it is conceivable that post-industrialism, by returning workers to their home base, may yet change preceding trends. Nevertheless, much as I disagree with the contentions of Muslim fundamentalists on the question of women and their position in society, I do see that what they offer—in terms of paid domesticity in the context of a relatively flexible and clearly delineated marriage contract—does have a certain logic and attraction for many women. Given the obvious failure of Western-style feminism to bring lasting liberation for Muslim women, for many the only way forward may be through a feminist reinterpretation of Islam itself.

But there is a major difference between male and female Muslim commentators of the new devout generation on the question of nature or nurture, with women seeing reproduction as natural and subordination as nurtured; most of the men, on the other hand, view women as naturally inferior and as physically and mentally unequal. Within a year of its establishment in Iran the new regime rejected all personal law improvements by decree. The veil was reintroduced, abortion made illegal, and a 'bantu' system of education introduced with women trained to become good mothers and banned from the faculties of science and engineering. Within three years, the Islamic criminal laws, *Qassas*, introduced in July 1981, formally relegated women to the position of second-class citizens and confirmed their apparent legal subordination. They were banned from practising law. Women became, legally, almost invisible. Their evidence, if uncorroborated by a male witness, could not be accepted by courts of law. According to the new laws of retribution, the murderer of a woman could only be punished if her male protector paid the blood money of the killer (articles 5 and 6). Women are strongly advised not to participate in the public domain; they have been barred from some professions, marginalized in others, and subjected to segregated work places.[33]

---

[33] Haleh Afshar, 'Women in Work and the Poverty Trap in Iran', in H. Afshar and B. Agarwal (eds), *Women, Poverty and Ideology in Asia* (London: Macmillan, 1989), pp. 43–69; and Haleh Afshar, 'Women and Work, Ideology not Adjustment

Thus, in practice, far from bestowing pride and glory on women, Islamic laws have proved highly oppressive. There is growing evidence that women themselves are beginning to realize this within Iran, despite the intense process of political re-education and Islamic propaganda currently addressed at women. So long as male fundamentalists are making the laws, women defenders of Islam can do little more than remain apologists for the regime.

---

at Work in Iran', in H. Afshar and C. Dennis (eds.), *Women and Structural Adjustment in the Third World* (Macmillan, 1992).

The South African Native Administration Act of 1927: Reflections on a Pathological Case of Legal Pluralism

MARTIN CHANOCK

This paper is an historical case study of the use by the state of legal pluralism. In 1927 the Government of South Africa, through the Native Administration Act (no. 38 of 1927), imposed upon the African population a national system of 'recognition' of African law, and extended and systematized the separate system of courts. This was to be one of the most fundamental institutional cornerstones of the development of the government's policy of segregation. This paper does not purport to describe fully the introduction, content or workings of this Act, but revolves around it, examining it in the light of assertions based on the legitimacy of the traditions of the oppressed, and of minority 'traditions' and cultural autonomy within state systems, and with state patronage of such assertions. (While it is obvious that black South Africans are not a minority in mathematical terms, they have been a figurative minority in terms of access to state power.) It considers the strategies and concepts of Africans, and of the state, in constructing versions of 'tradition', and looks at some of the features of the system imposed by legislation.

This paper describes a situation more than half a century ago. Much has since changed in South Africa. Proletarianization and urbanization have been intensified. The economic viability of the African rural areas has deteriorated well beyond the worst-case scenarios imaginable in the 1920s. Large numbers of people have been uprooted and forcibly resettled. Coherent resistance to oppression has led to the end of legal apartheid. The state's attempts to revive and manipulate traditionalism have largely collapsed and the institutional separation of black and white legal systems have been abandoned. In the circumstances of the disintegration of the apartheid state and in considering the South African future, focus has, rightly, been on transfer of power over central state institutions. The black liberation movements have given little attention to the questions of cultural differentiation and institutional separatism which concern minorities in plural societies elsewhere. The reasons for this are several, including their historical associations with Marxism; the need to avoid the taint of state-sponsored ethnicity; and their assertion of the legitimacy of a future political order without racial differentiation. Yet, in thinking about the shape of a future legal system in a black-ruled South Africa in the light of the experience of inherited legal pluralism based on racial and cultural differentiation in the rest of Africa, the place and content of black law needs to be considered. The question which must be posed is, 'Should a free South Africa have greater legal pluralism, or less?'

In this consideration of the Act of 1927 I will examine how ideological representations of African societies mutually constructed (though not necessarily with equally influential input) by Africans and whites were used by the state to construct an institutional system. The state, white ethnographers, and a range of African subjects produced differing versions, from differing standpoints, representing different interests. As Clifford remarks, 'processes rather than essences' are involved in the experience of cultures.[1] My purpose is to consider whose voices were heard in the processes; answering what questions; addressing what agenda? In constructing a system for a new South Africa, how will the pictures of cultures be created? Who will be asking what questions, and choosing, for what reasons of state, among the variety of answers? An appropriate regime of black law will not be lying waiting, ready to be employed. Boon has written that 'cultures continually fabricate . . . ideas of each other and of themselves'.[2] What range of cultural/legal 'fabrications' will be produced by black South Africans at the end of the twentieth century, and which, if any, will be seen as appropriate to a new state?

CULTURE AND POLITICS

In the history of South Africa equality and differentiation have been

[1] J. Clifford, *The Predicament of Culture* (Cambridge, Mass.: Harvard University Press, 1988), p. 275.

[2] J.A. Boon, *Other Tribes, Other Scribes. Symbolic Anthropology in the Comparative Study of Cultures, Histories, Religions, and Texts* (Cambridge: Cambridge University Press, 1982), p. 27.

in constant opposition. Oppression has been based on differentiation: liberation holds out promise of equality. In the South African context there are great problems in approaching equality as oppressive, and differentiation as necessary for freedom in culturally plural societies. Yet in many of the post-colonial states it is the assertions of cultural uniqueness and validity, and the consequent legitimacy of the claims for differentiated political and legal institutions, as opposed to the (usually unconfessed) messianism of liberal assimilationism, which is a core problem. In the current world this predicament has been dealt with on one scale by the proliferation of nation states and the legitimization of the ideology of national self-determination. But the nation states, of course, contain within themselves many competing assertions of legitimacy, and these have usually been subject to assimilationist strategies (ranging from oppression to neglect) by central governments. While the rhetoric and institutions of large scale nationalisms reign supreme, the assertions of smaller groups have an increasingly illogical and extreme appearance in a world in which the commanding heights of political rationalism are dominated by the discourse of international capitalism. Yet in some polities attempts are made to give expression (within an unchanged framework of majority domination) to aspects of minority cultures. The rhetorical debates in terms of universal values, rights and laws versus separate heritages and cultures, have their counterpart in South African history. (The obvious must be noted. In South Africa it is the minority which has ruled, not the majority. This made an assimilationist strategy impossible for the state, as it could not be combined with continued white rule). The great weight of cultural evolutionism which still sits upon these debates makes this even more obvious. The excluded minorities of the modern world are characteristically those which have adapted least to imperial and post-imperial transformations. (Many cultural minorities of a different type exist, of course, within the dominant polities, none of which are monocultural. But minorities of this sort, like the Scots, or the French Canadians, have aligned their fundamental rationales with modern state and capital.) The cultural assertions being made must not only validate themselves in political terms, but in terms of evolved rational equality with the dominant group. The politics of cultural condescension (which is its kindest face) has many reminiscent reverberations within South African history, where the assimilationist vs segregationist debate has been conducted in terms ranging from blunt racism to the most polite of cultural comparativist discourses. Between assimilationism, and the elaborate plans for cultivating the emergence of 'traditional' polities to a form of non-challenging separatism, there have been many constructions and manipulations of the content of the traditional heritages, by both white rulers and black leaders.

The subordinated minorities, where they face an overwhelming countervailing power or the crushing hegemony of racism, have been obliged to rely less on the force of their political assertions, and more upon a tactical moralism. They must assert their virtue and innocence: their case for liberation and recognition relies upon the acknowledgment by the dominant groups of the righteousness of the cause, and, therefore, of the virtue of subordinated cultural institutions. These conditions of political struggle have had profound implications for the understanding of, and presentation of, the cultures of the subordinate. While racist domination required the denigration of their institutions, the new politics requires their sanctification. The features of the latter have two important characteristics. First, they present indigenous institutions as existing in a pre-capitalist and pre-contact limbo, situating their essence outside history; and, secondly, they ignore the oppressions within and among the oppressed. This ultimate condescension of bestowing innocence on the subordinate (as if only their total virtue could qualify them to be free), has not usually been rejected by the entrepreneurial leadership of such groups who have, for sound tactical reasons, taken it up as a saleable feature of indigenous institutions. But ultimately these games are destructive: an appreciation of values need not be a bestowal of innocence. The bestowal of innocence has as much to do with the construction of a picture of the dominant societies as the dominated ones. As Clifford notes, colonial anthropology 'dichotomises and essentialises its portrayal of others and . . . functions in a complex but systematic way as an element of colonial domination'.[3] But this same process is to be found in the replying representations of the dominated: as with Primitive Man, so with Negritude. Both concepts function simultaneously as a celebration of the self and a criticism of the other. Cultures, as Boon notes, are contrasts, which 'can materialise only in counter distinction to another culture'. They keep 'symbolic track' of themselves by a selection of symbols chosen and valued as against the contrary arrangements of others.[4]

[3] Clifford, *The Predicament of Culture*, p. 268.
[4] Boon, *Other Tribes, Other Scribes*, pp. ix, 52.

We need to understand both the nature of pre-capitalist and pre-conquest differentiations, and also those created in the modern era. We need to know that while the state manipulates and ignores cultural traditions, so too do the people themselves, and often they do so in concert. For example, progressive elites and rural traditionalists can be shown over much of the South African material focussed on in this paper not to have had the same interests either instrumentally or ideologically. We must therefore ask about the conditions under which these two groups could come together to express a common interest, and in what idiom they could express their interests. In conditions of severe economic oppression, particularly where there is substantial urbanization, the ideological framework which has made most sense in interpreting the world for many people has been one of the forms of revolutionary Marxism. It became common for third world political movements to use this framework for a wide range of political ends, and also for elites to communicate with a wider audience in its terms. But where oppression is racial and cultural it may not be a sufficient medium through which to express meaning and mobilize support, especially where a substantial proportion of the oppressed population is not proletarianized or urbanized. In these circumstances the idiom of communication between elite and masses is that of traditional values and institutions. This is also a useful idiom where the elites are not themselves oppressed in anything but a cultural sense and shy away from Marxist rhetoric. Their natural language of opposition is in these circumstances cultural, and forms an ideal basis of communication with a wider mass, particularly when that mass has a limited engagement in the cash economy. But we must, of course, be aware that this does not mean that the communicating groups have congruent interests. And we must also be aware that ethnic assertions have became more prominent in the cold war era partly because Marxist assertions have not been acceptable in the political formations of the Western world or most of the Third World. While revolutionary rhetoric in Marxist terms guaranteed the unacceptability and crushing of a political movement, ethnic assertions could be 'heard' by Western powers. In liberal polities a discourse which, while not being revolutionary, can yet be emotionally and symbolically satisfying to cultural minorities, has an excellent chance of being established as ethnographic truth.

We must also analyse the different positions of traditional and modern leaderships in their relation to the dominant state. Which group can best make an impact on the politically dominant, or an alliance with them? In most of the history of the colonial period traditional leadership has been seen as being the most likely to adapt to new rulers, taking a subordinate share of state authority, and being of most 'use' to the state in its exercise of law and power. But in terms of the long term and symbolical legitimacy of new domination it is the modern, assimilated leadership which offers most to the dominant. While this leadership may compete most vigorously for a share of power in the new order, it has not usually rejected the transformations on which the new order rests. Once a successful political assertion has been made, the politics of cultural traditionalism have usually been abandoned. (One might consider here the spectacular case of the Mau Mau in Kenya). In the post-imperial world the politics of culture, therefore, have become associated not with the successful nationalisms which revolted against Empire but with situations of permanent subordination within entrenched states.

The individualistic concepts of human rights enshrined in international law through documents like the Universal Declaration of Human Rights have come under attack, particularly in the Third World, where they have been condemned as threatening and secondary to the stability of the state and the goals of nation building and economic development.[5] The economic and social rights of groups have been asserted as deserving of recognition in addition to, and often with priority over, the rights of individuals. Faced with the authoritarianism of governments and the difficulties of asserting individual rights within the domestic legal systems, the notion of group rights appears seductively adaptable to the leadership of cultural minorities. The demand for group as opposed to individual rights for the subordinate can be politically more effective. It can also be more intellectually coherent, when the minority community can present its own cultural rationale as being one of 'community' of a 'traditional' sort, rather than a modernist 'individualism'. But this communally justified assertion has also been a political tactic to secure advances within those legal systems in which individual rights are more easily recognized and secured, like those of Canada, the USA and Australia. 'Rights' are a point of intersection between law and politics and in the modern

---

[5] R. Nhlapo 'International Protection of Human Rights and the Family: African Variations on a Common Theme', Family Law Reform in Africa. Conference of the International Family Law Association, Harare, 1987.

state effective rights must ultimately be rights in law, as well as in politics or rhetoric. For this reason this paper approaches these questions through a focus on legal questions.

As the realm of law is one of the major parts of the 'content' of traditionalism, a look at the development of black law in the particular historical circumstances in South Africa may throw broader light on the construction and uses of 'culture' in relation to the state. Approaching African concerns through the customary law can produce insights into the preoccupations and conflicts within African communities. It also offers a corrective to a monolithic, unidirectional and teleological history. The realm of customary law also gives us access to the development of traditionalist and communalist ideologies which were formerly, and still are, at the heart of much of African politics not only of the traditionalist, but also of the radical kind. We should also note that notions about black law expressed by the dominant whites were important to the construction of white law. In this sense law can be seen as a particularly powerful form of ethnographic writing which concretizes and institutionalizes the contrasts between cultures. And, as we will see, certain social and legal institutions were picked upon for the construction of differences. Blacks were expected to assimilate in the areas of labour contract and commercial credit and debt, but to remain inherently different in the realm of marriage and family, economically perfectable, but reproductively different.

CREATING SEPARATE LEGAL SYSTEMS

I *African Resistance*

The state's version of African community and consequently of African law was not imposed on a population uniformly trying to shake off its heritage and integrate itself into economic life as individualist proletarians. While the system produced by the state was not the same as the (varying) versions of customary regime existing in African societies, it nonetheless depended for its workability on inhabiting the same universe of discourse and behaviours as the indigenous versions, and on being recognizable, plausible and acceptable to a wide-ranging constituency. The resort to African law as a measure of government must also be understood not as a form of super subtle statecraft by an all-powerful state, but as an index of the limits of its power. We shall consider first, therefore, the range of black resistances to white rule in order that we might understand something of the context, from the point of view of Africans and African leadership, in which the system was constructed.

There were a number of responses to white domination in South Africa on the ideological level. One was to accept the claims of the dominant group, but to press for equality for those Africans who met the qualifications of civilization, property ownership and Christianity. For the major part of the African leadership of the period about which I am writing this was the main ingredient of their politics. It made real sense in terms of the policy of token assimilationism which had been followed in the Cape Colony which extended the status of voter to such an African elite. It also made sense on a lesser scale in the light of the possibility of exemption from the operation of 'native law' (important for the Christians of Natal, and, later, of other provinces) and the pass laws. Nonetheless it was not possible for these people to forget that they were African—white South African racism made certain of that—and they could not be absorbed in any sense into the dominant racial elite. The more conservative of them therefore remained open to ideologies of traditionalism. Some of the more radical embraced versions of Marxism, and their engagement with the politics of the urban proletariat and trade unionism led them further away from ideas focussed on traditionalism.

In the rural areas, however, leadership was heavily invested in versions of traditionalism. The strength of this attachment to traditionalism, both ideological and instrumental, under circumstances of elemental social and economic change, must be positively accounted for and not simply assumed as a feature of backward rural life. The chiefs and headmen defended and, sometimes in co-operation with the government, extended their own powers. At the same time the bureaucratization of these powers, and their supervision by the Department of Native Affairs, rendered them considerably less 'traditional.' And the continuing existence of various forms of rural revolt and unrest reflected a complex mixture of traditionalism, independent Christianity, black nationalism and Marxism, much of it drawing strength from images of community. These were not random and naive confusions but responses which made sense in terms of the need to defend control over allocation of rural lands, and maintain viable families and households under the pressure of labour migration.[6]

[6] W. Beinart, *The Political Economy of Pondoland* (Cambridge, 1982); and

It has now become clear that there has been a concentration on urban life in recent South African historical scholarship, at the expense of rural life. The rural areas have been depicted as superseded backwaters, left behind by the flow of history. But it was in the rural areas that most of life was lived, and if it is given its proper place in the country's history, a greater emphasis on the adaptations and resistances and uses, of the realm of the customary will become necessary. Both government and the governed dealt extensively in the currency of custom. In South Africa, as elsewhere in Africa, it is not so much that this currency was devalued, but rather revalued and re-issued, more than once. This currency reform was crucial to the government of, and life in, the rural areas. It takes place within a framework well described by Beinart and Bundy:

The entrenchment and deepening of labour migrancy; the diminishing ability of the majority of the people to produce food for subsistence; the intensification of state control and constraints in everyday life; the limited, but increasing spread of Christianity.[7]

Rural families in African areas by and large retained access to land, though by no means in equal shares, and remained under the political authority of chiefs and headmen. Dependent on the chiefs for allocation of land and placed under their legal and political authority by the state, all rural dwellers were part of a 'traditional' system, and made their lives in accommodation with it. And while families were getting smaller and increasingly dependent on migrant earnings, the framework of 'traditional' law was still a necessary part of the formation and functioning of nearly all families.

But colonial legalism had other and perhaps more fundamental features.[8] Increased state intervention affected all areas of rural life—taxes, stock diseases, stock theft, forests and weeds—and pass and land legislation created an all embracing legal regime. State intervention to control cattle diseases and the introduction of compulsory dipping show that even the most 'traditional' area, cattle ownership, could not escape the new forms of control. Even in circumstances in which the government was gradually developing a sympathy towards traditionalism, administrative and economic logic led them to strike at basic social institutions.

W. Beinart and C. Bundy, *Hidden Struggles in Rural South Africa* (London, 1987)

[7] *Hidden Struggles in Rural South Africa*, p. 2.

[8] See in general, M.L. Chanock, *Law, Custom and Social Order* (Cambridge, 1985).

Furthermore, as elsewhere in colonial Africa, traditional leadership became 'enmeshed' in the new system of authority while at the same time, and in the dramatically altered environment, they continued to conduct 'traditional' business, the most important of which was the allocation of land. The chiefs remained 'symbols of communal rights to land' and, therefore,

some of the political processes and notions of legitimacy surrounding chieftaincy remained deeply embedded. These allowed for mass participation and provided a recognized system of justice for those who were excluded from, or would not accept, colonial courts and law . . . Perhaps most important of all, traditionalists found in the chieftaincy a means to define their rights to land—both the extent of the area they claimed as a group and the distribution of it among homesteads.[9]

Through their continued acceptance and use of the legitimacy of the chieftaincy the peasantry could resist the state's attempts to control the distribution of land, while the state, which sought to use the institution of chieftaincy, could not afford to undermine its most legitimizing feature. The chieftaincy underwrote the system of using the world of 'custom'. But there developed a very different chieftaincy from that which pre-dated white conquest. Under the Natal Code of Native Law, and later more widely under the Native Administration Act, the state clothed its own arbitrary and wide-ranging powers in chiefly garb. And while it was all too evident that this was a wolf in sheep's clothing, even the appearance of the sheep remained of considerable populist importance. In the years after the passing of the Native Land Act of 1913, which drastically reduced African rights to land, the most important issue affecting all rural Africans (and all urban migrant workers too) was access to land. While in the white farming areas the fundamental concerns of Africans were with the proletarianization of farm labour and the abolition of sharecropping and tenancies, in African areas things were different. Here the policy of segregation protected access to land based upon a regime of communal tenure and traditional authority over land distribution. Attachment to the chieftaincy, in spite of its transformation, and to an accompanying package of 'traditionalist' values, had a strong material rationale even though changing conditions were rendering many of the traditions onerous and meaningless.

The realities of rural life were those of an increasing population

---

[9] Beinart and Bundy, *Hidden Struggles*, pp. 11, 16.

without access to new land to meet its needs; overstocking of the confined space in which Africans could live; and soil erosion. Food production did not meet needs and there was increasing reliance on cash incomes from migrant labour. There was widespread debt and a growing number of persons who had no access to land, and as a consequence there were frequent disputes over allocation. Though allocation of land was unequal, with chiefs and headmen having the larger holdings, there was rejection of state initiatives to register land and redistribute it, because of fears that land held outside traditional constraints might be alienated by the holders. In addition the inflow of wages in the hands of the labour migrants, mainly young men, and occasionally women, was beginning to undermine the patriarchal households, and members of families found themselves in bitter disputes over family resources.[10]

In Natal, well before the law was amended to recognize the majority of men at the age of twenty-one, young men litigated in the courts in attempts to retain control over their wages (see below). In areas like the Ciskei three quarters of adult men were absent from their homes as migrant labourers for more than half the year. Women exercised a real day-to-day control over household resources which was unrecognized in law. The opening up of the households of the extended family to capitalist social and economic relations was undermining both the logic and the workability of the regime of customary law. Customary law had stark limitations in mediating family relations in the money economy. Yet it continued to be insisted on by the state and by all but a few Africans. This paradox needs explaining. We must consider how customary law not only retained its symbolic appeal but was adapted to become the instrument of new claims to new resources.

Black women were by no means passive in the face of state oppression and were prominent and active in many of the resistances in rural areas. Beinart and Bundy quote the prominent African leader Dr Jabavu on one such occasion commenting that 'the people with insight here are the women. They are the ones who wear the trousers because men fear the whites who have become rich from them'.[11] The

---

[10] See M.L. Chanock, 'A Peculiar Sharpness: An Essay on Property in the History of Customary Law in Colonial Africa', *Journal of African History* (31), 1991; and 'The Law Market in East and Central Africa', in J. Mommsen and J. de Moor (eds.), *The Expansion of European Law* (Leiden, 1992).

[11] *Hidden Struggles*, pp. 238–9.

suggestion here is that men were psychologically more subordinated to whites in the larger society. Yet black women, taken even less seriously than black men as political and cultural actors by the dominant system, had to build their opposition to the state around traditional cultural symbols. Also, progressive African political movements active in the rural areas, like the Industrial and Commercial Workers Union, had little political time or rhetorical space for women and this too tended to tie them ideologically to ruralism. The price that was paid for this was that it became very difficult for women to articulate an opposition to the gender oppression which was legitimatized by traditionalism.

It is necessary to distinguish, both for whites and for blacks, between the ideological and instrumental aspects of the customary law regime. For whites it served the ideological purpose of separating blacks from the mainstream of the country's legal and political institutions, and of placing them on a lower rung in the evolutionary scale. Instrumentally it served to construct a regime which would service the migrant labour system by governing gender and generational relations in the retained traditional sphere. For blacks the regime served the ideological purpose of preserving an element of Africanism in resistance to the overwhelming vilification of black culture by the dominant community. Instrumentally it provided men with the means to retain some power over the distribution of communal lands, and also over the property and labour of women and the young.

In what circumstances did the leadership of the modernizing elite adopt elements of the ideology of traditionalism, and how far could they really adopt it? In the latter part of the nineteenth century elite Africans in the Cape concentrated on reaping the benefits of assimilationism, and its promise of equal political rights. As a strategy for black advancement this was devastated by the colour bar in the Act of Union and by the rejection of the Cape policy for the country as a whole, and finally killed off by the rise of the Nationalists to political dominance. Since assimilationism could not become a strategy for Africans as a whole, 'progressive' leadership could not abandon its connections with other forms of African political expression.

When the dominant state policy was assimilationist, 'progressive' blacks and white liberals were aligned in their opposition to the customary regime. But by the 1920s the state had become segregationist: it abandoned its limited approval of black progressives and allied itself with traditionalism in African life. The progressive black elite essentially had to choose between the strategies of revolutionary rejectionism, or the development of a romantic version of 'custom' which would enable them to try to recapture and use that realm. Those most likely to break with assimilationism and turn to an Africanist populism were the marginal members of the elite, bruised by contact with the racism of the dominant group. Rural 'Africanism' defended traditional views on family and gender relationships in the face of the disruptions brought about by migrant labour. Its ideological outlook was centred on the desire to control communal lands, and, therefore, it gave support to the chiefs. It fused traditionalist expressions with those of both a growing African nationalism and independent Christianity. Significantly it provided for avenues of expression which were markedly different from the bourgeois aspirations towards improvement, progress and acceptance espoused by black elite. This did not provide a basis for the rejection of the imposition of the state's version of African law. Indeed the latter provided a framework in which to act. The state could not be ignored. Nor did it seem that it could be overthrown. This being the case it had to be used to achieve what limited ends could be reached, and this meant engagement with the state's customary law and the courts which enforced it.

II *The White Construction of Traditionalism*

The connections between knowledge and power, and the associated problems of how to 'know' anything about subordinate cultures in a world in which all knowledge of them has been created by the dominant, are by now common concerns of scholarship. The presumption of innocence is no longer applied to anthropology, which now has to struggle to prove itself innocent of association with racism, imperialism and colonialism, and the continued manipulation of dominated peoples.[12] In the South African context different anthropological traditions have had powerful political associations.[13] The connections between an anthropology based in the Afrikaans universities which emphasized the study of 'culture' and the uniqueness and appropriateness of each cultural system to its group, and the development of the ideological justifications for *apartheid*, have been noted. By contrast

[12] See T. Asad, *Anthropology and the Colonial Encounter* (London, 1973).
[13] See A. Kuper, *South Africa and the Anthropologist* (London, 1987); and M. Gluckman 'The Work of South African Anthropologists', in M. Fortes and S. Patterson (eds), *Studies in African Social Anthropology* (London, 1975).

a 'liberal' social anthropology has been credited with a refusal to emphasize differences. As Kuper has pointed out this dichotomy is too simple. My intention here is simply to emphasize the role which anthropology has had in constructing the terms of debate about traditional societies and to emphasize that those who study African societies in South Africa, knowledge about which has been largely produced by anthropologists, must use their work in full awareness of the intellectual and political circumstances of its production. We should note too that this uncertain body of knowledge has been used by government officials and by courts to interpret, construct, control and influence the development of 'traditional' institutions. The power to define what was in the cultural space of Africans had real long-term effects. The imposed cultural definitions led to imposed institutional frameworks created on the basis of these definitions. Within these, patterns of possible and meaningful behaviour led to the creation of new cultural realities, *which limited the cultural repertoire that could later be developed*. There was awareness of this in South Africa long before it became part of the fashionable currency of post-imperialist critiques. Edgar Brookes in 1934 wrote that 'all the influence of the older school of social anthropology has been thrown in the direction of regarding the urban native as an annoying intruder' and he noted its influence in creating in the public mind support for the idea that the urban African should go back to '"his own area"—the segregationist Utopia—where he will develop "along his own lines"—the anthropological Utopia'.[14]

South African anthropologists of the 'liberal' school have always been prickly about an emphasis on human and cultural differences. For them anthropology was there to demonstrate a common humanity, not to dwell upon cultural uniqueness. Gluckman[15] specifically and forcefully contrasted this position with that of Leach, who wrote of the course of anthropology:

We started by emphasizing how different are 'the others'—and made them not only different but remote and inferior. Sentimentally we then took the opposite tract [*sic*] and argued that all human beings are alike . . . but that didn't work either, the others remained obstinately 'other'.[16]

---

[14] M. Lacey, *Working for Baroko: The Origins of a Coercive Labour System in South Africa* (Johannesburg, 1981), p. 115.

[15] M. Gluckman, 'Anthropology and Apartheid', p. 28.

[16] E. Leach, quoted in ibid., p. 29.

What was seen and written about depended greatly on where the anthropologist stood in this debate, which is also crucial to the political acceptability of assertions of legitimate 'otherness'. Those striving to take part in, or to rule, a common society, will look for the academic support of similarity: those who search for a legitimized separateness, will take comfort from cultural uniqueness.

We must understand not simply the political context of the introduction of the Native Administration Act of 1927, but the larger totalities of discourse and world views of which it was a part.[17] The notions of 'difference' on which the policies of segregation were based were wholly distinct from those which legitimize approaches to 'difference' today, and must not be confused. The most important distinction is that the assertions of difference are today often made by the ruled, not by the rulers, and that they are premised upon a parity of esteem for cultures. Even the most liberal of the 'culture' minded of the anthropologists of the inter-war period, both in South Africa and beyond, did not seriously base their views on a parity of esteem. They were generous towards other cultures on the grounds that these were the most appropriate for people of their level of development. But they were not supposed to stay there. These anthropologists were, as Dubow points out, 'strongly associated with the demise of mid-Victorian liberalism and the ascendancy of racial science'. Social Darwinism; the horror of miscegenation; the fears of racial degeneration; the fear of 'swamping' by 'the rising tide of colour' were all fundamental to the white South African world view and lay behind segregationist discourse.[18] The emergence of urbanized Africans beyond the confines of rural traditionalism was not only politically and economically threatening, but in a fundamental sense a disease of the social order. For Africans a 'healthy' social structure was a traditional rural one; urbanism was social decay.[19] As Dubow points out, the

[17] See S. Dubow, 'Race, Civilisation and Culture: The Elaboration of Segregationist Discourse in the Inter-War Years', in S. Marks and S. Trapido (eds.), *The Politics of Race, Class and Nationalism* (London, 1987); and S. Dubow, *Racial Segregation and the Origins of Apartheid in South Africa 1919–1930* (London, 1989).

[18] Dubow, 'Race, Civilisation and Culture', pp. 74–6.

[19] There are tantalizing strands of this in some of the modern imagery of urbanism—cities as the running sores of capitalism—and in the anthropology of minority cultures which sees departures from 'culture' as derogating from social well being and wholeness and in which loss of 'aboriginality' is often associated with images of physical ill-health.

development of the anthropological notion of culture, or rather the way that that notion was used in the South African context, softened and made respectable the naked racism behind the policy of segregation and articulated it in a usable way for the state. The bureaucracy was given, and used, a usable version of African societies.[20] This is far from saying that either the newly developing 'discipline' or its practitioners were responsible for the policies of segregation, or, in this particular case, the enactment of the Native Administration Act of 1927. But they were an integral part of the construction of notions of 'difference'.

We cannot understand the development of the separate legal systems of South Africa outside the context of the contemporary constructions of anthropology and their political adaptations. For the simple desire to oppress did not create the tools which were used. The new formulations offered what was sorely needed, a path between assimilation and the overt embracing of repression. Henceforth it became possible to say that a good future for Africans was going to be built upon the basis of their own institutions. The departure from the Cape paradigm was complete. There was very little which distinguished South African discourse from that of British colonialism in Africa during this period. They shared the general discovery that traditional institutions and customary law were good for Africans, and that the emergence of Europeanized Africans was bad for governments. South African administrators spoke of the

middle way between tying (the African) down or trying to make of him a black European, between *repressionist* and *assimilationist* schools . . . which would take out of the Bantu past what was good, and even what was merely neutral, and together with what is good of European culture for the Bantu, build up a Bantu future.[21]

In similar vein Werner Eiselen (who later as Secretary of Native Affairs in the 1950s was one of the main architects of apartheid), stated in 1929: 'The duty of the native . . . (is) not to become a good European, but to become a better native, with ideals and culture of his own'.[22] Politicians were less likely to stress the cultural virtues of segregation and more likely to express its political necessities. As

[20] Ibid., pp. 80 *et seq.*

[21] The Government Ethnologist, G.P. Lestrade, quoted by Dubow in ibid., pp. 84–5.

[22] Ibid., p. 86.

Heaton Nicholls put it: '(T)he opposite policy of assimilation sub-stitutes class for race, and if continued on its present basis, must lead to the evolution of a native proletariat inspired by the usual an-tagonisms of a class war.' The major government commission to which this statement was made advanced the further point that it was 'not only the most reasonable but also the most economical approach to the native question'.[23]

III *Constructing the Customary Legal System*

(1) *The 1927 Act, the Common Estate and Native Courts*: We shall now turn to examine the circumstances in which law simultaneously became burdened with the construction of black identity and the pursuit of the administrative ends of the state. White conquest forced African law into a subordinate and subsidiary position to the common law (which was Roman-Dutch law) in the legal systems of the South African colonies. While all the colonies had this fundamental feature in common, there nonetheless had been, before Union in 1910, im-portant differences in approach. In the South African republic the basic position had been one of total non-recognition of African law, not because of a policy of assimilation, but because of one of total separa-tion and a denial of the existence of African legal institutions. By contrast the Cape had looked toward ultimate assimilation, and there-fore in theory administered its subject population by the imposition of the common law. But it had been forced, as it conquered and ruled greater numbers of Africans in the course of the second half of the nineteenth century, to give recognition to African legal institutions.[24] But this recognition remained subject to an assimilationist goal, and one tinged with a desire to change African institutions which did not accord with fundamental white views of public policy or morality. The Native Affairs Commission of 1903–5 pronounced that 'the object of improving Native Law, and, as far as may be, assimilating it with the ordinary colonial law should be kept in view as an ultimate goal'.[25] The major ideological targets of the Cape policy had been polygamy, bride-wealth and the coping stone of the traditional polity, the chief-tainship, though accommodation had to be made with all three.[26] Natal,

[23] Ibid.

[24] S. Burman, *Chiefdom, Politics and Alien Law* (London, 1981).

[25] Quoted in J. Lewin, *Studies in African Law* (Philadelphia, 1947), pp. 10–11.

[26] S. Dubow, 'Race, Civilisation and Culture', p. 79.

like the South African Republic, pursued separation as a goal, but gave full recognition to the separate legal system, codified it, and legislatively enforced its application.[27] It positively embraced the enemies identified by the Cape.

It was not until 1927 that a policy was legislated for the Union as a whole. The Native Administration Act was an important part of the overall policy of a government led by General Hertzog which was committed to segregation. But the Act was not a particularly radical piece of legislation. Of necessity, it incorporated aspects of what already existed, and it was also heavily influenced by the development of colonial policies in the rest of British Africa. African law was recognized as governing the personal relations among Africans and property relations arising from them, and limited recognition was given to the courts of chiefs and headmen. At the same time a separate superior court system for Africans, along Natal lines, was created for the rest of the country. But this system was not entirely sealed off from the common law courts, as in the last resort appeal could be had from the Native Appeal Courts to the Appellate Division of the Supreme Court. The Appellate Division thus exercised some influence over the development of the system, but it was for the most part in the hands of officials—the Native Commissioners—and others with 'expertise' in native affairs.

The belated recognition, and elaborated institutional separation, of elements of African law from the common law and court system of the white rulers was a political response to increased urbanization and proletarianization of the African population and the consequent growth of political assertions in various forms of socialist and communist rhetoric. These were accompanied by the increasing impoverishment of the African rural areas and the decline in traditional authority. The recognition of chiefs' courts was a part of the larger attempt to shore up traditional leadership with new powers in order to prevent the growth of the new mass political movements in rural areas, like the Industrial and Commercial Workers' Union. In pursuit of this Section 29 made it a criminal offence to act 'with intent to promote any feeling of hostility between Natives and Europeans'. The Act also made the Governor-General the Supreme Chief of Africans, giving him the power to make and amend law by proclamation. To these two great inroads into political freedom must be added the

---

[27] D. Welsh, *The Roots of Segregation* (Cape Town, 1971).

general observation that, in the words of the Native Representative
Council in 1945, judicial segregation itself 'violates the principle of
equality before the law . . . and it bolsters up the restrictive laws
differentially affecting natives'.[28]

The machinery and philosophy of the Act had curious and complex implications for conventional notions of legalism based on the
separation of powers and the 'rule of law' which continued to underlie
(in principle) the country's common law. On the one hand vast powers
were given to the Governor-General as Supreme Chief, and flowing
down through him to Native Commissioners, to rule by decree and
proclamation, and to issue orders affecting individuals, as well as
general laws. Legislative, executive and administrative powers were
unified, and the ways in which these were exercised went unchallenged
by the courts. The nature of judicial power was altered as Native
Commissioners' courts themselves became largely administrative
bodies, exercising powers which the Supreme Court defined as administrative, not judicial, and which were therefore beyond even the
weak tests of natural justice.[29] And there were also more far-reaching
implications for the nature of law itself. The common law was based
upon individual responsibilities, contractual capacities and property
rights. The ideology of the system of re-tribalization was hostile to
individualism and, indeed, believed it to be inappropriate for Africans
and not a part of tribal culture, which was presented as being based
on a firmly hierarchical communalism. In addition individualism was
picked out as a problem for administrative control. In the words of
J.A. Herbst, the Native Affairs Department Secretary:

Tribal rule has . : . been sapped of its vitality by the intrusion of European
individualism in advance of the habits and understanding of the people with
the result that there is confusion and doubt where order and coherence are
necessary.[30]

But while the operation of the common law could in many areas be
excluded from African life, Africans could not be separated from the

[28] H. J. Simons, 'African Marriage Under Apartheid', Family Law Reform in
Africa, International Family Law Association Conference, Harare, 1987. One
must note that their demand was not for a single system of substantive law, but
for an end to the segregated court system. The importance of this difference must
be stressed.
[29] M. Lacey, *Working for Baroko*, pp. 101 *et seq.*; and, therein, *R.V. Mabi and
others 1935 T.P.D. 408.*
[30] M. Lacey, op. cit., p. 95.

economic life of the country. Their economic transactions with each other, and with Europeans, were increasingly individualized by the operation of the common law governing proprietal and contractual capacity. This might be seen in the decisions of the Natal Native High Court which eventually led to the change in the Natal Code in 1932.[31] In customary law, and under the code, there had been a single estate for fathers, sons, brothers, and their women. But the men, and later the women, were increasingly engaged not only in wage earning, but in property dealings with outsiders. By the end of the 1920s the crucial economic core of the customary system, the common family estate, had collapsed. But the subordination of women remained. Courts adjudicating under Native Law continued to uphold the complete male control of female property, including the new form, money earnings.

The Native Administration Act applied customary law to Africans in a new court system. 'In consequence, both legislation and case law have produced a codification of the administration's view of acceptable aspects of customary law as it operated in 1927, with modifications to suit government policy'.[32] African custom was given institutional recognition at the price of being translated into the legalist discourse of the institutions.

But for many, mainly in urban but also in rural areas, its hold as the law in the sense that it was the only conceivable and legitimate way of ordering personal relations was weakening, and it came to be looked upon with attitudes ranging from suspicion to contempt, particularly by those women and young men against whose interests it operated.[33] Also, the attachment of elites to matters customary has not always been uniform. Christianized elites struggled vigorously against their inclusion in a customary regime[34] and urban elites generally looked down on customary law as rural, primitive and inapplicable to their new way of life. Indeed both groups identified very quickly just what the effect of a customary regime was, and the purpose of its imposition. The policy of which it was a part was designed to promote traditionalism, and the power of traditionalists at the expense of the

---

[31] See M. Chanock, 'A Peculiar Sharpness'.

[32] S. Burman 'Divorce and the Disadvantaged: African Women in Urban South Africa', in R. Hirschon (ed.), *Woman and Property—Women as Property* (London, 1984).

[33] See the analysis in M. Chanock, 'Neither Customary nor Legal', *International Journal of Law and the Family*, 1989.

[34] See D. Welsh, *The Roots of Segregation*.

aspirations and ambitions of the urbanized, detribalized and, therefore in the government's eyes, more threatening part of the African population. But even if the political thrust had not been so strong, the institutionalization of a separate legal regime and court system both entrenched and perpetuated the customary system. Recognition could not be a neutral or merely a convenient way of settling the disputes of the traditional. It not only entrenched a Native Affairs bureaucracy and a separately developing corpus of law, but it created assumptions about the law applicable to Africans whatever their way of life.

Bound up in the notion that African law was somehow inherently better fitted to Africans regardless of their class, location or way of life was the belief that it was a mysterious and complex subject, knowledge of which came only through a special and exclusive expertise among those who really knew 'the native mind'.[35] The Native Economic Commission of 1930–2 endorsed the greater powers given to chiefs and headmen under the 1927 Act as better than administration of native law by whites who 'know it only from books and are ignorant of its subtle implications . . . . [also] European procedure is wholly strange to natives and is certainly not adapted to bring out the true facts when applied to a primitive people'.[36] When Z.K. Matthews, a leading African nationalist intellectual, complained in 1945 that there was no reason why the ordinary Supreme Court should not administer customary law because there was 'after all. . . . nothing mysterious about native law' he was addressing far more than a problem of judicial administration.[37] For the idea of its 'mystery' placed it beyond the rationality of western law, and situated it as a racial rather than an intellectual construct and a necessary concomitant of and accompaniment to the racial peculiarities of Africans.

The 'native law' recognized by the courts was an essential part of the construction of the image of the 'native'. It was applied with a strong bias towards preserving the 'native' in the traditional realm. Section 11 of the Native Administration Act of 1927 was the statutory basis for the countrywide recognition of 'native law'. It read:

Notwithstanding the provisions of any other law, it shall be in the discretion of the Courts of Native Commissioners in all suits or proceedings between

[35] See M. Chanock, *Unconsummated Union: Britain, Rhodesia and South Africa 1900–1945* (Manchester, 1977).

[36] Quoted in Lord Hailey, *An African Survey* (London, 1938), p. 284.

[37] Quoted in Simons, 'African Marriage', p. 6.

Natives involving questions of customs followed by Natives, to decide such questions according to the Native law applying to such custom.

This did not, however, settle the question of which was to be given preference by the courts, the common law, or the 'native law'? Did it mean that the common law applied except in cases which were peculiar to 'native custom', such as bride-wealth marriage; or that 'native law' was normally to be applied to cases between Africans except in those classes of case where there was no 'native law' to apply because they covered transactions unknown to tribal life? Should, for example, a case involving the loan of money be settled according to common law because there was no money in traditional society; or should the principles covering loans in 'native law' be applied? (This was an important question as time limitations or prescription ran in Roman-Dutch law but the concept was held to be unknown to customary law.[38] Some early judgements leant towards the Cape tradition of giving priority to the common law, but on the whole the Native Courts took the view that Parliament had intended to give priority to the customary law, the law 'familiar and peculiar' to Africans, which was 'unquestionably the only system they contemplate and follow in their daily dealings and beliefs'. (Yako v Beki 1944 NAC (C&O 72)[39]. In *Monaheng v Konupi NAC (N&T 1930)* the court indicated its preference 'to avoid as far as possible getting away from a system of law which is more in harmony with the Native concepts of equity and justice whatever its shortcomings may be from our standpoint'.[40] (This latter was a case concerning damages for seduction to which the father had a claim in customary law.)

Even had the Appeal Courts not been inclined to give priority to customary law, there were other ways of trying to ensure that black litigants remained within the customary system. The instructions to Native Commissioners issued under the Native Administration Act in 1928 told them that they were to 'encourage natives to avail themselves of the facilities provided . . . for the simplified form of procedure in courts of Native Commissioners' and 'to hear and determine such matters with due regard to native law and customs and usages'.[41] In addition, section 12 (1) of the Act gave formal recognition for the first

---

[38] See J. Lewin, *Studies in African Law*, pp. 58 *et seq.*
[39] See J. Simons, 'African Marriage', p. 8.
[40] W.G. Stafford, *Native Law as Practised in Natal* (Johannesburg, 1935), p. 6.
[41] Regulations 5 and 9. See ibid., pp. 28–9.

time to courts of chiefs and headmen. In the pre-colonial state, in the absence of 'officials', the homestead heads exercised patriarchal powers over the members of homesteads. Now, as it was incorporated into the state, patriarchal authority became public power supported by state force. The patriarchs, transmuted into officials, were given the powers of a court to punish contempt and additional powers to impose fines for disobedience to their administrative orders. Section 18 read:

Chiefs and headmen have authority to require compliance by the people under their jurisdiction with their duties under native law and may give orders for that purpose. The enforcement of obedience to authority of the duty of children to their parents and of the obligations of inmates of kraals towards their kraal heads shall in particular fall within the scope of their authority.

The elaboration of these duties by the Courts completed the chain of confining authority.

(2) *Women and the Customary System*:   One of the fundamentals of 'customary' systems in Africa, including South Africa, was the denial of contractual capacity to most African women. Under section 27(2) of the Natal Code an African woman was 'deemed a perpetual minor in law (with) . . . no independent powers save as to her own person'.[42] While under the influence of modern law many states, including South Africa, have recognized the concept of an age of majority for single women, in South Africa this capacity is lost on marriage. The consequences have been, amongst others, to deny women control over their own earnings, either from waged employment or from the sale of rural produce, to exclude them from access to credit, and, in urban areas, to cut off their access to rental accommodation and housing finance. Yet the recognition of contractual capacity is no mere technical inroad into traditional systems, but strikes at their core. Accordingly such capacity is fiercely resisted by men as the economic stakes have grown with urbanization and market agriculture.

Urban South African women increasingly live in circumstances which have made the marriage laws enshrined by the 1927 Act more and more irrelevant, yet many still have to deal with their disputes under its framework. The entrenchment of bride-wealth payments as a fundamental legal necessity for marriage, and as a major transfer of (consistently inflating) resources, has been arguably the most crucial

[42] The Native Appeal Courts would not, however, recognize either the pledging of women for the value of their bride-wealth, or the enforced 'inheritance' of widows.

feature of African private law in South Africa. It is the lynchpin of the legal subordination of African women in private law.[43] And it has also been central to the legal ideologies of men, both white and black. During the nineteenth century it was the symbol of the moral degradation of African societies, a justification of the civilizing mission and the target of reformers. Africans responded with defensive vigour to European charges that their wives were bought and sold, constructing their defence of traditionalism, and stable family life, around the institutions of bride-wealth marriage. By the second decade of the twentieth century, however, the triumph of segregationist ideology and anthropology had virtually paralyzed the assault on bride-wealth. Indeed it might at first sight appear obvious that we have here a good example of the continuity of cultural and legal institutions, as the payments are widely regarded by Africans as a part of the legitimization of sexual unions. But it is not correct to consider the survival of the payment of bride-wealth, its entrenchment and inflation as being, somehow, a 'survival' of a traditional practice out of place in a modern society, and representing the continuation of a cultural pattern. The context of African family life was distorted by the necessity for would-be wage earners to leave the impoverished rural reserves and work in the towns, while state law forbade the urbanization of their families. Family relationships, including the control of children and the allocation of labour and resources took place within a context of spatial disruption and dislocation.[44] Bride-wealth became an important and integral part of the family system as it adapted to the economy built on migrant labour. Payments made to secure marriages by enlisting the support not only of 'culture' but of in-laws, were a response to the migrants' need to ensure that they could build up a stake in the rural sector against their return.

The institution of bride-wealth is an important part of cultural baggage, though experience in the rest of Africa can show how quickly it can be abandoned by those to whom it is of no further use.[45] In South Africa abandonment was difficult for 'technical' reasons. The state has insisted, and continues to insist, that the consent of a woman's guardian is necessary to her contraction of a valid marriage. Guardians had therefore, a monopoly over an important resource, which they

[43] For discussions of bride-wealth, see H.J. Simons, *African Women: Their Legal Status in South Africa* (London, 1968).

[44] S. Burman, 'Divorce and the Disadvantaged', pp. 119–20.

[45] See M. Chanock, 'The Law Market in East and Central Africa'.

continued to exploit. It is open to doubt whether bride-wealth would have survived, and become inflated, without the support it has received from the state in this way. It has been a support which went beyond simply 'recognizing' it as something that people do, and giving legal effect to it in state courts. It is a prime example of how a pattern created by state action can become a cultural reality and be defended as such. Yet, in its altered form, it came to be vigorously defended by most Africans, both assimilated elite and traditionalists. The tendency among nationalist elites to identify strongly with the values embodied in the family structure of independent pre-capitalist African societies, even though those values embody female subordination, has been noted.[46] That there was a male interest in the maintenance of the system of family law will be clear but there was little tendency for women, apart from a small Christian elite, to reject African family law. Non-payment of bride-wealth left women in a position where they and their children could be abandoned without any obligation of support, because without it, it could be asserted that no customary marriage had taken place.[47]

A brief examination of the position of those African women who found themselves on the borderline between legal systems, because of their conversion to Christianity, provides a rich vein on which to draw to illustrate both the dilemmas posed by pluralism for these women, and the terms in which alternatives were debated. The choice for women was not between subordination within a customary system and equality of status outside it. Those who commonly concerned themselves with the reform of the family law and its administration were usually connected to the Christian mission churches and were concerned neither with increasing the status or the liberty of women, nor with the protection of indigenous cultures, but with the protection and promotion of Christian family virtues.[48]

Some missionaries wanted Christian women to be freed from the guardianship laws which often placed them, and their children, under the guardianship of non-Christian traditionalists. Others, like the Bishop of Zululand, thought the continuation of the existing system better because in the long term 'paganism is dying, and, in the interim, nothing should be done to interfere with family life'. His archdeacon

---

[46] S. Burman, 'Divorce and the Disadvantaged', p. 129.

[47] Ibid., p. 127.

[48] D.W.T. Shropshire, *The Bantu Woman Under the Natal Code of Native Law* (Lovedale, 1941).

acknowledged that 'women want more protection than at present exists' but felt that 'the tremendous increase in divorce in the last few years points to the undesirablity of tampering with the Code and Native public opinion'.[49]

There was strong opposition to bringing the systems of marriage law together: on the African male side because it would mean a diminution in their control over persons and property; and on the European side because it represented an equalizing in the sphere of marriage as well as an acknowledgment that the institutions of 'tribal' society were no longer appropriate for regulating the lives of Africans. While it was acknowledged that there were a few Africans who might qualify for 'civilized' marriage laws, there was a particular hostility to those seen to be in-between 'tribal' and 'civilized' life. The '"intermediate class"' said one magistrate 'must of necessity fall within the unexempted class (i.e. those subject to "native law") until it is fit for promotion to a higher'.[50] The existence of polygamy and female subordination was vital to the portrayal of African societies as uncivilized, and was, therefore, important to European institutions as well as African ones.

CONCLUSION

I do not want to discuss fully the question of how the content of a legal system designated as customary or traditional gets to be known or established, as I have dealt with this extensively in another context.[51] But it is obviously germane not only to the way in which traditions are asserted, but also to their construction for use by the state. In the South African case it will be sufficient to point out here that there was a grotesque combination of the professed need for special expertise with its absence among those deemed to possess it. The vast and unbridgeable social distance between white officials and Africans prevented the rulers from acquiring a real knowledge of custom by contact with African life. They were dependent, therefore, on a barely developed body of white written knowledge. The authoritative and much quoted texts on 'Native Law' were dry, summary, technical and

---

[49] Ibid., pp. 11, 14, 16.
[50] Ibid., p. 20.
[51] M. Chanock, *Law, Custom and Social Order.*

legalist, and presented nothing of an appreciation of the working principles of customary law. These books tended to be used and applied, especially at the lower levels of the separate court system, with a rigid and bureaucratic legalism, though there were some thoughtful exceptions on the Native Appeal Courts. It is clear that the system of customary law that was made and applied was not 'custom' in any sense. (What is less clear is how custom could have been, or might ever be, utilized in the court system of a modern state.)

Africans in South Africa have been governed without any concern for, or representation of, their interests. It is far from surprising that, in the face of this oppression, and in the absence of means of amelioration through sympathetic legal reforms, Africans still have resort to 'custom' to express interests. The values, the vocabulary, the cultural baggage of 'custom', may appear to hold out little promise in themselves, especially for women. But they do provide a space for the manipulation of interests of both men and women, while the state provides no space at all. There are tools in the customary system for fashioning lives, stone tools perhaps, but better than none at all.

In the South African case, of course, the legal system of the 1927 Act was imposed, not requested, and was rejected from its inception by those among the most articulate representatives of the African people. A convention of chiefs pointed out in 1928 that while it was the policy of the government to govern Africans 'by means of their own law and custom', the new system was government by 'the wishes of the white race' and a 'violation of the Bantu system of government'. Lacey writes that, '(w)ith ghastly pseudo-science and pseudo-deference towards the group it intended battening under the hatches . . . the State forced an unnatural return by Africans to a bastardised form of "tribalism"'.[52] There may be no parallels between this and legal separatism based on a genuine acknowledgement of rights to self management.

The 'discovery' of subordinations within the subordinate system can be reacted to in a number of ways. They can be largely endorsed, as they were in South Africa, and, in the main, in colonial Africa. The rationale for doing this was both that they were useful to the state, and appropriate to the 'stage' of development of the subordinate. Or they can be rejected and judged against a 'modern' liberal yardstick of human rights. This can be done with the purpose of promoting

[52] M. Lacey, *Working for Baroko*, pp. 100, 285.

human rights, but it has also—again the South African context serves as an example—been used as the ideological platform for the rejection of all the values of the group involved, and the delivery of a general, and negative, judgement on their culture as a whole. South African state policy has tried to get the best of both these worlds. But it is possible to relate these subordinations to the historical conditions in which they developed, to situate them in time and circumstance, and not in essence. This involves rejecting the role of the social scientist as cheerleader to those cultural nationalists who seek to forward their aspirations on the basis of essence.

One of my purposes in this paper has been to draw attention to the construction of the debate about 'traditional' societies in the 1920s and 1930s in order to heighten awareness of our own construction of the problems of ethnic oppressions and assertions. We live in a time in which the dominance of class analysis of these problems is giving way to renewed emphasis on culture and gender and in which new paradigms of subordination are being born. We must ourselves be able to historicize this piece of intellectual history, which derives less from new understandings of the problems of the oppressed than from the political collapse of European Marxism.

There were several political trajectories possible in South Africa after the collapse of the central paradigm of liberal assimilationism in the 1920s. One was to move towards a politics of class rather than race, and the pursuit of the goal of a non-racial socialist society. This remained the core of the politics of African resistance. Another was to emphasize racial and cultural differences. For those whites who did this the logical conclusion was a divided, segregated and hierarchical social order of the sort pursued by the policies of apartheid. For blacks who went down this road there have been two directions: one towards a pluralist division based upon the national or 'tribal' identities established during the nineteenth century. The other has been towards the assertion of a united black consciousness and black nationalism. All of these latter routes have but one thing in common, which is the exploitation of varying versions of traditionalism to construct black identity.

Lacey has written of the 1927 Act that it had the effect of isolating the 'native question' from the rest of politics. There was created, wrote Margaret Ballinger, one of the special representatives of African interests in the South African parliament, 'a common illusion that Native Affairs are something apart from the mainstream of South African life

. . . a happy hunting ground for intellectuals and philanthropists'.[53] For those in other countries who advocate the dissolution of state policies based on a unified and assimilationist polity there may be lessons in the collapse of these assumptions in South Africa. Whatever the context in which institutional separatism is developed, and whatever the weaknesses of the arguments for unified legal systems, these political effects of separatism must be of concern. Institutional autonomy may not necessarily be a political prison as it was in South Africa, but it is all too likely to be a political playpen.

[53] Ibid., p. 117.

The Peoples of the Soviet North: Recent Developments

JOHN MILLER

I Introduction

The disadvantages suffered by the 'subordinated' peoples in the title of this volume are manifest; yet I find it difficult to pin down their essence.[1] Some would argue that certain types of disadvantage or oppression, and certain disadvantaged groups, are in such a distinct category as to deserve a distinct label. It is a suggestion that has some intuitive appeal, especially to observers of the Australian situation. In what way might some disadvantaged groups be in a distinct category of disadvantage? Because they are severely, rather than moderately disadvantaged? This would have little analytical value; it would be absurd to suggest, for example, that groups which have been the object of attempted genocide need have any other characteristic in common than the fact of having been persecuted. No—if there are distinct categories of group disadvantage, their features should rather be sought in the *relationship* between oppressors and oppressed.

One such relationship does present itself as noticeably distinct, and as a useful basis for analytical distinction. This is the relationship—usually an unhappy one—between, on the one hand, nomadic or hunter-gatherer economies and cultures, and commercial-manufacturing ones on the other. Often the clash between these cultures has been made more conspicuous by the fact that representatives of the commercial-manufacturing system are immigrants from another continent—the Europeans in Australia, or in North or South America, for example. Two features in particular seem to make this sort of culture clash distinctive.

[1] I am indebted to Terence Armstrong and Piers Vitebsky (both of the Scott Polar Research Institute, University of Cambridge), Murray Feshbach (Georgetown University, Washington DC), Kathleen Mihalisko (Radio Liberty) and R. H. Mole (Oxford) for helpful comments on aspects of this paper, or for drawing my attention to materials.

First, there were relatively few aspirations or criteria of success that Europeans shared clearly with Aborigines when they first made contact—considerably fewer, for example, than those they had in common with the Indians of India, or with the Bantu. So mutual incomprehension and lack of sympathy were strengthened, and it became easier for each group to perceive the other as scarcely human —too absorbed in achievement to appreciate life, too sunk in depression to take opportunities.

The second distinctive feature was usually the extremely unequal powers of the two cultures, powers physical, economic and psychological. Economic development is a juggernaut that sweeps all before it, not just because of its superior technical and organizational resources, but because of its *appeal* to outsiders who would like to share in its goods. People who stay loyal to a nomadic or hunter-gatherer culture can come to feel that they cannot compete, but must face either assimilation, or an isolation which is as good as fossilization—by grace and favour of the developed culture, and subsidized by it. One cannot but feel sympathy for Svensson's judgement that '[t]ribal culture, even in the process of its disintegration . . . , may perform a final, critical function for tribal people by protecting them from the direct and overwhelming impact of the modern world'.[2]

On the face of it, the clash between nomadic or hunter-gatherer cultures and the developed economies is a syndrome worth keeping distinct from, say, clashes between manufacturing and peasant economies, or general ethnic or class-based competition for scarce resources. But before accepting this, it is worth asking how much my generalizations so far reflect, not so much the clash of economies, but the more specific consequences of the migration of people from one continent to another. It would be natural if the features and characteristic problems of land-based empires differed from those of seaborne imperialism; yet it is the latter with which we tend to be more familiar.[3] Is the clash between a hunter-gatherer and sedentary eco-

---

[2] Frances Svensson, 'The Final Crisis of Tribalism: Comparative Ethnic Policy on the American and Russian Frontiers', in *Ethnic and Racial Studies*, vol. 1, no. 1, January 1978, pp. 100–23, this reference p. 102.

[3] If the British had developed their empire in a similar way to the Russians (starting perhaps in France in the Hundred Years War?), that empire might have stretched at its height from the North Cape of Norway to the Muslim areas of Northern Nigeria! This fanciful analogy does not exaggerate the range of geographical and cultural diversity to be found in the Soviet Union, and it hints at

nomy as pronounced if we look at the 'Old World' of Europe and Asia, territory where immigration has not played so great a role in settlement? This is the context of the present chapter; like that of Ramachandra Guha, it examines the clash between the manufacturing and non-sedentary economies in a context where the manufacturers are not recent immigrants from overseas.

My focus will be on the indigenous peoples of the Soviet North, mainly of Siberia. I propose to survey their interaction with the expanding Russian culture and economy, historically and especially in this century, and briefly to compare some features of this interaction with Russian/non-Russian relations elsewhere in the Soviet Union. At the back of my mind will be this question: does our provisional hypothesis—that there is something special about the clash between a manufacturing and a non-sedentary economy—hold true in the very different conditions of the USSR?

II   FEATURES OF RUSSIAN EXPANSIONISM

The first Russian state was organized by Vikings; and probably at all periods since then the Russian state has embraced a fair number of people whose native language was not Russian, but who used Russian as a *lingua franca*, and thus were readily absorbed into the Russian culture. This experience may have set the tone for Russian relations with non-Russians when the principality of Muscovy began to expand. Crucial also was the fact that this was a land-based expansion into contiguous, and not unfamiliar territory; in this it differed significantly from sea-borne imperialism. There were two early landmarks in Muscovy's acquisition of a non-Russian population.

The first was the annexation of the commercial republic of Novgorod in 1478. This gave Muscovy its first access to the sea and to foreign trade, with the acquisition of the White Sea coast around the later port of Archangel. It also brought into the state the Christian, Finnish-speaking groups who nowadays are called Karelians and Komi.[4] And it involved Moscow directly in the fur-trade, and so

---

some of the characteristics of land-based imperialism, and of the problems it leaves for contemporary government.

[4] The Komi had been Christianized a century earlier by Saint Stephen of Perm', who—most unusually—developed a Komi script and founded a literary language.

focused attention on routes into Siberia, and on problems of using them. Among the latter were the successor-states to the Tatar empire, Russia's former overlords.

The second major step was the defeat of the Muslim Tatar khanates of Kazan' (1552) and Astrakhan' (1556), and the acquisition of the Volga basin and the Urals. Immediately after this Ivan the Terrible commissioned the Stroganov family to embark on what was to be the colonization of Siberia. Because furs were a major objective of the enterprise (and doubtless because the Tatars were still formidable opponents), colonization followed routes through Perm' and Tobol'sk —somewhat to the north of present-day routes into Siberia. By 1645— that is in less than a century—the chain of Russian forts and trading posts had reached Okhotsk on the Pacific coast opposite Kamchatka.

Conducted in so short a time, the initial penetration of Siberia must have been superficial in the extreme. But it is worth noting *how long* the Russians have been in Siberia: they reached the Pacific before they reached Kiev or St Petersburg (1654 and 1703), while most of the non-Russian regions of the Soviet Union were acquired later still, by the partitions of Poland (1772–1795), or during the nineteenth century. The Russians had also reached the Pacific before the British and French had left the Atlantic seaboard of America.

It has always been tempting, and usually appropriate, to compare the Russian colonization of Siberia with the American opening up of the West, and with similar colonial enterprises such as the Australian. But the specific and distinctive features of Russian colonization are also marked, and for our present purposes need to be scrutinized more carefully.[5]

In the first place, starting as early as they did, and moving into territory contiguous with their own, the Russians did not possess a technology that was markedly superior to that of the Siberian natives. True, they had firearms; but for many other purposes, especially those connected with hunting and trapping, and with survival in an extreme climate, they adopted techniques from the natives, so that there developed a frontier culture which drew on both ways of life.

[5] This account is based particularly on Svensson's succinct analysis (pp. 103–9), but most of her arguments are echoed by others. See, for instance, Terence Armstrong, *Russian Settlement in the North* (Cambridge, 1965), pp. 95–121, 154–71; his 'The Administration of Northern Peoples: The USSR', in R.St.J. MacDonald (ed.), *The Arctic Frontier* (Toronto: University of Toronto Press, 1966), pp. 57–88; Caroline Humphrey, *Karl Marx Collective: Economy, Society and Religion in a Siberian Collective Farm* (Cambridge, 1983), pp. 23–32.

Second, while the Russians evidently considered themselves masters in a political and military sense, they did not (at this time) make great efforts to impose their religion or culture on others, and they lacked much of the arrogance or aloofness that we associate with racial prejudice. Intermarriage between Russians and natives was not uncommon; native landowners often employed poor Russians; and in some remote areas (notably Yakutia) Russian settlers adopted not only native techniques but native languages, and forgot Russian.

Third, Russian government was by design authoritarian, centralized and harsh. But central directives and harsh methods applied to Russians and natives alike, in an 'equality of subordination'. This is illustrated by the facts that in some areas central policy was left for implementation to native chiefs, and that many of the Russian settlers came there as convicts (sometimes from among the 'politically aware'!). Further, a corollary of harsh centralization was that the demands made on subjects were demands of obedience and passivity; they did not include pressure to participate, or to compete, or to develop—all of which might have fostered social differentiation among the communities of a region like Siberia.

Behind all these features of Russian colonization lies what is the overriding fact of life in Siberia—the ferocity and intractability of its environment: the most elementary operations in farming, building, travel or communications can be impossible for much of the year, and can cost many times what they do in Europe. Any centralized government—let alone one located outside the region—will have to struggle to get itself obeyed and to get policy implemented in any recognizable form; the opportunities for local people to evade, frustrate, or manipulate policy during its transmission or execution are immense. And the Siberian environment has not only blunted the efforts of would-be totalitarian politicians; it has also delayed the impact of technological innovation, and kept the technological gap between natives and immigrants narrow.

That has been Siberia's well-deserved image throughout history. Only recently has another aspect of the Siberian environment become apparent: the fragility and vulnerability of flora, fauna and permafrost. Plants grow, and pollutants dissipate, more slowly in the climate; food chains are shorter and more easily severed. It seems that it was not until the second half of this century that human technology became effective enough to challenge—rather than adapt to—Siberian conditions, but that impact has been very damaging. The widespread use of helicopters in the last thirty years may well have started an unprecedented revolution, both social and environmental: for the first time large numbers of people have been brought into Siberia without having to come to terms with it.

III NON-RUSSIAN NATIVES OF NORTH EUROPE AND SIBERIA

The indigenous non-Russians of Northern Europe and Siberia—all of them, incidentally, within the Russian union-republic or RSFSR—can be classified into two broad groups, depending on their position relative to the line of permanent sub-surface ice, the *permafrost* line. South of this line an economy based on agriculture or animal husbandry is viable. North of it agriculture is usually seriously impeded, and the traditional economy has therefore been based on hunting and fishing, fur-trapping and reindeer herding. These are occupations which have favoured the retention of small-scale organization and often of nomadism, as herdsmen followed the migrating reindeer. It is thus in the permafrost zones of Russia and Siberia that we may look for analogues of that clash of radically different economies that characterized relations between Europeans and North and South American Indians or Aborigines.

There is a permafrost zone in northern Europe, but it is small: a belt of territory north of the Arctic Circle running across the Kola peninsula and along the north coast as far as the Urals. But east of the Urals the permafrost line dips southward so as to include in the zone all of northern, and most of central Siberia—the greater part of the territory.

Non-Russian peoples whose geographical location does not preclude agriculture may be found in Europe almost as far north as the Arctic Circle, and especially between the Volga and Urals; their equivalents in South Siberia live approximately along the present line of the Trans-Siberian railway. We can assign more than thirteen million people in 1979 to these nationalities, ranging in size from the Tatars, with more than six million, to groups with less than 100,000 people. The names of the more significant are: (i) in the north of Europe, the Karelians and Komi, both speaking languages related to Finnish; (ii) in the Volga-Urals region, Tatars, Bashkirs and Chuvash (speaking Turkic languages), and Mordva, Udmurt and Mari (Finnic); (iii) in South Siberia, Buryats (Mongolian) and Tuvinians (Turkic).

The present study will be concerned with these three groups for purposes of comparison only.

When we turn to the population north of the permafrost line, almost all of it in Siberia, our focus immediately becomes narrower: we are dealing with some thirty groups totalling (on a generous interpretation) no more than a million persons. Of these groups, two amount to more than 300,000 each;[6] of the rest, none exceeds 35,000, and most are much smaller. The latter groups are normally referred to as the 'Peoples of the North'[7] in Soviet writing, and it is of these in particular that we think if we are looking for a Siberian equivalent of the American Indians or Aborigines. Table I gives some ethnographic,[8] and Table II some demographic data on them,[9] and the map shows the approximate location of the larger groups.

A comparison of these tables and the map shows a number of things about the natives of the Soviet North. First, with the exception of the Yakut and Komi, these are extremely small groups. Individual names and details have been given concerning the eight largest of them—those with a population above 7000 in 1989. At the beginning of the century approximately twenty more groups were distinguished, though often according to confused and fluctuating criteria; many of these now number a few hundreds only and some have been dropped from the census. At the same time, as we see from the map, some of them live dispersed over vast distances; the Nenets and the Evenk each span four time zones!

[6] These are the Yakuts and the Komi. The latter have been included among the agricultural peoples also; they live both north and south of the permafrost line and include some whose traditional economy was reindeer herding. Without the marginal case of the Komi, the 'non-agricultural' natives of Siberia do not exceed half a million.

[7] Or more formally, 'Peoples of the North, Siberia and the Far East'.

[8] Source for most of Table I: Bernard Comrie, The Languages of the Soviet Union (Cambridge: Cambridge University Press, 1981).

[9] Sources for Table II: (i) for the censuses of 1897 and 1926: Vsesoyuznaya perepis' naseleniya 17 dekabrya 1926 goda: Kratkie svodki, Vypusk 4 (Moscow: 1928), pp. xxiv–22, 134–8; T. A. Zhdanko, in Yu V. Bromlei (ed.), Sovremennye etnicheskie protsessy v SSSR (Moscow: 1975), pp. 36–7; Armstrong in The Arctic Frontier, p. 184. Interpretation has drawn also on Armstrong, Russian Settlement, pp. 184–6; and Frank Lorimer, The Population of the Soviet Union: History and Prospects (Geneva: League of Nations, 1946), pp. 55–61, 138–9; (ii) for the censuses of 1959, 1970, 1979 and 1989: Itogi vsesoyuznoi perepisi naseleniya 1959 goda: svodnyi tom (Moscow, 1962); Itogi . . .1970 goda (Moscow, 1973), vol. IV; Chislennost' i sostav naseleniya SSSR (Moscow, 1984); Vestnik statistiki, no. 10, 1990, pp. 69–75.

TABLE I

NATIVES OF ARCTIC EUROPE AND SIBERIA: ETHNOGRAPHIC DATA

Name	Former Name	Language Group	Traditional Religion	%Natives in Titular Territory (1979)
Larger Nationalities				
Komi	Zyryan	Finno-Ugric	Orthodox	25.3
Yakut		Turkie		36.9
Peoples of the North				
Nenets	Samoyed	Finno-Ugric	Shamanist	17.6
Khanty	Ostyak	Finno-Ugric		3.0
Mansi	Vogul	Finno-Ugric	(Superficially	3.0
Evenk	Tungus	Tungusic	Christianized)	20.3
Even	Lamut	Tungusic		na
Chukchi		Palaeo-Siberian		9.0
Koryak		Palaeo-Siberian		22.6
Nanai	Gol'd	Tungusic		na

plus some twenty smaller groups

TABLE II

NATIVES OF ARCTIC EUROPE AND SIBERIA: POPULATION AT CENSUS
(THOUSANDS)

	1897	1926	1959	1970	1979	1989	Growth 1959–89
Larger Nationalities							
Komi	153.6	226.4	287.0	321.9	326.7	344.5	1.20
Yakut	226.2	235.9	233.3	296.2	328.0	381.9	1.64
	379.8	462.3	520.4	618.1	654.7	726.4	1.40
Peoples of the North							
Nenets	15.9	16.4	23.0	28.7	29.9	34.7	1.51
Khanty	19.7	17.8	19.4	21.1	20.9	22.5	1.16

	1897	1926	1959	1970	1979	1989	Growth 1959–89
Mansi	7.6	5.8	6.4	7.7	7.6	8.5	1.31
Evenk	c48.7?	38.8	24.2	25.1	27.3	30.2	1.25
Even	c8.8?	7.0	9.1	12.0	12.5	17.2	1.89
Chukchi	11.8	12.4	11.7	13.6	14.0	15.2	1.30
Koryak	6.1	7.4	6.3	7.5	7.9	9.2	1.47
Nanai	c6.7?	5.3	8.0	10.0	10.5	12.0	1.50
	c125.3?	110.8	108.2	125.8	130.6	149.5	1.38
Smaller Groups	c23.3?	33.6	23.3	27.4	27.7	35.0	1.50
Peoples of the North							
Total	148.6	144.4	131.5	153.2	158.3	184.4	1.40
Grand Total	528.4	606.7	651.8	771.4	813.0	910.9	1.40

Soviet ethnic policy allocated to most ethnic groups of any size a 'titular' autonomous territory with a title such as 'Autonomous Republic', 'Autonomous District', etc.[10] Until 1937 there were also 'National Counties' (*natsional'nye raiony*) and National Settlements for particularly small or isolated groups. In the Soviet North, Yakuts and Komi were each given an Autonomous Republic (or ASSR) bearing their name; in addition most of the ordinary provinces contain Autonomous Districts (*avtonomnye okruga*) named after one or more of the larger Peoples of the North. Usually these districts occupy the sparsely populated northern portions of provinces, whilst the numerically preponderant Russians are concentrated in the south. Indigenous people are nowhere in a majority. Even in their 'titular' territories they are never more than half the population, and in the total population of central and northern Siberia they are more like five per cent—or one per cent if we exclude the Yakuts and Komi.

It is less easy to speak with confidence about the population

[10] The authorities of these territories administer all residents in them, 'titular' and 'non-titular', and indeed in many the titular inhabitants are no more than a small minority. And their autonomy has usually been more a matter of ceremony than of substance. Nevertheless, non-Russians have often shown marked attachment to these structures. One reason is that, even in conditions of severe centralization, and even when they were greatly outnumbered, the system conferred some advantages on 'titular' inhabitants; even the emptiest of ceremonies have to be conducted by someone!

THE PEOPLES OF THE NORTH: Geographical Distribution

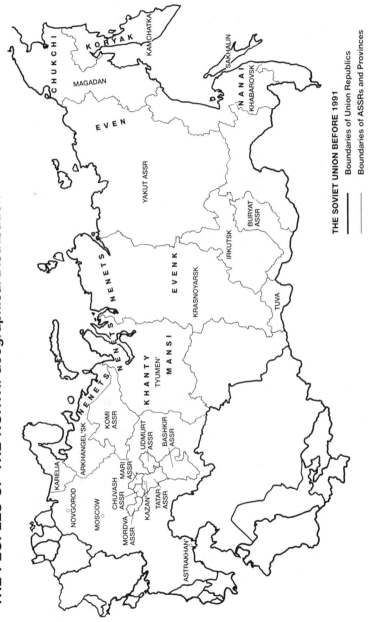

THE SOVIET UNION BEFORE 1991

Boundaries of Union Republics

Boundaries of ASSRs and Provinces

CHUKCHI

KORYAK

KAMCHATKA

SAKHALIN

MAGADAN

NANAI

KHABAROVSK

EVEN

YAKUT ASSR

BURYAT ASSR

IRKUTSK

NENETS

EVENK

KRASNOYARSK

TUVA

NENETS

KHANTY

MANSI

TYUMEN'

NENETS

KARELIA

ARKHANGEL'SK

KOMI ASSR

UDMURT ASSR

BASHKIR ASSR

NOVGOROD

MARI ASSR

MOSCOW

CHUVASH ASSR

KAZAN'

TATAR ASSR

MORDVA ASSR

ASTRAKHAN'

dynamics of natives of the North. Censuses since the Second World War have been reasonably reliable, if not very detailed, and they show that over the thirty year period 1959–89, the Peoples of the North increased by 40 per cent, the Yakuts by 64 per cent, and the Komi by 20 per cent. The comparable figure for the USSR as a whole is 37 per cent, for Russians 27 per cent, and for non-Russians 48 per cent. This does not sound particularly alarming for the Peoples of the North, though one notes that some groups, particularly the Khanty and the Evenk were doing badly in the 1970s and 1980s. If the analysis is extended back to earlier censuses, the suggestion emerges (it can be no more than a suggestion) that the Peoples of the North were declining in number in the first half of this century. The data from the 1897 census must be treated with the greatest caution;[11] but with the 1926 census (probably the most detailed there has ever been) we are on firmer ground, and its results suggest that indigenous peoples suffered some kind of demographic setback between 1926 and 1959. It is tempting to think of the collectivization of 'agriculture', which in the case of nomads amounted to compulsory settlement, but again caution is in order: we have no means of telling the impact of assimilation in these figures. There have never been insuperable barriers to assimilation to the Russian identity, even for people with non-European physical features. It is also probable that Evenks are assimilating to the Yakut identity,[12] and that the Nenets have been recruited from among the smaller Peoples of the North.

Table III shows the distribution of natives of the Soviet North across the most northerly provinces of European Russia and Siberia. Komi and Yakuts are concentrated in their titular ASSRs, whilst the Peoples of the North are spread thinly and fairly evenly across an immense tract of land—two-fifths of the earth's circumference at this latitude! There is one exception to this: almost a third of the Peoples of the North live in Tyumen' province, the region which since the early 1970s has become the Soviet Union's principal source of oil and natural gas, and which has experienced a massive influx of population in consequence. It is evident from Table I that the Khanty and Mansi

---

[11] For two reasons: (i) the classification was of language, not of ethnic self-identification; and (ii) the boundaries between groups were drawn differently in many cases and it is hard to make the data comparable with later censuses. The effect of the first of these is likely to have led to undercounting of the Peoples of the North.

[12] More than a third of Evenks cite Yakut as their native language.

TABLE III

GEOGRAPHICAL DISTRIBUTION OF NATIVE PEOPLES IN SOVIET NORTH (THOUSANDS, 1979)

Province	Komi	Yakut	Nenets	Khanty	Mansi	Evenk	Even	Chukchi	Koryak	Nanai	Other	Population	
												Native	Total
Arkhangel'sk	7.1	–	6.7	–	–	–	–	–	–	–	–	13.9	1466.0
Komi ASSR	280.8	–	–	–	–	–	–	–	–	–	–	280.8	1110.4
Tyumen'	–	–	19.0	18.8	6.7	–	–	–	–	–	2.0	46.5	1885.2
Krasnoyarsk	–	–	2.5	–	–	4.2	–	–	–	–	7.1	13.8	3198.6
Irkutsk	–	–	–	–	–	1.3	–	–	–	–	0.8	2.1	2558.0
Yakut ASSR	–	313.9	–	–	–	11.6	5.8	–	–	–	1.1	332.4	851.8
Khabarovsk	–	–	–	–	–	3.6	1.5	–	–	9.3	6.3	20.7	1558.0
Magadan	–	–	–	–	–	–	–	11.9	–	–	5.9	17.9	476.9
Kamchatka	–	–	–	–	–	–	–	1.3	6.3	–	3.1	10.7	383.5
TOTAL	287.9	313.9	28.2	18.8	6.7	20.6	7.2	13.2	6.3	9.3	26.3	738.6	13488.4

of Tyumen' province are particularly outnumbered in their home territory; this is a relatively recent outcome of immigration.

A final question arising from the demographic data: how to explain the striking differences in size and growth between the two large groups, the Yakuts and the Komi, on the one hand, and the rest, the Peoples of the North, on the other—differences all the more puzzling in view of an apparently uniform geography?.

Concerning the Komi we have already learnt that they straddle the boundary between agriculture and permafrost, and that they acquired a literary language, and the sense of distinct identity that goes with this, as early as in the fourteenth century. The Yakut case is less straightforward. Most Yakuts live in and around a sheltered basin on the middle course of the river Lena, between the tributaries Vilyui and Aldan, and this basin turns out to be geographically most unusual. Though within the permafrost zone, the climate here is drier and the summers warmer than anywhere else in Siberia; grain may be grown, and cattle and horses raised.

Here the Yakuts had developed an economy based on animal husbandry before contact with the Russians, and with it an awareness of interdependence and common identity that transcended the clan organization, and was relatively immune to Russian influence. Under Russian rule Yakut cohesion and the features of Yakut life were maintained with some success into our own times: a native-language literature was developed in the nineteenth century; there were the beginnings of a nationalist movement before 1917; armed resistance to the Bolsheviks continued until 1923; and at the end of the 1920s, alone among the groups in this study, the Yakuts could be accused of 'bourgeois nationalism' by Stalin.[13] By contrast, to the west, east and north of Yakutia there has been nothing in the natural environment that encouraged any other social organization than the loose, decentralized and small-scale structures of hunter-gatherers and nomads. There could hardly be a neater illustration of the socio-political implications of different economic orders.

[13] Walter Kolarz, *The Peoples of the Soviet Far East* (London: George Philip, 1954, reprinted Archon Books, 1969), pp. 102–13. It is worth adding that, although there is a considerable Russian population in the Yakut ASSR, most of it is in the gold and diamond mining regions south and west of the main area of Yakut settlement.

IV NATIVES OF THE NORTH IN THE SOVIET PERIOD

The revolution of 1917 seemed to promise great things to the non-Russian majority of the old empire, though almost from the outset there was disillusionment. Disappointment arose partly from the too easy Russian assumption of leadership in the new system, and from the reassertion of old boundaries for what was basically Russian *raison d'etat*. A further factor was the Bolsheviks' lack of serious thinking and policy on ethnic relations.[14] What later came to be lauded as 'Lenin's Nationality Policy' (but surely this glosses over Stalin's major contribution to it, from the very beginning?) boils down essentially to two things. First was an unexamined adherence to the Marxist—and liberal—notion that economic development would simply mitigate ethnic tensions. Second, until this should take effect, competitive activity among ethnic groups—that is ethnic politics in a strict sense—was suppressed. Minority cultures were encouraged, but in isolation from each other; comparisons and contrasts might not be drawn in public. With this went the freezing of the administrative boundaries of the early 1920s. Substantial evidence emerged during the 1980s that this did not dissipate ethnic perceptions, but merely relegated them to an underground subculture.

But for the first decade of Soviet power the developments that affected the native peoples of the North were distinct from the run of nationalities policy, whether because the natives offered no political challenge, or because some Bolsheviks (former exiles) had favourable experience of them. This atypical policy is worth tracing, as its legacy is still important today.[15]

[14] Like it or not, one can hardly deny the serious and thorough-going radicalism that went into the policy of the 'vanguard party'. Set against this, the nationalities policy seems to be marked by unexamined assumptions and short-term expediency.

[15] Such pluralism was not quite so unusual in the 1920s as it now seems to us. Svensson (pp. 108–11) argues that in the case of the North it allowed considerable continuity with nineteenth century policy. She also surveys the reasons why the Northerners in particular should have been the object of a distinct programme. In addition to the familiarity that political exiles had with natives, and the absence of political threat from the latter, she points out that they seemed to be examples of 'primitive communism' and so were likely to be naturally socialist. Possibly from such perceptions there emerged, as a distinct theme in Soviet publicity, the romantic and paternalist treatment of the Peoples of the North. This was to outlast the distinct policies of the 1920s, and indeed may have made ordinary Russians

Above all the new government was content to leave policy towards the natives of the North largely in the hands of a self-selected group of experts, many of them anthropologists and linguists familiar with Siberia. At first these were part of the People's Commissariat of Nationalities under Stalin, but from 1924 to 1935 they formed a distinct, quasi-ministerial body known as the Committee of the North.[16] The Committee saw its task as a combination of administration and scientific study, and as including at least some measure of protection of natives from European pressures; some of its members, notably the ethnographer, V.G. Bogoraz, favoured setting up reservations from which all except a few categories of Europeans should be excluded, but this policy did not prevail.

The Committee of the North set up an administrative system of Native Soviets, Tribal Assemblies and Tribal Congresses based on the existing social structure, and separate from the administration of Europeans in the same territory. Alphabets (in Latin, not Cyrillic, until 1937) were created, and then a system of native-language primary schools and of specialist training at the Institute of the Peoples of the North in Leningrad. A network of medical centres was developed. The Peoples of the North (but not, significantly, the Yakuts or Komi) were exempt from some taxes and from military service. In all this we can see elements, though not a fully fledged policy, of separate development.

By the end of the 1920s the activities of the Committee (like those of all other autonomous or eccentric institutions) began to be aligned with central priorities. The territorial principle of ethnic administration was now extended to the North, so that a region with a significant non-Russian presence, rather than the group itself, was designated as a 'nationality' area, and its government was of all the resident population, native and immigrant alike. Further, in 1937 the smallest units of ethnic administration (National Counties and Settlements) were abolished. All this coincided with accelerated immigration into the region, and it meant that the small access of indigenous people to local politics became increasingly handicapped.

Much more important was the general collectivization of agricul-

---

somewhat more receptive to the case of the northerners that emerged at the end of the 1980s.

[16] In full, the Committee of Cooperation with the peoples of the North (*Komitetsodeistviya narodnostyam Severa*). For treatment in English, see Armstrong in *The Arctic Frontier*, pp. 66–75, and Kolarz, pp. 65–7.

ture. Applied to natives of the North this entailed state regulation of hunting and fur trading, and, more serious, the 'denomadization' of reindeer herdsmen—a body blow to this kind of economy. It is clear that collectivization in the North was a crude and traumatic enterprise, and probably a violent one:[17] the number of reindeer fell by a third, and by a half in some places, and it would be reasonable to associate some at least of the population losses of the 1926–59 period with this episode. On the other hand, there is some evidence that central policy was recognized to be counterproductive in the North, and that its pace was deliberately slowed; in some places collectivization was not deemed to be complete until after the Second World War, and in others existing structures were simply relabelled 'collective farms' with the minimum of real change; there are still some 13,000 nomads in the north of Siberia. In all this we may suspect that the Committee of the North succeeded in blunting the impact of central policy.

One aspect of this 'compromise' that emerged from collectivization is of importance today. Once it was recognized that reindeer must migrate, a so-called 'production nomadism' became acceptable: herders, almost all men, followed the reindeer while women and children remained in villages, the formal collective farm headquarters. This may have preserved the herding economy, but its effects on the birthrate, family life, and retention of language and culture have been devastating.[18]

The Committee of the North was abolished in 1935, and its responsibilities were transferred, either to routine provincial administration run from southern cities strung along the Trans-Siberian Railway, or to a group of centrally subordinate economic directorates, of which the most significant were *Glavsevmorput'* (Directorate of the Northern Sea Route) and *Dal'stroi* (Directorate of Far Northern Construction). *Dal'stroi* was an economic arm of the NKVD, a vast mining, timber and construction empire, which controlled economic life in the North-East using slave labour brought in during the Great

[17] On collectivization in the North, see Armstrong, *The Arctic Frontier*, pp. 70–2, and Russian Settlement, pp. 167–8; Kolarz, pp. 70–2; Svensson, p. 112; and Piers Vitebsky, 'Reindeer herders of northern Yakutia: a report from the field', *Polar Record* 25 (154), pp. 213–8 (1989). Casualties do not seem to have been as severe as in the other case of 'denomadization', that of the Kazakhs: see my summary in Archie Brown (ed.), *Political Culture and Communist Studies* (London: Macmillan, 1984), pp. 52–3.

[18] See Vitebsky, pp. 214–15.

Purge.[19] Among the material on prison camps we catch only occasional glimpses of the native peoples on whom the camps had been imposed—to the effect, for instance, that useful prison guards could be recruited from among them, or that they were rewarded for turning in escapees.[20]

The secret police subordination of *Dal'stroi* has rightly earned particular attention, but for our purposes the advent of the big economic directorates heralded another drastic change for the North, and one that survived the dissolution of *Dal'stroi* in 1953. This was the subjection of *all* other policy concerns in the North—social, legal, cultural, ethnic—to the priority of economic development, usually in the form of resource extraction, and usually subcontracted to a single, general-purpose and monopolistic development agency.

The Soviet economy was centrally planned and directed. The notion of *centralization* must be emphasized here; it had wider-reaching consequences than any other socialist priority. Economic policy was devised at the political centre, to further what central politicians saw as the national interest. It did *not* constitute an amalgam or consensus of local interests, and local interests were sometimes violated, and more often ignored in the execution of central economic policy. Indeed some features of this centralization allowed a rapacity and exploitativeness (as perceived at the local level) to match any under capitalism.[21] This had the following effects on local economic life.

First, economic enterprises in any locality had to meet the demands of central ministries, and their success or failure was measured only on the centre's terms; the localities had no recourse or sanctions against the planners, and the planners had little reason to consult local opinion or knowledge in drawing up plans. Second, an enterprise might have a position of near-monopoly locally, or else the activities of enterprises with different ministerial masters might not be co-ordinated; neither of these situations encouraged responsibility towards local people or the environment in the course of operations. Third, if an enterprise wished to take account of local interests, centrally fixed prices, bearing no relationship to demand, were poor signals of eco-

---

[19] See Kolarz, pp. 67–70; Armstrong, *Russian Settlement*, pp. 146–53; N.C. Field in *The Arctic Frontier*, pp. 178–81.

[20] Kolarz, pp. 69–70; J. Scholmer, *Vorkuta* (London: 1954), p. 58.

[21] Consider what is brought out about West Siberian oil, or Central Asian cotton later in this chapter.

nomic opportunities or felt needs. Finally, success was measured and rewarded in terms of output only; enterprises had little incentive to promote services, facilities, the local community, or workforce satisfaction.

The result was a narrowly extractive, in some places quasi-colonial process of 'development', and the creation of economic and occupational profiles which often did not meet local aspirations. At the same time the policy was until recently immune to challenge or criticism.[22] Students of Soviet local government are familiar with the phenomenon of the 'company town'—one in which a central economic ministry (or a small group of them) offer almost all available employment and control almost all local infrastructure, services, finance and planning, while the local soviet (which cannot tax central enterprises) is a powerless bystander.

In the North this kind of impact of *Dal'stroi* and its successors must have been especially severe: there were almost no facilities there which were not owned by the central agencies, and their employees (convict or free) would have shared the developers' unwillingness to go on from resource extraction to the building of viable, all-round communities. Policy seemed to have forgotten the natives. No-one until recently challenged the assumption that native policy was a second-rank spin-off from economic development.

In 1953 the present pattern of administration of the North was introduced: subordination in political terms to provincial centres in the south (the exceptions were Murmansk and Magadan), and in economic terms to the central economic ministries.[23] At the same time, public relations treatment of the Peoples of the North underwent a change; the fascination with them as something romantic and exotic[24]

[22] But (it must be said) it was also a policy that had considerable support in society at large because of what it seemed to offer in terms of training and social mobility. Only comparatively recently have new perceptions gained ground: that social opportunities have declined, while the costs of development have become more obtrusive.

[23] A group of Northerners give a vivid illustration of the effects of these administrative changes using the example of civil aviation: after the 'Polar Administration of Civil Administration' was abolished (as late as 1970), its tasks were left to organizations in the south who had neither the skills, the specialized equipment nor incentives to tackle the problems of Polar transport. See 'Beskryl'nyi Sever', *Pravda*, 22 October 1989.

[24] Kolarz gives many examples, especially on pp. 79–84. The fascination may well have been Stalin's own.

faded away, and under Khrushchev and Brezhnev they received much less attention, and this attention seemed stilted and perfunctory, focused in particular on the career achievements (in Soviet terms) of named individuals, on high indigenous representation in soviets and the Communist Party,[25] and rarely on society.

Statistical information improved under Khrushchev and Brezhnev, and from this we can glean a certain amount about social trends among natives of the North, particularly in the fields of language and education. Available data for the Komi, Yakut and the four largest Peoples of the North, with some comparisons, are consolidated in Table IV.[26]

One of the main developments of this period was the abandonment, apparently during the 1960s, of native language teaching among the Peoples of the North, and its replacement by instruction in Russian; to the Komi it is available up to the age of ten; to Yakuts to the age of fifteen.[27] This was almost certainly connected with the widespread

[25] Examples in Armstrong, *The Arctic Frontier*, pp. 76–7 and Svensson, pp. 111–12. Non-Russian nationalities were generally over-represented in soviets —but these had little power before 1989. If the Peoples of the North could be shown to have had a higher *Party* membership than the average, that would be a claim with rather stronger implications for their integration into Soviet society and politics. Comprehensive data on Party membership among the Peoples of the North were first divulged in 1989 (see Table IV), and they show that it was *high* among the Pacific seaboard peoples of Kamchatka and Magadan provinces, but otherwise generally low, and *very low* in Tyumen province. Of the seven Autonomous Districts and two ASSRs designated for the indigenous peoples in this study, only two (the Yakut ASSR and the Evenk AD) had native Party first secretaries in 1989.

[26] Sources: as for Table II, with, in addition: (i) on schooling: Bromlei, pp. 272–3; and B.D. Silver, 'The Status of National Minority Languages in Soviet Education: An Assessment of Recent Changes', *Soviet Studies*, vol. XXVI, no. 1, January 1974, pp. 33–4; (ii) on publishing: various issues of the statistical annuals *Narodnoe khozyaistvo RSFSR* and *Pechat' SSSR*; (iii) on party membership: *Izvestiya TsK KPSS*, 2/89, pp. 140–1, and 7/89, p. 113. The percentages in Table IV, obtained by dividing party membership into *total* (not adult) population figures from the 1979 census, give no more than an approximate indication of the state of affairs.

[27] The trend is general to most indigenous minorities of the Russian Republic; only the Tatars and Bashkirs retain some native language instruction throughout primary and secondary schooling. Armstrong, *The Arctic Frontier*, p. 81 reports the Koryaks and Chukchi petitioning for the change. The process may not always have been as simple as that suggests, because Russian-language instruction suits both education bureaucrats and immigrant Russians (who are often in a majority); but it is true that elsewhere in the USSR 'upwardly mobile', non-Russian parents may press to have their children taught in Russian.

TABLE IV

NATIVES OF THE NORTH: SOCIAL DATA SINCE STALIN

| | Komi | Yakut | All | Peoples of the North | | | | USSR | | |
				Nenets	Khanty	Evenk	Chukchi	All	Russians	Non-Russian
Language										
% Claiming Russian as Native Language										
1959	10.5	2.4	14.8	5.5	22.3	8.7	5.7	59.4	99.8	10.8
1970	17.2	3.7	23.0	9.0	30.5	16.5	16.9	58.7	99.8	11.6
1979	23.7	4.6	28.7	14.0	31.8	20.7	21.2	58.6	99.8	13.1
% Claiming Russian as Second Language										
1970	63.1	41.7	52.5	55.1	48.1	54.9	58.7	17.3	0.1	37.1
1979	64.5	55.6	54.0	65.3	52.8	54.5	61.3	23.3	0.1	48.9
% Claiming Knowledge of Russian										
1970	80.3	45.4	75.5	64.1	78.6	71.4	75.6	76.0	99.9	48.7
1979	88.2	60.2	82.7	79.3	84.6	75.2	82.5	81.9	99.9	62.0
Schooling										
Grades in which Native Language served (1972) as:										
Medium of Instruction	1–3	1–8	–	pso	none	none	none	–	–	1–10

| | Komi | Yakut | All | Peoples of the North | | | | All | USSR | |
				Nenets	Khanty	Evenk	Chukchi		Russians	Non-Russian
Second Language	1–10	1–10	–	0–3	0–1	0–3	0–3	–	–	–

(0 = pre-school; pso = pre-school only)

Qualifications
% of Population with Tertiary Qualifications

	Komi	Yakut	All	Nenets	Khanty	Evenk	Chukchi	All	Russians	Non-Russian
1959										
Male	1.3	1.6	–	0.3	0.5	0.5	0.2	2.7	2.8	2.6
Female	1.1	0.7	–	0.3	0.2	0.4	0.1	2.0	2.3	1.6
1970										
Male	2.2	4.1	–	0.4	1.2	1.2	0.8	4.8	5.0	4.6
Female	2.1	2.5	–	0.8	0.9	2.4	0.5	3.7	4.2	3.1

% of Population with Secondary Specialist Qualifications

	Komi	Yakut	All	Nenets	Khanty	Evenk	Chukchi	All	Russians	Non-Russian
1959										
Male	5.2	4.1	–	0.6	2.1	1.8	1.4	4.8	5.6	3.9
Female	5.8	3.5	–	1.2	4.4	3.2	1.4	4.9	5.9	3.7
1970										
Male	5.4	5.2	–	1.5	3.0	3.1	3.6	6.5	7.2	5.7
Female	8.4	6.6	–	3.1	7.2	9.3	4.3	7.1	8.5	5.4

		Peoples of the North						USSR		
	Komi	Yakut	All	Nenets	Khanty	Evenk	Chukchi	All	Russians	Non-Russian
Publishing										
Books and Pamphlets,										
Vols per 1000 persons per year										
1940	1139	–	–	–	–	–	–	2725	3491	1649
1960	432	2563	–	435	–	–	1364	5938	8907	2361
1980	150	2177	–	204	–	–	1214	6715	10543	2497
Newspapers, Copies per 1000 persons per day										
1960	77	330	–	–	–	–	–	328	c457	174
1981	52	442	–	34	48	–	71	675	1003	315
Party Membership										
% of Population in Communist Party										
1989	7.1	5.8	5.5	4.3	3.5	6.0	9.5	7.4	8.3	6.5

requirement in the North that children move to remote, centrally located boarding-schools (*internaty*) for education.[28] The trend is clearly the background to the declining knowledge of native languages in the North, and declining publishing in those languages. About 29 per cent of the Peoples of the North claimed Russian as their *native* language in 1979 (twice what it had been in 1959), and more than 80 per cent claimed to know Russian; the figures are similar for the Komi.[29] In the Komi, Nenets, Khanty and Chukchi languages some native book or newspaper publishing can be identified, but in per capita terms its quantity is very small and on the decline. The connection between these processes and assimilation to Russian identity does not need spelling out. The exception to this pattern is, not surprisingly, the Yakuts: less than five per cent claim Russian as their native language (though some 60 per cent claim to know it), and per capita publishing rates in Yakut are as high as the average for all languages other than Russian.

Data on educational qualifications may perhaps fill out this picture. Those used in Table IV are tertiary and 'secondary specialist' qualifications—the latter being something like a trade or craft certificate obtained after secondary schooling beyond the legal minimum. Peoples of the North and the Komi show considerably fewer tertiary graduates than the national average (or the average for non-Russians), fairly respectable levels of secondary specialist education, and *high* rates of secondary specialist education among females; on all these counts the Yakuts come closer to the national average. The pattern is repeated among many of the smaller nationalities of the Volga-Urals region and of south Siberia. Interpreting it is by no means clear, but the following, very speculative combination of factors would be plausible. Schoolteaching in an unfamiliar language, and usually far from home, is likely to be of poor quality, arduous and uninspiring. Girls stay at school beyond the legal minimum because they aim to get jobs in towns, or at least in the 'villages' which are the centres of collective farms. Boys expect to take up traditional duties, for which Soviet schools provide no preparation,[30] and which they must begin to learn

[28] Vitebsky, p. 217, says almost 100,000 native children from the North may be in *internaty*.

[29] These figures are among the highest for non-Russians, but are not unique: knowledge of Russian is even higher among the Mordva and Karelians.

[30] See Vitebsky, pp. 215 and 217.

before military service intervenes. Hardly anyone is able—whether through low levels of training or of aspiration—to break into the fiercely competitive, and Russian, tertiary sector. Yakutia, by contrast, with its relatively unscathed and confident culture, and somewhat greater autonomous rights, will offer schoolchildren a somewhat easier passage.

When we turn to statistics on matters other than language and education, there is a striking lack of information. We should like to know more about the occupations people turned to as alternatives to the traditional ones, and much more about how they cope nowadays with the climate and the environment. But there are no data, ethnically or regionally specific, about the distribution of occupations or incomes, nor about health, and virtually no demographic data, other than the crude population growth rates already cited.[31] From the 1970 census, age distributions for the separate Peoples of the North were published, and these suggest, either that birth rates were very low, or child mortality very high, in the 1940s and early 1950s, and that rates improved from the mid-1950s.[32]

One more factor from the Brezhnev period needs to be brought out. What must rank as one of the world's great mineral booms began in the early 1970s with the development of massive oil and gas reserves in Tyumen' province, and chiefly in its two northerly Autonomous Districts. Since 1972 oil production there has increased sixfold, and natural gas more than twentyfold, much of it piped to Eastern and Western Europe; and the population of the Autonomous Districts has increased fivefold, from 350,000 to 1.75 million—virtually all of it, of course, by immigration. Nor does population increase tell the full story: teams of skilled workers are flown in and out by helicopter on short stints, and unskilled labour turnover is notoriously high; the number of people who have had fleeting, low-cost contact with Siberia has been put at five times the number of long-term immigrants. Anecdotal and circumstantial evidence suggests that the boom has attracted many 'no-hopers' and drifters, and that—as in the gold rushes—infrastructure and quality of life have deteriorated. The changes that

[31] It is claimed in *Izvestiya*, 15 June 1989, that such information about the Peoples of the North was kept 'for official use only'. Under Brezhnev limited vital statistics were published concerning the *union-republics*, but not about lower-echelon administrative units; and even the former information was suspended for a decade from 1975.

[32] See *Itogi*, vol. IV, pp. 374–7.

have swept over the native Khanty, Mansi and Nenets must be among the most drastic in their history.

V RECENT MATERIAL ON THE PEOPLES OF THE NORTH

The increasing obscurity of the natives of the Soviet North was dissipated by a remarkable burst of media coverage that began in mid-1988. The tone of the coverage is that of an exposé—and like an opening of floodgates; its portrayal of the situation of the northern peoples is grim, and its account of past policies very hostile.[33] The authors are typically natives of the North, like E.D. Aipin (from Tyumen' province), M.I. Mongo (Krasnoyarsk), E.A. Gaer (Khabarovsk), V. Ledkov (Arkhangel'sk) and V. Sangi (Sakhalin), or scholars employed on Siberian matters, like A. Pika and B. Prokhorov. They have utilized the assembly of the Congress of People's Deputies (May–June 1989), and the formation of a new government, to popularize their cause very effectively, and especially among those with environmentalist sympathies.

One of the most notable contributions by the Khanty writer, Aipin, was printed in the English language *Moscow News*. It is worth quoting extensively from this article because of what it conveys, not just of Aipin's argument, but of his tone and feelings:

The land of my ancestors has been ruined. My 76-year-old father realized this long ago, one night in January when a truck speeding ahead of him turned suddenly and stopped, barring the way on a lonely winter road. My father's reindeer sled also stopped. Two men climbed down from the cabin and made their way to the sled. One held the old man from behind by the shoulders while the other pulled off the old man's fur boots. The two leisurely walked back to the truck and then drove off. My father returned home in his socks. He was perhaps glad that they had not harmed the reindeer and that his home wasn't far away because otherwise his feet could get frost-bitten.

This happened when the conquerors of oil-bearing wilderness cut a winter road across our own pine forest from Nizhnevartovsk to their base in Novoagansk. Once a month my father used the road to fetch his pension money . . .

The next winter his sled, pulled by three dogs, was stolen from him in the logger village.

---

[33] References to this material are listed in the Appendix.

The timber-felling enterprise cut down all the trees on the tribal cemetery thus ruining the final resting-place.

My father can't understand many other things which happened during his 76-year lifetime, during which he not once plucked a fir needle or leaf, not a blade of grass unnecessarily on his land, on the land of his ancestors. He can't understand why they cut down his pine grove if the logs still lie in stacks needlessly rotting. Why have the oil prospectors left behind upturned soil and mountains of metal scrap? Why do the machines choke up the small streams with pipes and sand bars, making it impossible either for fishermen or fish to go through? Finally why do they pump oil out of the earth if it is allowed to float two fingers thick along the way? . . .

'I don't want anything,' he says . . . 'Only my land. Give me my land back where I can graze my reindeers, hunt game and catch fish. Give me my land where my deers are not attacked by stray dogs, where my hunting trails are not trampled down by poachers or fouled up by vehicles, where the rivers and lakes have no oil slicks. I want land where my home, my sanctuary and graveyard can remain inviolable . . . '

The land of our ancestors is no more and this has ended our tribe that used to settle along the entire middle course of the Agan, the right tributary of the Ob . . . Our tribe of the Makha, the tribe of the Beaver, is at an end. Our tribe is at an end. Our tribe is at an end, as I know now, from the feeling of doom. Nearly all of my first and second cousins died at age 35–40 from alcoholism . . .

What's happened to the kids? . . . They haven't amounted to anything . . . There is nobody there to teach the boys how to hunt game, catch fish or graze reindeers . . . Neither have they made 'the great leap from shabby patriarchal times into socialism' . . . They have not made oil workers, geologists or builders . . . This gave rise to the lost generation of my nephews and nieces who know neither the language nor culture of their nation . . .

We earnestly ask the government to save our small nation before it is too late. To leave for us the living space along the Bolshoi Yugan and Maly Yugan rivers. To stop oil production on these rivers. No settlements, oil derricks or oil pipelines should be built beyond the village of Ugut up the river . . . Our settlements should be declared a national preserve.

Neither the opinions nor the sympathies of the above would have been conceivable in print under Brezhnev.

The substantive content of these complaints by and on behalf of the Peoples of the North may be classified as follows.

Demography and Health

The stagnant or falling native population is attributed unambiguously, not to assimilation, but to a falling birth rate and a very high death rate. The latter is said to be two to three times higher than that of the Russian Republic as a whole, which would put it somewhere between 20 and 30 per thousand; it would require very high birth rates to offset this and leave a natural increase. Family breakdown is blamed partly on alcohol, and partly on boarding-schools, resented because they alienate children from the traditional way of life; girls in particular do not return to village—and still less to nomad—life. (We should clearly add a third factor here: the absence of herdsmen for most of the year). Infant mortality among indigenous Northerners is claimed to be two to three times the national average, or between 50 and 75 per thousand —high figures, but of the same order as in some southern regions of the USSR. Life expectancy is put at 45 years for men and 55 for women, about eighteen years less than the national average. Half of all deaths are the result of accident, poisoning, murder or suicide, with deaths from alcohol presumably included under poisoning. Dysentery and viral hepatitis are said to be widespread, and morbidity from tuberculosis ranges from 108.8 to 404.5 per hundred thousand—the last nine times the national rate of 44.2.[34] Plainly, behind these figures lies a demographic disaster.

Employment, Income and Living Standards

Between 13,000 and 15,000 indigenous Northerners are still nomads, and, we are told, since they are not sedentary, the planners of services and facilities do not make provision for them. About 43 per cent make a living from fishing, furs or reindeer farming (down from 70 per cent in 1959). But it is clear that, whilst the traditional economy has been wrecked for the majority, they have not made any successful transition to 'modern' patterns of occupation; most accounts stress that they are concentrated in part-time, casual or seasonal unskilled labour, and that many are unemployed. Pika and Prokhorov refer to 'lumpenization', and suggest that it is nothing for socialists to be proud of.[35]

[34] Details from Gamov, 'Arkticheskii konsilium', from Pika & Prokhorov, p. 80, or from Mongo. I am indebted to Dr Murray Feshbach for help in interpreting the TB statistics. Still worse infant mortality and TB rates (as well as a serious incidence of a range of cancers) are claimed for the Chukchi in Lupandin and Gayer, and are linked there with nuclear testing in north-east Siberia in the 1950s and 1960s.
[35] Pika and Prokhorov, pp. 77–80.

Aipin refers to an 'average monthly pay of an indigenous worker' in his district of just over 26 roubles in 1989, and to 'indigenous women workers' in a fish processing factory on 13 roubles a month. These are astonishing figures[36] when set beside a supposed legal minimum of 70 roubles per month in the state sectors of employment; they could just be plausible if they pertained to pensions or the poorest collective farms, but it is explicitly said they do not. It is possible the author is giving an average that includes casual employees[37] and the unemployed, but he also hints quite clearly that there are lower rates of pay for the indigenous. This is confirmed in part—as regards the penalty rates for severe climate—by a senior official of the Khanty-Mansiisk Autonomous District.[38]

An appalling picture is likewise painted of living conditions: numerous homes are without electricity or sewage, less than one per cent have piped water, only three per cent (in the gas fields!) have piped gas; the average living space in native settlements is 4 square metres per person, as against a legal minimum of nine.[39] The connection with TB and dysentery is obvious. Mongo labels the conditions 'primeval, with TV'.

Economics and the Environment

General hostility to economic development, at least in the rapacious and degrading form in which it has occurred, is standard to these accounts. References abound to 'occupiers', 'predators', 'interventionists',[40] and to the 'onslaught of technogenic civilization'; the tundra's enemies are 'the wolf, the bear and the oil-driller'. The fragility, rather than the ferocity, of the Siberian environment begins to be singled out.[41] M.I. Mongo, in a speech to the Congress of

[36] Aipin, *Moscow News*, 8 January 1989. I can find no hint of pay rates so low in Mervyn Matthews, *Poverty in the Soviet Union* (Cambridge: Cambridge University Press, 1986).

[37] Sangi refers to 'two or three workers' sharing a single wage, and Shinkarev to workers on half-pay of 35–40 roubles a month.

[38] R. Il'ina in 'Rodom s Severa'.

[39] Pika and Prokhorov, p. 77; see also Tabeev.

[40] An allusion to foreign intervention against the Bolsheviks after 1917.

[41] See in particular the articles by Kotlyakov and Agranat (with response by T. Armstrong in *Pravda*, 14 August 1989), Sleptsov, Lupandin and Gayer, and Denisov. Such appraisal often singles out the vulnerable nature of moss and lichen reindeer pastures.

People's Deputies on behalf of other deputies from the North, tries to classify and rank his objections, and hence to suggest an answer to the obvious question: is this a complete rejection of modern technology, or just of some of its forms? He lists, first, the physical destruction of the means of life and livelihood; second, the neglect of infrastructure and services; and third, the absence of native rights. His second and third complaints could be remedied (in principle) much more easily than the first; that they are still listed second and third shows how close Mongo—a Party member and chosen as spokesman by the northern deputies—comes to an outright rejection of northern development. The general opinion seems to be that the traditional economy and crafts (*promysel*) have not only proved themselves to be *the* viable and effective techniques for this environment, but are also indispensable to the social well-being and group identity of the original inhabitants; insofar, at least, as it interferes or damages, imported development should give way.

The concern with environmental impact comes out in another way. In much of this material there is condemnation of collectivization and in general of outside attempts to push people 'a thousand years in a lifetime'. But it is striking how much specific blame is laid on policies of the last thirty years, as if to say that the collective farm organization had little impact until then, or was basically tolerable—until something else threatened more vital interests. It is clear why these perceptions should prevail in the Tyumen' gas fields. But spokesmen from other areas attack the intensification of technology since the early 1960s: in particular, the resettlement of people from outlying, 'condemned' villages, but also the conversion of collective into state farms, and the centralization and mechanization of fishing and other occupations.[42] The result, they claim, has been the squeezing of indigenous people out of both their employment and their traditional homes. The preference for skilled immigrants over locals has had the same effect. This preoccupation with events in the present generation suggests that pressures on the Siberian environment, and European ability to penetrate remote areas, may have reached a critical level in that time, and that only now do indigenous people see their immunity collapsing.

[42] For example, Sangi (from Sakhalin), Gaer (from Khabarovsk), Ledkov (from Arkhangel'sk) or A. Nemtushkin (from Krasnoyarsk) quoted in Mihalisko, 'Discontent...'. Tabeev gives official endorsement to many of these complaints. Resentment at the village consolidation policy is general all over northern Russia.

Perhaps for this reason the spokesmen for the Peoples of the North tend to alternate between concern for the traditional economy, and talk in a much grander vein about the planetary ecosystem; Mongo calls the Siberian *taiga* 'an oxygen factory for the whole planet'. They tend (at least in this writer's judgement) to underrate detailed questiions of the medium term economic relationship between the North and the rest of the Soviet Union: Should the North have a trading relationship with the exterior? How should indigenous welfare and infrastructure be financed? By increasing prices paid for the products of the traditional economy, or by a limited measure of resource extraction? If so, controlled, financed, staffed and marketed by whom? And what of the majority, immigrant population?

Some, it is true, are beginning to address such questions. Aipin calls for deductions from oil and gas profits to go into the local budget. Ledkov suggests raising the official price on a hectare of reindeer pasture thirty thousand times! But in general it is outsiders, like the specialists Pika and Prokhorov, Kotlyakov and Agranat or Il'ina who tackle such intricate and practical questions—and perhaps they are the ones best in a position to do so. Pika and Prokhorov point to government prices for fur (most fur farms operate at a planned loss), and propose obliging the 'developers' to pay compensation, not in money, but in the form of services and facilities. Agranat protests against 'apparent' prices for land of 10–100 roubles per hectare in the tundra, and 15,000–20,000 roubles per hectare in the fertile Black Earth of Kursk. Il'ina castigates the illusion of 'cheap' resources and the ministerial attitudes fostered by this, and attempts to put a price on some of the hidden costs.[43] The First Secretary for the Khanty-Mansiisk District Party Committee, V.A. Churilov, a Russian, offers a perspective different from that of the Northerners on matters of migration: he sees his committee as having to reconcile two main tasks in ethnic relations, 'the survival and salvation of the native peoples of the North, on the one hand, and the transfer of a large mass of Russian speaking "industrial nomads" to settled life, on the other'. No hint here that the oil ministries might withdraw!

Though they advocate higher payments for products of the tradi-

---

43 Aipin, *Moscow News*, 12/89; Ledkov; Pika and Prokhorov, pp. 78 and 83, Kotlyakov and Agranat; Il'ina. Arguments justifying substantial rises in the prices charged for raw materials—plainest in Il'ina—would not have been unwelcome to the government of the RSFSR, which was campaigning at the time for the right to charge manufacturing regions more for their inputs.

tional economy, there is no suggestion in the present material that this could save the North; the consensus seems to be that improvements must depend *either* on the North paying its way in the modern economy, or on outside subsidies. Irrespective of what happens to economic development, it is probable that the RSFSR authorities would not be averse to subsidizing the Peoples of the North; it is much less easy to gauge what the Northerners themselves think of this prospect. Some may assume that the relationship should appropriately be one of subsidy (and perhaps Mongo was hinting at this with his reference to the oxygen factory?). It will be remembered that Svensson was sombre about the prospects of this sort of arrangement.

Culture and Spiritual Life

There is despair among the present generation of Peoples of the North at the possibility that they may be the last generation to use the native languages and to live the traditional way of life. Children brought up away from their parents, among Russian teachers and child-minders, soon lose their native language. Seventy years of unsolicited social engineering have bred into Northerners (as well as into many other Soviet citizens) a powerful conservatism. The refrain in this material is that *ancestral* ways and values, ancestral skills, ancestral lands are best and that modernity has brought nothing but doom. In the case of Aipin's father we can see this taking on distinct tones of paganism, and Aipin himself—a Party member—inclines to a 'Pan-Finno-Ugric' mysticism ('our land Ugra', 'our common Ugric Home').[44] Coupled with this nostalgia is the desire to be left alone by the Europeans; one Northerner says she 'would prefer to live on a reservation, so that we could have a policeman at the gates'.[45] After so long an association, and in such thinly populated territory, it would be unrealistic to expect nationalism or an independence movement, but there is an urgent desire for breathing space and for separate development.

Political Proposals

The authorities seem to have been aware that this publicity campaign was in the offing. In or about March 1988 a State Commission on Arctic Affairs was set up—an interdepartmental co-ordinative body

[44] *Moscow News*, 19 March 1989.
[45] Quoted by L Shinkarev in *Izvestiya*, 15 June 1989. Gaer in *Moscow News*,

of thirty senior officials, drawn mainly from All-Union (Federal) and RSFSR ministries, and chaired by Yu D. Maslyukov, the head of State Planning. In March 1989 a spokesman for this Commission warned that its task should not be perceived as one of keeping the ministries out of the North, and that the state could not manage 'without the northern treasure houses'; nevertheless, ecologically safe techniques must be developed, and he cited one project (on the Yamal Peninsula) that had been suspended for failure to meet standards.[46]

Compromise of this kind is brushed aside by virtually all the recent spokesmen for the North, natives and scholars alike. It is not so much that they urge genuine and effective local self-government for the autonomous districts of the North. In this they are going no further than citizens elsewhere, and simply to urge it does not grapple with the fundamental problem: real local government is incompatible with central planning and unthinkable without some autonomous power to raise finance locally—which the economic ministries are likely to resist or obstruct. The Northern claims go further in two ways.

In the first place a special deal should be sanctioned for the natives of the North, distinct from general arrangements for local government and ethnic minorities. Pika and Prokhorov argue this most systematically when they write that the northern population will lose out if it is given no more than *equal* rights and opportunities.[47] There is a consensus that such special arrangements should include the power to restrict developmental projects and exclude outsiders. As to the form of the new arrangements, Aipin, Mongo and Ledkov call quite explicitly for the re-establishment of the Committee of the North, 'groundlessly liquidated in 1935', or of some government body with equivalent powers, status and staffing.[48] Many also support the revival of National Counties and National Settlements.[49]

---

25 June 1989 expresses cautious interest in foreign experience with reservations.

[46] There seems to have been no contemporary announcement of the setting-up of this body, though it was apparently referred to in *Nedelya*, 9 September 1988. The March 1989 interview is in *Pravitel'stvennyi vestnik*, 6/89, pp. 11–12. Tabeev (*Pravitel'stvennyi vestnik*, 13/89, p. 7) refers to a somewhat similar commission formed by the RSFSR Council of Ministers.

[47] Pika and Prokhorov, p. 82.

[48] Aipin in *Moscow News*, 19 March 1989, Mongo in *Izvestiya*, 8 June 1989, Ledkov in *Sovetskaya Rossiya*, 18 June 1989. An implication seems to be disparagement of the existing State Commission on Arctic Affairs, an interdepartmental body composed mainly of ministers, meeting quarterly, and with a permanent staff of no more than four (*Pravitel'stvennyi vestnik*, 6/89, p. 12).

[49] For example, Aipin, Mongo and Sleptsov. The re-establishment of a National

Second, Pika and Prokhorov argue that it would simply repeat past folly if such special rights were handed down to the Peoples of the North from above; the population of the North should *themselves* work them out and implement them, from start to finish. On this question the response of the Northerners themselves is (in print) not quite so clear; but we notice Mongo's role as spokesman for the deputies 'from the majority of the autonomous districts of the Russian Federation'. Sangi proposes an 'Association of the Peoples of the North', a lobby to represent the Northerners' case to government and, administration, and such an organization, with 26 participant groups and with Sangi as president, was set up in August 1989.[50] Several of the articles raise the need for ideas and moral support from organizations of indigenous peoples overseas.[51]

A Balance Sheet as of Late 1989

Merely to have brought so much to public attention, to have placed so much on the political agenda in the space of just over a year is a considerable achievement. But how much progress has been made towards solution of these problems, and how much progress *could* realistically be expected? What are the apparent prospects for the Peoples of the North?

County for the Even population around Verkhoyansk (Yakutia) was announced in *Sovetskaya Rossiya*, 19 August 1989.

[50] For the proposed lobby, see Pika and Prokhorov, p. 82, Shinkarev, Gaer, and Mihalisko ('North American-Style...'); for the Association, *Sovetskaya Rossiya and Pravda*, 9 August 1989. Churilov reports on a first Congress of Northern Peoples of the Khanty- Mansiisk AD, and the setting up there of a local association for 'Ugric Salvation'. For a stimulating interpretation of the context and prospects of the Association (perhaps rather more optimistic than my own), see Paul Goble, 'Ethnic Politics in the USSR', *Problems of Communism*, July–August 1989, p. 10.

[51] See the articles by Ledkov and Shinkarev. A debate on the word 'reservation', reported by Mihalisko in 'North American-Style...' contains explicit references to North American experience. Gaer reports that one of her first acts when she came to Moscow as a deputy was to consult documents on International Conventions regarding indigenous peoples (*Pravda*, 26 June 1989). Churilov quotes from the ILO 'Convention on Native and Tribal Peoples of Independent Countries'. W. Reese, in *Report on the USSR*, no. 33, 1989, 18 August 1989, pp. 15–16, reports on the first Soviet participation at a meeting of the Inuit Circumpolar Conference.

Two kinds of policy are at issue here. First are ameliorative responses directed at the symptoms of the Northerners' plight, as manifested in such areas as health, education and living standards. The government of the RSFSR has indeed been prompt with the recognition that the North, for the time being, has to be subsidized, and with the announcement of an emergency social development programme from its own budget.[52] This programme sets out to inject more funds into infrastructure, to encourage traditional crafts and to ensure employment among the native population, among other means through the leasing and sub-contracting arrangements that became policy in 1988. More specific measures include the raising of state prices paid to farmers and traditional craftsmen; increase in compensation for reindeer pasture by five hundred times; mobile medical clinics; more teaching by trained natives in the native languages; and the replacement of boarding-schools by a large number of one-teacher schools, if necessary with as few as half a dozen pupils.

This is the kind of programme that the RSFSR, despite its economic woes, should be able to afford, and the cause has considerable public support.[53] There is in Russia a fund of (perhaps romantic) good will towards the Peoples of the North, and, more important, they pose no kind of political threat: the contrast with, say, Estonians or Uzbeks is not lost, either on officials or the public. But welcome as such measures are, they hardly touch the core of the problem: who holds what rights in the North?

On this score initial reactions from the authorities have not been uncompromising. As early as in June 1989 the State Commission on Arctic Affairs was quoted as favouring the creation of zones set aside

[52] Main details from Tabeev, *Pravitel'stvennyi vestnik*, 13/89, pp. 6–7; from the speech of V.I. Vorotnikov in Anadyr' (Magadan province), *Sovetskaya Rossiya*, 18 August 1989; from an interview with Vorotnikov, ibid., 3 September 1989; and from an interview with A.V. Vlasov, *Izvestiya*, 1 September 1989. Vlasov was at the time Chairman of the RSFSR Council of Ministers, Tabeev his First Deputy, and Vorotnikov Chairman of the Presidium of the RSFSR Supreme Soviet. Vlasov, who grew up in East Siberia, expresses himself in particularly sympathetic terms towards the Peoples of the North.

The note 'Detyam Chukotki' (*Sovetskaya Rossiya*, 2 September 1989) has some details on changes in indigenous education at the start of the school year.

[53] See, for example, Denisov, who seems to be a Russian, and note 15 above. Note however that there have been complaints that the aid is not actually getting through to villages; see Gaer in *Pravda*, 26 June 1989 and *Krasnaya zvezda*, 19 December 1989.

for natives and closed to industrial development.[54] This represents a considerable shift, no doubt under the impact of the Congress of Peoples Deputies, from its cautious approach of March. In September 1989 the CPSU Platform on Nationalities Policy (only a draft policy document of course) devoted a section to the Peoples of the North, which were, it stated, in need of 'special state defence and assistance'.[55] The soviets of their territories should have the 'exclusive right to their economic exploitation'—with specific mention of pastures, forests, inland waterways and shores, and craft resources—and to the 'creation of reserved zones for the purposes of restoring and maintaining their peoples' places of residence'. National Counties and Settlements should be re-established, a 'Congress of Representatives of Native Peoples of the North' convened, and a body formed which would 'represent their interests at all levels of administration'.

The main purpose of the CPSU Platform was to defuse rising ethnic pressures for separatism, and its recommendations concerning the Peoples of the North were unlikely to face serious challenge. Yet it is important to note what the Platform, with its formal, legal language, does not say or face. The list of economic resources does not specifically include subterranean minerals.[56] The body which would hold exclusive economic rights would not be an association of the original land-users, but rather the local soviet, on which native interests would not normally prevail. And a reservation based on a people's place of residence does not sound like one that could accommodate nomads. It would be hard to read support in the Platform for any substantial withdrawal of central ministries from resource extraction in the North, or for the payment by ministries of something like 'royalties' to traditional land-users.

This analysis must be concluded at the end of 1989, whilst political developments were still in full swing. Things to watch for in the future

---

[54] See Mihalisko, 'North American-Style . . .', quoting *Komsomol'skaya pravda*, 15 June 1989. She also reports debate as to whether the resultant 'restricted zones' will amount to 'reservations'.

[55] In draft form, *Pravda, Sovetskaya Rossiya*, 17 August 1989; after acceptance by the Central Committee, ibid., 24 September 1989.

[56] This is noted by First Secretary Churilov in *Pravda*, 14 September 1989; it is an article sympathetic to the Peoples of the North, but—as his remarks about settling Russian immigrants reveal—there is no doubt of his assumption of responsibility for *all* the population in his district. Mineral rights *are* included in many contemporary claims of economic sovereignty, for example those from the Baltic union-republics.

are, first, the development of indigenous organizations and the degree of their political access, and, second, the evolution of local government rights: will the latter include any say in matters of local economic development, and will indigenous communities gain any rights distinct from those of the rest of the population? What the Peoples of the North have going for them is a considerable sympathy vote, which is the stronger because sympathizers know immediate relief would not be costly. But beyond that they face powerful economic pressures, in a context of increasing Soviet dependence on resource extraction. My personal prediction is that an institution weaker than the old Committee of the North will be set up, probably attached to the Russian Supreme Soviet and without executive powers; it could be a standing committee of this Soviet on northern problems, or a weaker body with no more than advisory and consultative functions. Some reservations will probably be established for indigenous Northerners, off-limits for Europeans, and supported by external subsidies, but one suspects that they will be limited in extent. It would be a major achievement indeed for any lobby to succeed in modifying oil extraction in the North: even if the central oil ministries were broken up or privatized (so that policy could be made in Tyumen' or Tomsk), it is still hard in the current economic climate to foresee Russian politicians or managers accepting a deal which imposed added costs on resource extraction, let alone one which led to a withdrawal from it.[57]

A Note on Reliability

Overall this is a very disturbing portrayal. But how reliable is it? Caution is clearly aroused by the fact that such an abundance of material should emerge suddenly and all at once, and after decades of silence. One surmises immediately that specific censorship restrictions on this kind of topic must have been lifted around the time of the XIX Conference of the Communist Party in June 1988. This would have

---

[57] The message that the ministries are under pressure to maintain oil output emerges clearly from 'A Mere 0.5 Per Cent', *Moscow News*, no. 42, 15 October 1989, p. 5. That the ministries have support in this is suggested by *Izvestiya*, 8 September 1989, 'Konflikt v Pripolar'e', a report on an industrial dispute in the north of Tyumen' province, prompted by very preliminary cuts in ministerial outlays, and directed particularly against labour flown in from the south. It is for this reason that I am not as confident as Goble about the prospects for a Northern lobby attached to the bureaucracy.

been in the interests of the developing programme of M.S. Gorbachev: he was a politician still involved in the process of building a coalition; he saw the vested interests of the powerful economic ministries as one of the main obstacles to reform, and welcomed ammunition against them; and since the Chernobyl' disaster and what it revealed about official negligence, he had been happy to encourage social pressure in environmental causes.

So his regime stood to gain from an exposure of ministerial rapacity and native despair in the Soviet North. And if this is the case we must reckon with the temptation to exaggerate or distort the state of affairs, and especially on the part of people who see in this their first chance for decades to speak out. Our hesitancy could be strengthened by other considerations. Some of the claims are difficult to evaluate as long as we lack comparative material from other parts of the USSR. The authors sometimes quote each other's statistics inaccurately. And some of this critique has been available to interested parties for centuries; Armstrong quotes condemnation from the mid-nineteenth century that is strikingly similar to today's[58] (except that it does not mention oil!).

Some points tell in favour of the recent accounts, however. With small exceptions, the new material complements, but does not con-tradict what was published under Khrushchev and Brezhnev.[59] And when we try to put the natives of the North in comparative context, we find that their situation fits into a general pattern: the claims about them are certainly extreme, but they are not implausible, and oc-casionally worse cases can be found elsewhere.

VI COMPARISONS AND CONTRASTS

Two regions offer revealing comparisons and contrasts: first, that between the Volga and the Urals, with its substantial Finnic and Turkic populations; and, second, Soviet Central Asia.

North European Russia between the Volga and Urals (and south of the permafrost zone) contains a variety of non-Russian peoples living dispersed and intermingled among a Russian majority. Of Finnic

---

[58] *Russian Settlement. . .* , pp. 118–19.

[59] It has often been commented that the censors prefer to suppress coverage of unwelcome matters rather than fabricate it.

speech are the Mordva, Udmurt, Mari and Komi-Permyaks (southern relatives of the Komi); it is convenient to add here the Karelians of the north-west. Turkic in language are the Tatars, Bashkir and Chuvash. The Finnic groups, and especially the Mordva, Komi-Permyaks and Karelians, show many of the signs of cultures under threat that have been discussed concerning the Peoples of the North. As ethnic groups they are declining or static in size; from a quarter to a half of the population claim Russian as their first language, and about 90 per cent can speak Russian; native language school teaching and publishing are at low levels and on the decline, and in the case of Karelia seem to have been discontinued altogether. On all these counts the Mordva and Karelians show figures worse than any quoted in Table IV.

We have little hard data on employment and incomes. Anecdotal evidence suggests a concentration in blue-collar, low-status occupations and a propensity to migrate to the rougher and more remote development projects; the education statistics, which are very similar to those for the Peoples of the North, confirm this picture. Communist Party membership tends to be somewhat above average—suggesting ready reception (on whose initiative, we cannot be sure) into Soviet ways of doing things. One writer, referring to the Mordva, uses language that will be familiar to readers of this volume: '[they] come to [Russification] of their own accord, for the sake of convenience, but mostly because [they] have no historical cultural heritage to defend—and to defend *them*'.[60]

No ethnically specific health or demographic statistics are available. It would come as no surprise if the incidence, for example, of tuberculosis turned out to be high, even if not as high as among the Peoples of the North. It seems that the decline in their population owes more to assimilation—that is to self-identification as Russians, and to rearing of children in Russian—than it does to low rates of natural increase.[61] If this is the case, then it constitutes the most important

[60] Helene Carrere d'Encausse, *Decline of an Empire* (New York: Harper, 1978), p. 189.
[61] See B.A. Anderson and B.D. Silver, 'Estimating Russification of Ethnic Identity among Non-Russians in the USSR', in *Demography*, vol. 20, no. 4, November 1983, pp. 461—89, and 'Demographic Consequences of World War II on the Non-Russian Nationalities of the USSR', pp. 207–42 in Susan J. Linz (ed.), *The Impact of World War II on the Soviet Union* (New Jersey: Rowman & Allanheld, 1985).

way in which the plight of the natives of the North differs from that of the Finns of the Volga-Urals area. The former, as we have seen, are suffering a demographic disaster, and it is accompanied by great anguish at the collapse of a culture. The latter—even if we think Dr d'Encausse is too sweeping—do not seem to face the prospects of assimilation with such resistance.[62] At the back of this difference one cannot help but decry the difference between a peasant economy and a hunter-gatherer economy.

The case of Soviet Central Asia offers further interesting contrasts. Here, in the cotton-growing valleys and oases, morbidity and infant mortality statistics have been reported which are comparable with those of the Peoples of the North, and may exceed them in particular areas.[63] But this is against a background of rapidly increasing non-Russian population, and declining knowledge and influence of Russian. From the beginning of the Five-Year Plans the Soviet authorities imposed what amounted to a mono-culture in cotton production on the union-republics of Central Asia. For a time this brought the local population a prosperity not found in the collective farms of Russia proper, and the rising birth rates may owe something to this. This prosperity proved ephemeral. There was massive investment in irrigation for cotton, and little in piped drinking water or sewage, with the result that drinking water is increasingly contaminated by bacteria, fertilisers, pesticides and defoliants. Health has been affected by the promotion of cotton at the expense of food crops and livestock; and medical, and other infrastructure has not kept pace with rising population. The pressure to produce cotton has encouraged corruption also; many of the local leaders have returned falsified production figures

---

[62] I.T.. Kreindler in *The Mordvinian Languages: A Survival Saga*, pp. 254–7 rejects the pessimism of Carrere d'Encausse et al, but has little optimistic argument to offer in its place. See I.T. Kreindler (ed.), *Sociolinguistic Perspectives on Soviet Nationality Languages* (Berlin: Mouton de Gruyter, 1985), pp. 237–64.

[63] For infant mortality, in some union-republics rising since the 1970s, see *Narodnoe khozyaistvo SSSR v 1987 g*, p. 357. For comparisons of these figures with other material on Central Asia, see Aaron Trehub, 'New Figures on Infant Mortality in the USSR', *Radio Liberty Research*, RL 438/87, 29 October 1987; Annette Bohr, 'Infant Mortality in Central Asia', ibid., RL 352/88, 4 August 1988; Annette Bohr, 'Health Catastrophe in Karakalpakistan', *Report on the USSR*, vol. 1, no. 29, 21 July 1989, pp. 37—8. T he picture they paint has been confirmed publicly in the USSR since then; see, for instance, the speeches to the Congress of People's Deputies of T. Kaipbergenov and R.N. Nishanov, *Izvestiya*, 1 June 1989, pp. 5, 9.

to Moscow, and paid bribes to cover this up. Unemployment is high and is rising, and Party membership is declining. Taken together it amounts to a major political problem for the central leadership.

The comparison with the situation of the Peoples of the North lies in the obsession with economic output, pursued without local knowledge or consultation, and with woeful consequences for welfare and the quality of life. The contrast lies in the resources of the indigenous Central Asians: their numbers, the coherence of their settlement in a strategic area, their Muslim culture and their near-monopoly on cotton production. They have the means to make a political fight of it, because these are resources that their European opponents have to reckon with. Again the exceptionally weak status of the hunter-gatherer economy stands out.

VII CONCLUSIONS

What broader conclusions can be drawn from the situation of the natives of the Soviet North? Two, I think:

First, the Peoples of the North include groups who are perhaps the most disadvantaged of ethnic groups in the USSR—but to make this judgement is not a clear-cut thing. We have examined a number of dimensions of disadvantage—demographic, linguistic, economic, environmental—and in almost all cases the natives of the North lie at the end of a spectrum. But along each of these spectra they have near neighbours, peoples who are nearly as badly off as they themselves, and often these are peoples whom we would not intuitively want to call 'subordinated'. It would be difficult to draw a line on any of these spectra and say, 'beyond lie subordinated peoples', more difficult (I suspect) than such a task might seem in the case of Australia, Brazil or the United States. The reason would seem to be the long term interaction of peoples living side-by-side in a land empire. In this sense the hypothesis that land-based imperialism may be less damaging than the maritime variety seems thus far to be supported.

On the other hand, the Peoples of the North—but *not*, say, the Yakuts—seem to be in a situation of peculiar and comprehensive disadvantage. They lie at the extreme ends of most spectra. Theirs is the only case where population decline seems to have other causes than assimilation, and in these groups alone do we observe attempts positively to reject European development. Although there can be doubts about appropriate nomenclature, they—alone of Soviet nationalities—might qualify as 'subordinated' peoples.[64] Furthermore, their situation seems to have become worse during the twentieth century.

What is distinctive, both about the Peoples of the North and about their relations with the other peoples of the Soviet Union, can be traced to their hunter-gatherer economy. And their plight would seem to be worse than that of some other remaining tribal and nomadic peoples in 'Old World' Europe and Asia: Lapps in Scandinavia, Vlachs in the Balkans, Indian tribals or the hill peoples of South East Asia. Perhaps the hypothesis about land-based imperialism is not so very helpful after all? If this is so, I suspect it is for two interconnected reasons. For centuries the Peoples of the North were sheltered by the Siberian environment (as New World aborigines were by the ocean) and they got on reasonably well with the Russians of Siberia. But the irruption of the manufacturing economy, when it became technically feasible, was sudden and massive—the equivalent of an invasion by total foreigners. Second, this irruption coincided with the temporary sway of Marxism-Leninism in Russia, a creed which saw economic development as a panacea and which was as rapacious and as intolerant of human variety as any sea-borne imperialism.[65]

APPENDIX: SOVIET SOURCE MATERIAL FROM THE 1988–9 PERIOD

Below is a bibliography of Soviet material of which I am aware from the 1988–9 period, arranged in chronological order. I am sure it is nothing like an exhaustive list. Material that I have *not* been able to consult is marked *.

Lyubov' Nenyang, 'Pyatna v geografii', *Sovetskaya Rossiya*, 19 May 1988.
*Yu Rytkheu, 'Lozungi i amulety', *Komsomol'skaya pravda*, 19 May 1988.
*E. A. Oborotova, *Sovetskaya Etnografiya*, no. 5, 1988, pp. 146–51.
*A. Nemtushkin, *Komsomol'skaya pravda*, 17 June 1988.

[64] A report in *Moscow News*, 25/89, 18 June 1989, p. 13 (on ethnic violence in the Fergana basin of Uzbekistan) mentions a figure of one million unemployed in adjacent regions. If this is taken to apply to Uzbekistan it would represent about one tenth of adults.

[65] I have sought in the present chapter to draw attention to the socio-economic roots of conflict between hunter-gatherer and manufacturing societies. The word 'subordinated' with its suggestions of status does not do this.

*——— Stoit li mnozhit' oshibki?', *Sotsialisticheskaya industriya*, 28 June 1988.

A. Gamov, 'Kak zdorov'e, severyane?', *Sovetskaya Rossiya*, 28 July 1988.

*A. Nemtushkin, 'Bol' moya, Evenkiya!', *Sovetskaya kul'tura*, 28 July 1988.

*V. Sharov, 'Mala li zemlya dlya malykh narodov?', *Literaturnaya gazeta*, no. 33, 1988, p. 10.

*I. Levshin, 'Surovaya realnost' surovoi zemli', Literaturnaya Rossiya, 3 September 1988.

'Chto volnuet . . . ', *Pravda*, 8 September 1988.

Vladimir Sangi, 'Otchuzhdenie', *Sovetskaya Rossiya*, 11 September 1988.

A. Gamov, 'Arkticheskii konsilium', *Sovetskaya Rossiya*, 22 September 1988.

A. Pika and B. Prokhorov, 'Bol'shie problemy malykh narodov, *Kommunist*, no. 16, November 1988, pp. 76 -83.

*Yu Shestalov, *Literaturnaya Rossiya*, 23 December 1988.

Yeremei Aipin, 'Not by Oil Alone', *Moscow News*, no. 2, 8 January 1989, pp. 8-9.

**Sovetskaya kul'tura*, 11 February 1989.

*A. Nemtushkin, *Literaturnaya Rossiya*, no. 9, 1989.

Ye Aipin, 'Halt the Exodus to Nowhere', *Moscow News*, no. 12, 19 March 1989, p. 6.

'Osvoenie Arktiki', *Pravitel'stvennyi vestnik*, no. 6, 1989, pp. 11–12.

'Kak zhivesh' severyanin?', ibid., no. 7, 1989, p. 8.

'Rodom s Severa', *Sovetskaya Rossiya*, 31 March 1989, together with correspondence, 'Pod pressom progressa', ibid., 18 June 1989.

V. Kotlyakov and Dr G. Agranat, '"Tropiki" severa', *Pravda*, 9 May 1989.

Speeches to the inaugural Congress of People's Deputies: of M. I. Mongo, *Izvestiya*, 8 June 1989, p. 4; of E. A. Gaer, *Izvestiya*, 10 June 1989, p. 4.

L. Shinkarev, 'Tundra', *Izvestiya*, 15 June 1989.

*F. Sizyi, 'Drama bez okhoty', *Komsomol'skaya pravda*, 15 June 1989.

Vasilii Ledkov, 'Zagovoril Sever', *Sovetskaya Rossiya*, 18 June 1989.

F. A. Tabeev, 'Na krayu sveta—del cherez krai', *Pravitel'stvennyi vestnik*, no. 13, 1989, pp. 6-7.

P Sleptsov, 'Esli ne okruglyat', *Sovetskaya Rossiya*, 24 June 1989.

E. A. Gaer interviewed in 'New Person at the Top', *Moscow News*, no. 26, 25 June 1989, p. 16; and in 'Khotela by dobavit' k skazannomu . . . ', *Pravda*, 26 June 1989.

*V. Sangi, *Sovetskaya kul'tura*, 29 June 1989.

Visit of V I Vorotnikov to Magadan and Kamchatka, 17–22 August 1989, reported in *Sovetskaya Rossiya*, 18 August 1989; and interview, ibid., 3 September 1989.

T. Il'ina, 'Ekonomika minus ekologiya', *Sovetskaya Rossiya*, 18 August 1989.

V. Lupandin and Ye Gayer, 'Chernobyl on the Chukot Peninsula', *Moscow News*, no. 34, 1989, 20 August 1989, p. 5.

V. Denisov, 'Rany severnykh shirot', *Sovetskaya Rossiya*, 25 August 1989.

A. V. Vlasov, interviewed in *Izvestiya*, 1 September 1989.

'Detyam Chukotki', *Sovetskaya Rossiya*, 2 September 1989.

V. A. Churilov, 'Zhivye korni Severa', *Pravda*, 14 September 1989.

The CPSU 'Platform' on nationalities policy, 'Natsional'naya politika partii v sovremennykh usloviyakh', published for the Central Committee Plenum on that theme, *Pravda*, 17 August, and as approved after the Plenum, ibid., 24 September 1989.

M. Mongo, V Etylen et al., 'Beskryl'nyi Sever', *Pravda*, 22 October 1989.

E. A. Gaer interviewed in 'Deputat Gaer', *Krasnaya zvezda*, 19 December 1989.

Of the above authors, Nenyang, Rytkheu, Nemtushkin, Sangi, Aipin, Mongo, Gaer (Gayer), Ledkov, Sleptsov and Etylen are indigenous Northerners.

Many of these articles have been analysed in English by Kathleen Mihalisko: 'Discontent in Taiga and Tundra', *Radio Liberty Research*, RL 296/88, 7 July 1988; 'SOS for Native Peoples of Soviet North', *Report on the USSR*, vol. 1, no. 5, 3 February 1989, pp. 3–6; 'North American-Style Native Reservations in the Soviet North?', *Report on the USSR*, vol. 1, no. 29, 21 July 1989, pp. 31–4.

Index

119305

323.11
RIG